Complete Guide
to
Real Estate Financing

Complete Guide to Real Estate Financing

by

Jack Cummings

Prentice-Hall, Inc.

Englewood Cliffs, N.J.

Prentice-Hall International, Inc., *London*
Prentice-Hall of Australia, Pty. Ltd., *Sydney*
Prentice-Hall of Canada, Ltd., *Toronto*
Prentice-Hall of India Private Ltd., *New Delhi*
Prentice-Hall of Japan, Inc., *Tokyo*
Prentice-Hall of Southeast Asia Pte. Ltd., *Singapore*
Whitehall Books, Ltd., *Wellington, New Zealand*

This publication is designed to provide accurate and authoritative information in regard to the subject matter covered. It is sold with the understanding that the publisher is not engaged in rendering legal, accounting, or other professional service. If legal advice or other expert assistance is required, the services of a competent professional person should be sought.

. . . From the Declaration of Principles jointly adopted by a Committee of the American Bar Association and a Committee of Publishers and Associations.

Fifth Printing . . . . . May, 1980

Library of Congress Cataloging in Publication Data

Cummings, Jack,
Complete guide to real estate financing.

Includes index.
1. Real estate business--Finance. 2. Real estate investment. I. Title.
HD1375.C85 658.1'5 77-12018
ISBN 0-13-160481-3

Printed in the United States of America

Dedication

This book is dedicated to my wife Gloria, and our two children Robert and Anne Marie, who, with understanding, have suffered through long nights with a pounding typewriter; my co-brokers and associates at Cummings Realty, Inc. who must have felt at times they were being used as test cases; and to the thousands of dedicated professional people that make the real estate profession as exciting and challenging as it is.

What This Book Can Do For You

This book is a problem solver for all areas of real estate financing. It offers methods you can apply to any type of real estate to help you to close more transactions. This will mean, of course, greater commissions and more profitable transactions.

This is primarily a reference book. You will be able to use it as a tool to provide you with guidelines on how to approach the problems you must solve—a reference tool which will not only give you essential background information, but also the exact step-by-step procedures.

This book is dedicated to the how, when, where, the what works and the what does not work, of real estate finance. It is an every-day reference providing on-the-job advice for the tough financial problems.

All big problems start out as little ones. The foundations you lay in approaching any situation will be most important in keeping those small problems from growing. This book gives you methods that keep small problems small, then shows you how to eliminate them altogether.

Simply stated, the objectives of this book are:

1. *To provide a one-stop reference for real estate financing.* All types of financing are covered, all sources of loans, plus how and where to get them.
2. *To assist you in becoming more comfortable with the use of "unusual" techniques.* Financing is not a matter of black and white. There are many ways to reach the same objective. The impact on you and your clients could well depend not only on reaching the solution to a problem, but on exactly how you do it.
3. *To give you an easy-to-use problem solver.* You do not have to be a mortgage broker to understand these methods. The step-by-step procedures, checklists, and key factors involved in the various situations are clear, easily workable, and best of all, they get results.
4. *To help you make more money.*

Now that you know the objectives of the book, what can you expect to find within its pages?

There are 17 chapters devoted to making your job easier and more productive. The first chapter deals with the Ten Goals of Financing. There are limitations to finance, and you must accept the fact that not every problem can be solved by just one technique.

The foundations you establish with your clients are very important. Chapters One and Two stress the methods of developing a working relationship with a client that will last. One of the key factors in this lasting relationship is the discovery of the principal's goals. It is important that you don't superimpose your goals onto those of your clients. Seven tips for getting things started with your clients show you how to stay in control of the qualifying process.

The basis of all financing is leverage. Chapter Three deals with this topic in a way you have probably never seen before. You will see how to find the amount of leverage, and how to use this key factor in comparing two or more properties. Six key factors you must watch for when making this decision are shown.

Chapters Four and Five cover the conventional first and second mortgages—what they are, where to find them, and how to get them.

A special section on *How to Deal with the Savings and Loan Associations* gives you six advantages, four disadvantages, and a step-by-step approach to dealing with these crucial loan sources.

Commercial banks are also covered in detail. Then there are the other sources, such as mortgage brokers, the insurance companies, the real estate investment trusts and the pension fund.

Chapter Five covers the secondary loan market. This is the place where deals are often made or lost because of a few thousand dollars of needed capital. The chapter shows you where to go for secondary financing, and how to deal with the secondary lenders.

Chapter Six presents a complete, yet concise breakdown on how to use government-insured loans to finance real estate. It covers the Veteran and GI oan, tne major FHA programs to help you make small transactions, and large government housing-project loans.

Chapter Seven deals with the use of development and construction loans. It begins with why the loans are important and ends with where to go to obtain the loan. In this chapter, you will see how one broker made a four million dollar deal by using the techniques shown.

The blanket mortgage is covered in Chapter Eight. This widely used technique can have some dramatic results when used creatively. What blanket mortgages are, where to get them, and how to use them to your clients benefit, are discussed. Most importantly, you'll see how you can increase sales by using the blanket mortgage as a selling tool.

Chapter Nine introduces a less widely used technique, the discount sale. This technique is unique and can mean the salvation of deals that seemed to have no solution. Not only that, the discount sale can profit everyone. Because this technique is rather unusual, special details have been given to show you how to sell both the seller and buyer on its use.

Chapter Ten covers all aspects of the sale lease-back . . . how to structure the land lease-back, what and how to use subordination, values of leasehold and fee simple values, how you establish leasehold value, and of course, how to determine when the lease-back is effective.

Chapter Eleven on pyramiding will show you how you can have your cake and eat it too. Pyramiding is that fantastic path by which many people have started with almost nothing and become extremely wealthy. One example shows how one man started with $30,000 and in a few years had not only over half-a-million dollars, but also real estate giving him an income and continued appreciation.

The pyramid is the most risky of all techniques. Therefore, care is taken to show you what not to do, as well as how to present offers to sellers when dealing with a pyramid client. But the pyramid is not just a buyer's tool. Sellers can use it to great effect and I've shown you how to make property more saleable by using the pyramid. You will see how a pyramid sale got the seller his full price of $250,000 and at the same time made a second sale for the broker.

Chapter Twleve deals with exchanging. Exchanges are a form of finance that often work wonders when all else fails. You'll see how to get started in exchanging, and the seven key steps in the pre-exchange procedure, along with marketing-session presentation checklists that give you an edge, perhaps making the difference between the acceptance of your property and that of someone else.

How to get the offer, how to present it, how to balance equity, and how to calculate the tax consequences of the exchange are also covered. The effect exchanges have on depreciation is illustrated with several actual case histories.

Chapter Thirteen covers wrap-around mortgages. This most misunderstood form of finance is defined, then broken down into its basic steps. Twelve most common uses of the wrap are discussed. Then you will see how the wrap-around functions to create fantastic yields to the mortgagee. Finding and understanding the effective rate earned is not a simple matter. Yet, by use of the yield calculation forms I have provided, these calculations can be completed with the minimum of effort.

You will find interesting the discussion of the advantages and disadvantages of the wrap-around, and how to protect the mortgagor and the mortgagee.

Avoiding usury in wrap-arounds is a matter of great interest today, so I've included a section on this, as well as calculating the effect of earned income on the wrap for tax accounting.

When, why and how to discount a mortgage is the topic of the fourteenth chapter. Discounting mortgages is a key factor in all kinds of selling, but has a special function in real estate. You will learn how to determine the amount of a discount, and you will probably be surprised to find the yield that can result from a well-bought mortgage with even a slight discount. The methods in determining which mortgages will bring the greatest yield are given in easy steps. You will find how sellers can use the discounted mortgage to help them market their property, and of course, how to find buyers for discounted mortgages.

Chapter Fifteen presents five additional key methods of financing real estate. These methods are: mortgage and lease insurance; leasehold financing; percent of income; land leases; co-ventures and syndications. Each method has its special use in the world of real estate finance.

Most brokers and salesmen think of financing as a part of the sales and investment process, and most of the time this is where you will use the techniques covered in this book. However, Chapter Sixteen will show you what to do when you have to refinance a property. Sometimes the solution to your client's problem isn't to sell the property he has, but merely to refinance it. One example will show how a client was able to solve his problems by keeping a property he thought he had to sell. A list of the twenty ways you can refinance will help you apply this technique in many situations.

Sometimes however, all attempts to finance fail. When this happens, and there is an existing mortgage on the property, the result might be foreclosure. I have approached foreclosure as seen by the lender, covering the four foreclosure periods, and why the lender will avoid foreclosure if at all possible. The suggestions on what a mortgagor should do if he feels he may go into default are invaluable. The steps given for holding off foreclosure can delay that event and possibly save the client . . . and your deal.

This book should sit on or near your desk. You will be able to use it as a direct sales tool in helping you get across your points. When you are describing a wrap-around mortgage, for example, you might open the book to that chapter and show your client, either buyer or seller, the advantages and disadvantages.

But for the most part, you can use the book to tell you exactly what to do and how to do it. Charts and forms may be copied and run off in quantity for use. You will find that if you develop the habit of using the techniques given in this book, you will be closing more transactions. But even more importantly, you will be sure you are considering all of the many possible ways to finance real estate.

JACK CUMMINGS

Contents

Chapter 1

The Goals of Real Estate Financing: What It Can and Cannot Do

This chapter is divided into five sections which are designed to help you develop a clear understanding of what financing should do and to enable you to lay the foundation for a long-lasting, profitable relationship with a client.

All success must begin somewhere, and when it comes to real estate financing it starts with the ten goals of what financing can do for your clients. You can use these ten goals as your first approach to a problem to ascertain whether financing can provide an answer to that problem or not.

The solution to the problem financially does not depend as much on knowing the immediate answer, *but in knowing whether financing can provide an answer*. You will not be able to arrive at an answer without a clear understanding of the *goals*.

THE TEN GOALS OF FINANCING—AND WHAT THEY WILL DO

1. CREATE THE BEST VALUE: Financing should be able to enchance the value of a property. From a buyer's standpoint, it should provide the best terms and offer the highest yield possible. The seller, on the other hand, will look to financing that will give him the best market value.

There is a well-worn adage which applies here: "I'll pay your price, if you'll take my terms." In other words, price is often a fluctuating factor, depending on the terms of the sale. It is clear that a property may be difficult to sell if all cash is required with no financing available. That same property, however, offered at twenty percent down, with reasonable pay-out on the balance, may sell quickly.

2. CONSOLIDATION: Financing can be used to consolidate existing financing that is overburdening the property, and its owner, with high payments. The ability to refinance some or all of the existing mortgages may lower the total payments and increase the cash flow position on an income-producing property, or ease the cash outlay on other property.

A property with three or four mortgages, each with a different interest rate and term of years, can have excessive debt service. More often than not, the more junior the loan the shorter the term. A fourth mortgage, therefore, may run for only a few years, while the first mortgage will still have 20 years to go.

The refinancing of this type of property for the owner would be accomplished if the results offered some solution to the original problem. There is no need to seek consolidation as a goal unless one or more of the following situations are present:

A. A need to reduce total debt service payments by refinancing short-term loans into long-term loans.
B. The property is not readily marketable with the present financing structure, and new money at a more favorable constant is available.
C. A cash-out situation, where the owner can mortgage above present financing and put cash in his pocket, without overburdening the property in excessive debt service.
D. A need to raise immediate cash to retire a note or loan due.

There are many ways of consolidating existing financing. Almost any form of financing will lend itself to consolidation of the existing debt. Naturally, some forms of financing will give better results than others.

3. MAKE PROPERTY MORE SALEABLE: One of the major aspects of financing is the ability to make property more saleable. This touches on the first goal to some degree, but is not quite the same.

Creative financing may be the only way to take a difficult property into the market and find a buyer. Often, more than one form of financing must be put to work. For example, a sale and lease-back, with the seller holding secondary financing as cross collateral, may help give the additional security needed to make the deal worthwhile for a buyer.

4. INCREASE THE MARKET POTENTIAL FOR THE PROPERTY: The difference in this goal over and above the previous one is very subtle. It is one thing to make a property more saleable, another to broaden the market to include more buyers. A good example of this slight difference is seen below:

The Client and the Property: Mr. Wallace entered his broker's office and offered an exclusive on a 25-unit apartment house. "The price," said Mr. Wallace, "is $500,000." It sounded like a nice round figure. As it turned out, the price was fair. The NOI on the property was about $53,000, and for a normal market, this represented a good ratio of NOI to value.

The Problem Part of the Property: However, the city was about to launch a major road and sewer project right in front of the apartment house and there was every prospect that the complex would lose all its tenants for at least a year. Naturally, once the work was complete, the situation would be greatly improved and the property value would be increased.

The first goal in this situation was to *make the property more saleable.* This was done by creating a sale and lease-back for one year. The property had a first mortgage of $250,000, payable at $26,500 per year. The seller contracted to lease the property back from the buyer for one year on a net annual lease of $52,000. After the mortgage payment, the buyer was left with a $26,000 return on his capital investment of $250,000. Of course, the seller had to suffer during the lease-back year—or did he? As this creative financing permitted a sale, it solved his immediate need—*cash!*

Thus far, financing, by way of the sale and lease-back tool, took a problem property and made it acceptable in the present market.

Can Another Goal Be Reached? To go one step further, I suggested that the seller broaden his market, or *increase the market potential for the property,* by holding some paper on the sale.

This did two things: First, the seller-held paper would be pledged as security to the lease and strengthened it. Second, because the seller held more paper, a greater number of prospective buyers were attracted as the initial investment was reduced.

A Key in Selling the Seller is Tax Savings: An installment sale was determined to be of special tax interest to the seller, and the down payment was held to $140,000. This meant the seller would hold $90,000 in paper.

The terms of this seller-held paper were kept open for the initial offering of the final sale and set the terms at 10 years at 8% interest.

While it wasn't necessary, further steps to *increase the market potential for the property* could have been taken. The client, however, became motivated to the marketing plan—and saw that it would be a part of a way to solve his problem.

5. INCREASE THE CASH FROM MARGINAL PROPERTIES: This can be the most important goal for a buyer of income property. Because of its importance to buyers it also becomes very important to sellers. While cash flow is not the only criterion for determining acceptability of one property over another, it is necessary to create a spendable yield on investment. Generally, a high cash flow produces a more stable price. The causes of a low cash flow can be many: rents too low, expenses too high, debt service overburdening, high vacancy factors, poor management, or combinations of these and other factors. Financing can be used in various forms to lower the debt service either permanently or for a short period of time, which in turn can provide time to enable the new owner to correct the other factors.

6. GENERATE IMMEDIATE CASH WHEN NEEDED: This goal is often overlooked. Because existing mortgages may decrease and value increase through appreciation and equity build-up, it is often possible to refinance and pick up ready cash. Many times, this can be accomplished without affecting the cash flow on property. For example: The mortgage payment for $150,000 over 15 years at 8% is $1,434 per month. If a new mortgage can be obtained at 8½% over 30 years, the same payment of $1,434 would amortize a principal of $186,475. The increase of $36,475, even after the cost for the new loan, may give the needed cash desired.

7. HELP SOLVE TAX PROBLEMS: This goal serves two masters—the buyer and the seller. Often, when it solves a tax problem for one, it will create a problem for the other. The motivation of the seller will generally enable him to accept a small tax problem (or even a large one) if it will help sell the difficult property.

Therefore, from the buyer's point of view: Financing which gives the seller interest which would be earned income in place of capital gain income will add to the tax credits of the buyer in the year given.

For example, Jones, an investor, needed to raise $100,000 cash and would sell his 30 units for $450,000. All that is needed is $100,000 down, as Jones will hold paper above the existing mortgages for the balance of his equity.

Bradshaw agreed to pay the $100,000 cash, but wanted Jones to hold a $404,624 wrap-around mortgage, receiving 18 months of interest in advance. If the interest rate is 9%, this would total $54,624 in interest. Of the $100,000 paid at the closing by Bradshaw, only $45,375 would represent principal. The balance of $54,624 would be interest. The interest would be a tax credit to the buyer, but income to the seller.

In the long run, the buyer would be paying only slightly more for the property, even though the mortgage would appear to be greater by the amount of the interest paid in advance. Yet, as this is advance interest, the payment now will ultimately be offset in the reduction of interest later on. In the meanwhile, the immediate use of this tax credit may enchance the return for that year by sheltering other income.

It is important to note that the IRS will allow advance *interest only payments* for the time that remains in the tax year. A closing on the last day of January, therefore, would allow eleven months of interest. This is a dramatic change from the previous tax law and should be watched, as interest deductions are under constant attack as a primary item of tax shelter to be reduced.

8. CREATE TAX DEFERRED TRANSACTIONS: The goal here is to pass on, as far into the future as possible, tax. The installment sale is one such method. The best way is by exchanging one property for another. If the client moves up in base, the gain is transferred to the newer property. The tax is not paid until that new property is sold. If the client never sells, but continues to trade up, the capital gains tax is never paid and instead an estate tax, at the time the client dies, becomes payable.

Other forms of real estate transactions which pass on this tax are seen in the move from one residence to another. If the new property is of equal value or more to the base of the old one, there is no taxable gain on the sale of the first residence as long as the IRS time plan is adhered to. This deferment lasts until the second residence is sold.

The installment sale and exchange are only two methods of financing being used to defer tax. In some situations the wrap-around mortgage can be used to hold off gain.

9. CREATE NEW WAYS TO ALLOW THE INVESTOR TO EXPAND HIS PORTFOLIO: Creativity is the application of the science of financing. You must look beyond the obvious solutions to new ways to market and close. You will find a multitude of new forms of financing which will benefit your clients. New ways of creating saleable properties out of problem properties will depend on your awareness of changes in the motivations of your buyers and sellers. In doing this, you will be making more deals than before—out of situations you previously would have thought impossible. Being creative generally means testing your ideas with other solutions, looking to see what benefits will occur.

10. PROVIDE THE FINISHING TOUCH TO A GOOD MARKETING PLAN: This is where you put it all together to sell a property. Having the idea of a way to apply financing is not enough. You must be able to sell the concept to the seller, the buyer, and often the lender. Good, sound financing is a must to any marketing plan and should be included in all programs. It is a marketing tool, and will work for you and your client. Financing is a part of real estate—but it is merely a part.

KNOW THE LIMITATIONS OF THE TOOLS OF FINANCING

The preceding ten goals are the keys to your use of financing as a problem solver. Yet, from time to time, there are situations which cannot be solved by financing. The knowledge of the use of financing techniques must include the ability to understand when they will not work the wonders you and your client desire. In the chapters to come, each special technique is described as to its drawbacks as well as advantages. The limitations of these tools and their failure in some cases to meet the goals of financing should make it clear to you that financing will become a secondary consideration in the solution of the problem.

Here are some important points to remember when approaching a situation you feel may be solved with one of the financing techniques:

1. At least one of the ten goals must be met for financing to have any real benefit to the parties involved.
2. There will be different points of view by the buyer and the seller in their interpretation of these goals. Often, the results of the form of financing used will affect these two parties differently.
3. Theories which work on paper are only valid if they work in real life. Remember, there are often three parties to financing—the owner, the buyer, and the lender. Each has interests which can conflict with the other's concept of "the ideal situation." The broker's job is to mediate this conflict to solve the problem at hand.

HOW TO DEVELOP A WORKING RELATIONSHIP WITH A CLIENT THAT WILL LAST

This means money in your pocket.

First of all, you are in a service profession. Developing a knowledge of the tools of financing will be of little use to you or your client unless you can put them to work. You will have little chance of doing that unless you are able to develop a working relationship with a client.

A look into this mysterious ability which some salesmen seem to have naturally, while others can never grasp, will reveal a system that is remarkably simple. It is simplicity that is the key.

A lasting relationship in the real estate business is a mixture of friendship and service. It is impossible to have a long business relationship without some mix of the two. Which is the more important? The service. You should never think of friendship as a substitute for your inability to render service.

THE FIVE KEYS TO MAKING THE RELATIONSHIP LAST

1. *Always think of yourself as a friend to your client.* If you have difficulty doing this, the business relationship will not last.
2. *Maintain the constant service your client deserves.* Treat him as you would a new client whom you are most anxious to serve.
3. *Never take advantage of a friendship that may develop.* If you can't render a service say so, and help him find someone who can. Don't try to muddle through a situation you can't handle.

4. *Keep in touch.* Don't let the time between business calls grow too long. An old client you have not kept up with may no longer be your client, even though you may be social companions on a frequent basis. Never assume that he will call you when he needs your service. Keep in mind that there are other live-wire brokers out there trying to get that client away from you.
5. *Worry about your competition.* That's right, they are hot, and they want as much as you—if not more. If you don't provide service, or lag behind for a moment, you may find your client in their lap.

DEVELOPING THE RELATIONSHIP AND KEEPING IT IS A FULL-TIME JOB

There is nothing worse than a superficial salesman. The guy who has his speech canned and the smile temporarily imprinted on his face may fool some clients, and even himself, some of the time. But in the long run this will tire, and the job will be overbearing for even the strongest salesman.

THE PROBLEM-SOLVING APPROACH

Along with every client, there is a problem. Problems come in a variety of sizes and the solutions are equally varied. Usually, the problem is not as evident as many salesmen believe.

The reason for this is easy to understand. Clients don't like to admit they may have made a mistake. Nonetheless, there is a way for you to find out what the problem really is and take the proper actions to solve it.

The important task is to know how to isolate the true problem, to separate the *real* reason from the reasons clients often give. Accept the fact that few sellers will come into your office with a signed affidavit stating their real problem. You are the expert in real estate, but your client is the expert in his problem. The more involved you let him become in finding the solution, the closer and more profitable your relationship will be. If you are to effectively put the tools of financing to work, you must first develop this rapport.

HOW TO FIND THE PROBLEM QUICKLY, THEN SOLVE IT

1. Qualify
   then
2. Qualify some more.

The concept of the qualification of your prospects and clients and, of course, the property can never be over emphasized. It is a must. The overzealous salesman will not take the time to sit down and qualify the client. This type of salesman will gather up his prospective buyer and rush out to look at property that most likely will not suit the client or solve his problem.

Always remember that the only quick way to get to the solution is to first understand the problem. The client is calling for help. All you have to do is recognize the signals.

WHAT TO DO IN THE QUALIFYING PROCESS—THE 14 KEY STEPS:

1. Never rush anything. Set the proper stage for your qualification process. When you meet your client don't dash out to show him property, or assume that if he is talking about selling the sale is the best solution. Don't jump to conclusions. You need to hear and learn more. To do this you must get the client to talk. Remember his most favorite topic is himself. So, don't talk about yourself, let your client do most of the talking.

The more you listen, the smarter your client will think you are. If you ask a question, wait for an answer. The fact that it may not come immediately is no reason to fill the gaps of silence with more of your own talk. After all, some people like to think—so let them. However, watch your client while he is thinking. He needs to know you are being attentive.

I often say to my clients very early in our first conversation: "Mr. Client, I know that sooner or later, together we can come to grips with the situation at hand. What I need to know before we can even start is to understand what you feel needs to be done. From that point on I can be of service." Naturally, when I say that I don't know what the problem is or if I can solve it—but I am confident that I can be of service. After all, if I find the problem to be beyond my capacity, I will tell the client so and recommend someone I feel could help. That is service.

2. Ask your client to help you. You will be surprised how often a simple request for help will get a wandering session back on the right track. Most people don't like to be lectured to or feel they cannot assist in the solution of their own problem.

Some salesmen take the position that only they can come up with the answer. Generally, this is a cover-up for their lack of self-confidence—or an overabundance of false confidence. The fact of the matter is that you will not be able to solve the client's problem without his help—so ask for it early. "Mr. Seller," I often say, "there are many aspects to your situation, and the property you want to dispose of you know far better than anyone. Together we can make one heck of a team."

3. Don't accept the first reason or problem. This will apply more to sellers than to buyers, but the same rules should be used in each case. People are honest for the most part, but too often the truth is hard to get to.

There are several standard *first* reasons that sellers present for wanting to sell: (a) ill health, (b) lack of knowledge of the present type of property, and (c) desire to obtain another property elsewhere. Of course they may be valid reasons, but then, they may merely be symptoms and not the real reasons at all.

Do not change the reason given, but move into the qualification session and look for signs that you don't have the full picture.

4. Keep the good rapport moving. This is very important. It is not practical or fruitful to be introduced one moment and to start asking personal questions the next.

Qualification depends on the rapport you are able to develop. Some salesmen can do this more quickly than others. Much will depend on the situation. If the client came to you by referral, some of the barriers of confidence are already removed. If the client is a cold call or walk-in, you may have to spend some time establishing confidence in both yourself and the firm.

In any event, the amount of confidence you show is of great importance. You should not be overly confident in your ability to serve him before you learn of his problem. Yet, you must show confidence in your ability to solve problems.

5. Press for the important answer. In your qualification session you are bound to ask questions that the client may balk at answering. When this occurs you must assume two things: (1) You have not made it clear that you must know all about the problem and client before you can be of service, and (2) Your question is not being answered because the client does not believe you need to know the answer.

The first assumption will require you to back off for a moment and explain that you cannot be of true service unless you can see the entire picture. The second will require you to be persistent.

To ask a question you feel you need to know the answer to, then to accept anything less than the answer will only reinforce the client's feeling you did not really need the answer anyway. This pattern can continue and will cause more problems later in your dealings with this client.

"I appreciate your interest," I say in a situation where the client has just balked at one of my questions, "in wanting to know if the answer to that question will be kept in the strictest confidence. Let me assure you that I feel the answer to be most important for me to see the total situation." At this point I will let him talk. Often, he will go ahead and answer. If not, I will go on to another subject, only to come back to the same question in a few minutes. However, I would not let much time go by without pressing, softly, for the answer.

The danger here is making sure you are pressing for an important answer. If the question is not pertinent and the answer, if ultimately received, is not relevant, then you are on thin ice. Nonetheless, if you feel that you must know the answer stick to your guns and get it.

6. Don't be afraid to ask the same question more than once. In fact, all important questions should be asked more than once. It does not matter if you have received an answer the first time or not.

In the situation where you did receive an answer the first time, wait awhile. Let the rapport continue to develop. Get more information. Then ask the same question again. You may be surprised at the answer.

In the second situation, and in relation to the fifth key, you should not neglect to reask the question that was left unanswered earlier. By now the confidence may be enhanced and you will get the answer.

7. Ask the spouse or partner the same question. Don't worry if the other partner is in the room at the time. If you get a different answer, point up that difference and seek an explanation. Generally, you will get a similar answer but with a different point of view. This may help you ascertain if the answer you received in the first instance is a straight and candid reply.

One point of importance here, don't ask the same question immediately. Let the session develop before you go back to the same topic. The short time-span between questions can be a simple forgetful act on your part—easily explained if it creates a problem.

8. Use the word "why" often. No word is as foreceful as "why"—with the exception of "why not." So use them both. You will find that if you ask a "why" question, and have done so as a very interested person, you will never offend the client.

"Why" questions are usually the natural step to follow up on a negative reply to an earlier question. It is a good idea to ask the "why" after an intermediate question, rather than move immediately into it after you have received a "no."

"Earlier, Mr. Seller," you might say, "you said you didn't think you were in a position to hold any purchase money mortgages in the event of a sale. May I ask you *why*?" Often, clients find it easy to say "no" to a question they do not understand. Of course, they may have misconceptions about the question or be misinformed as to the reasons on which they base their answer.

If you don't ask "why" you will never know what the reason is, and cannot find the logic behind the motivation for the "no" in the first place.

On occasion, a client will act offended if you persist in the "why" or "why not" approach. Keep in mind that this could be the result of: (1) You have offended the client, not so much in the question but in the way it was proposed. Back off if that is the case and bring up the topic later on. But remember Keys 5 and 6; obtain an answer if you feel you need one. (2) You have touched on a very sore topic. This is generally the real reason for someone to act offended. This will tell you a lot about that person and the question. It may be he is trying to hide something from you, himself, or a partner who may be in the room. Do not push if you have any idea that this is the case. Back off for awhile and the answer may come out in later questions. If not, ask again when the client is alone or has calmed down.

It is typical that in asking for financial data on some types of businesses the answer will be: "Mr. Cummings, I don't want to give out that information except to a qualified buyer." Of course you did not ask to give the data to a buyer, you want the information for yourself. "To be sure Mr. Seller, I agree with you that much of the financial data should be confidential. Because of that, I feel we should discuss the income and expenses of the operation so I can get a feel for it. *Why not* go over the basic data with me?"

Asking "why" and "why not" is not hard if you follow these pointers:

A. Before you ask "why" or "why not," restate the earlier answer in a softer tone than it was given.
B. Agree that there is a valid point in the statement as you have understood it.
C. Ask the "why" and "why not" to ascertain the reason the client doesn't wish to discuss that question.
D. *Do not* present a "why not" in such a way that it will call upon the client to defend himself. This is usually the danger in this form of qualification. It is easy to ask "*Why* don't you want to exchange?" when he has just replied to your question, "Would you be interested in an exchange?" Instead, ask "*Why* do you feel an exchange would be to your disadvantage?"

9. Show a good reason for needing the answer. You will often be asked: "*Why* do you want to know that?" You should have a good answer. If you blow that one you will have a hard time explaining yourself. Never say, "Well I guess I don't need to know that after all."

Preplanning as to what you need to know will help. With this in mind you will find various checklists presented throughout this book for various types of properties for sale.

10. When you get the wrong answer don't go on the offense. Be positive. There are times you can be sure you have been told an untruth. Do not confuse this with a lie. Many clients may not know the truth, or they may have misunderstood the question. But when a red flag goes up, don't go on the offense. *Never infer you have been lied to.* Instead, question your understanding of what was said. Look back into the answer and try to see why there is a discrepancy in what was said and what you feel the correct reply should have been.

If you have been told the expenses on an operation are $10,000 per year, for example, and you think it should be double that, tell the client this amount of expense is way below the normal figure. "Mr. Seller, you stated earlier that your expenses were $10,000 per year. While I find that obviously a reflection on your ability to be a good manager (or operator), the amount nonetheless is well below the *trend*. So that I am able to explain this below average cost of operation, let's go over the expenses in detail.''

It is rare to have a qualification session without this situation occurring. Look for it, and be ready to handle yourself when it does. A client will lose respect for you if you accept an obvious misstatement without some challenge.

11. Move into a difficult topic in a positive manner. You may have to ask questions that are personal in nature. Of, you may have uncovered a touchy topic that you need to get into. Start your questions in a positive mood. ''Now, Mr. Seller, we are getting somewhere. I don't believe I have ever dealt with such a straightforward person.'' Or simply, ''I am beginning to see where we are now, let's get into the next step.''

You will be able to find something positive about almost any situation. As you are the only one who knows what the next question is that you will ask, you can set the stage.

12. Praise the client for his candor. If you feel your client is giving it to you straight, tell him you appreciate his candor and honesty. You may find the story will change slightly after you make that statement. Guilty conscience perhaps, but pat him on the back and let him know you appreciate being able to get down to the nitty-gritty early in your dealings with him.

This *praise* is in fact a reinforcement that he is doing the right thing by confiding in you. You will want to promote this feeling all through your dealings with any prospect or client.

It will not help you, however, if you call attention to his mistakes. Of course you should never agree with a client who volunteers the fact that he should not have done something. ''I don't know why I did it,'' a client may begin, ''but I believed that son-of-a-gun when he told me the roof was in good repair.'' ''I know,'' the uninformed salesman will counter, ''you should have known you can't believe a thing that guy says.''

13. What is said in jest is often a basis for the truth. To shake off an embarrassing question, the client may give a fairly correct answer then joke about it. Many salesmen may overlook this natural trait and miss the point completely.

When you ask a question and your client gives you such a reply, make a note of it and come back to the question again later on. Many people can laugh at their mistakes, no matter how painful. (Some of these people don't mind others laughing with them, but be careful. The joke after all is on them, not you.)

In every client relationship I have had, this situation has occurred some time or another. In each event the joke has been most revealing. Learn to look for this type of answer. It is a special plea from your client. When it comes make sure you do go back to the topic at a later time. However, it is best to wait a day or so to be sure you are clear about the reply.

14. Be truthful yourself. You can hardly expect your client to lay it on the line if you fill the dialogue with stories that are a bit above the truth. If your client comes up with a fish story, let it pass without attempting to better the ending.

"And so," the client is concluding his story of the deal he closed last year, "I took the property over in March, and within 6 months got a new buyer to give me a profit of $25,000 over the $15,000 I had put down." Many salesmen are already thinking of what success story they can invent that will top that one. Don't let yourself be led into the trap. Your client will only try to out-do your story.

You will gain few points, if any, in a story swapping match. It is far better to listen to his story and make some comment that indicates you were attentive, and that it was indeed an amazing tale.

UNDERSTANDING THE PROBLEM MEANS YOU HAVE TO UNDERSTAND THE PERSON

Thus far this chapter has covered the ten goals of financing. At least one of the ten goals must be met if financing is to be a part of the solution to your client's problem. Moving into a step-by-step procedure is important if you are to effectively utilize the tools of financing which will appear later in this book. All is to no avail if you are unable to *establish the proper relationship with your client*, then *keep that relationship.*

But you are still several steps away from that final result. The 14 key steps in the Qualifying Process will move the client toward the solution of his problems. Yet, a complete understanding of these steps is lacking unless you know what you need to ask to enable you to apply the various techniques of real estate financing.

What you need to know about the person. It is obvious that there will be two sets of facts you will need to know, depending on your client. Is he a buyer, a seller, or both? Some of the information will be the same in either case, so we can all it *general information.*

This general data is important for all clients. The importance of this information may not be apparent at first, but as you learn of the variety of financing tools available to you, you will see that it may be difficult to plan ahead without full details on your client.

GENERAL INFORMATION YOU NEED ON ALL CLIENTS AND HOW TO OBTAIN IT

1. Who is your client? Naturally you need his name. But go beyond that. Is he acting alone or are there others? A wife? Partners? Or, is he a corporation? Get a clear understanding right off the bat as soon as you get into the qualification session.

2. *Where does he live?* This may simply be an address. But it will tell you a lot.

3. *How long has he been in the area?* If he was born in your area you may not have to acquaint him with the same aspects of your community as you would someone from out of town. But don't assume that simply because someone has been in an area for a long time that he knows more than a newcomer.

4. *How can you reach him by phone?* You will need to know this as soon as possible. It is a great qualifier. Reluctance on the part of a client to give this information will mean you could be wasting your time.

5. *What caused him to seek you out?* You may already know the answer to this. Of course, you may have contacted him. If he was referred to you by someone you will want to drop that person a note thanking them, no matter what happens.

6. *The client's approximate age.* This answer may not have to be asked directly. It is sufficient that you make note that the client is in his early 30's or in his late 60's. It is obvious that the motivations of age will vary the solutions you may apply to the problem.

If your client is nearing retirement age, that information could be of great importance. Because age is difficult to ascertain in many cases, you may ask directly: "How soon do you plan on retiring?" This will generally start the conversation in the desired direction. I have found that the older the client, the easier it is to have him tell you his age without asking directly.

7. *The client's total obligations.* This covers a number of subtopics, such as: (A) Does he have a family? (B) How many children? (C) What are their ages? (D) How many are nearing college age? (E) What about dependents? (F) Does he have heavy financial burdens you should know about?

Finding out a person's obligations is not as difficult as most salesmen think. All that is necessary is to get the client to begin talking. If you ask a few simple questions about his family, where his children go to school, and through a few comments about *how expensive* that must be, the data will often flow out like water over a dam.

You will also want to know who his accountant is—if he has one. Make note of the accountant's name for later reference.

8. *What real estate does he own?* This information can provide you with new ways to solve a problem. You need to know what he owns since it will tell you what type of buyer or seller he is. "Do you own a lot of real estate?" is the best way to get into this topic. It will start him talking.

If he does not own any real estate, or at best only the one piece he wants to sell, it is important that you ask "why." The reason will help you deal with this client more effectively.

9. *Has he taken capital gains or losses in the past two years?* If he is a seller this will be very important. The carry-over of losses or build-up of gains may be

pertinent in a solution. A buyer may have other problems or a need to offset a gain which is carried over. Normally, a good lead into this topic would be: ''Mr. Client, it would be helpful for me to know what capital gains or losses you may have to work with. Are there any?'' I have never failed to get a correct answer from that one.

10. Does he have other types of tax shelter. Don't forget that there are many forms of tax shelter other than real estate. If you follow up on the gains question with this topic it seems like a logical progression. But it will often tell you what else he invests in. ''Yes,'' they will often say, ''lots of losses in the stock market.'' If there are gains in this area you will find out later.

A buyer with a lot of other tax shelters may be able to buy on terms that will minimize the shelters and maximize cash flow. On the other hand, a seller with a large tax shelter may be able to take earned income in the form of prepaid interest as a part of the down payment without any tax effect. Giving these two examples will enable the reluctant client to speak freely on this question.

11. What is his overall average tax rate. Keep in mind that many people don't know what their overall average tax rate is. Some won't want to give this information, but keep at it until you get some idea. It will be impossible for you to make any accurate projections showing the results of your proposals unless you have this data. A seller with a high tax rate may want to put off as much earned income until later years. If he has a low tax rate, it may be more desirable to maximize gains early.

A buyer with a high tax rate will need to maximize tax credits, whereas a low rate (due to shelter or lack of income) may require the need for cash flow. One good way to guide the client into this topic is by making this statement: ''From what you have told me, I'd assume you are paying an average of 30% of your annual earnings in real estate tax.'' Of course, you should adjust this percentage to fit what he has told you thus far. If you are met with silence, continue: ''Would it be safe for me to assume you are in the 30% overall rate?''

12. What is his approximate annual income? This is a bit more specific and may call on all your abilities to obtain the answer. A buyer will have to disclose this information if he is to apply for a mortgage, and sellers should plan ahead to take the greatest possible advantage of some of the selling tools of financing.

13. Does he see a shift in his annual income in the future? This may not mean retirement. He may have a mortgage that will be satisfied in the near future. It may be an expected increase in salary or a loss of a job. If she works, his wife may be leaving her position. There are many reasons for shifts, up or down, in income. If they are anticipated they can play an important role in planning a sale or a purchase.

14. How much can be set aside each year above his living expenses and other obligations? This is not easy to ascertain. Most people don't know what can safely be set aside in a savings account. Certainly, some of their possible savings should be reserved for emergencies and not committed to investments. This information will be good to know, but not absolutely essential except when the client is a young buyer who is looking to make money or a seller who wants to take a profit and move up.

In later chapters the steps that will help you ascertain this information will be covered in more detail.

IMPORTANT QUESTIONS TO ASK SELLERS

1. *How long have they owned the property they want to sell?*

2. *What capital improvements have they made since their purchase?*

3. *What are their obligations, or mortgages, on this property?*

4. *What do they feel their needs are?* This will tell you a lot about the motivations of sellers. How candid are they in answering this question?

5. *When did they decide to use you as their agent?* This is a great leading question. In the first place, it assumes they have made that decision and gets them thinking in a positive mood. There are numerous ways of asking this question, and much will depend on the tone of the conversation. But don't fail to get into this topic if the listing is one you want.

6. *All the details on the property itself.* Get all the data as soon as possible, as sellers are most receptive to answering questions when they are in a qualifying session. If you have to spread the fact-finding sessions over long periods of time it will give the impression you are not a pro. Get the data then go to work with confidence.

IMPORTANT QUESTIONS TO ASK BUYERS

1. *How much cash can he invest now?* There is no sense attempting to sell a property that you know will take twice the down payment your client has to work with. In asking this question, watch out for the answer "I can come up with more if needed." Get to the bottom. What is the maximum they can come up with if you find the right property?

2. *What are his capabilities?* This is not financial information but actual capabilities. What type of business or real estate are they able to take over. If they will need outside management, then that will have to be taken into account when you show them property.

There is a tendency for a retiring couple to want to get into a business they know nothing about. Part of your job may be to point out the problems in that and suggest another type of realty.

3. *What is his timing?* Buyers often given the impression that they need to act right away or that there is no hurry at all. These are two extremes that are

rarely adhered to. The middle-road approach is best, of course, but get your buyer to give you some timetable with which to work.

4. Is he currently working with another agent? This question is usually not asked because the salesman is afraid of knowing his competition. Ask the question. If the answer is "yes," you will try to get the client to work with you exclusively. If the answer is "no," then commend the client on his choice. Knowing your competition will help you serve your client better. Keep in mind that even if he is not working with another agent today, he may tomorrow.

To summarize the *ten goals of financing* are a must and should be examined each time you approach a problem in real estate. But, as real estate problems are tied to people, the step-by-step method of *developing a working relationship with a client that will last,* becomes your foundation to success in putting the tools of financing to work.

The fact-finding sessions and the checklists given in this chapter will be very helpful to you. The ability to have this data flow into your files will depend on the presentations you give and the impressions you make on your clients.

Chapter 2

How to Determine The Goals Of the Principals

Even the best salesman will have a difficult time meeting the goals of his buyer or seller unless he knows what those goals are. To make the situation more difficult, the discovery of these goals can be a hard task. More often than not, neither the buyer nor the seller knows exactly what the goal is or should be. This chapter will show you how to help the parties ascertain their goals.

THEIR GOALS AND NOT YOUR GOALS SUPERIMPOSED

"Do you know what I think you should do?" You have heard this type of statement before. It precedes advice that is someone's idea of what you should do. Generally, it is what they might do if they were in your shoes. It could continue as follows: "I'd take $50,000 and get a nice bar at a good location and make a killing."

It is so easy to have an idea and to overlay that idea on the goals of others. Your idea may be the best, the right thing to do, but it is still *your* idea. The goals of your clients must be brought out into the open as their goals. At times, you will have to prod, pull, and be patient in arriving at these goals, but always remain silent as to your own goals.

THE BUYER'S GOALS—UNDERSTAND THEM AND YOU WILL MAKE MORE SALES

Goals and motivation are separate. Prior to moving into the buyer's goals, a brief explanation of the two from a selling point of view is necessary.

Goals are the stepping blocks into the future. These blocks are set by logic as well as emotion. Some people don't set any definite goals, others set unrealistic ones. Some goals are too high, others too low. Everyone has goals, even if they are nothing but dreams in the sky or lost hopes.

Motivation is the emotion that drives people to seek out their goals. The more definite the goals, the stronger and more pronounced the motivation. Motivation, however, is not always working in a straight line. Some people are full of drive (highly motivated), but lack defined goals. They are always moving and are standing still at the same time.

Often, it is easier to see the motivation that is moving your client than the goal. To act on the motive without understanding the goal is not prudent. Because of this, it is far more important to see the goal than the motivation. Once the goal is in sight, your selling capability can be directed to the attainment of that goal. When you start to sell with the goal clearly in your mind, a remarkable result will occur—you will make more sales.

OVERLOOKING THE GOALS WILL MEAN TIME WASTED

It will mean lost sales as well.

The first encounter between a buyer and the salesman may result in an unsatisfactory conclusion, simply because the salesman fails to spend time counseling the buyer. If a buyer walks into the office and announces he wants to buy an apartment house, what occurs next? It takes great restraint on the part of the salesman to sit this buyer down and ask a few questions about his reasons for wanting to buy an apartment house. The average salesman, in fact, will be so anxious to get out and drive to the nearest apartment complex in his listing book, that all he will get from the prospect is his name and about how much cash he can invest.

Once the salesman realizes that an hour spent in the office will be worth days in the field, the building of a sale can begin. The qualification process is the time to set out the client's goals.

HOW TO HELP THE BUYER DISCOVER WHAT HIS GOALS REALLY ARE

You want to find out what the buyer wants to accomplish and why he wants to buy what he thinks he wants. The prospect who announces he wants to buy an apartment house may really mean that as far as he knows, that is the type of property he wants to own. This knowledge may be the result of the imposed goals of others, or it could be based on a genuine experience in owning apartment houses.

To start the process of qualification, you will begin by establishing the rapport that will carry you through future dealings with this prospect. A mistake at this stage may never be rectified.

SEVEN TIPS FOR GETTING THINGS STARTED ON THE RIGHT FOOT

1. Be in surroundings that are comfortable. You want to keep the prospect still for a while, so if your office is not quiet or comfortable go out for a cup of coffee.
2. Privacy is important. This does not mean you must lock your door or find an empty corner in a coffee shop. Simply isolate yourself from the normal humdrum of your surroundings. Have your phone calls held or joke to the waitress that you and your guest have some serious business to discuss.
3. Seek an early, central ground of mutual interest. Don't invent one, but find one you both have. It is there if you look for it.
4. Soft sell, but sell. What you are selling at this point is your ability to help once you know what is needed.
5. Control the conversation by letting the prospect do the talking. It is a fatal mistake to think you control a conversation by doing all the talking.
6. Ask pertinent qusetions to bring out the goals and abilities of the prospect. "Mr. Prospect," you may say, "have you owned any apartment houses before?" Simple, direct, and to the point.
7. Don't rush the prospect or let him rush you. You are doing your job, even though the prospect may not know it yet. If he seems anxious to get moving, you have overlooked a major part of the qualification process. Explain why you are talking instead of out looking at property.

This explanation of the qualification and goal-finding process is very important. It should come early in the encounter and should be filled with confidence. "Once I have a full grasp of your needs, I know we will find you what you need." Let the buyer know that you want to know his needs, and that by using this knowledge you will be better equipped to serve him.

Your ability to keep silent is important. Selling, after all, is really effective listening. If you will just listen to what is being said, you will be on the way to making a sale.

HOW TO STAY IN CONTROL OF THE QUALIFYING PROCESS

The learning process will develop at a fast pace as long as you control the conversation. To do this you will be doing more listening than talking, but keep in mind that just being silent is not listening. You must pay attention to what is being said.

Your guard is up and you are looking for the reasons the buyer has for his desired action. These reasons may or may not be goals. That is what you must determine. The reason someone gives could be a cover-up for his goal or a substitute for a real goal.

There is an old adage that "buyers are liars." This is not true. Buyers often don't tell it as it is simply because they do not know the correct answer. Or worse, salesmen don't hear the real meaning of what is said.

Once the rapport seems to be moving in the right direction and you feel the buyer is ready to get down to the nitty-gritty, you can begin to ask the all important questions: Why? Why not? When? What? and How?

"Why have you chosen apartment houses" is a good question to start the goal-seeking. "What do you feel you will want to do five years from now?" This is a great start to see if he has any long-range plans. You may be surprised to find he doesn't know, or has some vague idea about settling back to retire on his wealth. If you ask about the future and get no definite goal dig deeper.

"When do you plan to retire from your present line of work?" Again, you may be shocked to find he has given this no thought at all. "What future expenses do you feel you may have that we should plan for?" Children going to college, operations, balloon payment on a mortgage—there are many things that can cause a financial burden in the near future that should be incorporated into the client's goals.

MISREADING GOALS OR OVERLOOKING THEM ALTOGETHER

You will not hit on the correct goal 100 percent of the time, no matter what you do. Yet without the qualification process you will have a low batting average, and the trial-by-error procedure most commonly used is not very efficient.

The missed goal is not as disasterous as overlooking it altogether however, as you will probably be working close to the target. Adjustments in the course can be made in mid-stream to make the sale.

Recently, one of my salesmen was working with a Canadian buyer who said he was in the market for an apartment complex to convert to a time-sharing vacation program. The salesman was so convinced that this was the target that he spent weeks showing the prospect numerous complexes. The goal was seen as a desire to have a time-sharing vacation package. After a month of going back and forth from Canada and a dozen or so apartment complexes,the full goal was finally seen. The time-sharing was right, but the type of property was wrong. What the Canadian really needed was a hotel. This situation was a misdirected goal, or a superimposed goal. The Canadian had been told by friends that the best buy in Florida at the time was apartment buildings. The salesman, believing the Canadian was on target, went off with the prospect unable to understand why a deal eluded him.

It is typical for salesmen not to question the needs of a buyer. They fear that to do so will cost them the prospect. While this is far from the truth, it is hard to convince salesmen to seek goals early in the selling process.

Because goals are established by emotion as well as logic, the hidden goal is most easily overlooked. In this situation, the buyer presents more of a "rationalization" for buying than his true goal. Because the rationalization may be for his benefit as well as others, it will often be selected as a cover for the real goal.

Buyers of hotels, restaurants, and other glamour properties often hide their goals with these rationalizations. The buyer will say: "I would consider seasonal properties, but keep in mind they must show one heck of a return." The salesman may assume this to be only a warm approach to seasonal properties and spend time looking for other types of investments. The real goal, however, could well be that the buyer wants a hotel and is hoping the salesman will give him the amunition to sell himself and whoever else the rationalization is designed to fool.

There is no easy way to scrape away the layer of false reasons to find the real goal. One set of questions I often use seems to bring out a wide range of answers and helps me get down to the facts at hand.

"Mr. Buyer," I'll begin, "if you were to draw a picture in your mind of yourself ten years from now, what do you see?" At this the prospect may stop and think. He usually says, "I haven't thought about that" or "I see . . ." If he doesn't see something I'll ask, "Mr. Buyer, what would you want to see?"

Once you feel you have ascertained the goals and have gained insight into the motivation of the buyer, keep an open mind and be ready to change your opinion of this goal as time progresses. In working with a buyer you may learn new facts to indicate an even deeper goal than earlier anticipated.

A CASE HISTORY OF A GOAL THAT CHANGED IN MID-STREAM: Mr. John Barth came to our office highly recommended as an investor. In the first encounter with Mr. Barth it was discovered he was moving from his home in Ohio to Florida and would need to find a residence. Later, he said, he would be in the market for income property.

From a residential standpoint, the basics of his need were noted. The size of his family indicated he would require a four-bedroom home. He wanted most of the items buyers want in Florida: water frontage, pool, good area, modern appliances, and so on. He had ample cash to put down for such a home.

The salesman from the residential department went through the presale qualification in detail and set out to line up homes for Mr. Barth to see. The idea was this: Barth would approve several homes and then his wife would fly down from Ohio to make her choice.

Nine homes were viewed by Mr. Barth and of these he settled on two as being ideal for his needs. Two days later Mrs. Barth came to town. You will not be surprised to learn she did not like either of the two, or for that matter any of the seven others. But the strange part of this situation was her reason. "None of these homes really suit my husband," she told us.

As it turned out, Mr. Barth had set as the ideal home a mental picture of what he thought his wife would like. At this point Mr. and Mrs. Barth went through a qualification session together. There was give and take, and finally a new image of a home appeared to take shape. They decided they didn't want to be on the water after all, that a large, country-type setting was more to their liking.

The salesman, however, was not convinced that this was the real situation, so he asked the two prospects to write down all the aspects of their desired home. He then handed each of them paper and pen and said: "Only the five most important priorities, and when you have finished number them in order of importance."

Here is what happened:

Mr. Barth wrote:
1. 4 bedrooms
2. Large lot
3. Modern kitchen
4. Family room
5. Fully air conditioned

Mrs. Barth wrote:
1. Good area for children
2. Den for John
3. Room for garden
4. Near shopping
5. Master bedroom separate from childrens' bedrooms

Different priorities, but they were farther along toward a mutual ground. With this information, the salesman then launched into his "why" program. Why not 5 bedrooms? Why do you want a garden? What do you mean by a good area for children?

The answers to these questions enabled the buyers to understand exactly what it was that the other wanted. The salesman now felt he had the goal in mind that was *their* goal.

This example obviously points out the need to have both the husband and wife together in the qualification process. But, even more important, it shows the role the salesman can play in helping the buyers crystallize their own goals. It is not uncommon for a husband and wife to be unaware of the other's priorities.

INVESTMENT PROPERTIES PRESENT A DIFFERENT GOAL STANDARD

When working in investment properties the ultimate goal of a buyer can be more important than that of a residential sale. The reason is residential sales are of a transient nature. The ownership span in homes is much shorter than the term income property is owned. The goal of ownership of investment property is generally long range. A home may be merely a stepping stone, and buyers often feel they will eventually move up into something better. The exception to this would be a retired person who is seeking a home or apartment that will be his last. Oddly enough, this goal is often overlooked and salesmen will sell down to this type of prospect. If the retired person sees himself settling down for the rest of his life in an apartment (many do), the salesmen can upgrade by adding color to this mental picture.

Investment property is generally the means by which the end is to be reached. Because of this, the overall goal should be sought out. It is one thing to buy an apartment house or strip store for the immediate cash flow, another to build an estate for other future gains.

The goals of most buyers of investment properties are set by their limitations of experience in investing in real estate. Most buyers want a high return of cash as their first priority. Salesmen who spend weeks rounding up only the high yield, cash-on-cash properties may find to their chagrin that the buyer really wants to set up his estate so that in ten or so years he can upgrade his life style.

Follow this conversation and see how goals can change.

Salesman: "Mr. Buyer, you said your interest is in buying something that will show you at least a 10% cash flow."

Buyer: "Don't you think that is reasonable? After all, I can get close to that in the bond market. Besides, all I have ever read on investing in real estate seems to indicate a 10% return to be minimal."

Salesman: "Do you need the cash flow to live on?"

Buyer: "Not really, but what does that have to do with it?"

Salesman: "Tell me, Mr. Buyer, when you think about this idea of investing in real estate, what do you feel it should do for you five years from now?"

Buyer: "I haven't really thought about that."

Salesman: "Let's talk about this for a moment and see what you really want to accomplish by a prudent investment plan."

Force the buyer to give the future some thought. He has his dreams, all you have to do is to open the tap and they will flow out.

THE AGE FACTOR AND HOW IT WILL AFFECT GOALS

In the first chapter importance was placed on the need to understand and use the age of your buyer. A 35-year-old buyer will view the future in a different perspective from a 65-year-old buyer. Both may want the same thing, but for different reasons. Salesmen often overlook the long-term investment for their older clients, when the goal of those clients may well be acquiring wealth for their grandchildren.

The short-range goal or investment that may fit that philosophy of in-quick-and-out-with-a-fast-profit will suit most any age buyer. However, many younger buyers are preconditioned into the long haul and don't have the experience in real estate to accept the idea of a fast turnover. Your long-term service to this buyer will depend on your ability to grasp his goal, then to arrange the structure of the deal to fit his future plans. As you develop a comfortable approach to the many tools of financing, the varied ways to create different end results from the same deal will aid in this process.

GETTING THE GOALS DOWN ON PAPER

In your first encounter with the buyer you should use two data sheets. One will be for the prospect to fill out. An example is shown in Figure 2-1.

Figure 2-1: CONFIDENTIAL INFORMATION SHEET

NAME ____________ AGE ____ MARITAL STATUS ____________
NAME OF SPOUSE ____________ CHILDRENS'AGES ____________
PRESENT ADDRESS ________________________
PHONE ____________ MONTHLY RENTAL
OWN OR RENT ________ OR P.I.T.I. ON MTG
____

REAL ESTATE OWNED ________________________
____

OTHER ASSETS OWNED ________________________
____

EMPLOYMENT STATUS ________________________
FINANCIAL OBLIGATIONS ________________________
____

PERSONAL INFORMATION ________________________
____

NEEDS AND GOALS (1) ________________________
(2) ____________ (3) ____________
(4) ____________ (5) ____________
(List the five most important goals in order of their priority.)
HOW MUCH CASH IS AVAILABLE FOR IMMEDIATE INVESTMENT ______
(Without disposing of any present assets as shown above.)
HOW MUCH ANNUAL INVESTMENT CAN BE ADDED EACH YEAR ______
WITH NO CHANGE FROM THE PRESENT STATUS, WILL INCOME NEXT YEAR DIFFER FROM THIS YEAR? IF SO, BY WHAT AMOUNT ________
EXPLAIN ________________________
____

WHAT WAS THE OVERALL INCOME TAX RATE FOR THE LAST YEAR ___
HAVE YOU BEEN WORKING WITH OTHER AGENTS IN THE PAST FOR THE SAME TYPE OF PROPERTY?
____

The questions on this sheet may not seem overly important at first. Information of any kind is only important if you are able to utilize it for positive ends.

The key factors to look for in obtaining the answers for the information sheet are outlined below.

THE 15 KEYS TO THE BUYER INFORMATION SHEET

1. Is the buyer reluctant to give you any information? If he is, you will have problems in your relationship with this prospect. You should not spring the data sheet on the prospect too early in your session as this may cause some of the reluctance. Ease into it. Some buyers will fill the sheet in by themselves with no hesitation. Others will be more comfortable if you ask the questions and fill in the answers yourself. Play this by ear.
2. Make special note of the obvious answers, such as age, marital status, childrens' ages, and present address. These are all factors which will have bearing on the buyer's motivations and goals.
3. Does the buyer own or rent? If he rents, ask why. The answer could indicate inability to raise capital to buy or an unwillingness to get locked into a property. The amount of rent or mortgage payment also will reflect on his financial capability.
4. Real estate owned. Some buyers own vast properties, others only a few or none. An understanding of what knowledge your client has about real estate can save you headaches later. Don't fall into the trap, however, of assuming that ownership alone creates expertise.
5. Knowing what other assets the prospect owns is essential. Of course, you are interested in major assets and not the car or mink coat. A buyer heavy in the stock market, for example, may require special attention as he will be constantly comparing his real estate investments with the stock market. This is easy and will work in your favor if you speak the same language he is used to. Remember, stock market brokers sell the outlook of profit, the concept of: "It is selling at $5.00 a share today, could go to $7.00 in a day or so." Real estate is not that type of market.
6. Employment status and where he is employed. Or, does he own his own company? When will he retire? Is he insecure in his job? All factors you will want to know.
7. The financial obligations your prospect has go beyond his mortgage payments. Does he have two children in private school, or in college? Is he feeding a sick corporation? Does he have major business losses? Hit on this, but keep in mind you may not get all you need to know right away. Watch for new developments in this area as your rapport with the prospect develops.
8. The personal information question is a leading one. If you have your

prospect fill out the questionnaire (best way), don't give any lead-in as to how to answer this question. See what he puts down. If you are asked what it means, tell the prospect to put anything down that he may feel you should know about him.

9. The needs and goals are, of course, the basis for the qualification process. Tell your prospect to list the five most important goals, or needs, as far as the real estate investment at hand is concerned. However, this will be just your starting point, and you will build on these five goals until you are able to grasp the entire picture of what your prospect wants to accomplish.
10. How much cash? Question this answer, no matter what the amount. "Could you add more if the investment was exceptional?" If so, "How much?" Or you may take the other side, "Is this cash you have to invest over 80% of your net worth?" Some investors will overdo this answer, others will grossly understate the amount of capital they can invest.
11. The annual investment, or the amount needed to carry a land purchase or other form of continued investment program is important. However, the real reason for the question is to bring up the matter of annual earnings. You may naturally be talking about an annual investment, then have to help the prospect figure the amount by taking his annual income and deducting the normal living expenses he has.
12. Does the prospect expect to have any shift, up or down, in his earnings in the coming year? The answer could be many: a large capital gain to be received in the next year from an installment sale; A drop in expenses that would increase income. Look for the big increase as it may guide you to look for a shelter for the year it occurs, rather than the present year.
13. The overall income tax rate may not be known by your prospect. If he does not know, ask him if you could check with his accountant, or even look at his 1040. The overall tax rate is important only if you are going to do an in-depth analysis of income properties. But, that analysis will require you to know much more about the prospect that you will obtain in the first encounter, so do not press this question. In brief, it is good to know if he is in a high or low bracket. This data will prove useful no matter how technical you may get on later analysis.
14. Use the information you have. If you put the information sheet in a file and don't look at it after the first day, you have wasted the effort. Refer back to it from time to time to see if anything has changed. Update the goals whenever you feel they have changed.
15. What has he done in the market? Find out if he has been with a dozen other brokers before he came to you. If so, ask why he has changed. Don't be afraid to get into this. A prospect who switches agents every week may do so tomorrow.

THE RECAP OF THE FIRST ENCOUNTER

The Recap of First Encounter form will be used after your first meeting with the prospect. To be more precise, it will be used after the prospect has left your office. A blank form is shown in Figure 2-2, and covers several topics which you have dealt with in the qualification process. Once the prospect has departed, you can refer to the notes you may have taken during the session and go over the information sheet the prospect has filled out. Figure 2-3 shows this form filled out.

With the meeting still fresh in your mind, sit down and fill out this recap sheet. Make careful notes of what you feel are the client's primary and secondary goals. The abilities and obligations should be itemized in detail so you can refer back to them later on.

The personal observation of the prospect is crucial. Be honest with yourself. There are times when you will undoubtedly feel the prospect has been less than honest with you. Make note of these feelings.

Figure 2-2: RECAP OF FIRST ENCOUNTER

PRIMARY GOALS: ____

____

____

SECONDARY GOALS: ____

____

____

ABILITIES	OBLIGATIONS
1.	1.
2.	2.
3.	3.
4.	4.
5.	5.

PERSONAL OBSERVATIONS: ____

____

____

____

DO I FEEL I HAVE EXPRESSED CONFIDENCE IN MY ABILITY TO SERVE HIS NEEDS AND BEST HELP HIM MEET HIS GOALS? ____________________

____

____

Have you made a good impression? The last portion of the recap is designed for you to be self-critical. Like any criticism, it must be direct. If you feel you have left out something important, call attention to this and make a note that you should rectify the situation as soon as possible.

Figure 2-3: RECAP OF FIRST ENCOUNTER

PRIMARY GOALS: To build equity to enable possible retirement in 20 years with an annual income of no less than $75,000, without reduction of at least 75% of the attained equity at that time.

SECONDARY GOALS: To seek a secure financial situation in about 20 years with good income and financial backing for self and family.

ABILITIES

1. Age: 32
2. Has $55,000 in cash
3. Has home with $45,000 equity
4. Owns cars outright
5. Has $25,000 in stock
6. Has fairly secure job that covers present economic needs
7. Is in good health
8. Has $8,000 in equity in a residential lot in city
9. Can invest approximately $4,000 per year from present income
10. Present job pays $35,000 per year

OBLIGATIONS

1. Overall tax rate is 32%
2. Pays all $326 PITI on home
3. Other fixed annual expenses around $11,000 per year
4. Has wife and 2 children (kids in elementary school)
5. Feels he must put aside at least $2,500 per year for emergencies

PERSONAL OBSERVATIONS: Seems to be on the up and up. Has filled out the personal data sheet and has been candid with me as to his needs, wants, and goals. He may, however, not be as willing to speculate as he thinks at the moment. Have not met wife as yet. He states he worked with another agent several weeks ago, but has not been out with any other since. Said he will stick to me. We will see.

DO I FEEL I HAVE EXPRESSED CONFIDENCE IN MY ABILITY TO SERVE HIS NEEDS AND BEST HELP HIM MEET HIS GOALS? I feel sure he will stick with me until I can meet this requirement. Not too sure that he has as much confidence in me as I would like. I will work on that.

WEED OUT THE PROSPECT WHO WILL WASTE YOUR TIME

One of the important results of a carefully planned qualification process is to weed out the buyer who is not a genuine buyer. Some of these pseudobuyers are easy to spot, others are not as evident. Time will be saved if you can learn to determine which prospect will be a buyer and which will be a looker. The deadbeat prospect will drive you up the walls looking for the nonexistent property of his dreams.

Unfortunately, there is no clear signal to indicate many of the prospects you should put into the category of time-wasters. Some of these prospects are genuine buyers and will buy, but only after months of effort that in the end result is not truly productive.

We have all had this type of buyer from time to time and we can find some solace by telling ourselves that we finally did make the sale after all. Yet, the time and effort wasted in finding that unique property for this reluctant buyer caused many lost sales by making it necessary to pass up other, more qualified prospects. The percentage of sales made to the time-waster over the sales lost will work against you in the long run.

TABOOS—OR HOW NOT TO IMPRESS YOUR PROSPECT

Many of the mistakes salesmen make are made over and over again. I have narrowed this list down to the ten most common errors made. They are not in a priority order of importance, since salesmen will generally make more than one of these errors.

The Eleven Most Important Things Not To Do

1. Start an argument.
2. Rush out to show property before you are prepared.
3. Get your facts wrong, or overstate the facts.
4. Talk too much and not listen carefully.
5. Be late to your appointments.
6. Skip the qualification process altogether.
7. Work with a prospect you feel is a deadbeat to prove you can sell him something.
8. Put the amount of the commission in your mind the moment you meet your prospect.
9. Never ask "why," because you might find out.
10. Wait for your prospect to say, "I'll buy that, please write it up!"
11. Never try to top your clients "fish" story with a better one of your own.

WORKING WITHIN THE GOALS OF THE SELLER

One of the main objectives of working with sellers is to control the listing of the property. You know the advantage of the exclusive listing, and that the lower the price the better the chance of selling the property in a short time-span.

This objective can create a conflict of interest with the goals of the seller. A low price may be desirable from the salesman's point of view and market conditions, but this may not meet the seller's goals.

This is a matter of attitude for the salesman. If the seller has a strongly stated goal, then the entire effort of the salesman should be directed towards this goal—even if an outright sale is not the answer.

There will be times when a sale may seem to be the solution, whereas a re-financing of the property will generate the needed cash and be more in the seller's interest. It takes some upper-lip biting to move this motivated seller and ideal property off your inventory rolls and into the hands of a mortgage broker. This should be done if you feel it is best for the seller.

HOW TO DETERMINE THE SELLER'S GOALS

As with the buyer, the seller will often approach a situation with a predetermined decision which he feels is the solution to his problem. This decision is often based on outside influence, either sound advice or the superimposed goals of others. Your approach to these sellers will depend somewhat on their origin. Knowing the origin of your seller will aid you in the goal-seeking process. The sources of sellers follow.

SIX SOURCES OF SELLERS

1. *Expired Listings:* The salesman locates a known seller from a list of expired listings and attempts to relist the property. The motives and goals of the seller are rarely questioned in this case, as the salesman assumes the sale is the goal or at least the means to fit the goal. This failure to seek goals may account for the fact that the property did not sell in the earlier listing.
2. *Cultivated Sellers:* A live-wire salesman will no doubt have a campaign of farming new sellers. The methods vary and the productivity of farming depends on the effort, perseverance, and rapport the salesman is able to develop. These sellers are people who may not have thought of selling before, but because of the conditions of the times may now decide to sell for any of dozens of reasons. A salesman that uses "Goal Seeking" as part of the farming process will increase his percentage of motivated sellers and number of sold listings.

3. *Cold Calls:* The seller calls the office and simply states he wants to sell his property. The majority of salesmen that work with this seller will not question the goals or the motivation. They are most anxious to get the price low enough to make the job of selling easier. A cold call listing is generally more motivated than any of the others. He has called you. Of course, his reason for calling you may be a result of efforts made by you or your firm. Nonetheless, failure to seek the goals of this or any prospective seller will result in a marketing program that may have problems in the long run.
4. *Referrals:* There are two forms of referrals. The first, and most productive, is the satisfied client who will bring you new clients or who recommends you to someone he knows. The second is a referral by a friend or satisfied client of a third party known to be interested in selling.
5. *Previous Buyers:* This is the cream of the crop. A buyer will generally become a seller if you give him enough time. Because this type of seller is without a doubt the best, salesmen will be greatly rewarded by understanding the goals of their buyers to know when they should become sellers. The reverse is also true. Sellers become buyers, and again the goal process is crucial in understanding this phenomenon.
6. *Friends and Relatives:* Often overlooked by even the best salesman are his own friends and relatives. Some salesmen fear they will lose a friend or get business involved with social activities. Lack of confidence in one's abilities plays a major part in this fear. Yet, at times it is difficult to sit down with a friend and dig into his goals. The older the friend the more difficult this process can be.

All sellers can be classified into one or more of these six categories. The first three comprise sellers who are new to you, and you must spend the necessary time to develop the rapport that is so important to all aspects of selling. The latter three categories deal with preestablished confidence to varying degrees. Obviously, the previous buyer is already a client and knows your service. You will not keep him as a seller unless you have maintained a good rapport or provided good service in the first instance. Therefore, as in dealing with buyers, the first step in the goal-seeking process is to establish rapport and confidence. Now move into the goals themselves.

THE SELLER'S GOALS: WHAT THEY ARE AND HOW TO GET THEM OUT INTO THE OPEN

To begin with, there are six key points to keep in mind as you move into the goal-seeking process. I will assume you have taken all the proper preliminary steps for establishing good raport and the seller has enough confidence in you to list his property with your firm.

The Six Key Steps Toward Discovering Seller's Goals

1. Lay the ground rules for the goal-seeking process: You will want to establish the reason for the questions you will be asking. It is much better to do this right away than wait until the seller questions your intent. You may begin by saying:

   "Mr. Seller, I understand your interest in selling your property. However, because there are over ____ ways to dispose of real estate, and each method has a different impact, I want to understand all I can about what you wish to accomplish in the sale. I want to spend a few minutes with you in ascertaining your goals."

2. Restate the seller's desire to sell, in stronger terms than presented: This is the opposite technique of restating the objections of buyers covered in the first chapter. For example:

   Seller: "My wife and I have decided to sell the 15 units we are operating."

   Restatement by Salesman: "I understand from what you say, *both you and your wife* want to dispose of the 15 units you own."

   What you are doing is inviting a remark to explain what he originally said. You have not asked, as you will later, *why* he wants to sell. You have merely restated in stronger terms what he first said. His reply may be:

   Seller: "Well yes, but the reason is . . ."

   You need to listen very carefully to his reply. Keep in mind that after your restatement you should stop and await his reply. It will come and will be significant.

3. Ask the seller why he wants to sell the property: He may have told you already, but ask him again anyway. If he did give a reason, *restate the reason:*

   Seller: "We want to sell the 15 units because we feel we can operate more units just as easily and want to own more."

   Salesman: "I understand that the reason for selling is to enable you to own more units." Pause, wait for a reply. If it doesn't come, ask why.

   Seller: "As I said, we feel we can operate more units."

   Salesman: "I see, your goal then is to own more units."

   You are trying to get the seller to accept what he is telling you as his goals. If they are his goals he will accept them, if they are merely reasons he may back off. Should he fail to take the goal as his, then dig for another.

4. Paint a future picture: This is similar to the same technique you use with the buyer. You are reaching out to see if your seller has thought about the future in concrete terms. Again, you may use restatement.

   Salesman: "I understand from what you have told me, Mr. and Mrs. Seller, that your desire is to own more units after you sell the 15 you presently have. Tell me, what do you see yourselves doing five years from now?"

   The mental picture your sellers have is important for their goals.

5. Expand on these goals. Once your seller begins to think of the future, you can get him to expand the dream into specific goals. In this stage you are getting down to the nitty-gritty. The dream may be unrealistic or not high enough. Usually, your early goal assumptions will fall into one of these two extremes. A goal that you feel is too low or too high can be brought into clearer focus by simply stating it so the sellers can hear it for themselves.

   Salesman: "Mr. Seller, I understand you see yourself and your wife moving up into a 20-unit apartment house instead of the 15-unit one you presently have."

   There is something about hearing your goals stated by someone else that makes you think of them in more concrete terms. Normally, you can expect a reevaluation of the goals to follow.

6. Go beyond the stated goal: So far, all you may have is a vague generalization of an intermediate goal. A seller wants more units. But why? What does he really want to accomplish? Again you can use the restatement process to dig deeper.

   Salesman: "Mr. Seller, I understand you want to move up into more units. What do you want to accomplish by this move?"

   Such a question may bring a defensive reply as, "We just feel we can make more with a larger complex." Such replies should not be challenged at that moment. An argument could result. Instead, back off and move into another topic for awhile. Then, come back to the question in another way: "I want to help you reach your goals in investing in real estate. Because of this, I want to understand all the things you wish to accomplish." Again, pause and see if that gets some results. Then proceed. "A move up into larger units is a positive move to be sure, but where do you want it to end?"

At this time you may introduce the list of Methods of Disposing of Real Estate (Figure 2-4). This list is a good lead into the topic of goals because most sellers are not aware of the many facets of selling. Those methods that are new to you will be covered in later chapters or in the glossary. It is not unusual to combine several methods into different concepts altogether, making the list even longer.

Figure 2-4: METHODS OF DISPOSING OF REAL ESTATE

1. Acquisition (additional property)
2. Adverse possession
3. Bankruptcy
4. Build to suit
5. By will
6. Charitable contribution
7. Chattel
8. Condemnation
9. Conversion
10. Demolition
11. Development
12. Discount sale with recapture of lease-back
13. Easement lease
14. Easement sale
15. Eminent domain
16. Escheat
17. Exchange complete
18. General corporation
19. Gift
20. Joint venture
21. Holding
22. Insurance lease
23. Insurance mortgage
24. Improvement of building
25. Lease—air
26. Lease complete
27. Lease—sub
28. Limited partnership
29. Mortgage out—foreclose
30. Option—sale
31. Partition suit
32. Prescription
33. Pyramid
34. Reclamation
35. Refinancing
36. Rent
37. Rezoning
38. Sale—air rights
39. Sale by auction
40. Sale—contract back
41. Sale—improvements only
42. Sale—land only
43. Sale/lease riparian
44. Sale—lease-back
45. Sale—lease-back with recapture
46. Sale or lease leasehold
47. Sale—riparian rights
48. Sell complete
49. Subdivide
50. Subordination
51. Subordination mortgage
52. Syndicate
53. Tax sale
54. Trust

WHAT TO DO ONCE YOU HAVE A FEELING FOR THE SELLER'S GOALS

Knowing what the goals are, then doing something about it is the next step in the listing process. Remember, the reason for knowing the goals is to utilize that information to your best advantage in setting up a marketing program that will come closest to helping the seller attain his goals.

The best way to start is to begin with the goal itself. Write it down in as detailed a way as possible. Go over the list of the Methods of Disposing of Real Estate and ask yourself this question for each method: "Will this method help the seller reach his goal, and if so, why, how quickly, how effectively, and what are the drawbacks?'' As you go down the list, you will find many methods which may give affirmative answers. List them in the order of importance from the standpoint of the seller's most pressing need, and then again from the market position. One method might be the best from all aspects except local market conditions. Since you must sell the concept in the market, this criterion will eliminate methods that would otherwise be best for the seller.

With this information, and the answers to your own questions, you are ready to apply the final touch to the goal process.

EXAMINING THE IMPACT YOUR SOLUTIONS MAY HAVE ON THE SELLER'S GOALS

This is where you will bring all your expertise into play. The more you know about the Methods of Disposing of Real Estate, the better you will apply the impact. A case study on this process follows. Follow through with the salesman to see how he made a study of the impact of his solutions.

Upon the completion of the first meeting, Jeff felt he had a good understanding of what the sellers wanted to accomplish. He wrote their goals down:

1. Sellers want to eventually have management-free income so that in 10 to 15 years they can have an income of around $50,000 per year plus a free and clear condo on the beach. Want to travel and have no ties.
2. Sellers feel their present 15-unit complex to be too small and that with their equity ($175,000) they could get a larger complex.
3. Sellers feel that a sale will give them cash to invest in a larger complex.

With this data down on paper, Jeff checked the sellers' capabilities and noted they also had about $60,000 in cash or stock to be used as possible investment capital. He then went over the list of Methods of Disposing of Real Estate. From that list he made these notes:

1. Outright sale: Could generate cash. As the market is strong, should sell quickly. Because of high gain, however, reinvestment capital will be reduced substantially. Sellers may have to hold paper.
2. Exchange: Could move sellers directly into larger unit. Time, however, could be longer than direct sale, and limited choice for exchange. Possible third leg on sale and exchange, however. Some problems in value equivalent as present owners are making more cash flow than a new owner would.
3. Syndicate: Could generate greater cash. Time problem, however, may take longer than sellers are willing to wait.
4. Refinancing: Will generate immediate cash. Mortgage rates are lower than they have been or may be for some time. No tax problems. This does not get

rid of the 15 units, but gives about the same after-tax cash to reinvest. Why not keep the 15 units and get 20 more?

Jeff had other solutions which were rejected. The sale and lease-back, for example, was considered as an adjunct to refinancing, but the low rates in the mortgage market made refinancing more acceptable. Pyramiding also was examined, and rejected as the limitation of reinvestment possibilities and time to pyramid did not suit the sellers.

The next step was to examine the impact of each of these four possible solutions on the sellers' goals. Each solution was fairly equal as far as the local market conditions. The time factor was weighted in favor of refinancing as the quickest, and then sale, exchange, and syndicate following in that order.

Jeff then reviewed the goals. Of the four, the refinancing solution seemed to be the best way to accomplish the long-term as well as intermediate goal. The sellers, he decided, should not sell at all, but refinance. With the cash from the new mortgage they could become buyers immediately—buying more units and therefore achieving their goal.

He then set out to document the basis for his decision. In a subsequent meeting with the sellers he showed them how it was to their advantage to keep what they had, using the equity gained in cash from a new mortgage to buy a larger complex. While Jeff did not list a property, as the 15 units were not sold, he did sell the converted sellers a 23-unit apartment complex. The 38 units enabled the sellers to build up enough equity to fulfill their goals.

KEEP YOUR ANALYSIS SIMPLE

Statisticians devise analytical forms that require a C.P.A. to decipher their meaning. Your analysis should be direct and to the point. At this stage of your listing process and goal seeking, all you should do is examine the goals and attempt to fit a marketing format into the program. The long-range goal should be kept in mind, but it will be the intermediate goal that will be most important for both you and the seller. Long-range goals will change, and hence it can be dangerous for you to rely on them. Analysis over a prolonged time period will also be subject to greater error. In fact, any projected analysis over five years will be wrong 99% of the time.

Application of your solutions to the seller's goals will require assumptions to be made. The depth of your goal searching will narrow down these assumptions, but will never eliminate the need for some guesswork. It would be best for you to hone in on two or three possible solutions to the problem, then confer with the seller to get his ideas. Have a detailed statement of how each of the solutions will affect the seller. The Impact Form shown in Figure 2-5 can be used. To learn how this impact analysis can be used, see how Jeff filled it out in Figure 2-6.

Figure 2-5: IMPACT FORM

STATE THE GOAL: ____

____

____

POSSIBLE SOLUTION: ____

____

____

1. HOW WILL THIS SOLUTION HELP IN REACHING THE DESIRED GOAL?

   ____

2. WHAT IS THE APPROXIMATE AMOUNT OF NET REINVESTABLE CAPITAL THAT CAN BE GENERATED FROM THE PROPERTY USING THE SOLUTION SHOWN? ____

   NOW? ______________ LATER? ______________

3. HOW LONG MAY IT TAKE TO OBTAIN THE DESIRED RESULTS? _____

4. WHEN COMPARED TO OTHER POSSIBLE SOLUTIONS, HOW EFFECTIVE IS THIS SOLUTION?

____

   ____

5. WHAT SHOULD BE DONE TO IMPLEMENT THIS SOLUTION? ________

   ____

6. MARKET SITUATION AS IT APPLIES TO THIS SOLUTION: __________

   ____

7. WHAT ARE THE DISADVANTAGES OF THIS SOLUTION? ___________

   ____

Figure 2-6: IMPACT FORM FILLED OUT

STATE THE GOAL: Develop investment program which will enable clients to have $50,000 in management-free income in approximately 15 years, with immediate move into more units.

POSSIBLE SOLUTION: Refinance existing apartment complex; add some cash to refinance proceeds and buy larger unit while keeping the existing one.

1. HOW WILL THIS SOLUTION HELP IN REACHING THE DESIRED GOAL? Will give best overall cash flow potential and use clients' abilities to their best advantage.
2. WHAT IS THE APPROXIMATE AMOUNT OF NET REINVESTABLE CAPITAL THAT CAN BE GENERATED FROM THE PROPERTY USING THE SOLUTION SHOWN? $120,000 in net loan proceeds.
   NOW? all LATER? ____
3. HOW LONG MAY IT TAKE TO OBTAIN THE DESIRED RESULTS? approximately 30 days
4. WHEN COMPARED TO OTHER POSSIBLE SOLUTIONS, HOW EFFECTIVE IS THIS SOLUTION? Seems to be the quickest; also best if owners are confident in the existing property.
5. WHAT SHOULD BE DONE TO IMPLEMENT THIS SOLUTION? Shop for new loan. At same time look for new complex. Suggest owners make offer on complex subject to new loan proceeds.
6. MARKET SITUATION AS IT APPLIES TO THIS SOLUTION: New money available now at attractive interest rates and terms of years. Good time to take advantage of that situation. The property seems to be able to support new loan to throw off the net proceeds of $120,000.
7. WHAT ARE THE DISADVANTAGES OF THIS SOLUTION? Sellers will keep existing base for tax accounting. Means keeping the existing property. Are sellers willing to do this? Or, do they have other reasons for selling?

Chapter 3

How to Maximize Leverage In Real Estate Financing

It is often thought that leverage and risk go hand in hand. The greater the leverage the higher the risk. This axiom is not without merit, but does not hold true in most real estate transactions. Yet, because leverage is one of the main factors in real estate investing, a clear understanding of its function is a prerequisite to the application of the tools of financing.

Leverage is the result of borrowing money at a constant rate lower than the Net Operating Income rate generated by the property. For example, say an investor buys a strip store for $200,000 cash and has no mortgage. The NOI of this free and clear property was $20,000 each year. The investor has a 10% yield before tax adjustments, cash on cash, but there is no leverage because there is no financing.

On the other hand, he could have purchased the same property with $25,000 down and obtained a first mortgage in the amount of $175,000. The annual payment of principal and interest amounts to $16,000 each year. This represents a 9.14% constant on the amount of the loan. The NOI rate in each situation is 10%, as $20,000 is the cash flow, and the price is $200,000. Yet, he has a mortgage payment of $16,000 which leaves him with a cash flow of $4,000 after debt service. This time he has leveraged his investment of $25,000 so that his yield, cash on cash, is 16%.

It is obvious that if he were to purchase eight such strip stores, on these same terms of $25,000 down on each and spending the same $200,000 as he did in the first example, his cash flow would be $32,000 rather than $20,000.

This chapter will delve into leverage and how you can put it to work for you and your clients. It will also cover overleverage and when leverage should be kept at a minimum or maximum. The pitfalls of overleverage and the extreme danger of overextension will also be discussed.

Remember that leverage is always examined with the effect the constant rate has to cash flow rate, and in turn the NOI rate. The combined principal and interest amount, as reflected by the total principal owed, is a constant annual percent that holds true through the term of the mortgage. For example: a loan for 20 years with an interest rate of 8½% per annum will have a constant payment of 10.4% of the principal amount at the beginning of the loan. As the loan progresses and matures the annual payment remains the same, but the constant rate is increasing. If the NOI is less than the 10.4% in the first year, the yield (cash on cash) will be reduced or eliminated altogether.

For example: a strip store sells for $200,000 and the NOI is 10% or $20,000 per year. If the buyer borrows $175,000 and the constant at the time of the closing is 10.4%, he pays $18,200 each year in debt service leaving a cash flow of $1,800 per year. As the cash down was $25,000, the yield is on 7.2%. Because this yield is less than the return the buyer would receive had he paid all cash, leverage is working against the investor.

WHY LEVERAGE IS IMPORTANT IN REAL ESTATE FINANCING

Investment properties are valued to a great extent by the cash flow they produce. A buyer will pay for a return based on the yield. If the risk demand for strip stores indicates a need to have a minimum of 10% cash on cash, it will be your job to find or market properties that can meet that demand return.

The use of the various tools of financing will allow you to increase the cash flow yield, thereby increasing the value. You will accomplish this feat because you have increased the leverage on that property.

Buyers are cash flow conscious and usually look for the immediate return on their investment. They will, at times, sacrifice the higher leverage, when the long run is more advantageous to them to accept a low or negative cash flow. But the overall leverage is still important. Leverage calculations will make no distinction in the tax advantage one property may have over another, nor will they pinpoint one property out of many as the right property to buy.

SIX KEY FACTORS IN REAL ESTATE LEVERAGE

First: the structure of financing will affect the amount of leverage you receive. A short pay-out of a mortgage may have a very high constant and may eliminate the cash flow entirely. On the other hand, an interest only mortgage will bring the constant to a lower level for the early term of the loan, even though it can create havoc in the cash flow in later years. The goals of your buyer will form a basis for the amount of leverage you will use in the solution you find.

Second: leverage calculations themselves are merely a comparison of yield increases, and should be used to show differences between financing methods and leverage capabilities of various properties. To accept a transaction by saying the leverage is 13.23%, so that is better than a 9.58% leverage could be short sighted. Why there is a difference can be most important. You will see how to make these comparisons later in this chapter and how to use leverage to your advantage.

Third: maximum leverage possible and maximum leverage feasible are two different aspects. After all, the maximum leverage in any transaction may or may not be available due to the circumstances of the property. Maximum leverage feasible depends on the investor. Again, the goals involved play an important part of your analysis of leverage.

Fourth: leverage by itself should not be the major criterion for analysis of a property. If the transaction is a bad one, the best leverage in the world may not make it a good deal. On the other hand, low leverage for a fantastic deal may be acceptable.

Fifth: leverage is the biggest advantage in investing in real estate. This is because there are factors that apply to real estate not usually found in as complete a package for other types of investing. These factors are: (1) The availability of financing at reasonable rates. (2) The relatively higher appreciation available in real estate as compared to other types of investments. (3) Cost of living rates that give the effect of paying off presently used monies, which are borrowed, in cheaper dollars in the future. (4) A wide variety of financing tools to increase the percent of leverage. (5) Greater loan to value ratios in real estate. (6) A vast multitude of financing methods highly suited to real estate.

Sixth: understand leverage and you are able to put more deals together. This means more money in the form of commissions.

HOW TO FIND THE AMOUNT OF LEVERAGE

To use leverage as a comparison to the forms of financing, it is necessary to arrive at a percentage which will represent the amount of leverage available in the applied situation. Fortunately, the calculation is very easy to do and can be done on the Leverage Calculation Chart (Figure 3-1). In looking at the Leverage Calculation Chart, it should be evident that the NOI rate is a direct function of the leverage. An error in the NOI will affect the cash flow, and, of course, the leverage calculations. However, as you will use the same NOI rate for all comparables, the leverage for all examples would be in error by the same percentage as the original error. This consistency is sufficient for the purpose of the comparison. Of course, you should attempt to be as accurate as possible in any projections.

Figure 3-1: LEVERAGE CALCULATION CHART

ASKING PRICE	$______	NOI	$______	NOI RATE ______%		PROPERTY	______
PRESENT FINANCE	$______	DEBT SERVICE	$______			DATE	______
EQUITY	$______	CASH FLOW	$______	CASH FLOW YIELD	______%		
				NOI RATE	______%		
				LEVERAGE	______%		

LEVERAGE CALCULATIONS

Method	Amount of Mtg.	Years	%	Constant	NOI	Debt Service	Cash Flow	Cash Down	Add. Cash for Financing	Total Cash Down	Yield on Cash	NOI Rate	Lev-erage Rate
1													
2													
3													
4													
5													
6													
7													
8													

EXPLANATION OF FINANCE FORM USED ABOVE

1. ____________________
2. ____________________
3. ____________________
4. ____________________
5. ____________________
6. ____________________
7. ____________________
8. ____________________

Prepared by: ____________________ Date: ____________

THE LEVERAGE CALCULATION CHART

In Figure 3-1, a blank Leverage Calculation Chart is shown. This chart enables you to chart out one property with given standards, utilizing up to eight different financing methods and constants. The constants, or various methods of financing, will be described by you in the analysis of the chart in the Explanation of Finance Form Used in the lower section of the chart.

In the upper portion of the chart, prior to the analysis of financing and its effect on the yield and leverage, you will fill in the specific standards to be used—the Asking Price, Present Finance, NOI, and so on.

It is important to note the Cash Flow and to be as accurate as possible. The present leverage is merely to indicate the present situation based on existing financing.

HOW TO USE THE LEVERAGE CALCULATION CHART

A case study of the Leverage Calculation Chart follows.

Mr. Johnson is the prospective purchaser of an income property, and after the goal-seeking process it is felt he should not invest more than $35,000 in a small apartment complex. One of the properties the salesman felt was well suited was examined and placed on the leverage chart shown in Figure 3-2. This property was fairly priced at $100,000 and had an NOI of $11,000.

Refer to the chart and you will see how the data was filled in. The salesman first ran the chart on the existing financing. In the first method, notice the existing situation and the leverage resulting for the present owner, assuming his equity to be his investment. The negative 3% leverage means that because his present financing is at a high constant, he is losing 3% of his potential yield in cash flow due to his debt service. Arguments can be given in favor of a negative leverage, as in this case the property will be free and clear in 11.2 years. Yet, only the most conservative investor will trade present cash flow for a future free and clear property that far in advance.

The other forms of financing that may be possible have been put down in items 2 to 8. Each of these forms is briefly described in the lower portion of the chart, and all but the last two involve new financing. The last two involve seller-held financing.

The percentages and constants needed to fill out this chart are available in many handbooks, as well as in this book. Some of the new portable calculators will calculate this information in seconds.

In the third method, the salesman begins with a conservative loan of $70,000. The loan is payable over 25 years at 8½% per annum. Based on local

Figure 3-2: LEVERAGE CALCULATION CHART FILLED OUT

ASKING PRICE	$ 100,000	NOI	$ 11,000	NOI RATE	11 %	PROPERTY	units
PRESENT FINANCE	$ 50,000	DEBT SERVICE	$ 7,000			DATE	Jan. 4, 19xx
EQUITY	$ 50,000	CASH FLOW	$ 4,000	CASH FLOW YIELD	8 %		
				NOI RATE	11 %		
				LEVERAGE	−3 %		

LEVERAGE CALCULATIONS

Method	Amount of Mtg.	Years	%	Constant	NOI	Debt Service	Cash Flow	Cash Down	Add. Cash for Financing	Total Cash Down	Yield on Cash	NOI Rate	Lev-erage Rate
1	50,000	11.2	8¼	14	11,000	7,000	4,000	50,000	0	50,000	8	11	-3
2	65,000	20	8½	10.41	11,000	6,766.50	4,233.50	35,000	2,600	37,600	11.25	11	.25
3	70,000	25	8½	9.66	11,000	6,762	4,238	30,000	2,800	32,800	12.92	11	1.92
4	70,000	25	8¾	9.87	11,000	6,909	4,091	30,000	2,800	32,800	12.5	11	1.5
5	80,000	25	9¼	10.28	11,000	8,224	2,776	20,000	3,200	23,200	11.96	11	.96
6	80,000	30	9½	10.09	11,000	8,072	2,928	20,000	3,200	23,200	12.6	11	1.6
7	80,000	—	—	11.75	11,000	9,400	1,600	20,000	0	20,000	8	11	-3
8	70,000	—	—	9.59	11,000	6,713	4,287	30,000	1,500	31,500	13.6	11	2.6

EXPLANATION OF FINANCE FORM USED ABOVE

1. The existing situation.
2. New Loan, over 20 years at 8½%, closing cost 4%.
3. New Loan, over 25 years at 8½%, closing cost 4%.
4. New Loan, over 25 years at 8¾%, closing cost 4%.
5. New Loan, over 25 years at 9¼%, closing cost 4%.
6. Maximum Loan from S & L, over 30 years at 9½%, closing cost 4%.
7. Second above existing first held by seller, interest only on 5 years at 8%, balloon.
8. Extend existing to 20 years at 8½%, seller holding second for $20,000, interest only, 8%, 5 years.

Prepared by: ______________________ Date: ______________

information, closing costs for this and all new financing were set at 4%. A quick check in the Constant Annual Percentage Chart for Monthly Payments will show the constant of 8½% over 25 years to be 9.66%. The NOI has been filled in and it remains the same for all items.

The debt service is found by multiplying the constant percentage by the amount of the loan. In this case, 9.66% times $70,000. By deducting the debt service of $6,762 from the NOI, the remainder is the cash flow of $4,238. The cash down is the difference between the loan amount and the purchase price, or $30,000. To this amount is added the cost of the loan, predetermined to be 4% of the loan amount, or $2,800 for a $70,000 loan. This gives a total cash at purchase of $32,800. The yield on cash is found by dividing the capital investment ($32,800) into the cash flow ($4,238) resulting in a 12.92 cash flow yield.

Because the NOI rate is 11%, indicating that the owner would receive 11% on his investment if he paid all cash for the property, and the yield on cash, due to financing, is now 12.92%, the leverage is found by subtracting the NOI rate from the yield rate (12.92% less 11% equals 1.92%). The leverage percent in method three, therefore, is 1.92%.

This rate by itself is meaningless, and the salesman must continue to carry the forms of financing out further to ascertain the effects of other methods. He did so with several other methods, as shown and described on the leverage chart.

Upon completion of the eight methods used, the salesman then examined his results. He has a spread that ranges from a negative 3% to a positive 2.6%. Several of which are well within the buyer's means from a capital standpoint, and all but two (methods 1 and 7) show a good yield rate on the invested capital.

The last method, while showing the highest yield, has the distinct disadvantage of having a balloon in five years. Unless there is reasonable assurance that the property can be refinanced to produce the needed capital to pay off the balloon, this form will be rejected in favor of method 3. Method 8 is a good example of overleverage to push the early yield, and may be used providing the buyer understands and will accept the fifth-year consequences.

The salesman found the comfortable area for financing. He can see the distinct advantage of several different forms and is able to weed out those that give little leverage to the buyer. The rising constant on the debt service, as the loan amount increased, erased the advantages of paying less down. It is not uncommon to find that the interest rate, and term of years for a 70% loan, will result in a lower constant payment than a 80% loan. While leverage is often thought to indicate the least possible down payment, it can clearly be seen from the chart that this is not the case. Naturally, if the salesman had been able to obtain an 80% loan at the same constant as the 70% loan, the leverage would have been greater for the larger loan.

It would appear, therefore, that finance methods numbers 1, 2, 5, and 7 can be eliminated because of the low leverage. The later comparison then of 3, 4, 6 and 8 becomes a matter of individual point of view, with the final choice, in my opinion, narrowing down to 3 and 8.

The Leverage Calculation Chart has made a clear choice in the form of financing, and has been used to distinguish between the various forms of financing available.

USING THE LEVERAGE CALCULATION CHART TO COMPARE TWO OR MORE PROPERTIES

The best use of the chart is to compare several properties so that you can get your buyer into the best leveraged property.

It is wise, however, not to offer the comparison unless your buyer is having problems deciding between two or more properties. You could have the leverage chart prepared on each of the likely properties to show the best form of financing you can use, should he decide to purchase either. Yet, certain properties may offer the opportunity for greater leverage than others and this advantage can be used as a selling point, if and when needed. For example, in the case history, another property was shown to Mr. Johnson. This was a larger complex priced at $150,000. It had an NOI of $16,500, giving it the same NOI rate of 11% as the previous property. However, in using the calculation chart, the salesman noted several interesting aspects. Refer to Figure 3-3 showing the second property.

The salesman had several of the savings and loans give some quotes on probable loans, and he put them down in methods 2 through 5. The leverage for methods 3 and 4 proved interesting, and available in the first property, but the cash required was above the amount the buyer had to work with. Digging deeper, however, the salesman discovered the seller was not overly anxious to have cash and would rather have income postponed until his later years. As the seller knew this was an ideal situation for a wrap-around mortgage, he applied such a method in item 7. The resulting leverage of 5.36%, with only $30,000 down, proved to be an ideal situation all around. He pointed out this fact to Mr. Johnson and the result was a sale.

It is important to note that when you use the chart for comparisons of several properties, you should attempt to keep the cash investment at a nearly constant level. Using a percent-of-loan-to-purchase-price as a constant will work only as long as the values are similar. Increases in value will obviously raise the cash down and could move one property out of reach, even though the leverage is greatly increased.

Figure 3-3: LEVERAGE CALCULATION CHART FILLED OUT

ASKING PRICE	$ 150,000	NOI	$ 16,500	NOI RATE	11 %	PROPERTY	Complex
PRESENT FINANCE	$ 75,000	DEBT SERVICE	$ 10,000			DATE	Jan. 4, 19xx
EQUITY	$ 75,000	CASH FLOW	$ 6,500	CASH FLOW YIELD	8.67 %		
				NOI RATE	11 %		
				LEVERAGE	−2.33 %		

LEVERAGE CALCULATIONS

Method	Amount of Mtg.	Years	%	Constant	NOI	Debt Service	Cash Flow	Cash Down	Add. Cash for Financing	Total Cash Down	Yield on Cash	NOI Rate	Leverage Rate
1	75,000	12.1	8¾	13.33	16,500	10,000	6,500	75,000	0	75,000	8.67	11	−2.33
2	110,000	20	8½	10.41	16,500	11,451	5,049	40,000	4,400	44,400	11.37	11	.37
3	115,000	25	8½	9.66	16,500	11,109	5,391	35,000	4,600	39,600	13.61	11	2.61
4	115,000	25	8¾	9.87	16,500	11,350	5,149.50	35,000	4,600	39,600	13	11	2.00
5	120,000	25	9¼	10.28	16,500	12,336	4,164	30,000	4,800	24,800	11.96	11	.96
6	120,000	—	—	11.48	16,500	13,776	2,724	30,000	0	30,000	9.08	11	−1.92
7	120,000	—	—	9.66	16,500	11,592	4,908	30,000	0	30,000	16.36	11	5.36
8													

EXPLANATION OF FINANCE FORM USED ABOVE

1. All new loans at years; interest rate + closing costs shown
2. ” ” ” ”
3. ” ” ” ”
4. ” ” ” ”
5. ” ” ” ”
6. Existing financing, seller holds 25-year second at 8½%, principal of second, $4,500
7. Wrap for 30 years at 9%
8.

Prepared by: ____________ Date: ____________

SIX KEY FACTORS TO WATCH FOR WHEN COMPARING PROPERTIES WITH THE LEVERAGE CALCULATION CHART

1. *Use common standards.* Keep the total cash down as close as you can to the comparison. Don't worry about the loan percent to value at this point. The importance is the effect the financing has on the cash invested, not the reverse. Watch for overestimates in any projections, so be as conservative as possible. Remember your buyer may hang onto these charts, and if your projections were to his disadvantage you will hear about it in the future.
2. *Have a realistic basis for the forms of financing you use.* Don't come up with forms not feasible due to the market condition or any other reason. However, try some creative forms to see how they will affect the deal. Check around with the various savings and loan associations to see what they will do. Ask them about varying years and percent down to see if the constant will change. Get to know the seller to see how far he will go in holding secondary financing or wrap-arounds.
3. *Always remember the amount of leverage gained or lost is merely a number.* By itself it means nothing. Only when you compare it to other forms of financing will the significance of leverage begin to play a role in the formation of the best form of financing for your buyer.
4. *Know the goals of your buyer.* If you don't, you may chose the least effective leverage for his situation. Leverage can be increased temporarily by interest-only mortgages, balloons, and so on. This may fit your client, or it may be to his disadvantage.
5. *Look beyond the short term.* The overall view is most important, no matter what the goal of your buyer may be. Extremely high leverage obtained by passing a burden to a future year must be examined as to what will happen the year the burden hits. Never assume a refinancing in later years can bail the new owner out of a ballooning mortgage.
6. *Use the leverage chart to compare several properties.* If your prospective buyer is leaning toward one property for reasons other than the leverage, don't attempt to use the leverage chart to switch him, unless you feel you have judged his goals correctly and are convinced he should buy the other property. Then the chart becomes part of your selling material.

Deciding Between High Leverage and Low Leverage

Should your buyer look for high leverage in all deals or are there times when low or even negative leverage should be sought? This will depend for the most part on the existing financing available on the property. If, for example, the property has a low interest rate mortgage that is several points below the current rate available, it may be wise to accept the higher constant that may come with that mortgage. A $100,000 balance outstanding on a mortgage that is ten years old may have a 6½% interest rate. But, as the mortgage may have only ten years to go the constant payment percentage would be 13.6%. This constant would be above that available in current financing.

This fact is magnified by the shorter the term of the existing financing. This same mortgage six years later would have an outstanding balance of $47,831. Yet, the annual payment would be the same as on the $100,000 balance. This payment of $13,632 now shows a constant of 28.5%. This will throw the leverage chart into a tailspin if you were to look at the first year only.

FACTORS TO WATCH FOR TO EQUALIZE LEVERAGE

When you see short pay-out and high constants, look to see what will occur when the final payment is made on the short-term loan. In the case above, the cash flow would increase upon satisfaction of that mortgage by the amount of the payment—$13,632. This additional cash flow, when seen over the future holding period, may be highly advantageous to your buyer.

This tends to lead you back to the goals of that buyer. So, ask yourself these questions:

1. *Do I understand the goal of my buyer?* Then state the goal as you understand it to be. Check to see if you are still on the right track.
2. *Does the low or negative leverage cause a cash drain?* If your high constant is not supported by the NOI, then the buyer will have to dig into his pocket to make up the difference. If this is improbable or impossible, then you will reject the low leverage without further question. On the other hand, you should proceed if there is still a positive cash flow.
3. *How long a period will the leverage be low or negative?* This is important. If the span is a year or two, you will be able to show the buyer the gain in cash flow which will occur with the sacrifice of low leverage now. But, if the term becomes longer than five years, this future increase in yield may be difficult to project. Too many other factors can come into play to react on that yield, and projections begin to break down beyond five years.

There is no set answer to the question: Should your buyer have high or low leverage? The amount of leverage should fit his situation and be reasonable for the property. Yet, no buyer should reject a deal that will show low leverage if there is a good sound reason for this kind of leverage.

HOW TO AVOID THE DANGERS OF OVERLEVERAGING

Excessive leverage is often present in properties that fail, but the real illness is overextension. Overextension is the result of using high loan ratios to value. This high ratio of loan to value may or may not give high leverage. In overextension, a decline in the market, a slip in the NOI, or a stagnation of the status quo can cause financial disaster. Overextension is not always associated with high leverage and can have a negative leverage, as seen below:
Property Value: $1,000,000; NOI 12%; Loan is construction 3% over prime, which is now 9%.

LOAN AMOUNT	CONSTANT	NOI	DEBT SERVICE	CASH FLOW	TOTAL INV.	YIELD ON CASH	NOI RATE	LEVERAGE RATE
$950,000	12%	$120,000	$114,000	$6,000	$50,000	12%	12%	0

In this situation the leverage is 0, so the transaction is not highly leveraged but is most certainly extended to the breaking point. The construction loan is interest only, and unless a permanent with a reasonable constant is found the results will most likely be economic disaster.

In the above transaction, the leverage could also be considerable if there was a low capital investment. Many builders find it possible to establish phantom equity to increase a value. With this paper value of $1,000,000, they may borrow the $950,000 and have nothing or very little invested. To show what may occur, assume the same facts as above, except $10,000 is the only real dollar invested. A $40,000 phantom equity exists only on paper.

LOAN AMOUNT	CONSTANT	NOI	DEBT SERVICE	CASH FLOW	TOTAL INV.	YIELD ON CASH	NOI RATE	LEVERAGE RATE
$950,000	12%	$120,000	$114,000	$6,000	$10,000	60%	12%	48%

Here we see the extreme example of ultrahigh leverage and what would appear to be overextension. The owner of such a property will do very well if everything goes his way, and there are no slips in his NOI and a permanent at a lower constant is found.

It can be said that high leverage does not cause problems. It is the combination of high leverage and overextension that creates a dangerous mixture. Whenever the loan to value ratio exceeds 80%, there is a possibility the property is being extended beyond its loan carrying capacity. A good test or rule of thumb for determining the danger of a potential overextension is shown below.

OVEREXTENSION TEST

Rule: For each 100 percentage points of the loan to value ratio, reduce the NOI rate by one point. Then apply this reduced NOI rate to the leverage chart and test for positive leverage. A negative leverage of 15% or more will indicate a high probability of overextension.

For Example: In the case of the two situations shown where the value was $1,000,000 and a $950,000 loan was attained, the loan ratio is 95% of the value. The NOI rate will be reduced by .95 points (12% less .95 equals 11.05). The new NOI rate will now be 11.05%.

LOAN AMOUNT	CONSTANT	NOI ADJ.	DEBT SERVICE	CASH FLOW	TOTAL INV.	YIELD ON CASH	NOI RATE	LEVERAGE RATE
1st: 950,000	12%	110,500	114,000	(3,500)	50,000	−7.0%	11.5%	−18.5
2nd: 950,000	12%	110,500	114,000	(3,500)	10,000	−35%	11.5%	−46.5

With a slight drop in the NOI rate, from 12% to 11.05%, the leverage situation changed drastically. In the first case, the leverage went from zero, as shown on the previous chart, to a negative 18.5%. And most dramatically in the second situation, it went from a positive 48%to a negative 46.5%. There is little doubt about the second situation being overextended. Any negative leverage will create serious doubt as to the soundness of the form of financing used.

These two examples illustrate what can occur when there is no apparent leverage, as in the first situation, and high leverage, as in the second. Leverage itself is not the contributing factor to the overextension, and overextension is not always throwing off high leverage. This is a fact that you should note very carefully. High percentages of loan to value will not always give prudent leverage.

SOUND METHODS OF GENERATING HIGH LEVERAGE

1. *Refinance to the lowest constant, with the highest loan to value ratio which you feel warranted.* Test for overextension. If the leverage remains positive, you are at the peak of leverage without moving into an accelerated risk. Any negative leverage at all will be a warning that you are pushing the financing. Use caution when you have an early or temporarily high leverage due to balloon-type financing, and make sure the future consequence can be accounted for.

2. *Consolidate the existing financing, along with new financing which will lower the constant.* If this reduced constant will hold for more than five years, and the test for overextension remains positive, you are moving in the right direction.
3. *Increase the NOI.* This is the most advantageous way to increase the leverage for any property. But it is often the most difficult as well. You saw what occurred with a slight drop in the NOI in the overextension test. The increase of the NOI would have boosted the leverage to extremely high percentages. Even though this method is difficult, in some properties it is highly feasible and your projections can show this fact. In this type of leverage analysis you would examine the property as it presently stands, then show the highest form of financing best suited for the property, apply an increased NOI as your *pro forma* would indicate, and obtain a new leverage percent.

WHAT YOU SHOULD EXPECT LEVERAGE CALCULATIONS TO DO FOR YOU AND YOUR CLIENT

In the first place, leverage will be of little use to you from an analysis point of view unless you apply the techniques given in this chapter. Using the leverage chart may seem to be unnecessary and time consuming. As for being unnecessary, that point is argued simply by saying you must try it to see what it will do. I am confident that by using the leverage chart you will gain a fuller understanding of the effects of the various forms of financing. As for time, this is something you must work out for yourself. The leverage analysis and other analyses which will be covered in this book are designed to save time in the long run. Time means money, so the real function of leverage calculations is to help you make more money.

Leverage is the only factor which can be used to bring various forms of financing into focus. The analysis, therefore, will serve only one real goal from your standpoint: *It will enable you to ascertain what your solutions will do and to help you choose the correct method of financing.*

Your client is the direct beneficiary of these efforts. He will respect what you do and the interest you take in him. Carefully checking leverage and overextension will guide you in the right direction toward solving your client's problems and helping him reach his goals. The ultimate sale and commission you earn will be because of these efforts.

Chapter **4**

Conventional Financing: The First Mortgage, Where to Find It and How to Get It

The purpose of this chapter is to clearly define first mortgages which are obtained from conventional sources, and to then tell you where and how to get them.

Conventional financing of any sort is generally understood to mean loans obtained from sources such as savings and loan associations, commercial banks, insurance companies, pension funds, and any other source that will lend on the same terms and standards as these institutions.

The term "conventional financing" is often misleading because it applies to the nature of the loan rather than its source. Often, the conventional loan is referred to as an "institutional loan." This term has come about because most conventional financing comes from one of the institutional sources. Yet, for a loan to be "conventional," it need only meet the terms and conditions of a loan which would be given by one of these more standard lenders. A private lender may give a conventional loan even though he is not a lending institution. Therefore, when we speak of conventional loans it is the *structure* of the loan that is important.

This chapter will cover the first mortgage conventional loan and will explain the various differences in the types of terms that can be obtained. The art of expanding on these terms from the lender will be a major part of this chapter.

THE FIRST MORTGAGE

A first mortgage, or first deed of trust as it is called in some states, is a document which gives the lender a right, or lien, to the title of the property pledged as security to the loan. The mortgage document itself is not evidence of the money owed, only of the security which has been given. The note, which is generally attached to the mortgage document, is the evidence of the debt.

When a mortgage is given to the lender, the lender then advances a sum of money and the borrower signs a note (promise to pay back) indicating the terms of the loan. The terms will tell both parties how the payment or payments are to be made, the due dates, amount of interest, and any other data which may be pertinent to the loan.

As title has not passed to the lender, the borrower still owns the property. The lender however has obtained this right, or lien against the property, which is now the security for the loan. In some situations involving sale of land, a "Contract for Deed" is used. This term is sometimes confused with a first mortgage. In a Contract for Deed the buyer of the property owes a sum of money to the seller, for which there is a term of payments and usually a sum of interest paid on the unpaid balance. This is a debt, but there is no mortgage as the title remains with the seller. And until the total owed is paid, the buyer may not attain title.

The first mortgage, of course, can be satisfied simply by paying off the amount owed, plus any interest or penalty which may be due, thereby releasing the property as security. At times, the lender will specify that the loan cannot be paid off in full or limit the amount of prepayment the borrower may make. This factor is one which should be stated in the mortgage note, and is often overlooked as a negotiating point in obtaining favorable terms.

Unlike the Contract for Deed, if the borrower fails to make payment the lender cannot simply refuse to give the buyer the deed. Because the borrower has the deed, the lender must go through the foreclosure proceedings to attach the security.

It is this act of attachment that separates the strata of liens which are recorded against the property. The first mortgage becomes the first lien which will be paid off in the event the property is sold at a foreclosure sale. There are some other liens which can come ahead of the first mortgage, but for the most part they are limited to tax liens.

All other mortgages or liens filed against the owner, for which judgment has been given against the property, will line up in the order in which they were recorded. This will cause the subsequent mortgages and liens to take an order of precedence behind the first mortgage. Assuming there are sufficient funds from the sale of a property at foreclosure to pay the first mortgage balance, the balance will go to the second mortgage next and so on down the list of liens.

Foreclosure is often very cumbersome, and most lenders will avoid it if at all possible. Nonetheless, it is the final step which a lender can take when all reasonable methods to collect what is owed him fail. You should not, however, anticipate that a lender will not take the legal steps to enforce that right to foreclose. Quite often the second mortgage holder will be quicker to foreclose than the first, forcing the issue to come to a head.

This first position or right over other subsequent loans and lenders is what makes the note and mortgage a first mortgage. However, the name ''first mortgage'' by itself is meaningless. A mortgage is not a first mortgage because it is called that. It must be recorded correctly in the property records, ahead of any other mortgage or lien, to attain that position. There is one exception to this: A subordinated interest recorded ahead of the mortgage can take a position junior to the mortgage.

This fact has caused most lending institutions to enact procedures which enable them to check the title prior to placing the mortgage on the records. They will often examine the title twice to make sure there are no long-range problems in the chain of title. Once the lender is satisfied as to the condition of the title, he will then proceed to close the loan, have the mortgage and the note signed, and check the title once more to be sure there have been no other mortgages recorded since the last time he checked.

WHO IS THE MORTGAGOR AND WHO IS THE MORTGAGEE?

When you are dealing with lenders, the terms ''mortgagee'' and ''mortgagor'' will come up from time to time. These terms are often confused and should be set straight. The easiest way to remember which gives the mortgage and which makes the loan is to think of the sounds'' or,'' and ''er.'' These suffixes which come at the end of such words as mortgagor, lender, grantor, and so on, indicate a giving. The grantor is the one who grants something. The lessor is the person who gives up property to another (for a fee). The mortgagor, therefore, is the person who gives the mortgage. As a mortgage is evidence of a security for a loan, then the lender will give money to the mortgagor.

Banks don't give mortgages, despite the common misconception. You don't go to a bank for a mortgage. You go to a bank for money, and the bank will lend you the money on the mortgage you pledge as security.

STANDARDS WHICH MAKE A LOAN "CONVENTIONAL"

When you are dealing with the conventional loan market, you will find a standard which tends to prevail throughout the country. There will be little variance in terms or conditions wherever you go to seek a loan.

A large part of this standard is government imposed. The amounts a savings and loan or commercial bank can lend, for example, are part of this control with which these lenders must contend. Yet, there is a broad spectrum within which the lenders can extend themselves, if they want to. Once you know just how far the lenders can go legally, then you should push them to the hilt to better the terms and conditions needed.

It is only realistic to believe that lenders are aware of what their competition is doing in the market. Some lenders even quote you the rate they believe their competitors are giving, if they know they can beat it. However, because there are restrictions within the conventional market, a look at these regulations would be worthwhile. Keep in mind that some of these regulations may vary from time to time, and I would suggest you check with the various lenders in your area to keep abreast of the current trends and new regulations.

LOAN CONDITIONS COMMON TO SAVINGS AND LOAN ASSOCIATIONS

MAXIMUM LOAN	MAXIMUM TERM	TYPE OF PROPERTY	CONDITIONS
90%	30 yrs.	Single family and condos	Percent of loan is based on the contract price or an appraisal, whichever is the lower amount. The total loan is usually under $45,000.
95%	30 yrs.	Single family and condos	Same as above, except private mortgage insurance is required. These loans usually are below $40,000.
80%	30 yrs.	One to four multifamily dwelling units	Appraisal value will take market conditions of rental area and vacancies into account.
75%	25 yrs.	Five or more units Commercial real estate	Greater emphasis on the person behind the loan. Appraisals will also be more detailed and the term of years reduced.
75%	3 yrs. 5 yrs.	Developed lots Developed lots	Terms for builders more than two lots. Terms for individuals are longer. Usual provisions on which the lots are built within the term of loan.
100%	12 yrs.	New mobile homes	Based on invoice price.
100%	8 yrs.	Used mobile homes	Wholesale value.

It is interesting to note that almost all loans over 80% must also follow these limitations:

1. Monthly payment must include principal, interest, and a pro rata build-up for an escrow of taxes and hazard insurance.
2. If a residence, certification that the property will be the borrower's home.
3. No secondary or junior loans.

INTEREST, POINTS AND COST

Interest rates are not regulated except by state law setting usury, which then establishes the maximum rate which can be charged. Interest charged is generally somewhat competitive, but will not vary much between lenders.

All savings and loan associations have what is called the "point system." Most other lending institutions also have a similar system. This is a fee charged for making the loan. In essence this fee is a form of discount, although the lending institutions will often go to great lengths to persuade you otherwise.

The points charged are a percentage of the total loan taken. If the lender quotes his fee as 4 points, this means he will deduct a fee of 4% of the total loan amount at the time it is disbursed. Naturally, the borrower is receiving only 96% of what he wanted and must pay back 100%.

The problem is not just the points, but other costs. It is important for you to be sure the savings and loan associations and other lenders which make conventional loans tell you what other costs may be involved. It is not uncommon for there to be considerable "other" costs. The recent truth in lending laws make disclosure mandatory in almost all situations. But the disclosure is only required to be made to the applicant for the loan. If you, as a broker, don't get it straight before you take one of your clients down to the savings and loan, you could be in for a surprise. Ask for full details before you submit your client to the ordeal.

The savings and loans have the most stringent lending requirements to contend with. Commercial banks, while restricted, have slightly greater leeway with their lending. In fact, in some communities the commerical banks are able to compete rather strongly with the savings and loans in the home market.

HOW TO DETERMINE WHICH SOURCE TO APPROACH

This will depend on the situation at the time. There can be no real answer which will fit all occasions and all transactions. You can, however, become familiar with some of the advantages and disadvantages of each of the major sources, and some of the special ways to approach each of the lenders. You will find that you are dealing with people, and no matter what the institution or how large or small the company or bank, the person you meet, face-to-face, can be the deciding factor.

It is rare for any mortgage board to grant a loan which the loan officer tells them he has "a funny feeling" about. The attitude of the lender—at least the one or two people you may meet—will affect how well you do with that institution in getting the best for your clients. At the same time, your attitude will have equal bearing on your success.

Because this is a fact, you should center your attention on the single most important factor in dealing with lenders' representatives: *Understand that the person you talk to is not lending you his money—it's the money of the people he works for. A mistake on his part is a red mark against him. He will avoid red marks.*

This may sound trite, but I have never dealt with a loan officer who was not overly cautious. The bigger the loans, the more cautious they often become. Not because the amounts of money are staggering, but the red mark that would go against them is bigger.

Their attitude is often determined to some degree by the demands of the institution for which they work. If the lender wants to get out a lot of money he will ease up on his requirements.

Establishing a good working relationship with the person you will deal with is most important. This relationship must be businesslike. The wine and dine days (and nights) still play an important role in some types of deals, but that is a game few play well.

HOW TO DEAL WITH THE SAVINGS AND LOAN ASSOCIATION

When you are in the market for a first mortgage, the first source you should look at is the savings and loan association in your area. We have already seen some of the basic restrictions of the savings and loan association. However, check with the associations in your area to be sure of their full legal requirements and restrictions.

A loan obtained from a savings and loan association will have certain advantages and disadvantages over a loan obtained from other sources. Knowing the restrictions is important, but knowing the advantages and disadvantages is imperative if you are to make a judgment as to where you want to devote your time and efforts in obtaining a loan.

Six Advantages In Dealing With A Savings And Loan

1. Unlike some sources, the savings and loan is local in nature. The loan officers are on the spot, and working with them will normally not require mortgage brokers or outside help. If the going gets rough and the owner has a hard time making payments, the savings and loan is more apt to bend slightly to accommodate the borrower. The local aspect of the savings and loan can overshadow all other benefits in many cases.

2. The ability to appraise property in the local area is unique to the savings and loan. They are often far better equipped to gather information on the property than any other lender. Naturally, this can have some drawbacks in some cases. But for the most part, the more the lender knows about a property the better your chances of obtaining a satisfactory loan.
3. Confidence in the area. This goes hand and hand with the first item mentioned. Savings and loans must lend within a tight area, and are "forced" into having confidence in the community. As they receive deposits, that money becomes ear-marked for loans in the area. Remember, this is the reason for savings and loans in the first place.
4. The loan pay-out term is generally longer in the number of years the borrower has to pay off the loan. This fact will often give a lower monthly payment than a loan from another source. The difference between a 20-year loan, and a 40-year loan, with the same principal of amount and the 40,000 annual interest rate of 8% will be: a $334.60 monthly payment on the 20-year loan and a $278.13 monthly payment on the 40-year loan. The decrease in monthly payment may allow the buyer to buy the property.
5. The percentage of loan to market value is higher in most cases than with other sources. This is important when the buyer needs the largest loan possible. The standard percentage for home loans may be 80%, but it is not impossible to obtain up to 95% through coinsurance on the upper 15% of the loan. A relatively new source of conventional loans, the mortgage REITS, rivals the savings and loans in this aspect, but in many cases the savings and loans will still provide the highest percent of loan to market value.
6. The savings and loans are, in their qualification of the borrower, often the most lenient of all sources. This does not mean the savings and loans are not diligent in their qualification procedures, but only that they are not as strict as some of the commercial banks and out-of-town lenders. The qualification of the property itself becomes an advantage as well, and this stems from their ability to appraise quickly and rather accurately. Few lenders are as current on the area as are the savings and loan associations located in the community.

Four Disadvantages Associated With The Savings And Loans

1. In comparison with the other sources, the points, or loan fees, are generally higher at savings and loans than at other lenders. These costs come under several titles, and often it may be difficult to ascertain a direct comparison without looking at the full cost of the loan. For example, some savings and loans separate points as a loan fee, while others tend to lump that cost in with out-of-pocket. Out-of-pocket costs are generally attorneys' fees, surveys, accounting, and the like. When shopping among several savings and loans,

the best method of ascertaining the full cost is to take the gross loan requested and deduct all costs that the savings and loan is charging, including the points. This will tell you what the net loan proceeds will be. Such things as escrow funding, where the borrower must fund an advance deposit to cover future costs, should not be considered. Points are simply a form of discount to raise the overall yield to the lender. If, for example, the points total 4% of the loan proceeds, then a loan of $100,000 will net, before other costs, $96,000. Yet the interest rate charged to the borrower is based on the original $100,000 amount. And, of course, the pay-back is $100,000 of principal. The other costs will vary from lender to lender and are not standard, even though some are. These standard items will include tax escrow, recording, stamps on the note, and other governmental requirements.

2. Personal liability is almost always required in the savings and loan mortgage. This may not present the borrower with any problems, but is something to consider when the larger commercial type of loan is received.
3. The present trend in savings and loan mortgages is for these loans to be nonassumable. A new owner must requalify for the loan. This gives the savings and loans the opportunity to adjust the interest rate to the present market conditions, or to turn the new owner down all together. In many cases, a new loan is written and costs and points are collected by the lender. A loan with the nonassumption clause can present problems when the property is to be resold and should be avoided if at all possible. Try to negotiate this clause out of the mortgage commitment. Naturally, the savings and loans have taken this posture for good reasons (for them), and you may be forced into accepting this condition.
4. In addition to the nonassumption clause, another trend is a penalty for prepayment of principal. The thought here is that if you borrow money at what the savings and loans feel is a top rate, they will want to protect that return over a long period of time. A sudden drop in rates might prompt the borrower to refinance elsewhere at a more favorable rate. If the lending market has caused rates to drop, the first savings and loan could not return the money to the market at the same rate as on the now prepaid loan. Generally the penalty decreases as time passes, and if the owner feels he will keep the property intact with the new financing for a reasonable time period, the penalty may not be of importance.

You will find that each association in your area will approach a given situation differently, and one association may become very interested in making a loan another has just turned down. The method you use in going through the steps of a loan application for your client is most important. You don't want to spend too much time in the wrong place, and, unfortunately, you may find you have to shop around to find the right place and the best terms.

Steps in Approaching and Dealing With A Savings and Loan

1. Research the regulations governing the savings and loans in your area. The best way to do this is to stop in at one of the savings and loans in your town and get to know one of the loan officers. Tell him that you want to know as much about the institution as possible.
2. Develop a rapport with at least one person in the major savings and loan in your area. If you are in a large city and there are many, then pick at least four associations and at least two branches of the same association (if there are any). You will need to develop these contacts before you call on them for a loan. If you happen to be dealing with a person with whom you cannot establish a rapport, then call on another loan officer at the same institution. If you make your first contact in a general, informative way, you can make a change without offending the first loan officer or embarrassing yourself in front of a client. It is important that you hit it off with the loan officer, so work at this.
3. Learn their procedures. Each savings and loan will vary slightly. They will have different loan application forms and will want different material on those forms stressed. Find out when they meet to approve loans and who does the appraisals. If the association has its own appraisal staff, and most will, give the appraiser a call and see what you can find out. How do they appraise various properties? If they are real sticklers for the economic approach, then you will want to know that and have some idea as to CAP rates they use for various properties. If they pay more attention to the market value, when you submit the application you will have more data on that part of the form.
4. Plan your submission well. The Loan Request you will have to prepare is a complete document summary of the property, the improvements, and the person. Now that you know what they are looking for, you are one step ahead of them. You want to answer all possible questions that may come up in the loan committee in your report. Keep in mind that in various requests you may want to stress some points and de-emphasize others, depending on the nature of your lender. It is best, however, to include all the basic information: (1) the property, (2) the person, (3) the Loan Request.
5. Make your loan requirements known. You should, of course, be able to justify the amount and work the terms to fit with their requirements. It would be useless to ask for 80% when you know they can only lend 75% on commercial properties. On the other hand, if you can justify a higher value than that on the contract, then the increased funding may be obtained. Nonetheless, there is flexibility in many aspects of the loan and you will

want to ask for the best terms and conditions you think you can get. Then work hard to get them.

6. Make the application for the loan in time to allow ample study of your presentaiton before the committee meets. Do not rush in the day before the monthly meeting, unless there is no other choice. Find out how many members sit on the committee and be sure you have a copy of your submission for each of them.
7. If you don't receive a favorable reply from the loan committee don't take that as the final answer. You can sit down with your loan officer, or even have his superior sit in on your meeting and go over the reason for the denial. If the terms of the loan or the amount differ from your request, try to find out why. Often it may be a matter you can alter, correct, or negotiate. Sometimes the lenders will not divulge the reasons and you are hampered in second attempts. If they don't want to play ball, the only thing you can do is try another lender.
8. Use your influence. But don't abuse your hospitality. If your firm deals mostly with one bank or association, try to let the bank or association know that you appreciate the interest it takes in your loan applications. No association will grant a loan to an unqualified person, or overappraise a property because of any influence you could bring to bear. However, if it comes down to your loan over another, and each stands on similar qualifications, then your influence can help.
9. Remain calm. If you are turned down, and your strongest counter to the objections fail, then let it go. Know when to back off from that lender. You will get all those you come in contact with angry if you press the issue beyond that "extra effort." However, do try to be sure you know why you were refused, as this problem may come up again with another lender and you might be able to counter earlier. The best thing you can do in a situation where you are denied a loan, after you have given the extra punch, is to call those you have worked with at that association and thank them for the attempt "on your behalf." They will appreciate your thoughts that they gave extra effort, even if they did not.
10. Try to involve the associations you deal with in the other things you do. If you belong to a professional or social club, see if you can invite one of the association's officers to speak at one of the functions. All savings and loan associations will have someone ready to give a lecture on some topic of finance or general community information. It will help you round out the rapport you want to maintain.
11. Never try to barter one lender against another with direct confrontations such as: "If you don't let me have this loan at 8½% over 30 years then I know XYZ will jump at the opportunity." Competition is fair, and most lenders anticipate that their applicants will shop around.But it goes against

the grain to be told they have to do something because one of their competitors will. Be sure you let the lender know that you are making submissions at other savings and loans, or elsewhere, if you are in fact doing that. A statement such as the following may be used: "We are limiting our request for this loan to only three savings and loans in the area. We feel you will find the request for the amount and terms to be within the standards and capabilities of your institution."

These 11 steps in approaching and dealing with a savings and loan association are not easy. They will be used for most of your local lenders as well. The normal process followed by the average broker or associate is to hand his client a form from the savings and loan and tell him the address. The more astute salesmen will go down to the institution with the client.

You will find out many things about the various institutions you will deal with by getting to know the people and the procedures involved. You will begin to learn where to push and how hard you can argue.

When you are dealing in larger commercial transactions, or even usual residential situations, you must often use your own creativity. Your suggestions might be picked up and used if they can legally incorporate some of the ideals of creative financing. There is considerable creativity, by the way, that can be worked into a complicated transaction, as is shown in the example which follows.

Recently, I sold an expensive single family property. The price was $200,000, and the property consisted of an oceanfront site with a 35-year-old frame house on it. The house was livable, but at best in need of considerable work. The most conservative estimate, just to put the home in good condition, was over $150,000. The buyer was well qualified and had a good personal statement. His intention was to buy the property and either tear down the existing structure and rebuild or remodel considerably. But he had to sell his existing home before he could pay the major part of the purchase price and have cash available for remodeling. His existing home was to go on the market for $150,000 and he had a low first mortgage of about $30,000. The sale, after fee and closing costs, would give him about $110,000.

What he wanted to do was buy the property with as little cash down as possible—sell his existing home and make the transition. Because he didn't know just how far the remodeling would go, he was not in a position to apply for a development loan. The submission to the savings and loan showed a value of $200,000 to be justified on the property as it presently stood. Everyone knew the greatest part of the value was in the land—in fact *all* the value was in the land.

The association said they would lend 75% of the contract price, which was substantiated as the market value. A loan of $150,000 was therefore obtained.

This meant that the buyer needed $50,000 plus out-of-pocket to close on the property. He didn't want to part with that right at the moment, because he knew he would have to spend hard cash on construction or remodeling.

In the sale of the property, the seller was willing to accept a contract that called for $100,000 at closing, and he agreed to hold paper for $100,000 payable in one year. The lenders said they could not permit any secondary loans against the property they were using as security. Through negotiations, we were able to convince the seller to hold the paper as a second mortgage on the buyer's existing house. In addition, the buyer made a personal guarantee that the payment would be made. This meant that when the savings and loan made the loan of $150,000, the buyer had not spent any money and in fact had pocketed nearly $50,000 after the loan costs. This cash, and other cash that may have had to go towards the purchase, went into the remodeling of the home.

The savings and loan was aware of the situation, as they had a copy of the contract which spelled out the terms of the sale of the property and the terms of the $100,000 balance owed. They could loan on the property, however, as the $100,000 was not a second or junior loan on the same property.

Often, your buyer will have other property he can pledge to the seller as security to remove the "second mortgage" stigma from the financing package. This method will create a form of second financing and does not hamper the transaction as far as the regulations affecting the savings and loan. By doing this, it is possible to finance above the money requirements of the purchase.

HOW TO DEAL WITH A COMMERCIAL BANK

While savings and loans are the major source of first mortgage funds, there are times when the commercial bank, both state and federal, will be most interested in your submissions. Commercial banks differ from savings and loan associations in many ways, but are one of the sources for conventional loans. FHA and VA loans are generally arranged with a commercial bank, and such banks provide a vast wealth of services that can make them viable and competitive to the savings and loan and other sources.

The Plus Factors Of The Commercial Bank

1. Like the savings and loan, the commercial bank is local in nature. They are in the community and like to work within it. This local aspect is always important, and the commercial banker has a number of advantages over the savings and loan by the virtue of charter and government regulations. Their loan capacity in certain areas, namely land, development loans, and construction lending, can make them more than competitive to their local counterpart.

2. To a lesser degree than the savings and loan, however, they do have good insight as to real estate values in the area and this can be important. Also, confidence in the community is a positive aspect which rubs off on the commercial bank. But as their loan area (the distance from their front door in which they can loan) is often greater than that of the savings and loan, this local communal feeling can be less important and may swing over to the other side of the fence and become a disadvantage.
3. The biggest advantage to the commercial bank is the lower loan fees. The points charged by the savings and loans are not a factor for commercial banks as they are generally lending a lower ratio and have counterbalancing factors that will show up in the disadvantages. Nonetheless, commercial banks generally charge less for their money.

Disadvantages Of Commercial Bank Conventional Loans

1. Commercial banks are older than the savings and loans and have always had a more conservative approach to lending. This approach, which is often more conservative in some banks than others, provides some distinct disadvantages to the borrower. Such as:
   A. A low loan to value ratio. The bank will look hard at the value of the property, and then grant a loan that can often be far below that considered by the other sources. Whereas the savings and loan may go to 95% of the appraised value, commercial banks are more apt to stay below 75%.
   B. Often, the borrower must be a client of the bank or become a client. This may mean that he must put aside the other bank that he deals with and deal in a substantial way with the lending bank. This may not cause any problems, but on the other hand could be a definite disadvantage.
   C. Interest rates granted are often higher than the current rates available from other sources. This factor, however, must be considered along with the points charged, as the overall rate on the net loan proceeds may not be higher.
2. Prepayment penalty is generally a negotiable point with commercial banks, and only if it is required could it become a drawback.
3. The term of years is normally shorter at commercial banks, and the annual payment therefore higher for a similar loan when compared to a longer term.

How To Approach And Deal With A Commercial Bank

To a great degree, you will find that many of the same steps used in dealing with the savings and loan will be used for all lenders. Review the eleven steps given earlier in this chapter and adapt them to fit the characteristics of the commercial bank.

In addition to these eleven steps, there are some areas that will require other approaches and other opportunities will present themselves.

Special Key Steps In Dealing With A Commercial Bank

1. Start with the commercial banks with which you deal. There should be more than one. You will have an account under the firm name in one or more banks (the escrow account, operating account, etc.). This gives you immediate access to the bank and its services. You should, however, have your personal account with another bank to broaden the number of your contacts. Other associates in your firm will, no doubt, have other banks with which they deal, and they can be your liaison with those institutions. Commercial banks feel they have an obligation to deal with their own customers first. The presidents of commercial banks are often more accessible to you because of this "account status." You should be on speaking terms with the president of the commercial bank you are to deal with.
2. When you are to present a loan request to a commercial bank follow this special procedure:
   A. Know the limitations of what the bank can do, and have some idea as to the amount of the loan you can expect and the terms they will offer.
   B. Call and make an appointment with the president of the bank. Have several copies of the loan request with you. You need not have the completed application or even the part on the person at this stage. Ask the president who you should talk to (this is not necessary if you already know which loan officer you need to see). Have the president of the bank introduce you to the correct loan officer. Invariably, the president will say something complimentary about you in front of this loan officer. The impression this will make on that loan officer will help.
   C. Spend the first few moments talking about how you and the president of the bank have gone over the basics (I assume you have and so will the loan officer) of the loan you or your client needs.
   D. See how far he will commit himself without your having to bring the buyer into the picture. If you can soften the lending procedure at this stage, you will find that when you come in with the buyer you will have a much easier job of obtaining the loan.

HOW TO DEAL WITH THE MORTGAGE BROKER

There are other sources of first mortgages. However, because these institutions are not readily accessible to the average buyer or mortgagor, you will find that you will be dealing through a mortgage broker. Use his services to the best advantage of your client. But shop around for a good mortgage broker. Find out the names of some from friends that have used them in the past. Visit them, and most important, read the chapter in this book on how to deal with mortgage brokers.

Because you will not be dealing directly with these next few types of lenders, I have not included the intricacies of direct dealings with them in this chapter. That's the mortgage broker's job. You will still have to do your homework however, and the mortgage loan request will be most useful. Keep in mind that the more remote the lender, the more detailed the loan request must be.

THE INSURANCE COMPANIES

Insurance companies are a good source for funds. But getting the money from them is another question. In recent years, the insurance company has not been as important a lender in the home market as in the past. To some degree, the savings and loans have cut into this market and insurance lenders have looked to other forms of lending, such as permanent loans on large commercial transactions. These transactions are, of course, conventional. As lenders, the insurance companies are a major source for that type of loan. The larger the deal, the larger the role the insurance company will play.

Advantages Of The Insurance Company

1. The biggest advantage is the amount of money they have to lend. If you are a big borrower, the savings and loans or commercial banks may not have the capacity to make the loan. In smaller loans, the insurance company, through its outlets, does compete in the lending market.
2. The loan fee, or points, is often the lowest of all sources. This becomes more important in the smaller loans.
3. The interest rate is also generally the lowest of all sources. This fact alone can make the insurance company the most sought after lender.
4. Often, the permanent loan does not carry a personal guarantee. In other words, the borrower does not become liable for a default on the loan. The lender looks to the value of the property for liquidated damages.

The preceding advantages make the insurance company a highly sought after source for loans. But some disadvantages are also present in dealing with insurance companies.

The Drawbacks Of An Insurance Company Loan

1. Most insurance companies are not local and you must deal with them through an intermediary, such as a mortgage broker. This is not, however, always a

disadvantage. But it does separate the lender from the borrower. There may be no personal contact at all except for the broker making the loan.

2. Because of the favorable terms, there are many borrowers looking for a limited amount of funds. This causes lenders to be much more cautious and the demands on qualification are the highest in the lending industry. This reflects on both the borrower's ability and background, as well as the property. Insurance companies prefer to deal with winners and will seek to maintain a group of borrowers with whom they have had good success. This is only natural, but can leave out a qualified borrower if the choice is left between a past performer and a newcomer.
3. The time it takes to process a loan with an insurance company can often be the blow that kills the deal. To some degree this is by design. The marginal deals will not wait, while the good ones will. Nonetheless, the time to get the commitment is long, and the commitment is often full of loopholes for the lender that must be carefully analyzed by the borrower.

There are other disadvantages of dealing with insurance companies, depending on the type of loan requested. For the most part, however, the advantages outweigh the disadvantages, and insurance company loans are the most sought after in terms of larger loans.

THE REAL ESTATE INVESTMENT TRUSTS: REITS

In the recent years, a new source of money has come on the scene through the creation of Real Estate Investment Trusts, or REITS as they are known. This form of institution is relatively new to the lending market, and as REITS were formed to serve several purposes, some explanation of the types of REITS and their function is necessary.

TYPES OF REITS: WHAT THEY CAN DO AND CAN'T DO

1. The Equity Trust. As the name indicates, this REIT is formed with the main goal of investing in equities. They do not lend money as a general rule, but buy properties for investment and income return. They may or may not be connected with their brother, the Mortgage REIT. Equity Trusts are not a source for loans.
2. The Mortgage Trust, on the other hand, is designed for lending. These trusts grew to immense proportions in a very short time, and by the early 1970's were lending billions of dollars of short- and long-term funds. However, the bulk of the loans were construction or development monies, and not permanent in nature. This trust, and to some degree the third category, the Hybrid

Trust, suffered greatly in the construction decline that began around 1974. Nonetheless, the Mortgage Trusts are to be reckoned with, and you should not overlook them as a source for funds.

3. The last type of REIT is the Hybrid Trust. These trusts formed a small portion of the entire REIT industry in the early stages of the development of Real Estate Investment Trusts, but have grown as the Mortgage Trusts have become Equity Trusts in nature by virtue of acquisition of properties from foreclosures. The Hybrid Trust is a mixture of both the Equity Trust and the Mortgage Trust, and involves a bit of each form of investing. They are not, however, a major source of conventional lending. Yet, they could become more important in the future of conventional loans.

Special Advantages of the REITS

When you look at the advantages of the REIT loans, they will follow the same pattern as shown for insurance companies. But they do, however, extend into some special areas of advantage not often found in most insurance companies.

1. In the past, the REITS have been less conservative than any other source of funds. This practice may have been part of their problems, but it is doubtful they will ever convert to the staunch conservatism that abounds in most insurance companies. This freedom of movement makes the REIT a good source for the unusual deal, providing the outlook for success is economically promising. The REIT grew fast, and to some degree it was this urge to place loans that added to their monumental growth.
2. The loan terms are often much more flexible, and the REIT is not adverse to such innovative ideas as land leases, advance funding, land banking, and other necessary financing concepts in an expanding market. The Hybrid Trust is a good candidate for a joint venture or participation loan.

On the reverse side of the picture, the REIT has drawbacks like the insurance company, but with a different twist.

Disadvantages Of Dealing With The REIT For Mortgage Funds

1. The REIT is generally a short-term lender. This means they like the construction loan and the high interest rate that is attached to that form of lending. This does not mean they will not lend on long-term rates, but they do prefer the in-and-out of a short term.
2. Loan processing takes time, although not as much as with the insurance company. Nonetheless, until the REIT as an industry pulls itself out of the hole, they will look long and hard at prospective loans.

3. Because they, like insurance companies, are not local, there is the lack of personal contact. The impersonality of loans may be good business when you are about to foreclose, but it is difficult for the borrower to deal at a distance. Mortgage brokers provide about the only contact with the home office, and once the loan is closed some mortgage brokers seem to fade into the sunset.

THE PENSION FUNDS: THEY HAVE MONEY TO SPEND

This is a growing source of funds for coming years. To be sure, they have been around for a long time, but their loans have not been readily available to the general public. Pension funding comes in numerous packages and can be association funds, such as the firemen's funds, teachers' funds, labor union funds, and the like. For the most part they invest in package deals. Banks will make loans and sell a package of many loans to the funds. In this way the fund is in the lending business in a secondary way, not making the original loan but merely buying the paper from the bank.

Some funds actively seek loans through mortgage brokers or mortgage bankers. The mortgage banker, a firm that handles such funds rather than their own money, establishes the loan to suit the requirements set by the fund putting up the money. A borrower may never know the initial source of money when dealing with a mortgage banker, as his job is to place the loan and then sell it to whoever will buy it.

The average home loan that is financed by these funds is not, therefore, done on an individual basis, but in mass. You can discount dealing with the funds on home loans, but if you are looking for large construction or commercial monies, the pension and trust fund can be the best source available. Also, with the growth of personal pension funds, banks and institutional investors are developing large funds. This money must be invested and large amounts will work their way into real estate lending. They vary in their advantages and disadvantages, but for the most part have the same plus and minus factors as the insurance companies and the REITS combined. With one difference. . . .

The One Difference With The Pension Funds

Pension funds have a more stable fund of money than insurance companies or REITS. Money managers of pension funds are able to plan more effectively for the return to the investors in the fund. And as the return to the fund is usually at a lower "demand rate" than that demanded by a profit-making institution, this can ease the lending rate and terms on the loan desired. Pension funds are not as free and fancy with their lending as the REITS however, but they are not as conservative as most insurance companies.

If You Are A Big Borrower, The Pension Fund Can Be The Only Way To Go

No one will disagree with this statement, except the other lenders hoping to make the same loan. The only answer, of course, is to shop around and find out for yourself just who is the best source for you at the time you need the money.

A SUMMARY OF ADVANTAGES AND DISADVANTAGES

	Advantages	*Disadvantages*
SAVINGS AND LOANS	Local and on the spot Know property and area Have confidence in area Long pay out High percent of loan to value More lenient in qualifying both the property and the borrower	High points Personal liability Nonassumable at times Prepayment penalty
COMMERCIAL BANKS	Local and on the spot Know property and area Have confidence in area Lower points Construction and land loans	Low percent of loan to value Want other business Higher interest rate Sometimes prepayment penalty Shorter term of years
INSURANCE COMPANIES	Have ample money Like big borrowers Lower interest rate (often) Low points Permanent loan usually not personally guaranteed	Not local Can be impersonal Highly selective Demand greatest qualification on property and borrower Long processing time
REITS	Same as insurance companies Less conservative Loan terms more flexible	Not local Can be impersonal Generally short-term lender Long processing time
PENSION FUNDS	Same as insurance companies	Same as REITS
THE SELLER	Depends on the situation and the seller No points at all Usually best rate No processing time to worry about	Seller may be limited in the amount he can hold Term usually shorter

AN OVERLOOKED SOURCE FOR FIRST MORTGAGES

One of the best sources for first mortgages is the seller. There are many advantages to this source, and oddly enough it is the seller that is often the first source that is overlooked. The biggest advantage to you and your client is that there is no middleman. You are the middleman, and the saving of loan points and time are valuable to all parties of the transaction. This chapter will not deal with the methods of approaching the seller. Other chapters will cover this aspect in greater detail. Yet, you should never overlook this as perhaps the best source of all.

MORTGAGE SOURCE CHECKLIST:

WHAT KIND OF LOAN NEEDED	WHERE TO GO TO GET THE MONEY	WHEN TO USE THIS SOURCE TO ITS BEST ADVANTAGE	HOW TO GET THE MOST FROM THIS SOURCE
	Start with the local savings and loan association and make at least two or three applications.	When you need between an 80 to 90% loan and total loan is under $50,000.	Follow the procedure given in this chapter.
Single family residence (first mortgage under $80,000 in value	Your commercial banks. Pick one the buyer deals with first, then try the ones you deal with.	For loans over $50,000. Or when your buyer is well respected by his commercial bank or you struck out at the savings and loan.	Follow the procedure given in this chapter. Remind them how much they respect the client —your buyer.
	Insurance companies: Deal with your mortgage broker. Often, they will be in the market for single family loans.	When you cannot get anywhere with the other sources. Or, if you know the mortgage broker is hot to make a deal.	Deal only with a reputable mortgage broker. Do not try to deal directly with an insurance company.
Single family residence (first mortgage over $80,000 in value)	Start with the local savings and loan and make at least three applications.	When you need no more than 80% loan to value ratio and total loan is under $100,000.	Have more details on the buyer, as well as comprehensive sales data.
Residential lots for ready development—single buyer	Commercial banks. Same as previous mortgage.	For loans over $100,000 you may find the commercial bank the best bet.	Negotiate for good terms and use the buyers' good financial statement.

WHAT KIND OF LOAN NEEDED	WHERE TO GO TO GET THE MONEY	WHEN TO USE THIS SOURCE TO ITS BEST ADVANTAGE	HOW TO GET THE MOST FROM THIS SOURCE
Multifamily (up to 5 units)	Start with the local savings and loan. Make as many applications as possible.	Maximum loan possibel is 80%, but your chance is improved if if you ask for only 75%.	Have detailed loan request ready for each savings and loan.
Residential lots for builder-developer use	Commerical banks—talk to them first. If they have money available, make several other applications.	When you need only 70% loan to value ratio or less.	Have detailed loan request and stress the buyer as much as the property.
Multifamily (6 to 20 units)	Start with the local savings and loan. Make at least three applications.	When the loan to value ratio does not exceed 75%.	Have detailed loan request with past years' statements available.
Commercial properties up to $500,000 in value	Commercial banks may be good market here; but this will depend on the bank, the property, and the person. Check around.	If you can get the seller to hold some paper and only need a 50% loan.	Show strong management capability of buyer and good past history.
	Insurance companies: REITS and funds.	When the value is over $300,000 these sources may be interested.	Use good mortgage broker and detailed loan request.
Multifamily (20 to 100 units)	Savings and loans. Make at least three applications.	Will find 70% of economic value with conservative approach the best loan ratio.	Do your homework and have detailed loan request.
Commercial properties ($500,000 to $2,000,000 in value)	Insurance companies, REITS and pension funds.	If the value is over $1,000,000 these may be the only source.	Mortgage broker and loan requests are necessities.
Multifamily (over 100 units) and Commercial properties (over $2,000,000 in value)	Insurance companies, REITS, pension funds, and trust funds.	You have little choice: these are about the only sources you have.	Mortgage broker and very detailed loan request.
Shopping center development with major tenants (over $1,000,000 in value)	Commercial banks	Very rare; but if you are close to one you might have luck.	Pray.
Restaurants and special single-use properties	Commercial banks	Loan to value ratio 50%.	Detailed loan request, and heavy input on ability of buyer and past records.

PRIVATE MONEY: WHERE IT IS AND HOW TO FIND IT

Because private money is not institutional, it is often not classified along with conventional financing. But as conventional financing is a type of loan, and not limited by the source, I have chosen to include a brief section on private money. Because the use of private money varies greatly in its advantages and disadvantages, it is safe to say that it can have both the advantages and the disadvantages of all other sources.

Each private lender is an independent lender, and reacts to a loan request by seeking the most profitable deal based on what the market and his requirements dictate. In general, rates will be the highest and the amounts limited. Some private sources seem to be well financed, but these are few.

However, finding the private money is easier than getting it. A look in the Yellow Pages or newspaper classifieds will be a good start. Many mortgage brokers and stock brokers know of private money.

Deal with private money very carefully. It is best to advise your client to have any and all mortgage documents examined by an attorney.

HOW TO PUT TOGETHER A LOAN INFORMATION PACKAGE WHICH WILL GET THE BEST TERMS AND THE MOST MONEY

Whenever you have a loan request in excess of $100,000, and always when you are putting a commercial venture together, you will need to have a loan request package. This folio of information will be used by the lending institution to help justify the loan, and to give you the best advantage at improving the amount of money you get and the terms offered.

The information used in the package should already be known to you. If the property is your listing, then you most certainly will have the data. If, on the other hand, the property is the listing of another office, you may have to do some digging to get all the information needed. All the data pertaining to the property and the improvements can be, and should be, part of your selling tools. The only additional data you will need to add to the package will be the portions that refer to the loan request amount and terms and personal data on the buyer. Naturally, other supporting documents, such as copy of the contract, bank forms, and so on will be added as well.

I have included in this chapter an outline which you can follow in the preparation of a Mortgage Loan Request (Figure 4-1). The request you formulate should be as complete as possible. Because the outline can become the index to all your loan applications and requests, you should have several of them run off in your office. A quick review of this chapter prior to making up a request will aid in preparing a more complete and professional presentation.

Figure 4-1: OUTLINE FOR MORTGAGE LOAN REQUEST

I. THE PROPERTY
   A. General Description
   B. Legal Description
   C. Location
   D. Location Sketch
   E. Aerial Photo
   F. Location Benefits
   G. Location Drawbacks
   H. General Statistics
      (1) Demographics
      (2) Average Rent
      (3) Traffic Count
   I. General Site Data
      (1) Legal
      (2) Size and Square Feet of Land and Site Coverage
      (3) Use of Site
      (4) Zoning
      (5) Utilities
      (6) Access
      (7) Sketch of Lots Sharing Building Location
      (8) Survey
   J. Land Value
      (1) Estimated Value of Site
      (2) Comparable Land Sales and Values
II. THE IMPROVEMENTS
   A. Description
   B. General Statistics
      (1) Date Built
      (2) Year Remodeled
      (3) Type of Construction
      (4) Other Structural and Mechanical Data
      (5) Floor Area
      (6) Parking
      (7) Other Data
   C. Sketch—Ground Floor
      (1) Show Tenants
      (2) Show Square Feet
      (3) Show Approximate Sizes
      (4) Building Plans (if new building, or if lender is not in area, or if requested)

D. Sketch—Second Floor
  (1) Show Tenants
  (2) Show Square Feet
  (3) Show Approximate Sizes
  (4) Building Plans (if new building, or if lender is not in area, or if requested)

E. Sketch—Third Floor
  (1) Show Tenants
  (2) Show Square Feet
  (3) Show Approximate Sizes
  (4) Building Plans (if new building, or if lender is not in area, or if requested)

F. Personal Property
  (1) Inventory
  (2) Value

G. Statement of Condition of Property

H. Replacement Cost of Structure
  (1) Original Cost
  (2) Replacement Cost

I. Comparable Sales of Improved Property of Similar Nature in the Area

J. The Economics (Actual)
  (1) Income
  (2) Expense
  (3) Net Operating Income
  (4) Economic Value
  (5) Rent Roll
  (6) Sample Lease
  (7) Past Records of Income and Expense

K. Opinion of Economics
  (1) Relationship to Average Square Foot Rent for Area
  (2) Average of Square Foot for this Building
  (3) General Opinion
  (4) Estimated Future Income

L. General Summary of Value
  (1) Land Values
  (2) Replacement Value
  (3) Personal Property Value
  (4) Estimated Present Value
  (5) Economic Value at Present Income
  (6) Comparable Value
  (7) Contract Price
  (8) Copy of Contract
  (9) Value Justified

III. THE PERSON
   A. Name
   B. Address
   C. Occupation
   D. General Data
   E. Net Worth
   F. Supporting Documents
      (1) Net Worth Statement
      (2) Schedule of Assets
      (3) Schedule of Liabilities
      (4) References
      (5) Position of Employment
      (6) Verification of Salary
      (7) Estimated Annual Earnings
      (8) Credit Report of Applicant
      (9) Other Forms Supplied for Application
IV. THE LOAN REQUEST
   A. Amount
   B. Terms and Conditions

Four Key Steps In Formulating The Loan Package

1. Keep your sales material up-to-date and accurate. This will mean knowing all there is to know about the property you are to sell.
2. Accumulate the various sketches, photographs, past records, and other supporting documents you will use. These are shown in the Presentation Index as you go from listing to marketing.
3. Develop an understanding with the lenders you will approach to make sure what parts of the presentation they want emphasized. Remember, some lenders pay more attention to the person, others the property. You will want to know just how far you should go with the economics on the property. I prefer to limit the economic data to a minimum. Past records going back two or three years are helpful, and of course current data is a must. Expenses are almost more important than income and should be realistic. In most cases, you will have to increase the expenses the seller gives you. Avoid *pro formas* showing the next five years or more. Some of the new computer printouts enable you to run a ten year, or longer, projection of income and expenses. This is a waste of time on two counts. First, no one will read them with any real belief that they are correct. Second, they will not be correct. You cannot effectively project into the future, so don't go beyond one or two years at most.
4. Get into the habit of using the package on all your loan applications. This accomplishes four things: First, the more you do the easier it is to do them.

Second, the loan officers will get into the habit of knowing how to examine your material. If you are taking a sound approach to your analysis and the data contained in the package is readable and to the point, they will appreciate what you are doing. Third, the package will be effectively helping you get more money at better terms. And fourth, the data compiled will be more accurate and your sales ability increased.

Chapter **5**

Secondary Real Estate Financing: The Deal Maker

All mortgages that are not recorded as a first lien against the property pledged as security are "secondary" or "junior" loans. These mortgages follow behind the first mortgage in priority of claim against the security, and will not be satisfied in the event of a foreclosure until the higher ranking mortgages are paid off.

Mortgage rank is the numbering of the mortgages according to their position of claim against the security. This placement is really the order in which the mortgages were recorded. The first mortgage, and highest ranking, will be recorded ahead of all others (except in the event of a subordinated interest allowing a new mortgage to move ahead of a prior one). The second mortgage would be the next to have been recorded, the third mortgage behind that, and so on.

As in first mortgages, the term "first mortgage" or "second mortgage" does not indicate the position. This is dependent on the order of recording or registry.

SECONDARY MORTGAGES CLIMB UP THE LADDER OF RANK

When a superior mortgage is satisfied, the mortgage below moves up in priority. For example: If the property has three mortgages, a first, a second, and a third, satisfaction of the first will move the second one into a first-rank position and third will become the second. Satisfaction of a mortgage in the middle rank will still move the lower mortgage up. If the second mortgage was paid off, then the third automatically becomes a second mortgage.

The importance of this fact is that a mortgage can move up in priority, but not back. If there is an existing third mortgage, the property owner cannot place a new second mortgage once the old second one is paid off. Some people find out too late that the document that had *second mortgage* in bold print on it, was not in fact a second mortgage. However, it is possible to have subordination of position within a mortgage. This would enable a borrower to recast the superior mortgage without the junior mortgage moving up in position. While this technique is not often used, it can provide excellent results in situations where the existing first mortgage on a property being sold is low, and ample cash is received on the down payment. A second mortgage held by the seller behind the first mortgage may allow the buyer to refinance in a few years to a specific limit, without having to pay off the purchase money second mortgage. With the exception of a junior mortgage being subordinated to new superior mortgages, the secondary financing will move up the ladder as those mortgages above it are satisfied.

SECONDARY FINANCING AS A DEAL MAKER

In the resale of property, you will often need some form of secondary financing to make the real estate saleable. The reason for this secondary financing may be to take advantage of an existing mortgage that has a low interest rate, but a low loan-to-value ratio. You need additional extension in this ratio, and you can achieve this by some form of secondary financing.

The primary use of secondary financing in the sale of real estate is to bring the down payment down to an affordable level for the buyer and/or to increase the leverage on capital invested. Yet, there are other aspects that are of equal importance, depending on the seller's point of view. Without the seller holding some form of secondary financing, the property may be very difficult to sell. Conditions may require a drastic reduction of price or offering terms that will entice a buyer to consider the property. The saying, "I will pay your price, but you have to take my terms" is often a very real buyer's concept. The terms, however, needed to enable a buyer to meet the price, are not always advantageous to the seller.

ADVANTAGES AND DISADVANTAGES OF SECOND MORTGAGES

This is how second mortgages look to lenders and borrowers.

The institutional or private lender:	The borrower:
1. More risky the higher the position (seconds more than firsts, thirds more than seconds, etc.).	1. Can reduce equity in the property and leverage up the return.
2. The more the risk, the higher the rate.	2. Can mean a high rate on the money borrowed.

3. Borrower should be strictly qualified.	3. May be hard to get.
4. Keep the term short.	4. Term too short to make a reasonable payment schedule.
5. Obtain other security.	5. Other security can tie up other property.
6. Be quick to foreclose.	6. Even slight default can bring pressure.

A lender will examine all superior financing when considering making a loan on a property. The value of the property and the percentage of existing financing will dictate the amount of risk he is taking. Obviously, the lower the percentage of existing financing to total value, the lower the risk to the lender. If the property is valued at $50,000 and the first mortgage is $20,000, a second mortgage of $10,000 is a fairly safe gamble for the lender. The rate and term of years can be adjusted to account for this risk or lack of risk.

Lower-ranking mortgages, such as third or fourth mortgages, will command even higher rates as the risk increases and as the position or rank decreases. From a practical point of view, there are few institutional or private money sources that will lend on third or fourth mortgages. When you have a client that is in need of such funds, it may be best to look to some other form of financing to solve the problem.

WHEN SECONDARY LOANS ARE NEEDED

Because not all real estate transactions involve the use of secondary financing, it will be helpful for you to know when you should look to this form of financing as a deal maker. The first step in ascertaining when the secondary form of financing is needed is to fully understand what the second loan can do.

Six Things A Secondary Loan Can Do

1. It can enable the buyer to structure the total financing so that he can afford the required equity down payment. Because the terms of the secondary financing may vary, the overall debt service may require lower monthly payments due to the combined financing, when compared to other alternatives. Of course, there are times when the new first mortgage money market will not permit the loan to value ratio needed, and the secondary financing may be the only way to achieve that ratio.
2. It can increase the cash flow yield on the cash invested in an income property transaction by reducing the amount of cash to be invested; and by establishing a constant rate of payment on the secondary financing which is lower than the prior cash flow yield, then the new cash flow yield will be increased.
3. It can leverage a seller's return on the paper. If a seller were to receive $50,000 in cash, where could (or would) he invest the sum of money and at

what interest rate? On the other hand, if the seller were able to obtain a 15% return or better from a secure second mortgage on his previously owned property, he might be interested. The wrap-around may do this, and is one of the better forms of secondary financing.

4. It can spread risk and separate values. Because secondary financing covers such a broad spectrum, it includes such creative forms of financing as: land leases, wrap-around mortgages, blanket mortgages, cross-collateralized purchase money financing, subordinated interest, interest-only payments, moratorium on all payments, percentage override sale of divided interest, and on and on. These various techniques, that are covered in this book, are used in secondary financing. You will be able to sell a building, for example, but keep the land, which is then leased to the purchaser (this is a form of secondary financing).
5. There may be a limit to other choices. If the new money market is tight, seller-held secondary money may be the only possibility for structuring a high loan to value ratio.
6. The secondary loan can substantiate value. If the seller will hold a substantial second or third mortgage, at good terms, a sale at a higher price may be attained. There is normally a trade-off in this situation. The seller accepts lower than current interest over the term of the mortgage and the buyer pays more for the property than he might have if he had more cash invested. The judgment of which is better for the buyer or the seller depends on the alternatives that are actually present. It will do no good to assume it would be better to take cash instead of a mortgage, unless someone actually is offering cash and someone else is offering a mortgage.

Of the six things that secondary financing can do, not all may be present in every situation. In fact, to have two or three would be exceptional. Now that you have seen what secondary financing can do, look at the circumstances that will cause you to look to it as the most effective method of financing a transaction.

When To Use Different Types of Secondary Mortgages

THE CIRCUMSTANCES—1.
New money is tight and expensive. Closing costs and points are high,

THE TYPE OF SECONDARY FINANCING TO USE—1.

* * *

Start with seller-held secondary financing. If the seller won't hold a normal secondary loan, then approach him with a wrap-around structure.

* * *

A land lease subordinated to existing financing will separate values and reduce the cash needed for the down payment.

and loan to value ratios are 80% or less. The property has an existing financing that totals 50% or more of value and has a reasonable constant rate of payment. The buyer has a limited amount of cash to invest and must raise the loan to value ratio.

* * *

If the seller will not take the paper, look to other markets for the secondary loan.

* * *

Possible cross-collateralization of other property may provide sufficient equity to support the loan for the seller or other lenders.

THE CIRCUMSTANCES—2.

New money is tight and expensive as in the previous situation. Loan to value ratios are not sufficient to give the amount of financing needed, and the lender will not permit secondary financing on the property. The existing mortgage is very low (below 30% of value) or the property is free and clear.

THE TYPE OF SECONDARY FINANCING TO USE—2.

* * *

Use other property the buyer has for the security of the secondary financing, and go into the new money market for a first mortgage.

* * *

In some situations the lender will not look at a land lease that is subordinated to the first mortgage as secondary financing, and this alternative can be used.

* * *

Leaving the seller in the deal, with a right to buy him out in the future, is a form of secondary financing.

* * *

Establishing a royalty fee on overages of income can provide income to a seller, and will not affect the lender's restrictions on new money.

THE CIRCUMSTANCES—3.

New money is available at reasonable rates. Loan to value ratios are high, and the property is free and clear or has a low percentage of existing financing. However, the buyer still needs extra financing.

THE TYPE OF SECONDARY FINANCING TO USE—3.

Look to the seller as the prime secondary lender.

* * *

If the amount of the secondary financing needed is small, and the commission substantial, the broker will often hold the paper.

* * *

The land lease and other provisions mentioned earlier may be useful in this type of situation.

The above three situations are most frequently encountered. There are many variations, of course, and secondary financing can be used in any deal. However, there are times when secondary financing is not effective and you should be aware of these.

When Secondary Financing Should Be Used Only As A Last Resort

1. Avoid using secondary financing when the buyer is financially weak and the transaction must be forced to meet his economic ability. If a buyer is putting down his last dime on an income property, he may be destined for trouble. Overextension of loan to value ratios will create debt service that may be more than the property or the buyer can handle.
2. Avoid seconds if the new money market is good, the existing financing on the property is low, and the equity needed with this type of financing is available from the buyer. Do not use secondary financing simply to increase this extension at the sacrifice of leverage. You should, however, first analyze the leverage and extension of a property to be sure you are arriving at a proper level. Use the Leverage Calculation Chart discussed earlier.
3. If a property has a number of existing secondary loans, you may still use secondary financing, but see if it is possible to eliminate some of the current loans with the cash down or from a new first mortgage.
4. Avoid a package of combined financing that has a constant rate which is more than 3 points above the possible existing financing, unless there is a good reason (such as an existing mortgage that is to retire in a few years, and the cash flow can be sacrificed for the period of time for future gains).

Remember that the greater the percentage of loan to value ratio, the more risky the secondary loans become. There are exceptions to every rule mentioned about secondary financing. The needs of the parties involved, their capabilities, and their willingness to risk capital need to be considered.

WHERE TO GO TO FIND SECONDARY FINANCING

The few sources of secondary financing are listed below:

1. *The Seller:* He is the best. (See sections of this chapter which follow for more detailed information.)
2. *Commercial Banks and Savings and Loans:* These sources are available for secondary financing in the form of home improvement loans. These loans should not be overlooked, because a buyer often anticipates additions to a property and plans on using cash after the sale for these improvements. Transfer cash to the down payment and finance the improvements with a home improvement loan. Some commercial banks are good sources for personal loans secured by real estate. This is a changing market, however, and will depend on the bank and the person.

3. *Mortgage Companies:* Most communities have several mortgage companies that deal in the secondary loan market. They are effective, although often expensive. Check your area to locate them. Then use the same methods of establishing rapport with them as you would for a lender (discussed in the previous chapter).
4. *Private Investors:* This source is hard to find, and often there are investors that deal with the mortgage companies. Sometimes, however, you will find them advertising in the classified section of the local newspaper. They should be found before you need them. Your commercial bank may know of some.
5. *The Broker:* In the large commercial transactions, brokers are often asked to hold a part of the risk in the transaction by holding some of the paper. Some brokers will, and others will not. You must decide on the situation as it presents itself.

HOW TO DEAL WITH SECONDARY LOAN MAKERS

Each of the preceding five sources will require a slightly different approach. Not all five will be available for all transactions. The banks, for example, will not be very useful in secondary financing over a first mortgage that represents at least 75% of the value. The effectiveness of mortgage companies diminishes when there is existing financing of at least 80% of the value.

Therefore, in the order of their acceptability to the transaction, look at the major sources of secondary loans and learn how to deal with them.

Dealing With The Seller On Secondary Financing

The seller, after all, is the most motivated of all possible lenders. When you deal with the seller, you don't have to justify the value or pay points. But sellers require special handling.

Third party loans, made by outside lenders, banks, or private parties, are not highly negotiable. The end result will be a loan in the amount and at the terms the lender feels he can live with. The seller, on the other hand, is not bound by the same restrictions and can be more flexible. Some brokers mistakenly feel that the sellers who don't need the money (wealthy sellers) are the best candidates for purchase money secondary financing. Naturally, these sellers are good sources and are often receptive to this form of financing. However, they can sometimes be very independent. They may take the attitude that they will hold out until a cash buyer comes along. Wealthy sellers sometimes expect all buyers to have money.

The seller who doesn't have money and needs money is generally the one who will take the secondary financing. Why? Look back on the motivation. If he needs money, the sale of the property becomes the important aspect. It could be that he is being transferred, or just cannot afford to keep the home or property being sold. In this situation, the need to make the sale will motivate the seller to hold some reasonable paper. Many sales are lost because the salesman assumes the seller will not hold secondary paper, or the salesman is not comfortable in the use of purchase money financing. The fact may be that the seller cannot afford *not* to be flexible.

How To Lay The Groundwork For Secondary Financing To Be Held By The Seller: Four Key Steps

1. *First make sure you know the goals and needs of the seller.* If he needs a quick sale or money in a hurry, then your entire marketing program may take on a different approach than if he were not pressed. You may find secondary financing becomes more important and crucial as the motivation of the seller increases.
2. *Examine the property carefully.* If you believe the first or existing financing is good and adds to the saleability of the property, start talking about the possibility of the seller holding paper or other forms of secondary financing rather than new financing. When the money market does not provide suitable or reasonable terms for new financing, then seek a form of secondary financing as a solution to the marketing problems. Remember, the seller is the best such source.
3. *Sit down with the seller and explain the marketability of his property.* If the prices obtained on similar property have been lower than the price asked by the seller, show him the true facts. Most important, however, is what has *not sold*. Look at those listings in the same category of property that have been on the market and are still unsold. If you can, look into those properties that have sold and try to find out the terms of the sale. Was there secondary financing? Put the whole story before the seller. If the picture is gloomy, say so! But don't be pessimistic about your abilities.

   This is the time to go into the question of secondary financing with the seller. Do not present the situation as a question: "Would you hold some paper, because that sure would help make a sale?" *First, you must assume that the seller is not as knowledgeable about financing as you are.* If you have done your homework you should be able to say: "Mr. Seller, I have worked out a plan that I believe will offer you the best chance of marketing this property in the least amount of time." Then, move into how you feel the buyer should be required to pay so much down, assume the existing financing, and so on. Then, show the seller how the financing you have structured provides him with these advantages:

   * It will help reach the goal of selling the property.
   * It will provide a substantial part of the cash needed.

* It can help sustain the price.
* It can speed up the closing.
* It can have a favorable tax advantage to create an installment sale.
* It will relieve him of the burden of ownership.
* It will offer a flow of cash over the term of the paper or other forms of financing.
* It may be the only way to establish an effective marketing program for his property.

4. *Know the options you have in providing secondary financing for your client.* Do not forget that it is not a first mortgage, it is a secondary or junior loan. But secondary financing is not just mortgages. It can be a land lease or building lease. The combinations are many, and you can utilize this book as a reference source for reviewing those options.

How To Deal With Commercial Banks And Savings And Loan Associations For Secondary Financing

There are usually two forms of commercial banks in any area—state and federal. There are slightly different regulations that govern each of them, and the individual bank policy on secondary financing may vary widely. It is necessary, therefore, that you follow the guide below in order to obtain good secondary financing from these institutions.

The savings and loans also follow similar guidelines, so you may consider this section as a combined guide for both these institutions. Keep in mind, however, that each loan situation is different and, as with all loans, one bank or association will look for different criteria in their analysis of the risk. Here are five important guidelines:

* Know the policy of the institution before you go in to talk about a loan.
* When you make a loan presentation, have all the necessary back-up material you know the institution will require in order to reach a decision.
* Precondition your buyer to the possibility that he may need a cosigner for the note. Sometimes a relative will be glad to do this.
* Do not approach this form of secondary financing unless you could not arrange satisfactory financing with the seller or get new money.
* Find out, ahead of time, what additional collateral your buyer has that can be used as security on the loan needed. Often, stocks can be pledged, eliminating the need for a second mortgage on the property, or at least assuring the availability of a second mortgage.

How To Deal With Mortgage Companies

Mortgage companies are also regulated, but not to the same degree as normal banks or savings and loan institutions. These companies are either private firms or credit institutions. They may be a branch of a union dealing primarily with its own members, or backed by insurance companies or trust funds. Their interest rates vary—from higher than any other source to lower.

The first step is to locate them and the best place to start is the yellow pages of your phone book. They will be listed under "Mortgages," "Loans," and sometimes "Trust Funds-Credit Unions." If you fail to locate any in this way, contact your commercial bank and ask if they have a list of the public as well as private mortgage companies that are in the area.

Once you have found them, learn what their lending policy will be in various types of deals. Some of these lenders will not touch anything but single family, while others will go into hotels and other commercial transactions.

This source is large and seems to have a lot of money most of the time. However, before you deal with any such lender do the following:

* Sit down with one of their representatives and find out how their operation works.
* Ask if they will give you detailed information on their company.
* Get a list of their references.
* Check out the references they give, but also ask others about them.
* A check with the Better Business Bureau may disclose some interesting facts about the firm.
* Get a clear understanding of their charges and interest rates.
* Be sure that the mortgage company you are about to suggest to your buyer is indeed reputable.

Finding Private Lenders And Dealing With Them

This is the most difficult source of all to find, but can be one of the best. These investors are usually wealthy persons who have substantial cash and/or the ability to borrow cash at better rates than your buyer. They will then lend the cash out at a higher rate, picking up the leverage. Secondary loans that are secure are a good form of investment for many people and those who are in that field seem to do well. It is not, however, a market for the occasional investor, and you should avoid the casual investor who says he will take a second mortgage on a property if it is exceptional. Look for the full-time investor.

These investors are found in the most unlikely places. They will normally deal with mortgage brokers or mortgage lenders to some degree, but the mortgage broker or lender will guard the identity of this investor and you will not find out who he is. Sometimes they work from leads they cultivate with commercial banks, and this contact is more accessible to you.

Some advertise in the newspaper, usually in the classified section under "Venture Capital" or "Capital Available." Various newspapers have different headings for this type of ad so look around. You can, of course, advertise for this source yourself, but this is rarely very productive. About the only way is to keep your eyes and ears open and to ask your commercial bank president and other lenders.

Because the private lender uses a lawyer in closing his transactions, you may find that a letter to a group of attorneys in your area, asking them if they know of private investors dealing in first and second mortgages, will be the most productive method of locating this elusive investor.

The private lender has an advantage over you and your buyer. He knows it and takes advantage of that situation. He is, after all, usually the last person you and other borrowers will turn to. Because of this fact, the private lender will either take the loan or not.

The harshness of the terms will depend mostly on the general market for other investments. If the investor is able to obtain nonrisk investments elsewhere at a good rate, then the rate he will demand on a second loan will be considerably higher, depending on the risk involved. You can do very little to change the outcome of a loan from such a lender. Nonetheless, you may find that the need for the money will be great enough to warrant the cost.

There are times when the private lender will lend at comparative terms when all things are considered. Usually, the closing costs are a fraction of those available from commercial banks and mortgage companies.

When dealing with private lenders, keep the following three cautions in mind:

1. Be sure the lender's attorney does not represent your buyer in closing the real estate transaction.
2. Tell your buyer to have an attorney go over the loan document before he signs it.
3. Do not recommend any private investors. Merely inform your buyer that you know of one or more, and that you can introduce him to this source. Do not make direct remarks about the reputation of the lender unless you are very sure of what you are saying.

WHEN AND HOW THE BROKER CAN HOLD SOME OF THE PAPER

If the transaction has a substantial commission, and the buyer is just a little short of cash to close the deal, the broker may be asked to take some of the paper as a deferred commission. Of course, this situation, can come up in almost any transaction, and this becomes an individual matter that some brokers will agree to do while others will not. It is important, however, that certain factors be understood about deferred commissions.

* If the broker takes a note, or other form of loan equivalent to a deferred commission, it is likely the IRS will tax the full amount of the commission the

year the note was taken, rather than in subsequent years when payment is received.

* A fee conditioned on the future collection of a debt held by the seller may avoid the tax situation shown above, as the future payments are in a sense based on continued performance. However, if the payments are not made to the seller there could be problems in collecting the balance of your fee.
* Further commission payments have a tendency of being due when the person owing you the money would rather not pay. When you get the funds at closing that problem is solved.
* Have your lawyer and tax accountant advise you on the proper way to handle any situation where you decide to take future pay-out on the commission you have.

Chapter 6

How to Use Government Insured Loans to Finance Real Estate

The insured loan programs of the Veterans Administration and the Federal Housing Administration can provide reasonable loans for millions of people in the United States. The purpose of this chapter is to review these two programs offered by the United States Government and to show how you can benefit by making more sales. While this chapter cannot hope to make you an expert on either of the programs, it will tell you how to deal more effectively with this form of financing. You will find these programs to be very useful in many different types of real estate. They are not limited to single family housing.

These two programs overlap in some areas and enable lenders across the nation to provide real estate loans which may not have been available otherwise. In these mortgage programs the government does not lend any money at all, but merely insures the lender that the loan will be covered in full or the upper limits of the loan will be insured in the event of default. Because this insurance narrows or eliminates the lender's risk, they are willing to make loans that can be as high as 100% of the purchase price. The VA does not charge for this insurance, but the buyer of a property insured by the FHA will pay for this insurance over the life of the loan in the form of a monthly payment of ½% of the loan amount. The lenders for both types of loans will either hold the loan for their own portfolio or will package these loans and sell them to other lenders. Primary lenders are commercial banks and savings and loan associations, but they are not limited to these sources. A complete list of all lenders approved in your area can be obtained from the VA or FHA office serving your region.

THE VETERANS ADMINISTRATION AND THE GI LOAN

Veterans of the United States Armed Forces number over 30 million persons. This is a sizeable number of prospective clients in need of solutions to their real estate problems. The GI loan is only one of many benefits granted to veterans. In the pages which follow you will learn who can obtain a loan, what the loan will cover, what the maximum amount of the loan will be, and how to get the it.

WHO IS ELIGIBLE FOR A GI LOAN: According to the most recent guidelines available from the VA, the following people are eligible for guaranteed or insured GI loans:

(1) A veteran who has served a minimum of at least 90 days active service between the dates September 16, 1940 and January 31, 1955; providing that (A) the veteran was discharged under conditions other than dishonorable; (B) except that a discharge was due to a service-incurred disability then the active service could be less than 90 days.

(2) A veteran who served active duty for a period of 181 days or more than any part of which occurred after January 31, 1955 and was discharged or released under conditions other than dishonorable or who was discharged or released after such date for a service connected disability.

(3) Widows of men who served during the periods above and who died as the result of service.

(4) Any member of the Women's Army Auxiliary Corps who served for at least 90 days and who was honorably discharged for a disability incurred in the conduct of service causing her to be unable to physically perform service in the Women's Army Auxiliary Corps, or in the Women's Army Corps (Note: This provision is applicable only to discharges prior to the integration of that corps into the Women's Army Corps, pursuant to Public Law 110, 78th Congress.)

(5) Certain United States citizens who served in the Armed Forces of a Government allied with the United States in World War II.

(6) A serviceman who served on active duty after January 31, 1955 for at least 2 years for so long as he continues on active duty without a break therein.

(7) Unremarried widows of veterans or servicemen described in items (2) and (6), above, who died as the result of service.

(8) The wife of any member of the armed forces serving on active duty who is listed as missing in action, or is a prisoner of war and has been so listed for a total of more than 90 days.

(9) Any person who satisfies all basic requirements above, except discharge or release from active service, and who is hospitalized pending final discharge is also an eligible veteran.

The above nine categories indicate those persons who were, at least at one time, entitled to obtain a GI loan. Their continued eligibility to this entitlement depends on several factors. It is possible to use up the entitlement. At present the maximum guarantee offered is $25,000. Once this sum is drawn against in the application to secure a loan, the amount is lost unless restored. A veteran's entitlement may be restored if the total sum of the loan on which the guarantee applies is repaid.

However, there are other ways in which the entitlement can be renewed or excluded. These occur when the security for the loan has been:

(1) Taken (by condemnation or otherwise) by the United States or any State, or local Government agency for public use; or
(2) Destroyed or damaged by fire or other natural hazard to the extent that occupancy, use or restoration is impractical, which destruction or damage is not resultant from an act or omission willfully designed by the veteran to bring about such destruction or damage; or
(3) Disposed of because of other compelling reasons devoid of fault on the part of the veteran. (These reasons may include health, employment, voluntary conveyance in lieu of condemnation, or other reasons felt to be compelling.)

VA loans may be used for a number of different real estate ventures. For the most part the loan is used in the single family market. However, the GI loan does have these uses:

(1) To buy a home.
(2) To buy a residential unit in a condominium project.
(3) To build a home.
(4) To repair, alter, or improve a home.
(5) To refinance an existing home loan.
(6) To buy a mobile home.
(7) For farms, where the loan may be used to purchase land, buildings, livestock, equipment, machinery, etc.
(8) For business, where a loan may be used to purchase land, buildings, supplies, equipment, etc.
(9) Finance apartment complexes. Four units for one veteran plus one unit for every additional veteran that lives on property and cosigns mortgage.
(10) To refinance a property so it may be sold with improved financing.

INCOME REQUIREMENTS TO OBTAIN A LOAN: The VA has set a basic qualification formula which must be met by every applicant for a GI loan. This formula sets the maximum loan available in most cases. The essence of this formula is to assure the lender that the borrower has reasonable income and credit to repay the loan. Therefore, in addition to being declared eligible for a GI loan based on his period of service, the veteran must meet the requirements of the governing law in respect to income and credit. This income credit takes into consideration more than the property and the respective mortgage payments that will become due as a result of the financing. It also takes into account other obligations confronting the veteran, which include his dependents, and other expenses that he may have. At the time an applicant is filing for a loan, the pertinent data will be used in the final calculations as to the credit of the borrower. The wife's or spouse's income will also be included in the total family income. As a broker, it is wise to save yourself, your client, and the loan officer time and effort by predetermining the financial capability of your client.

The local conditions will depend on the actual requirements which the VA will look at. The ratio of income to mortgage payment will be between 4 to 1 and 6 to 1. Keep in mind that the mortgage payment includes the cost of the mortgage, interest, taxes, and so on. You should check with your local VA lenders to see what they will accept.

THE GI LOAN AND HOW IT WORKS: First, the amount of the loan possible is not limited to the amount of the guarantee. This fact is often misunderstood. The present accepted limit for a single family loan with 100% financing is $100,000. This amount, $100,000, is based on calculations of 4 times the present entitlement of $25,000. At this loan ratio, the buyer does not need to put any cash down. Higher loans are available and cash down is the fee needed. This means that with GI guaranteed loan, a qualified applicant could go to a lender willing to accept the maximum guarantee offered by the VA of $25,000 and obtain a loan. The lender is secured on the upper limit of the loan to the amount of 60%, or the maximum of $25,000.

This factor broadens the scope of these loans considerably. It is often thought that the GI loan is good only for the lower priced properties. This is not the case at all. In many areas where all qualifications are met as far as income and credit are concerned, the limits are not as much a factor as the competition or availability of other financing at more reasonable rates or terms.

Because an appraisal of the property is needed for both VA and FHA insured loans, this appraisal may be the first step necessary in selling property you list with these government loans. In fact, if you feel the property you are listing is in need of new financing, or that the marketability of the property will be enhanced by offering it for sale with a VA or FHA appraisal already completed, then there is no doubt that this step should be completed by the time your prospective buyer comes along. It is best to obtain a VA appraisal even if the idea is to go FHA, because the VA appraisal will often be higher than the FHA and this appraisal is convertible to an FHA loan whereas the FHA appraisal does not convert to a VA. It is not practical to have the appraisal made for all properties you may list. In the first place the appraisal costs, $50.00 (FHA) and $75.00 + $10.00 for each unit up to 4 units (VA), may not be effective for many properties over $100,000, even though loans on properties above that price are available through both the FHA and VA.

When you list a home with the idea of offering it on a VA or FHA, you should inform the seller of the conditions that are normal on a VA or FHA contract. The seller should be aware, for example, that he is expected to pay for the discounts on the financing. Some brokers and salesmen inform all their sellers about the possibility that a contract for VA or FHA financing may be presented. Have the sellers agree to pay the discount on the possible sale on a VA or FHA. If the seller is overly concerned about the discount amount, you can limit it by tying it to a set price.

Therefore, the first steps you should take are the VA appraisal and the agreement to sell under FHA and VA terms. With this you are ready to market the property.

During the normal operation of your business you may be dealing with prospective buyers who may want to buy a home listed by another office, one that may not be offered with FHA or VA terms and appraisal. If these buyers want to buy on VA or FHA terms, you will be making an offer on a property not presented with VA or FHA conditions and you should follow these 5 steps.

FIVE STEPS IN PRESENTING AN OFFER FOR A VA OR FHA HOME, AND GETTING IT CLOSED: First: Qualify your prospective buyer as to his eligibility for a VA or FHA loan. If he appears to meet the income and credit standards, then check his eligibility for VA entitlement. If he has used his entitlement or is not qualified by VA standards, then look to the FHA program for mortgage assistance.

Second: Explain the general terms and conditions of VA and FHA loans to your prospective buyers. Be sure the buyer understands what is being asked of the seller in these loan programs. Explain that the appraised value, as established by FHA or VA, may be less than the quoted price or even the offered price. The reason is that furniture and equipment not included in the appraisal will account for some difference. Personal property must be purchased under a separate agreement, even though it is often merely a memorandum that is attached to the deposit contract at closing and handled as a part of the overall contract. Nonetheless, the loan amount will be based on the appraisal and not the offered price.

Because the seller has expenses in VA and FHA closing, not customary in conventional closings, it is important not to low-ball offers to him.

Third: After showing the property, draft the contract on a form approved by the VA or FHA. You can get such forms from most lenders in your area. I recommend, however, that you establish a relationship with a local mortgage broker who deals in VA and FHA loans. This broker can be worth his weight in gold over the years of VA and FHA dealings and will assist with the paperwork. Nonetheless, make the offer at this point in time on an approved contract, paying careful attention to the items that are not usual in conventional contracts.

Fourth: Present the offer to the seller. Let the seller know that you have an offer for which the buyer should be able to qualify. Go over the costs which the seller will have in closing the contract, and the time limits which are normal for your area in closing (ask your mortgage broker as these vary). Pay careful attention to the provision that indicates the buyer can get his deposit back and that the contract will be null and void if he fails to be approved for financing or if the appraisal falls short of the value under the contract. This is why your prequalification will pay off. The seller will want to know your opinion of the buyer, and you will have one.

Fifth: Get the *seller's* acceptance of the offer, then immediately proceed to your mortgage broker or other source you use to assist with your VA and FHA loans to process the application, get the appraisal, and qualify the buyer.

The process for selling with VA and FHA is not difficult. Time is generally the most pressing problem. Sellers don't like taking their property off the market while the VA or FHA process grinds toward a closing that may fall through at the last moment, because the buyer cannot qualify or the appraisal falls short of the needed loan amount.

The advance appraisal will cut this time down considerably, but both buyers and sellers can get overly anxious about when they will be informed that the deal has been approved across the board.

The personal liability on the amount of the loan will exist until the loan is paid in full, or the borrower is relieved of the liability. The veteran will be relieved of this liability by payment in full, or under such circumstances as a forced sale, condemnation, fire, or even transfer because of ill health.

In conventional financing, if you sell to a new buyer and that buyer assumed your conventional mortgage and later defaulted, there would be no deficiency judgement against you for any amount of money not recoverable by the lender.

The GI loan differs greatly in this aspect. Your liability exists no matter how far down the chain the sale may extend. For example, say you, as a veteran, obtained a $30,000 loan on a home and two years later sold the home to Buyer A. Buyer A assumed the existing financing (your original GI loan). A few years later Buyer A decides to sell the home to Buyer B; and B does the same thing a year later in selling to Buyer C. Now, C gets behind in his payments and starts to let the home go downhill. The loan is finally foreclosed due to nonpayment of the mortgage.

In such circumstances you will have a possible obligation to the VA for the amount of any claim they may have to pay to the lender due to their insured coverage of that loan. The liability remains even though the property passed from you to A, B, and C. Of course, as long as you retain the property, the liability situation is no more extreme than with a conventional loan.

HOW TO GET INFORMATION: The following list includes all the regional offices of the Veterans Administration. Any correspondence should be directed to the *Director* of the corresponding office in your area. You may request additional data from the office to assist you in your use of the VA loan program. One caution, however. Much of the material they will send you is out-of-date, and you should not rely on this information if it applies to interest rates, dollar amounts, and current programs. Local lenders dealing with loans can provide this up-to-date information. The VA sends notices on minor changes on a very frequent basis, and there is no way you can keep abreast of these changes unless you have the time to sift through all the notices which the VA sends out.

VA Regional Office
Aronov Building
474 South Court Street
Montgomery, Alabama 36104

VA Regional Office
Federal Building
230 North First Avenue
Phoenix, Arizona 85025

VA Regional Office
Federal Office Building
700 West Capitol Avenue
Little Rock, Arkansas 72201

VA Regional Office
Federal Building
11000 Wilshire Boulevard
Los Angeles, California 90024

VA Regional Office
211 Main Street
San Francisco, California 94105

VA Regional Office
Denver Federal Center
Denver, Colorado 80225

VA Regional Office
450 Main Street
Hartford, Connecticut 06103
Note:
Loan Guaranty consolidated with Philadelphia.

VA Center
1601 Kirkwood Highway
Wilmington, Delaware 19805

Veterans Benefits Office
Veterans Administration
2033 M. Street, NW
Washington, D.C. 20421

VA Regional Office
P.O. Box 1437
144 First Avenue, South
St. Petersburg, Florida 33731

VA Regional Office
730 Peachtree Street, NE
Atlanta, Georgia 30308

VA Regional Office
P.O. Box 3198
680 Ala Moana Boulevard
Honolulu, Hawaii 96801

VA Regional Office
Federal Building & U.S. Courthouse
550 West Fort Street
Box 044
Boise, Idaho 83724

VA Regional Office
2030 West Taylor Street
Chicago, Illinois 60680

VA Regional Office
36 South Pennsylvania Street
Indianapolis, Indiana 46204

VA Regional Office
210 Walnut Street
Des Moines, Iowa 50309

VA Center
5500 East Kellogg
Wichita, Kansas 67218

VA Regional Office
600 Federal Place
Louisville, Kentucky 40202

VA Regional Office
701 Loyola Avenue
New Orleans, Louisiana 70113

VA Center
Togus, Maine 04330

VA Regional Office
Federal Building
31 Hopkins Plaza
Baltimore, Maryland 21201

VA Regional Office
J.F.K. Federal Building
Government Center
Boston, Massachusetts 02203

VA Regional Office
801 West Baltimore at Third
PO. Box 1117-A
Detroit, Michigan 48232

VA Center
Federal Building
Fort Snelling
St. Paul, Minnesota 55111

VA Center
1500 East Woodrow Wilson Ave.
Jackson, Mississippi 39216

VA Regional Office
Room 4705, Federal Building
1520 Market Street
St. Louis, Missouri 63103

VA Center
Fort Harrison, Montana 59636

VA Regional Office
220 South 17th Street
Lincoln, Nebraska 68508

VA Regional Office
1201 Terminal Way
Reno, Nevada 89502

Note:
Loan Guaranty consolidated with San Francisco. Loan Guaranty activities for Clark and Lincoln Counties, Nevada consolidated with Los Angeles.

VA Regional Office
497 Silver Street
Manchester, New Hampshire 03103

VA Regional Office
20 Washington Place
Newark, New Jersey 07102

VA Regional Office
500 Gold Avenue, SW
Albuquerque, New Mexico 87101

VA Regional Office
Federal Office Building
111 West Huron Street
Buffalo, New York 14202

VA Regional Office
252 Seventh Avenue (at 24th St.)
New York, New York 10001

VA Regional Office
Wachovia Building
301 North Main Street
Winston-Salem, North Carolina 27102

VA Center
Fargo, North Dakota 58102
Note:
Loan Guaranty consolidated with St. Paul.

VA Regional Office
Federal Office Building
1240 East Ninth Street
Cleveland, Ohio 44199

VA Regional Office
Second and Court Streets
Muskogee, Oklahoma 74401

VA Regional Office
426 Southwest Stark Street
Portland, Oregon 97204

VA Center
P.O. Box 8079
5000 Wissahickon Avenue
Philadelphia, Pennsylvania 19101

VA Regional Office
1000 Liberty Avenue
Pittsburgh, Pennsylvania 15222

VA Center
Barrio Monacillos
GPO Box 4867
Rio Piedras, Puerto Rico 00936

VA Regional Office
Federal Building, Kennedy Plaza
Providence, Rhode Island 02903
Note:
Loan Guaranty consolidated with Boston.

VA Regional Office
1801 Assembly Street
Columbia, South Carolina 29201

VA Center
Sioux Falls, South Dakota 57101
Note:
Loan Guaranty consolidated with St. Paul.

VA Regional Office
U.S. Courthouse
801 Broadway
Nashville, Tennessee 37203

VA Regional Office
515 Rusk Avenue
Houston, Texas 77061

VA Regional Office
1400 North Valley Mills Dr.
Waco, Texas 76710

VA Regional Office
125 South State Street
Salt Lake City, Utah 84138

VA Center
White River Junction, Vermont 05001

VA Regional Office
211 West Campbell Avenue
Roanoke, Virginia 24011

VA Regional Office
Sixth and Lenora Building
Seattle, Washington 98121

VA Regional Office
502 Eighth Street
Huntington, West Virginia 25701

VA Regional Office
342 North Water Street
Milwaukee, Wisconsin 53202

Note:
Wyoming consolidated with Denver.

HOW TO USE THE FHA PROGRAMS TO MAKE MORE SALES

The FHA covers far more ground than the VA. Therefore, it will offer more opportunities for selling real estate.

The Federal Housing Administration was created by the National Housing Act which was approved on June 27, 1934. The purpose of the FHA was to encourage improvement in housing standards and to offer lenders incentives to have a broader lending policy, thereby stabilizing the mortgage market. All these things were needed in 1934; and in retrospect, the FHA programs first offered to the public had considerable impact on lending policies.

In 1965, the office of the Federal Housing Administration was transferred to the Department of Housing and Urban Development. As a result of this move, the FHA is now an organizational unit within the Department of Housing and Urban Development (HUD). Like the VA loan program, the FHA does not give loans, but insurance on loans. The FHA provides insurance for private lenders against loss on mortgages which they give to finance homes, multifamily projects, land development projects, and other programs which will be discussed in this chapter.

Here is a list of some of the current, existing programs which indicate the involvement of the FHA in mortgage assistance.

Homes And Units Up To 4-Plex

TITLE II

Section 203 (b)	1- to 4-family housing units
Section 203 (h)	Disaster housing
Section 203 (i)	Low-cost homes in outlying areas
Section 203 (k)	Home improvement loans
Section 203 (m)	Seasonal, leisure, or vacation homes
Section 213	Sales of individual housing cooperative units
Section 220	Urban renewal housing
Section 220 (h)	Home improvement loans in urban renewal areas
Section 221 (d) (2)	Low-cost homes for families displaced by urban renewal, etc.
Section 221 (h)	Low-income rehabilitation housing
Section 222	Servicemen's homes
Section 233	Experimental homes
Section 234 (c)	Sales of individual condominium housing units
Section 235	Home ownership for lower-income families
Section 237	Marginal credit risk

TITLE VIII

Section 809	Homes for civilian personnel of military bases, etc.
Section 810 (h)	Sales of individual housing released from Section 810 (g)—Mortgages

Mortgage And Rent Assistance Programs For Multifamily Structures

Section 207	Rental project housing and mobile home parks
Section 213	Cooperative housing
Section 220	Urban renewal housing
Section 220 (h)	Rental project housing improvement loans in urban renewal areas
Section 221 (d) (3)—(4) .	Low- or moderate-income family housing below market rate—income not limited
Section 221 (h)	Low-income rehabilitation housing
Section 231	Housing for elderly
Section 233	Experimental housing
Section 234 (d) (f)	Condominium housing
Section 236	Rental housing for lower-income families
Section 241	Supplemental loans

Land Development

TITLE X	Purchase and development of land; ''New Towns'' development

Medical

TITLE XI	Medical group practice facilities
Section 232	Nursing homes and hospitals

You should become familiar with the titles of the various FHA programs by their section numbers. In conversation, FHA programs are simply referred to as ''a 236,'' ''a 203,'' and so on.

Because these programs may vary slightly from year to year as new programs are added or old ones changed, it is necessary that you continuously update the information contained in this chapter. This can be done simply by keeping in touch with the mortgage broker you plan to deal with in all FHA or VA matters.

Naturally, it is not necessary for you to deal with a mortgage broker. You can handle the applications yourself. However, unless you plan to devote a major part of your time to keeping up-to-date with FHA and VA regulations, I suggest you do not attempt to handle your own applications or the applications of your clients.

FHA Program Chart

I have included a chart, Figure 6-1, of the more useful FHA programs, showing the VA or GI loan as a comparison. You will find this chart helpful as a quick reference to the program number and the general aspects of that program.

Keep in mind that this chapter is not designed to make you an expert in FHA or VA financing. Books containing far more pages than this one could not accomplish that. The more you work with the VA and the FHA, the greater your understanding will be of the workings of these government programs. There can be no doubt that both VA and FHA are more complex than conventional financing. And generally, the time periods required to obtain the commitments and funding can be greater than those required in obtaining conventional financing.

In viewing the chart, you should take the minimums and maximums shown as the amounts or periods which can be obtained under ideal conditions. In some cases those maximum amounts can be altered upward, but such circumstances would be highly unusual and cannot be counted on. A lot of the actual funding has to do with the favor in which the particular program finds itself at any given point of time. For example, if the FHA has decided to cut back on the Title XI program for medical facilities, you can have the finest presentation and the worthiest cause and not get anywhere. On the other hand, if Section 207 is pushing mobile home parks and money is flowing into this area, it might be to your advantage to know this and to look for clients who may want to build mobile home parks.

How FHA And VA Programs Can Help You Make More Sales

Many real estate brokers deal with VA and FHA programs in a part-time way. That is to say, they make very few deals each year using these programs. On the other hand, some brokers use VA and FHA to a great extent, closing fifty percent or more of their sales through these governmental programs.

There is a third type of broker who is increasing in number: the broker or salesman that doesn't deal with FHA or VA because he doesn't know enough about the programs to know what they can do. FHA and VA will not be of help to you unless you use the facilities at hand. Once you understand the field of government assistance in financing, you will be broadening the services you can render to your clients. The loans that are available from these programs have lower down payment requirements than loans available from conventional sources without government insurance. This may make the difference between selling or not selling a home for your client.

If you are representing any type of property that fits into the FHA or VA format, you should examine the value to see if a government assisted loan will

Figure 6-1: SOME OF THE USEFUL FHA & VA PROGRAMS

FHA PROGRAMS	LOANS ON	MAXIMUM LOAN AMOUNT	Not Owner Occupied
Section 203 (b)	1 to 4 family homes; existing, under construction, or proposed	1 family: $60,000 2 or 3 family: $65,000 4 family: $75,000	$51,000 55,250 $63,750
Section 203 (h)	Disaster Housing	100% estimated value	
Section 203 (m) (Not often used. See 203(b) not owner occupied)	Second or Seasonal Homes	1 family: $18,000	
Section 203 (v)—with veteran buyer	One family homes; existing, under construction, or proposed	1 family: $60,000	

DOWN PAYMENT REQUIRED	MAXIMUM TERM	GENERAL INFORMATION
Construction approved by FHA for house over 1 yr. old: 3% of 1st $25,000 5% above $25,000 Existing construction, less than 1 yr. old and not approved by FHA before construction: 10% of the total cost to buy.	30 yrs.	+Single people are eligible. +In property not owner occupied, mtg. amount is 85% of mtg. amount for owner occupied (if over 1 yr. old & built to FHA requirements 85% or max. mtg. allowable if home not built under FHA requirements.
No down payment as property is generally owned	30 yrs. or ¾ remaining life	Mtgs. given to finance the replacement of homes destroyed or damaged by major disasters.
25% Maximum	30 yrs.	As these homes are not required to be lived in year-round, they need not meet full FHA restrictions. S&L's can loan $5,000 without secured high 1st mtg.
No down payment on 1st $25,000 5% above $25,000	30 yrs.	+Veteran must have had 90 days of continuous service on active duty in any branch at any time. Eligibility never expires. There is a minimum investment of $200 on the 1st $25,000 of value. This $200 can be applied toward costs. +National Guard and Reserves are eligible.

Figure 6-1 (continued)

FHA PROGRAMS	LOANS ON	MAXIMUM LOAN AMOUNT	Not Owner Occupied
Section 207	Mobile Homes and Mobile Parks	Mobile Homes—up to 100% Parks: $2,500 per space; $1,000,000 per park	
Section 207	Rental Housing—8 or more family units (new or re-habilitated)	90% of face value, max. established per project	
Section 213	Coops of 5 or more units	Varies—follows completed formula	
Section 220	Improvement Loans (1 to 4 units)	Usually follows 203 (b) maximums	
Section 221 (d) (2)	1 to 4 family; existing, proposed or rehabilitated; for low- and moderate-income families	1 family: $39,000 2 family: $41,000 3 family: $54,000 4 family: $64,800 Maximum loan amounts on 1 family homes may be increased to $25,200 ($28,800 in high cost areas) for a family of 5 or more, if house has 4 or more bedrooms	

DOWN PAYMENT REQUIRED	MAXIMUM TERM	GENERAL INFORMATION
No down payment required by FHA. Some lenders may however, require small equity.	145 mo.	While FHA will insure for over 12 yrs., such term is not generally available in the market.
Development provision will vary depending on size of park.	40 yrs.	In high cost areas, max. loan amounts can be increased up to 45%.
10% Minimum	40 yrs.	No discrimination permitted against families with children.
Varies as to maximum loan requirements	40 yrs.	Mortgagor must be nonprofit organization. Individual units to be owned by a closely defined group usually a part of the nonprofit organization.
Usually follows 203 (b)	40 yrs.	Mortgagor can seek funds through FNMA under this program when local lenders are not available.
If mortgagor is nonprofit organization there is a down payment required. Minimum of 3% of total acquisition cost, which may include FHA estimate of value plus closing costs and prepayables. (221 Certificate holders—minimum investment $200).	40 yrs.	+There must be family relationship by blood or marriage, except if mortgagor is 62 or older. +Single people not eligible unless mortgagor is 62 or older. +Some FHA offices have income limits, others don't.

Figure 6-1 (continued)

FHA PROGRAMS	LOANS ON	MAXIMUM LOAN AMOUNT	Not Owner Occupied
Section 222	One family; existing or proposed; home or condo, provided condo is insured under FHA Sec. 234 (c). For members of armed forces on active duty.	1 family: $60,000	
Title X	Land Development	$25 million ea. project. Based on: (1) 79% finished value, or (2) 50% of raw land value + 90% improvements; whichever is lowest.	
Title XI	Medical group practice facilities, medicine, optometry, dentistry	Up to $5 million per facility; 90% of costs	

VA PROGRAM	TYPE OF HOUSING	MAXIMUM LOAN AMOUNT
	1 to 4 family homes; existing, under construction, or proposed; owner occupied	VA does not set a max. mtg. amount. However, many mortgagees limit amount to $100,000.

DOWN PAYMENT REQUIRED	MAXIMUM TERM	GENERAL INFORMATION
Construction approved by FHA: 3% of 1st $25,000 5% over $25,000. Construction not approved by FHA: 10% of total cost to buy.	30 yrs.	+Servicemen must have served at least 2 yrs. on active duty to qualify. +Government pays ½% FHA insurance premium while serviceman owns property and remains on active duty.
Balance of equity required to acquire land and meet development formula.	10 yrs. (but can be extended in many cases)	Under this program, land can be brought to development to ready to build stage. Loan covers all aspects. Releases are made available at 10% *pro rata* lot to mtg. value.
10%	25 yrs.	Mortgagor must be nonprofit. However the facility can be leased to a profit-making group. This program can be used by practitioners who form a nonprofit organization then lease the facility as a profit-making group. Equipment can be included in cost.

DOWN PAYMENT REQUIRED	MAXIMUM TERM	GENERAL INFORMATION
No down payment is required by VA. However, a down payment may sometimes help chances for approval.	30 yrs.	See list of nine categories in this chapter. Must live in home.

aid in the sale of the property. You may find that it will be of no help, and you can then go on to seek other methods of financing. On the other hand, you should never overlook the programs because you don't want to get involved with red tape. There is not that much red tape, and if you are using a mortgage broker he will be doing most of the paperwork anyway.

The Advantages And Disadvantages Of Dealing With VA And FHA Financing

In the first place, it is necessary to find out the advantages and disadvantages of the three parties involved—the buyer, the seller, and the broker.

The pros and cons of VA-FHA for the buyer. Because financing has a long-range effect on the property, the buyer will generally see the majority of the advantages and disadvantages. Nonetheless, it is necessary to compare the VA or the FHA loan with alternatives. In many cases there are no alternatives, and hence no real comparisons to make. The VA, for example, is the only way to buy with no down payment, since no conventional financing is available to match that capability. On the other hand, if you have a buyer who has between 5 and 10% that he can put down, and he insists on going ahead with a VA loan, then you should show him the effect of going with a conventional loan, having coinsurance which will allow 10% down. Because the seller is to pay the discount under VA and FHA, the savings that can accrue to the buyer may make it feasible and desirable to buy conventionally, even though he must put cash down.

The long-term pay-out provided for in most VA and FHA loans can be most advantageous. Once the loan is placed with an interest rate (due to the discount policy) below the market rate, the loan becomes valuable in its own right.

The value of low interest and long terms is seen when the property is placed back on the market in a few years. If you buy a property worth $50,000 and have a $50,000 mortgage, and in three years hope to get $60,000, you can offer the property for sale with excellent financing already on it. Your VA-FHA loan will still have nearly $48,500 in principal, and will have up to 27 years to go at an interest rate which should be well below the market rate. In essence, you have over 80% financing available which can be *assumed* at no cost to close the loan. This type of financing on a home may well mean a better opportunity to sell at a higher price.

The ups and downs for the seller. The seller takes the big bite when he pays the discount on the VA-FHA loan. A minor disadvantage comes in taking the property off the market while the appraisal is made and the buyer is undergoing the qualification process. Time thus becomes the major nonmonetary stumbling block for the seller.

Nonetheless, the sale via VA or FHA may still be the best way to go, or the only way to go. The arguments made by the seller over discount are usually unwarranted, since he would have dropped his price anyway. But this usually means that sellers up the price to cover the cost. Of course, the appraisal must cover the overstuffed price, and generally does.

The biggest problem for the seller is the uncertainty of the whole transaction for a period of time. First of all, he does not know exactly what the discount will be when he places the property on the market, what repairs he may have to make, or when or if the buyer will be approved.

The advantage is the sale itself. When all is said and done, the seller has his money.

How to deal with the broker's problems. To some degree, the broker must understand all the pros and cons and help the buyer and seller appreciate what the other must do or accept. From the broker's point of view, however, the VA and FHA loans can be most burdensome—as well as most productive.

What are the problems? First, you are dealing with buyers who are tying up property with very small down payments—which they will get back if they don't qualify or if the appraisal is not reasonably representative of the price. You will find that unless you do a very careful job of qualifying your buyer, you will have a high incidence of "skips" (buyers who change their mind at the last moment).

Most broker problems can be eliminated by making sure each party does indeed understand the problems of the other. If the seller is told well in advance that the VA-FHA process is slow and cumbersome, then you will not have him on your neck every day. The seller should be aware of repairs he may have to make; and once they are known, he should proceed to have them done so the reappraisal can take place. If the repairs are an obstacle to selling the home, they should be made no matter what the outcome of the VA-FHA loan.

The advantage to the broker is that it provides an additional financing tool with which a sale can be made.

Where To Obtain FHA information

To obtain additional information about any of the FHA programs, you should contact the regional office of the Department of Housing and Urban Development serving your area. See Figure 6-2 on page 136 for a list of addresses.

Figure 6-2: REGIONAL OFFICES OF HUD

Region I 26 Federal Plaza New York, New York 10007	Connecticut, Maine, Massachusetts, New Hampshire, New York, Rhode Island, Vermont
Region II Curtis Building Sixth & Walnut Streets Philadelphia, Pennsylvania 19106	Delaware, District of Columbia, Maryland, New Jersey, Pennsylvania, Virginia, West Virginia
Region III 645 Peachtree—7th Building Atlanta, Georgia 30323	Alabama, Florida, Georgia, Kentucky Mississippi, North Carolina, South Carolina, Tennessee
Region IV Room 1500 360 North Michigan Ave. Chicago Illinois 60601	Illinois, Indiana, Iowa, Michigan, Minnesota, Nebraska, North Dakota, Ohio, South Dakota, Wisconsin
Region V Federal Office Building Room 13A01 819 Taylor St. Fort Worth, Texas 76102	Arkansas, Colorado, Kansas, Louisiana, Missouri, New Mexico, Oklahoma, Texas
Region VI 450 Golden Gate Ave. P.O. Box 36003 San Francisco, California 94102	Northern California, Guam, Hawaii, northern Nevada, southern Idaho, Utah, Wyoming
226 Arcade Plaza Building 1321 Second Avenue Seattle, Washington 98101	Alaska, Montana, northern Idaho, Oregon, Washington
Room 1015 312 North Spring Street Los Angeles, California 90012	Arizona, southern California, southern Nevada
Region VII Ponce De Leon Avenue & Bolivia Street P. O. Box 3869, GPO San Juan, Puerto Rico 00936	Virgin Island, Puerto Rico

Chapter 7

How to Use the Development Loan And the Construction Loan Effectively

The development loan and the construction loan are not exactly the same form of financing. The development loan is generally a loan that is given to a builder or developer to finance the cost of improving raw land.

The classic land development loan has accounted for the majority of development financing over the past twenty years. But land development alone is not the sole use of this form of lending. Redevelopment loans, where existing properties are reconditioned to provide new and often entirely different types of profits, are the more modern use of this form of lending. In this expanded form of the development loan, construction does take place.

The construction loan, however, is merely that part of the development loan that refers to the actual construction of new improvements (other than land enhancement). This segment of financing can occur as an integrated part of the development loan or as a separate loan on its own merits. One developer may take raw land and, with help from local lenders and funds by way of a development loan, bring that land to a stage where it is ready to have homes built on it. This would mean, of course, that utilities, roads, drainage, land plan, and so on would be the major improvements. This developer may then sell lots out to other builders, who would then construct homes with the help of other local lenders' construction loans.

The end of the cycle occurs when a buyer comes along and buys the finished home, replacing the construction loan with a permanent, long-term end loan of his own.

WHY DEVELOPMENT AND CONSTRUCTION LOANS ARE IMPORTANT

These forms of financing are important because they form the basis for all new development. Very few projects will get off the ground unless the cost of development can be financed. It is necessary, therefore, for you to understand the workings of these types of financing and how to find lenders willing to look at your presentation.

The ability to provide for development loans is also important. Many brokers are able to sell properties solely because they know what funds are available for specific projects. If you know in advance of the general market what can be financed, you will have a jump that may be sufficient to put you ahead of your competition. Naturally, this advantage will come as good news to your clients—both buyers and sellers.

Before we get to the fine points for developing this advance knowledge, let's examine these two forms of financing.

The Development Or Construction Loan Usually Depends On The Permanent End Loan

The permanent loan is the final mortgage which will be placed on the property. This loan may have a term of twenty years or as long as forty years on pay-back. These permanent loans are made by commercial banks, savings and loan associations, credit unions, insurance companies, REITS, pension funds, and other sources. These loans are the pay-off for the earlier development and construction loan.

The permanent loan is not placed on the property until construction is completed. Construction cannot start until the construction loan is made and advances issued. The construction loan cannot be made until the land is ready for building, which means the development loan began the sequence. It is very difficult, if not economically dangerous, to begin this sequence in the first place without having a commitment for the end, or permanent, financing.

Development and construction loans are predicated on the amount of the final permanent commitment. If you are going to build 100 apartment units and based on your submission to numerous lenders you obtain a commitment from one or more to lend $1,500,000, on the basis of the final product meeting the specifications of your submission, you will find the maximum development or construction loan available will not exceed the $1,500,000. In fact, it will generally be considerably below that amount, depending on the size of the project and cost overrun averages for the area.

Because the permanent financing has such a profound effect on the nature and amount of development and construction funding you may obtain, we will look at the proper way to examine new developments.

Nine Steps For Achieving Top Dollar In Development and Construction Funding

1. Feel out the market to see what the permanent lenders favor. Once some specifics are known in this area, the builder or developer can move to the other stages. For this example, assume the developer finds that the major permanent lenders are looking favorably at projects of single-family homes in the $40,000 range; shopping centers located in new and growing suburban areas; and mobile home parks that have a density no greater than six sites per acre.
2. The smart developer will follow the money. In the above case it appears that the favorites are single-family projects, shopping centers, and mobile home parks. There may be many other areas that will be open to funding, and it is natural for lenders to disagree on their favorite type of project. What is hot in one area of the country may be cool to cold in others. If the developer has the flexibility to move from one endeavor which is out of favor to another in vogue, he will do better in the long run than the builder who will only build warehouses—whether they can be financed or not. Our hypothetical builder has this flexibility, and wants to look at either mobile home parks or single family projects. This will offer him some choice as he looks for the site and in making the final project selection.
3. Armed with the advance knowledge of the type of project, the builder now attempts to find sites which the lenders may prefer. Remember, the builder is still concerned with the permanent lender. He will either use a mortgage broker or his own contacts with the permanent lenders to find out whether they have any areas in the community which they prefer. You will be surprised to find that many lenders maintain comprehensive statistics on the growth of areas in which they invest their funds.
4. The builder may still not know which of the two types of projects he will consider, or he may have narrowed it down to single-family homes. If this were the situation, he would begin to price out the competition in the areas in which he is looking. Brokers and salesmen reading this chapter will hope that by now he has aligned himself with a broker to help him in the final selection. But the fact of the matter is that he may not, and it is not uncommon for the developer to work with a mortgage broker at this stage of the game or to be on his own. Nonetheless, he is out looking for the right site.
5. A site is selected and negotiations begin. The developer may attempt to get an option on the raw land so he can take his package to some lenders to feel out the market for this site. The option may be for 60 to 90 days so he has time to obtain a response from the permanent lender. During the first week or so of the option, the builder, the mortgage broker, and usually a land planner or two enter the picture to lay out a master plan for the development. If the plan

is to go from raw land to finished product, including homes, the option will be longer than 90 days. On the other hand, if the site is ready to go now, then 90 days may be enough.

6. With a commitment in hand from the permanent lender, the builder is now ready to talk to a development or construction lender. At times, the permanent lender will also make the interim loans leading up to the permanet loan. In this case a combined package of construction and permanent loan can be arranged. But more often than not, there will be two different lenders on the large projects. *Keep in mind, however, that on small projects requiring less than one million dollars, the local savings and loan associations can compete favorably with other lenders by making a package development and permanent loan.*
7. In commercial projects such as strip stores, this stage would begin with negotiations on the terms of the construction loan. If the builder had a commitment for an end loan of $2,000,000, he would take this commitment to several commercial banks in the area and shop for the best terms on the construction loan. Because the terms of the end loan may call for placement not earlier than 24 months from the present date to no later than 36 months, the builder will look to the longest take-out construction loan possible, or 36 months.

   Many permanent end loans have a floor loan amount and a maximum amount. The spread between the two sums is generally based on the break-even rent roll as projected. The lender will calculate the projected break-even rent schedule, then deduct a percentage he feels is reasonable based on the market conditions. Based on the resulting net operating income, he will establish a floor or lowest amount which will be extended on the end loan. The maximum amount of the loan will be paid if a percentage of net operating income, as determined by the lender and agreed to by the builder in advance, is met. There is generally a time period in which the builder has to meet that rent roll, and if he fails to meet it he will never get a shot at the maximum loan again.

   This spread in the two sums often leaves the builder short of loan funds to finish the job. Sometimes this fact is known ahead of time. The construction loan will rarely exceed the floor amount, so if development costs are above that amount then shortages will occur prior to the end of construction and most certainly at the end of the construction loan. Other times, the builder feels he can build under the floor loan amount, only to be surprised at his lack of funds as the estimated cost does not resemble the actual expenditures.
8. This is where ''gap financing'' comes in. This is another part of the develop-

ment and construction loan process. The gap loan is a secondary form of financing that is used to literally fill the gap between the floor amount of the loan and the maximum, or the construction loan amount and the permanent loan. The source for these loans is often a mortgage banker or private party. At times commercial banks will take up the call here but these loans are often very expensive for builders and should be used only when absolutely necessary. The only redeeming factor on a gap loan is that it is usually for a short term. This means that even though the interest rate is high, it will not last for long.

9. With the end loan commitment obtained, the construction loan set, and the development loan tied down, the builder can now proceed with the expectation that he will not need any other financing. The project gets started, and as one loan is paid off by another, the progression of financing from development loan to end loan takes place.

There can be no denying the fact that the foregoing nine steps cover an ideal situation. All aspects of this development seemed to go smoothly. They often do, and when you are dealing with professional mortgage men all the way down the line you will usually have a smooth transition.

However, one clog in a loan progression and a mess can occur. These clogs can appear with amazing speed and never seem to disappear. They take the form of title problems, legal hassles, attorneys' errors, and nit-picking; fights over wording in legals, contracts, mortgage documents, or releases; delays caused by documents lost in the mail, pages missing from commitment letters, or documents not properly signed or witnessed. Yes, there is no doubt that if things don't go right, it can be a mess.

Of course, the fact that all went smoothly at first doesn't mean it will stay that way from the day construction starts until the day the end loan is placed. In the first place, the terms of the commitment must be met. That means that the building to be constructed must be exactly as the plans and specifications indicated when the commitment was issued. Any changes must be approved by the lender. This is where many loans have gone astray. A lender who wants to withdraw from a loan he committed himself to two years earlier when interest rates were 2 points lower than the current rate, will look very hard to see if there is a way to get out of it.

The construction lender gets very anxious about this type of talk from permanent lenders. The construction lender is in the project for a short time, he hopes, and enjoys the high interest rate he gets on the construction loan. But he is not ready to take over a project that fails to close on the end loan. If the end loan does not close because you did something wrong you will have made an enemy.

GETTING A DEVELOPMENT OR CONSTRUCTION LOAN WITHOUT AN END LOAN

This was very popular at one time, and as you might suspect, due to its dangers, has lost the favor it once had. This type of financing gained support when the permanent market all but dried up. Builders, sensing that the money market was very tight on a long-term loan but still relatively soft in the construction money market, went out on a limb and started projects without effective end loans.

Not many lenders would make development loans without the end loan commitment first. Then, some of the big builders persuaded their banks to go with them on the idea that by the time construction of a big project was finished one, two, or three years later, the permanent market would be back in the swing of things and that type of money would be available again.

Other builders took advantage of commitment letters from mortgage brokers, bankers, and other sources, who in effect sold these letters to the builders. In essence, the commitment letter would state that an end loan was available. This would satisfy the construction lender and the loan would be made. However, these commitment letters were for throwaway loans. The terms of the end loan under many of these letters were so onerous that to take the loan would have been a financial disaster.

The idea was this: pay for the letter to satisfy the construction lender that an end loan was available, then wait for better years ahead in the long-term end loan market. As the best plans of mice and men don't always work out, the commitment letter format was not very effective. The permanent money market remained firm and the commitment letters were called to take out the construction loans. In some cases, the commitment letters were found to be worthless and projects got into trouble one after the other.

The lesson to be learned is simple and sweet. There are few reasons to obtain a construction loan without having an end loan. It is much better to have the end loan before you start.

WHY THE SIZE OF THE PROJECT DOESN'T MATTER

The size of the development or construction project is not the main criterion for understanding and using this form of financing. It is natural, of course, that in projects under $100,000 the local savings and loan association may compete favorably with a duo-part loan—the construction loan which is replaced by the permanent loan. The combined package loan that most savings and loan associations and other lenders offer, puts both aspects of the two separate loans into one document. Still, builders of single-family homes will operate with separate construction loans rather than have this combination package of end loan and construction loan as an automatic event.

USING THE DEVELOPMENT OR CONSTRUCTION LOAN TO MAKE MORE SALES

Putting the whole ball of wax together may be your role. If you are dealing in developable types of land, the redevelopment of urban areas, or in any type of real estate that calls for some form of development or construction, then you must have a working knowledge of this tool.

To be specific, the ability to package a deal will require a considerable amount of expertise in many areas. In some of these areas you need only have the sense to get someone else on your team. Planning and engineering, for example, will no doubt be beyond the scope of most salesmen. To be sure, moving from a listing to a sale can be an immense task for some salesmen on some properties.

How One Broker Made A Four-Million Dollar Deal

Jackson had just listed a very interesting property in Fort Lauderdale. The site was about 15 acres of prime, business-zoned land located on a major highway. Its uniqueness was that it was the largest vacant property in the city that had deep water access to the Atlantic Ocean. The site was located in a high-income area of town and adjoined a major shopping center.

The drawbacks in marketing the property were the general economy and the price. The economy was still struggling to make a comeback and the price quoted by the sellers was eight dollars per square foot. The price was not high when compared to other smaller sites in comparable locations. In fact, smaller lots similarly zoned had sold for over fiteen dollars per square foot. However, the size of this tract and the fact that it could not be subdivided made prospective buyers scarce.

It was clear to Jackson that what was needed to entice an investor was an economic use. A use that could not be financed was not going to be productive, so Jackson had to find a use that *could* be financed. Therefore, Jackson tried to determine all the possible uses the site could be put to. He and others made a list of all the possibilities no matter how silly they sounded at the time.

Armed with this list, Jackson approached several lenders and mortgage brokers that he had dealt with in the past and presented the problem to them. He was not asking for money, only assistance in solving a problem. What were the possible uses for the tract which could be financed? Several new possible uses were added to the list by the lenders.

Then Jackson put this question to each of them: "Of all the possible uses on this list, which is most financeable assuming that the economics work out?" Many of the suggested uses were eliminated. Some sound ideas were cast off as being overbuilt for the area or impractical for other reasons. The list was narrowed down to five possible uses that could be financed if the economics did work out.

Jackson knew that for the economics to work out, a conservative approach to development, income, and expenses would have to show the project to be profitable. Once he had some possible lendable projects, he went to work to see if the numbers would work.

One by one the projects failed to work out on paper. Then, two concepts began to make economic sense. Jackson took his numbers to a mortgage broker. The mortgage broker went over the numbers and made some changes and suggestions, then sat back and agreed. It did look as though there were two types of projects that might work economically.

Jackson didn't stop there. He went to his builder and management friends and smoothed out the figures even further. With the refined projections, he returned to the mortgage brokers. Several brokers got excited about the two concepts. They could see the possibility of making a nice loan fee, so they in turn talked to several of their lenders. Before Jackson knew it lenders were hot to go. He knew that his job was now almost completed.

The result of Jackson's efforts was that the property was sold. He had developed two concepts that in turn attracted lenders and buyers' interest in the property. Interest that was prequalified, and able to recognize that the proposals were sound and feasible. What Jackson sold was not the land but the *concept*.

HOW TO INCREASE THE AMOUNT OF MONEY YOU CAN BORROW ON A DEVELOPMENT LOAN

It is possible to obtain 100% of the funds needed for the development and construction of many projects. In many cases, you can even include the land in this mortgage amount and enter into a development with little or no cash.

Your ability to do this will depend on several simple factors. Experience by the way, is not necessarily one of these factors. The following list will outline the factors which must be developed in order to obtain the highest possible loan.

Eight Factors In Getting The Maximum Loan

1. *Seek the lender's favorite type of project.* Follow Jackson's example of finding out what the lenders like and then go for that type of loan.

2. *Don't jump in too soon in asking for the funds.* Plan out your project. Some lenders will ask for a feasibility study if you move too quickly. Wait until you have done your own study. If you have done it well enough you may not need a feasibility study.
3. *Have the right numbers.* Don't take one person's advice on what rent you should be able to collect on a proposed office building until you have checked out the actual market as it now stands.
4. *Have the property tied up.* If you don't own it already, be sure you have some tie on it. You have a lot of work ahead of you, and unless you can hold onto the land you may end up with a commitment and then be unable to buy the property or have to pay more than you expected.
5. *When ready, act forcibly.* Bravado is important in asking for money, so have plenty of it (bravado is a nice word for guts). Don't, however, try to cover up lack of knowledge with smugness. Point out good features instead.
6. *Leave inexperience at home—yours or your client's as the case may be.* What is important is the project, the numbers, and ability. Note the word "ability" and not "experience." The fact that it may be your first shopping center or strip store, or ten times larger than anything you have ever built is not important.
7. *Negotiate for more.* Your lender will usually offer less than you ask for. Hold firm if you can and try to get what you feel you need. Remember, if you say you must have $500,000 you may then have to explain why you are willing to take $425,000.
8. *Offer incentives to the lender.* When the need for venture capital is overwhelming, you may have to resort to tradeouts with the lender. In order to increase the loan amount closer to 100%, you may often have to give the lender a percentage of the action. This can occur in many ways, which will be covered later in this chapter. Be careful, however, since the lender knows all the tricks and controls the purse strings.

HOW TO PUT TOGETHER A PRESENTATION FOR A DEVELOPMENT LOAN

In Chapter 4 the basic loan presentation was outlined. This format should be used in all loan presentations that cover existing properties. Its adaptation so it can also be used for presentations on proposed projects will be covered in this chapter. In essence, greater detail must be included to cover the potential of the project. You cannot rely on past performance, which in the case of a new development does not exist.

The presentation itself will take on the aspects of a feasibility study. It is often thought that all feasibility studies ascertain the best use of a given site. However, this is only one type of feasibility study. More commonly, a lender may request that a study be made to indicate the potential of success a given project may have. The lender's reason for requesting this study is to use the data obtained to help the money managers come to a decision as to whether or not the money requested should be lent.

Unfortunately, the whole system of feasibility studies has gone somewhat astray. There is the classic story of a major lender from the northeast. This lender was presented with a well-planned hotel project that looked fantastic on paper. The developers were experienced, the designers were well qualified, and all the right things had seemingly been done. But the lender needed a third-party reference, so the loan was not going to be granted unless a feasibility study was made. At considerable cost, therefore, such a study was hastily ordered and sent to the lender as soon as it came off the press.

The loan was made. But after several years of development, and one failure after another, the project developers went into bankruptcy. The lender had to take the project into his portfolio and finish the construction. Some time later, a bright young lawyer in the lender's office read the feasibility study. The study had predicted that the project had merit and, based on the then present statistics of competition, would be successful. However, the study continued, there were over 47 similar ventures currently on the drawing boards, which would no doubt enter competition around the time of the proposed hotel development. The study went on to disclose the statistics, the number of projects and their locations.

The mistake in this situation is obvious. The venture under consideration was a hotel, and the existing hotels in the area would not be able to handle the demand for rooms that the future Disney World complex would provide. So, what else but a hotel would be a good idea? Unfortunately, what's good for the goose is not always good for the geese.

The lender was anxious to make the loan, and once the study came in it was most likely glanced over and then filed. In reality, he had paid for a study that recommended that the project not be started in the first place.

HOW TO APPROACH A FEASIBILITY STUDY

In many respects, the feasibility study is similar to the loan request shown in Chapter 4. However, the differences are sufficient for you to follow a new outline. In Figure 7-1, I have provided an outline for you to use when compiling feasibility studies.

Figure 7-1: OUTLINE FOR A FEASIBILITY STUDY

I. THE PROJECT
  A. General Description
  B. Site Plan
    (1) Breakdown of project to square footage of improvements
    (2) Use of project
    (3) Stages to be built or developed
  C. Economics of Project
    (1) Cost estimates
      a. builders' bid on other supporting data
    (2) Operating expenses
      a. during development
      b. marketing expenses
      c. preleased agreements (if applicable)
    (3) Cash flow—expense vs. income chart
  D. Feasibility of Project
    (1) Economy of area
      a. aerial photo showing location of similar projects in competing area
      b. description of competing projects
      c. economics of competing projects
      d. future growth proposed and documented
      e. future demand on type of project (including supporting documents)
      f. summary of economics of competing projects
    (2) Opinion of use based on area economics
  E. Value of Completed Project
    (1) Estimated potential cash flow on finished project (if income property shows Operational statement, 12 month estimate after project completed)
    (2) Market value based on cash flow (capitalize at current investor demand rate)
    (3) Value of existing projects of similar nature (refer to same projects covered in earlier description of competing projects)

II. THE PROPERTY
  A. General Description
  B. Legal Description
  C. Locations

D. Location Sketch
E. Aerial Photo
F. Location Benefits
G. Location Drawbacks
H. General Statistics
   (1) Demographics
   (2) Average rent
   (3) Traffic count
I. General Site Data
   (1) Legal
   (2) Size and square feet of land and site coverage
   (3) Use of site
   (4) Zoning
   (5) Utilities
   (6) Access
   (7) Sketch of lots sharing building location
   (8) Survey
J. Land Value
   (1) Estimated value of site
   (2) Comparable land sales and values

III. THE DEVELOPER
A. Name
B. Address
C. Occupation
D. General Data
E. Net Worth
F. Supporting Documents (not included, but will be on forms institution supplies)
   (1) Net worth statement
   (2) Schedule of assets
   (3) Schedule of liabilities
   (4) References
   (5) Position of employment
   (6) Verification of salary
   (7) Estimated annual earnings
   (8) Credit report if applicable
   (9) Other forms supplied for application

IV. THE LOAN REQUEST (for End Loans)
A. Recap Value of Finished Product
B. Recap Development Cost
C. Add Land Cost to Development Cost

D. Show Relation to Total Estimated Value and Total Cost to Develop
E. Amount of Loan Requested
F. Terms and Conditions Requested
(for Construction or Development Loan)
A. Recap Value of Finished Product
B. Recap Development Cost
C. Add Land Cost to Development Cost
D. Show Relation to Total Estimated Value and Total Cost to Develop
E. Copy of End Loan Commitment
F. Amount of Construction or Development Loan Requested
G. Terms and Conditions Requested

V. SUPPORTING DOCUMENTS
A. Full Set of Working Plans (if available)
B. Topography (if needed)
C. Preleased Documents (if applicable)

WHERE TO GO TO OBTAIN A DEVELOPMENT OR CONSTRUCTION LOAN

Many lenders will provide such funds, and for the most part all normal institutional leaders have involved themselves from time to time in this type of financing. However, there are some sources which are better than others, depending on the size of the loan and the nature of the project.

I have provided a chart that illustrates the best lenders for the various situations which may appear. Keep in mind that much of this will have to do with the lending experiences of the lender. If the commercial bank has been burned with construction loans, they may not be ready to jump back into that market. Nonetheless, commercial banks tend to be the better source for short-term construction funds.

Never forget the private money sources. These funds can be available when all other sources dry up. In essence, they are costly monies to borrow, but can compete favorably in a very tight money market. When you have to borrow, the cost may be immaterial.

Examine the chart and use it only as a reference as to where to start first. The fact that savings and loans are not generally in the construction loan market will not mean that you should not ask them if all other avenues fail.

Seven Points To Remember In Negotiations With The Lender Or His Agent

1. DISTANCE REQUIRES MORE SUPPORT: The farther you get from the lender in the chain of command, the more the decision to lend is based on the

Figure 7-2: LOAN SOURCES

	LAND DEVELOPMENT LOAN	CONSTRUCTION LOAN	PACKAGE: DEVELOPMENT AND CONSTRUCTION	PACKAGE: DEVELOPMENT, CONSTRUCTION, AND PERMANENT
COMMERCIAL BANKS	Bank policy varies as to local situation. Dev. loans must generally be backed by high credit or take out from end loan. Rare to find loans which exceed one million dollars except from majors.	The ideal place to look when an end loan is already committed. Loan will be set at a rate depending on the project. Often very competitive.	Are available from some commercial banks. The end loan commitment will be a major factor here.	Long-term lending will vary from bank to bank. Rates and years to pay back may not be as good as other lenders.
SAVINGS AND LOANS			Some possibility here. Depends on bank policy, situation, and type of project—but very rare.	Ideal for single family or condo-type development. S&L's may bring in other S&L's to combine funds to make big deals.
INSURANCE COMPANIES	Some companies have been very active in this area in the past, primarily when the project is land sales rather than continued development. Good source. Funds are not limited, but prefer over $500,000.	Rare, but some companies have made such loans in the past. Better to look elsewhere.	Rare	For big projects this may be a good source. The lender often gets a piece of the action on this type of loan. Rates and closing costs may be lowest from this source.
REITS	When REITS have money they will look at almost anything. Some look only to the short-term loan (the development or construction loan). Others like the long-term loan. As of this writing, however, REITS have lost the potency they had in the early 1970's. But that is likely to change and they should make a comeback. Make friends now as they may well become the best source again—for all forms. They prefer the larger loan, and have made some of the biggest.			
PENSION FUNDS	Don't like high-risk deals, so won't be in this field except for closely connected loans.	Same as Development Loan	Same as Development Loan	Are becoming effective lenders in this area. Try them for deals over $500,000. Like proven track record.

Figure 7-2 (continued)

	LAND DEVELOPMENT LOAN	CONSTRUCTION LOAN	PACKAGE: DEVELOPMENT AND CONSTRUCTION	PACKAGE: DEVELOPMENT, CONSTRUCTION, AND PERMANENT
MORTGAGE BANKERS	Yes. Depending on the banker, funds are often available for good, sound developments that have end loan take out already committed.	Same as Development Loan	Same as Development Loan	Can fund many moderate size deals. Beyond that they will seek coventure funds. Can be expensive money, but often available when others are dry.
CREDIT UNIONS	Credit unions, like the REITS, vary greatly. They have growing masses of funds like the pension funds, but like to lend first within their own circle. Yet, their managers will often allocate percentages to long- and short-term lending. They can be good for developments within their own area: teachers credit unions lending to a textbook publisher and the like.			

opinions of other people. This is human nature. The loan officer at a local savings and loan will act without having to check with as many people as the mortgage representative of a major insurance company a thousand miles away. Because of this, try to obtain as many outside opinions yourself. Then document them in your presentation. These outside statements of market conditions, rental *pro formas*, expenses, and operating costs can be found without much effort. Fellow brokers, banks, property managers, owners of similar properties, and so on will often be glad to help. When you do get information from them, don't just refer to the facts—put a copy of the memo they sent you or the letter from the property manager in your report. This padding will become third-party support material that people who make the final decision can hang their hats on.

2. YOU CAN'T REALLY LOSE: Do as much of the initial work as you can yourself. The first time you make one of these studies you will be amazed at how little you knew about the area, the project, and your perseverance. By the time you have finished the study, you will know more than much of your competition about this type of property and development. That is not a bad side-benefit, no matter what happens to the development. After you have gone through several such studies you will have the formula down pat.

3. CONTINUE TO EXPAND YOUR ABILITIES: At first, there will be some aspects that you may need assistance with. If you are dealing with a mortgage broker, he can usually provide help. Brokers are often able to go over the numbers with you, and once they see a feasible project they will get excited as hell. If they can make the loan, then everyone will benefit.

4. BE READY TO NEGOTIATE FOR THE MONEY: When money is tight, lenders will take advantage of the scarcity of funds to make as favorable a deal as they can. This may mean they will demand a percentage of the action, which can take many forms. The most usual are shown here:

a. *An override*—This form of percentage-of-the-operation is based on the lender receiving a preset percentage of all income that exceeds certain amounts. For example: A $10,000 loan on a shopping center has a provision that the lender will receive 10% of gross income in excess of $2,000,000. Once the loan is satisfied, this provision does not continue.
b. *Land ownership*—The lender takes title to the land and leases it to the developer. The lease may be reasonable, and in essence the lender becomes a partner in the venture. The loan covers the development of the land. Once the loan is paid off, the land lease still goes on. This way the lender continues to benefit even though the loan has been satisfied.
c. *Coventure*—This can take many forms. The percentage of coventure will depend on the lender and the deal. It is not uncommon that a lender will put up all the money and then take 50% of a venture. Usually, only builders of outstanding reputation can get these deals. However, when money is flowing, these builders can make deals without having to give up any percentage to a lender, or at most very little.

5. DON'T TAKE "NO" FOR AN ANSWER: For the most part, you are dealing with very conservative people. They take lending the money of their employers very seriously. Therefore, you may get a "no," especially if you approach the lender prematurely. So, if you think you have a hot item, hang it on the possibility of getting the money. However, do not be overly pushy.

6. BOUNCE RIGHT BACK FROM A DEFEAT: Nothing should keep a good guy down for long. When you have made your most fantastic presentation for the greatest project you have ever thought of and on the hottest site in town, and can't get a lender to sound interested, try to find out why. One mortgage broker I have dealt with in the past may smile if he is very excited. The rest of the time he speaks of doom as though it came two hours ago. He tells me this is his way of maintaining his sanity in the business he is in. From your point of view, his negativism can sound like lack of interest. If one mortgage broker or lender gets to you in this way, go on to another. Always be ready to accept the fact that your idea is not sound—and if it's not, find one that is.

7. WATCH OUT FOR TOO MUCH PRAISE: This is the one thing that concerns me. If all I hear is good news about a project I am working on, then I start to worry. (I call my mortgage broker friend from Item 6 and know he will have something bad to say.) You need to find someone you can count on to cut the project you are working on to ribbons. You won't get ahead riding the crest of disinterested praise.

Chapter 8

How to Utilize Blanket Mortgages To Aid in Financing

The blanket mortgage is often mistaken or confused with the wrap-around mortgage. Blanket mortgages are mortgages that cover more than one parcel of property. Wrap-around mortgages are mortgages that encompass other mortgages. The purpose of this chapter is to take a hard look at the blanket mortgage and see how it can be used to assist in other forms of financing. Later on in this book, the wrap-around mortgage will be discussed in detail.

Any basic form of mortgage, including a warp-around, can be used to encompass more than one property. The moment more than one property is security for the mortgage, you have a blanket mortgage. For example, an investor I knew owned three duplexes that were side by side. He wanted to refinance the mortgages on two of them, but found it was to his advantage to refinance all three under one mortgage. The resulting mortgage was a blanket mortgage.

As you read through this chapter you will see the many advantages of the blanket mortgage. There are drawbacks as well, and these will also be examined.

WHO CAN UTILIZE THE BLANKET MORTGAGE

The criterion for using a blanket mortgage is easy enough. You must have at least two parcels of property. It helps if they are adjoining, but this is not necessary. It is not unusual to have a blanket mortgage on two or more properties that are neither adjoining nor in the same area. A home and a lot, an apartment building and a warehouse, or vacant land and a duplex are some of the many combinations of dissimilar properties which can be combined in a blanket mortgage. Some mortgages of a blanket nature can include *dozens* of properties.

Most investors seeking to obtain maximum leverage will find the blanket mortgage helpful in obtaining the highest yield on their invested capital. Because maximum financing is one of the benefits that is attained from its use, let's look at this as well as the other benefits which can be derived from the blanket mortgage.

WHAT BLANKET MORTGAGES CAN DO

1. Provide maximum financing. Generally, if you include more than one property as security for a loan, it is possible to borrow in excess of the value of a part of the total security. With this in mind, blanket mortgages can provide 100% financing for new ventures and throw off cash to boot. In the refinancing of several properties, the combined effect of the security can make the package presented to the lender more secure and thereby increase the amount to be lent.

2. Allow the mortgagor to obtain better terms and conditions on the loan. It follows that if the loan is more secure, then you have room to bargain for better terms. Of the terms to be considered, the interest rate and annual payment will be most important. If you can decrease the percentage of loan to value ratio, thereby decreasing the lender's risk, you will find the terms should ease considerably. For example, Simon, a local investor, wanted to purchase a 10-unit apartment house fairly priced at $145,000. The property had a low first mortgage of $30,000. The seller indicated he would hold up to $20,000 in a second mortgage, and wanted cash above that. Simon discovered that within the new money market, the best he could come up with, after mortgage cost, was $102,000. This left him short the difference needed to buy the property, even if the seller held the $20,000 paper. The best terms available from a local savings and loan association were 24 years at 9¾% with 4 points closing.

However, he did own a small lot that was across the street from the apartment house. It was free and clear and he hoped to build on it one day. Its value was $35,000.

He went to the bank again and offered to put the lot up as additional security on the loan. The lot was appraised at the $35,000 value, thus a total value of $180,000 was created. The bank was told a 72% loan to value ratio, or a $129,600 mortgage, was all that was needed. This ratio was lower than that which the bank was willing to lend, so they gave in on the terms. A 27-year mortgage at 9½% was obtained. Points came to only 3% instead of 4%. Simon was able to have provisions put into the mortgage that would enable him to release the lot once the principal was reduced by $26,000. This would enable him to build at a future date without having to pay off the entire amount of the first loan.

Simon ended up with the 10 units with no cash down, since the seller held the balance of the paper against the property.

3. Consolidate properties for refinancing. Some clients have put together a considerable array of properties over the years. Mortgages have different payment schedules and termination dates. Sometimes it is feasible to add several properties to a refinancing package of another property to provide a larger base and reduce the overall loan to value ratio. In this type of blanket mortgage the properties should be similar types of realty when dealing with institutional lenders. However, private lenders may not care.

Another local investor, Aston, had nearly a dozen small warehouses across town. Each of them was fully rented and none had a mortgage greater than 50% of its value. Two of the larger warehouses had mortgages that were at very high interest rates as compared to the present market. Aston decided to refinance them all under one blanket mortgage. He obtained an excellent commitment from one of the local savings and loan associations in the area, and another almost equally good from a local commercial bank.

I had the opportunity to see Aston just before he made his deal with the savings and loan. In looking over the package, I discovered he had two warehouses which had 5½% loans. While these loans were low in ratio of loan-to-value, their term was still 14 years to go. (They must have been FHA or VA in origin.) I suggested he keep these loans and let the lender hold second position on those two warehouses. This would lower the overall payment and probably not affect the amount of money lent.

The savings and loan did not go along with that idea, but the commercial bank did. The total loan was far in excess of the pay-off of the existing financing, and Aston withdrew from the property nearly $175,000—which was not taxable. His annual payment increased only $5,000 over his previous debt service on the earlier financing.

4. Lock property in. This can be an advantage as well as a disadvantage. If you were Aston and had ideas of selling some of the warehouses in a few years, you would have to have release provisions as a part of the mortgage terms. Some lenders will go along with this, but others won't. However, if you are selling property, the features of the blanket mortgage can be made to work for you if you are asked to hold paper. You can have the buyer include other properties which will become security to the transaction. This becomes both a buyer and a seller provision, depending on the circumstances and point of view.

5. Lock other assets in. There is no reason why the blanket mortgage should be limited to real estate. As in the above situation, the buyer or seller can offer or require other assets to be pledged as security. A liquor license, for example, may be tied to a bar in this way. Stocks or other collateral can be given as additional security via the blanket aspects of the mortgage.

In both of these examples, the assets can be pledged by the mortgagor or a cosigner. For example: Walters wanted to buy a home that had existing financing of $50,000 and $40,000 in equity. He had no cash to put down, but did have a father-in-law anxious to see his daughter move out of the guest house and into her own home. The father-in-law offered a second mortgage on his own home as additional security to the seller. In the end, the seller took a blanket second on the home being sold, with a second position on the father-in-law's home. The total equity was more than enough and this saved the deal.

WHERE TO GET BLANKET MORTGAGES

Not all lenders will consider a situation that calls for a blanket provision in the mortgage. However, the big lenders, such as insurance companies and REITS, have made such loans. Also, many of the more local lenders, such as commercial banks and mortgage bankers, will frequently lend with blanket provisions. The whole idea of blanket provisions is to make the loan more secure, and virtually all lenders will make blanket loans given the right circumstances.

The best place to look for money when you are willing to offer additional property as supplemental security is to the seller. The increased equity gained by virtue of this form of financing can often sway the seller into holding large amounts of paper. Other private sources, such as investors, private lenders, and mortgage brokers, also like the blanket mortgage and should not be overlooked.

WHEN TO USE A BLANKET MORTGAGE

When you are considering the use of a blanket mortgage, reexamine the 5 things it can do:

1. Provide maximum financing
2. Provide a stronger position for negotiating the terms and conditions of the loan
3. Consolidate properties for refinancing
4. Lock property in
5. Lock other assets in

Situations that call for blanket financing require the satisfaction of one or more of the above five items. Since items (1) and (2) are rather general, it is important to remember that there are many different forms of financing that can accomplish these two desired goals. But when the best form for the borrower is unacceptable to the lender, then a blanket mortgage may be the answer.

Providing maximum financing may not be worth the cost or the disadvantages that result from both excessive leverage and overextension. Because of this, the use of blanket mortgages must be compared to the other alternatives.

Once you have a basis for determining which form is the most advantageous to your client, then you can proceed to see if you can work out the transaction on those more favorable terms.

HOW TO DETERMINE THE ACCEPTABILITY OF A BLANKET MORTGAGE

The acceptability of a blanket mortgage can be seen from both sides of the transaction. As in all forms of mortgages the effect may differ from transaction to transaction and from buyer to seller. Unless you can pinpoint what makes the blanket mortgage acceptable, you may not know when to use it.

Blanket Mortgages As Seen From The Buyer's Point Of View

The buyer must understand that in order to use this form of financing, it is necessary to encumber more than one piece of property. If the transaction itself contains these separate properties, there may be no reason to hesitate —providing the buyer can obtain releases that may be necessary (such as purchasing four lots from one seller). It is not unusual for the buyer to add security to the blanket mortgage from property already owned.

The majority of blanket mortgages do occur with this extra outside security as a part of the transaction. The buyer uses equity in other property to assist in new financing. To some degree it is seen in pyramiding and other forms of high leverage and extension buying. Nonetheless, the buyer must understand the disadvantages, as well as the advantages, of this format, and must weigh these in determining whether it is wise to use a blanket mortgage.

Disadvantages in blanket mortgages for buyers.

(1) They place a burden on other properties. Whenever a second property is pledged as additional security on a blanket mortgage, that property is in jeopardy if the mortgage falters.

(2) They can make a separation difficult or impossible. Of course, this will depend on the terms of the blanket mortgage. But to some degree, the mortgagor is hampered in his ability to sell the other properties. A buyer can, however, buy subject to the blanket mortgage, and if the principal of the mortgage is less than the amount of financing held there is no disadvantage.

(3) Assets can be locked in. This works as both an advantage and a disadvantage. In this instance, the combined effect of tying two or more assets together can cause unforeseen hardships in the future if the mortgagor needs to separate those assets.

You can see that the main disadvantage is the combining of other properties with the inability to separate them when or if the need arises. With this in mind, you can then look to the blanket mortgage as a useful tool when the criteria which follow can be met.

Buyers' criteria for blanket mortgages.

(1) Other conventional forms of financing do not generate the viable financing required to meet the cash requirements of the buyer.
(2) Other properties exist which have sufficient equity that will be accepted by the seller or mortgagee as additional security to arrange the financing required.
(3) Total income generated from all properties covered with the blanket mortgage is sufficient to meet the pay-out requirements of the debt service to be created. A reasonable leeway should provide for a drop of income before the break-even is reached. This will depend on the situation of course. Some transactions may be approached with a deficit—the mortgagor coming out-of-pocket for a time until new income from the property can be generated (as in the case of a new development, construction, or other income increasing methods).
(4) The mortgagor can project that he will not need to separate the properties from the mortgage in the relatively near future. Even if he has release provisions, they will no doubt be costly, so it may be dangerous to enter into a blanket mortgage if he anticipates that early separation will be necessary. This will not be the case if the mortgagor is anticipating a complete refinancing and has confidence he can recast the mortgage and obtain separation in that way. Nonetheless, the risk remains that it may be costly to obtain separation.

In summarizing the blanket mortgage from the buyer's point of view, if the buyer can meet the four criteria and he understands the disadvantages of this form, then he can use the mortgage.

Blanket Mortgages As Seen From The Seller's Point Of View

Like the buyer, the seller and other mortgagees should know all the ins and outs of the blanket mortgage. Yet, because this format is designed to increase the security, the advantages are more often weighted in the seller's and the mortgagee's favor. However, disadvantages do exist.

Disadvantages in blanket mortgages for sellers and other mortgagees.
(1) The blanket mortgage may cause overextension of the property. This in turn could lead to the mortgagor failing to make his payments. The seller can

always look to the properties held as security, but to move into a foreclosure can be most unpleasant, costly, and to no one's ultimate benefit—if there is a choice. The mortgagee can take all precautions to see that this does not occur, but when the buyer is into the property with no cash, or at best very little, then the security may be dependent on what occurs with the other property.

For example: Curtis bought a 15-unit apartment house that had a fair market value of $200,000 and a good first mortgage of $140,000. He gave the seller a blanket second in the amount of $60,000 on the 15-units that also covered (by first mortgage) a lot he owned across town. The value of the lot was estimated to be $30,000. The seller felt secure that he had $90,000 of equity covering his $60,000 second mortgage.

As it turned out, the lot was worth only about $10,000. Curtis milked the apartments for a few years, got behind on his mortgage payments, and then walked away from a foreclosure. The seller had to step in and rescue the 15 units from the first mortgage, and spend several thousand dollars as well to repair them.

(2) Blanket mortgages generally reduce the cash at closing. This happens because the blanket aspect is used to supply additional security to a mortgage greater than the seller is willing to hold otherwise. The effect is to reduce the amount of cash he will receive. All things being equal, this in itself is not a disadvantage, but merely a characteristic of this form of financing. However, all things are rarely equal, and equity rarely equals cash.

The other disadvantages in blanket mortgages are of a more technical nature, and have to do with the possible legal terminology used in the document itself. I have found that most lawyers are able to draft a blanket mortgage which will adequately protect their clients. I suggest, however, that you never have the lawyer for the seller draw up the mortgage for both parties (or the other way around for that matter). Most lawyers will not do this, but I have seen some who will do exactly that. Each party should have separate legal representation for this and all mortgages.

Criteria for mortgagees holding blanket mortgages

SELLERS HOLD:	THIRD-PARTY LOANS:
1. Must have strong motivation to sell or hold the blanket mortgage. It is possible that the blanket is sold, and more than provides the security. Usually, the overwhelming motive is the need to be relieved of superior debt, or is sick to death of the property.	1. Is the security good, sound, and acceptable?

2. The security checks out. The combined equity which secures the blanket mortgage should be well over the principal amount of the mortgage itself. This will vary, depending on the type of property and the existence of superior mortgages. Do not rely on the value as stated by the buyer or his agent. Seek an independent appraisal, or at least ask the advice of other Realtors in the area.

3. Some cash can be a part of the deal. All buyers should put some cash into a transaction. Of course, the amount will depend on many factors. But it does have a solidifying effect.

2. Are the terms of the loan good, sound, and acceptable?

3. Is the return on the mortgage good enough, nonusurious, and acceptable?

4. Is the mortgagor good, sound, and acceptable?

HOW TO INCREASE SALES BY USING THE BLANKET MORTGAGE AS A TOOL

Blanket mortgages have a function as a sales tool in some types of transactions. If you are selling property from a large inventory within the same owner's portfolio, such as tract lots or other subdivided property, the seller can offer packages of lots or parcels to investors with the blanket mortgage. In this way, the buyers would have two or more pieces of land covered by one mortgage. The seller would agree to release some of the lots as the mortgage is paid down. The release would be the same kind that could be used in any form of financing that may provide for the division of a property. The actual wording of the release could be predetermined by the seller to afford him the maximum protection in this type of transaction.

The advantage to the seller in this type of mortgage is mainly the increased sales potential. The risk to the seller over other forms of financing is negligible, if the land in question is substantially worth the price. The buyer can compare the blanket mortgage to other forms of financing to see how it will affect him. In the following example, you will find one such comparison.

McMoore was a land developer and had over 50 lots remaining in his most recent subdivision. He was not a builder, so he preferred to sell the lots rather than get into the housing business. While homes were moving at a fair pace, he could not attract private buyers and home builders were not interested in his normal sales terms. McMoore had been selling his finished lots at about one a week and was asking $12,000 for each one. In the past, McMoore wanted and had gotten $3,480 down and was holding the balance for one year. Some buyers had paid cash, financing the paper with their own sources.

McMoore's broker, who had sold him the raw land nearly three years previously, suggested that he make a quick deal for a sellout and move on to the next land development program they had been working on. The broker reasoned that if the proper terms were given, they would be able to get some home builders to buy the remaining lots. They came up with this plan: The lots would be put into groups of five. This meant they had 10 packages to offer to the local builders or investors. The average price per package was $60,000. The down payment, however, was $6,000, instead of the $17,500 which was based on the normal down payment McMoore had gotten on the other lots. The mortgage terms offered were interest only for three years at 8% per annum on the balance. This marketing of the package at 10% down was bound to produce the desired results. McMoore knew this and wanted to make sure he was secure in the transaction.

What he did was to require that $12,000 be paid against the purchase price for a lot to be released from the mortgage. The releases were for the purpose of building homes for later resale. So McMoore took a second mortgage position on the home back into the blanket as additional security. That second would be removed when the next lot was released—and a new second would be placed on the second home. This would continue until the first four lots were released. On the last lot, only the remaining $12,000 plus interest had to be paid. Each builder had three years to build before the balloon came due on the unpaid balance.

HOW THIS TRANSACTION LOOKED TO THE BUILDERS THAT BOUGHT THE PACKAGES

It was a good deal. McMoore had priced the lots fairly and the housing market was strong enough to warrant tying up the initial cash. McMoore had also made the down payment reasonable, so once the builders had invested the $6,000 they could go ahead with preparations to build. They would arrange construction financing through local lenders to cover the cost of the home (plus a little overage). The excess of the loan, if any, would help pay off the lot. When they were ready to go, the mortgage to McMoore was reduced by $6,000 and the first lot was released.

The giving up of a second position to McMoore was no hardship to the builders. They knew that as soon as they sold the home they would merely move on to another one anyway. If they sold a new home from the model, they only had to pay down $12,000 cash and build on another lot. There was to be only one second lien at a time. In the meanwhile, the cost to carry the remaining lots was not overburdening them and they liked the idea.

The real key to this formula was simply the security for the seller. The blanket formula of holding all the unreleased lots into the mortgage was part of the security. The idea of adding the second mortgage on each new home as it was built, releasing the previous one, put the icing on the cake for the seller and didn't affect the buyer.

SUMMARY OF BLANKET MORTGAGES

The concepts inherent in blanket mortgages are also found in other forms of equity liens. If you remember that the ability to add other assets in order to bind the mortgage is the concept behind the blanket mortgage, then you can apply this idea to leases as well.

In the lease, the term used to cover this concept is cross-collateralization. The main use of the blanket lease is in sale lease-backs. In this situation the seller of a property becomes the lessee to the buyer. If the seller holds a mortgage as a part of the sale (e.g., sale price: $150,000—seller holds $50,000 in paper and takes $100,000 down), the mortgage may be given as additional security on the lease. This has a very strong affect in securing the lease.

Blanket mortgages can be in any position on the scale of superior or junior liens. The mortgage can actually take different positions on the various properties it covers. Usually, however, the same position on all the properties is attained, but the fact that this is not necessary is most important.

It is always possible to hold individual mortgages instead of a blanket. From the seller's point of view, if the two mortgages are offered at the same term, interest rate, and principal, then the only advantage in the blanket would be the lock-in provision. This would, of course, depend on the situation and what assets or property the seller wanted to lock into the transaction.

Buyers will use this form of financing to cover a down payment. However, even the buyer can take the alternative route and offer secondary paper on the existing property. Usually, the blanket mortgage is used in circumstances when the buyer is looking for the combined effect of one seller-held mortgage that is supported by his equity in other property, rather than an exchange of equity by virtue of paper offered on something else. It is a matter of negotiation. And, it often sounds better to offer a blanket mortgage secured by the purchased property and the buyer's equity in his vacant lot, instead of a mortgage to the seller and a mortgage on the lot. Of course, if several additional properties are used to add security, the blanket mortgage is easier to work with.

Chapter 9

How to Approach A Real Estate Discount Sale

A discount sale, as it applies to real estate, is a sale at a drastically reduced price in relation to the supposed value. This reduction must be for sound reasons, and not simply a ploy to save on capital gains or other taxes.

The Internal Revenue Service will review a discount sale with a careful eye to see if it has been contrived as a method of cutting the possible tax consequences or not. Of course, the sale may never come to their attention, but don't count on that because they may very easily examine such a transaction at some time in the future. The three-year statute of limitations on audits of past income tax returns will not hold if there is reason to believe that fraud was committed. If the discount sale was accomplished to eliminate tax, fraud may be claimed. You should be very cautious in the use of the discount sale and should follow the simple checklist shown below. If you can answer "no" to all of the questions, then you should be able to justify the use of a discount sale. In using this checklist, however, it is wise to check with the individual's tax advisor to see whether he has any special problems with the use of the discount sale.

CHECKLIST TO DETERMINE WHETHER A DISCOUNT SALE CAN BE USED

All questions must be answered "no." Even one "yes" answer may raise doubt as to the acceptability of using a discount sale as a method of selling a property.

1. Is the buyer a relative of the seller?
2. Is the buyer a close business partner or associate of the seller?

3. Does the seller owe the buyer money or any special favors?
4. Is the sale price below the assessed value of the property?
5. Is the sale tied to other terms or conditions involving other property?
6. In the event of a lease-back by the seller are the terms of the lease unreasonable for either party based on the market area.
7. Is there a mandatory recapture provision where the seller must become a buyer at a future date?
8. Is there reason to believe that the seller does not need immediate cash or other financial relief?
9. Are there buyers at a higher price, with reasonable terms?
10. Have similar properties been sold above the sale price within a reasonable time-span?
11. Has the seller taken a large (for him) long-term capital gain in the same year?
12. As a broker or salesman and listing agent are you the buyer?

Assuming you have answered "no" to all the above questions you can now proceed with the discount sale as a method of helping your seller accomplish his goals.

The discount sale has a real function. It can often be the only solution, short of financial disaster, for some clients and some properties.

A DISCOUNT SALE GENERALLY MEANS CASH

A sale at half the value may, after all, be the only cash price you can get due to market conditions. Because the reason for a discount sale is usually the need to produce immediate cash, it is generally associated with the "cash sale."

If you have a client in need of immediate cash who is not in a position or is not willing to borrow the required sum of money, and the sale of a real property becomes the only suitable solution, you may find yourself looking to the discount sale to satisfy his needs.

From the buyer's point of view, a purchase at a bargain price is more appealing than buying at a market price. Of course, the all-cash requirement may limit some buyers. But for the most part, the number of possible buyers will be increased when a "steal" is being offered.

As for the seller, it depends on what problems he is trying to solve. If his most critical need is for cash, then you can raise cash with more ease by utilizing the discount sale. Often, his need for cash is overshadowed by the necessity to "get out" or to be released from financial burdens he is unable to support.

Roscoe owned an apartment lot suitable for 10 units. In a good rental market the lot might bring $25,000. In fact, a few years ago this price may have been attainable. However, times are now tough and rental properties are overbuilt and have high vacancy factors. Roscoe has been hurt by the decline in the economy and is in need of some ready cash. The property cannot be sold at its past value. Some prospective buyers have indicated a willingness to pay $20,000, but only with a very low down payment and long terms on seller-held paper. Since Roscoe needs cash immedaitely the broker recommends the discount sale as a method of solving the problem.

Roscoe sells the lot for $10,000 cash. Because of the obvious "steal" at this price, a buyer was found almost overnight. But the discount sale has a buy-back option, so Roscoe retains the right to re-purchase the lot within the next 36 months for $16,000. If he fails to do so the option is lost forever.

The discount sale solved the immediate cash need Rosco had, and at the same time offered him an opportunity to buy back the property in the near future if the market reversed itself. Should the value return to the lot within the 36 months, or increased values make the lot worth more than the suppossed $25,000, then Roscoe will profit.

The buyer of the lot will have a limited gain should Roscoe recapture the lot within the 36 months. Yet, his gain will still be substantial. Hence, the bottom line for the buyer is the recapture. He may gain much more if Roscoe cannot or will not recapture within the 36 months.

LEASE-BACK, RECAPTURE OR OPTION: A NECESSARY PART OF THE DISCOUNT SALE

Lease-back, recapture or option—one of these methods is almost always used in conjunction with the discount sale to provide for future gain to the seller.

How can these methods be useful? First, accept the fact that the discount sale offers the most potential when the market for the type of property being offered is not at a peak. After all, when there is a demand for what you are offering you need not offer a discount. When the sale of apartment lots is down and not many buyers are around, it may be necessary to seek drastic measures in order to sell. Of course, the poorer the market the greater the discount required to make the buy a "steal."

At times, the discount by itself is still not enough to entice a buyer. You may have a floor under which you cannot go. The seller may have financial obligations to pay off or may simply be unwilling to sell below a fixed price. Many sellers have lost all rather than drop the price to a level at which the property would sell.

The lease-back can be brought into the terms of the deal to make the property saleable. In such a situation the seller will arrange to lease the property from the new buyer for a period of time. This is the same as a sale and lease-back, but with a discount on the sale.

If the seller has a use for the property and can produce income to pay the lease, the reasons may be sound. With the discount and additional income (in the form of rent), the transaction may proceed. The amount of the lease can usually be lower than an economic return on the price, as the buyer is looking at the discount as the major incentive for buying. This is another flexible aspect of this form of financing. You can negotiate different time periods of the lease, amount of the lease, and discounted prices. The variance on any one could alter the others in the market place.

The Recapture Allows The Seller To Recoup Value

With a recapture clause in the lease, the seller may, at a later date, buy back the land at a price fixed in the contract or at a price adjusted by other agreements.

The most common *extra* provision used with the discount sale is the option to buy back. Because the seller is taking a reduced price, he may want to buy back at a future date. This future price may be considerably higher than the price the property was sold for in the first transaction. Consider this case:

Astoff owns 200 acres of farmland outside the city in a growing area. Land nearby has sold for $500 per acre. Based on this information, the current value of the land should be $100,000. Astoff wants to get some cash to buy a yacht and spend a year or two at leisure. He paid $50 per acre 20 years ago and presently has no use for the farm site. The current market conditions indicate that there are not many buyers ready, willing, or able to buy this land today, or in the very near future.

EXPLAIN THE TRUE MARKET CONDITIONS TO YOUR CLIENT

As a broker, you will advise your client of the current market conditions and the time period you feel the property may remain on the market. It is important not to underestimate what you feel the normal time period may be. Too often, the seller is misled by the broker or salesman on this issue. Naturally, you don't know how long it will take to sell the property. But you can find out how long it took to sell a comparable property in the same area. This should be an indicator as to the market time needed. This time-span is important in many types of financing, as it may show the real urgency in the seller's mind.

In this instance, the last sale of a similar property required 12 months and there have not been any sales of similar property for the past several months. So, the seller may be faced with a 12-month or longer delay in order to sell the property at a reasonable price. Astoff, however, did have a time problem and time became the element to work against. He had made up his mind that if he didn't take time off now, he would never be able to in the future.

DISCOUNT SALE EQUALS A STEAL

At what price then do the 200 acres become a "steal?" When you can answer that question to the highest dollar amount you have the probable discount price. In this case it was $300 per acre. Remember, the discount sale may require all cash to suit the client's needs. If the $60,000 which can be generated by the discount sale is more than Astoff needs, then you may back off and sell only a portion of the property at a discount and hold onto the rest. However, we found that Astoff needed the $60,000 and we proceeded to market the property with this in mind.

In the future, Astoff's 200 acres may skyrocket in value due to a new subdivision nearby or for some other reason. If the value should go to $2,000 per acre, some of the new value of $400,000 could be recouped if Astoff had taken an option to buy back the land at the time he sold it.

An option to buy back, however, is normally not granted for a long period of time, except in lease-back and recapture situations. The reason is simply that the option is one sided, and the new owner does not want to be locked into the property for a lengthy period of time without being able to sell. As Astoff felt the land would appreciate greatly within a few years, he negotiated for a short option at a lower recapture price rather than a long option at a high price.

He settled for a four-year option at a $110,000 recapture price. This would give the new owner a $50,000 profit, less his carrying cost, for four years—should Astoff buy the land back at the end of that time. If the land went to $400,000, Astoff could buy it back at $110,000 with a profit of $290,000—plus the original $60,000 he received from the first sale. Had Astoff made the decision to sell the property for its top value of $100,000, that would have been the maximum top dollar he would have received—less the tax.

RECAP OF THE TRANSACTION

Astoff had land similar to that which had sold for $100,000. To get a quick sale, he took a discount and sold it for $60,000, but with an option to buy back within four years at $110,000.

Three years later, Astoff realized that a new subdivision nearby had opened up this farmland and that it could be sold for as high as $400,000. So, with time on his side (he had 12 months before the option came due), we put the land on the market. He knew that he could exercise his option to recapture the land if he got a buyer.

A year later a buyer came along, and Astoff sold his option to him for $260,000. The new buyer exercised the option for $100,000. Astoff sold the option rather than exercise it for capital gains reasons. He had held the option long enough to take a long-term gain; whereas, had he recaptured the land then sold it, he may have found he had a short-term gain.

It should be obvious that Astoff made more money with this form of financing than if he had sold the property for the $100,000.

ADVANTAGES OF A DISCOUNT SALE

There are 4 basic advantages of the discount sale:

1. Cash in a hurry
2. Fast closing
3. Action in a bad market
4. Very flexible

The Discount Sale Can Be Used Effectively In These Situations:

1. The seller needs cash in a short time
2. The market is difficult
3. The property is difficult to sell
4. The seller needs a fast transaction
5. A fast cash-out for an exchange is needed

The discount sale is a seller's and a broker's tool, but can be used by an astute buyer as well. The buyer can go into a transaction offering a reduced price. The later buy-back can become a negotiating point. It can follow many avenues and can be very flexible.

The discount sale and buy-back option offer the seller more possibilities for return when the property has the promise of fast appreciation. In the event of a property valuation decline, the seller simply does not use the option and walks away from the property.

DISADVANTAGES OF A DISCOUNT SALE

Many things can go awry in planning a discount sale. It may be that the price is reduced too low, or the terms of the buy-back are too high or for too short a period of time. The value in appreciation may not warrant the buy-back and the seller may have lost out on part of the gain. Many things can and do go wrong, but this is more often a fault of the planners and not of events. We cannot fit the discount sale format into all situations. In those cases where there is a threefold increase in the value of the property the year after the option is dropped, the planning was obviously wrong.

Because the discount sale is highly effective, the broker should not recommend its use unless he is sure that the seller has no other option available which can solve the problem. An overzealous broker can sell a lot of property with the discount method, but not always to the benefit of the seller.

A discount sale holds considerable risk for the seller if the market value of the property does not appreciate to cover the pick-up cost, or if his situation changes and he cannot exercise the option when the time comes. The amount of risk the seller is taking depends on the amount of the discount and the probability of appreciation. A reduction from $100,000 to $60,000 with a likelihood that the value will go to $200,000 in three years, is less risky than a reduction from $100,000 to $75,000 with little hope of an appreciation in value to $150,000 within four years.

Because of this risk factor, the discount sale can be used by the buyer with a certain degree of effectiveness. It is normally the seller who is telling the buyer how great the value of this property will be in a few years. In essence, the buyer turns that around and says: "I'll give you part of your price now, and if you are right about the future, a lot more later."

PUTTING THE DISCOUNT TRANSACTION TOGETHER

The only thing you must remember is not to offer a "good buy"—but a "steal." First of all, the price offered must be a bargain price. It should be a price which any able buyer will recognize as a "steal." By utilizing this tool you will develop a stable of such investors. They will know that when you offer them a discount sale there will be little to negotiate and that the price will indeed be a bargain. At first, until you find this stable of future buyers, visit a few of your better clients or your local bankers. If that fails, call on the owners of the adjoining property or owners of similar property, since they will recognize the discount quickly. If that also fails to locate a buyer, you may not have made the discount great enough for the market.

You will find that the most difficult part of making a discount sale, once you have convinced the seller, is locating the buyer. Until your buyers know that you bring them discount sales, they will question the value. You could offer them a $100,000 property discounted to $40,000, and they would want to offer $35,000. You must be firm, and then be ready to move on. You can go back to that buyer another time, but not on that transaction. You should not spend too much time in attempting to convince a buyer that your discount is real. If you have to show MAI appraisals or other value justifying data, other than usual comparables, your discount is not great enough. Only with the very rare property will such back-up data be needed. Your discount buyers should be sophisticated enough to recognize the discount.

HOW TO SELL THE SELLER ON THE DISCOUNT SALE

If you are convinced that the discount sale is the most practical method of solving the seller's problem, then approach him with that thought in mind. Sellers know that the lower the price the easier it is for the broker to sell the property. This will create a natural barrier for the broker in getting the seller to accept the discount. The seller must feel that the broker's interest is not in trying to make it easier to sell the property, but in solving the seller's problem as quickly as possible.

The following guide will be helpful in explaining the discount sale to the seller:

1. Keep in mind that the discount sale is effective when:
   A. Fast cash is needed.
   B. The seller has no other acceptable way to get the cash.
   C. A fast closing is needed.
   D. The property is very difficult to sell.
   E. A cash-out for an exchange is needed.
   F. The seller knows the value will increase substantially.

2. Qualify your client to see if his needs fit the above criteria. If one or more of the six preceding factors is not present, the discount sale will probably not be the best form to use.

3. Explain the ramifications of the discount sale to the seller. You should:
   A. Be candid about the disadvantages of the discount sale.
   B. Show the seller how the transaction may work out. However, never be overly optimistic about the future value. The best way to handle that is to have questioned the seller previously on what he feels the value will be in a few years. If his estimate is plausible, then reduce that and use those calculations as future value. Be sure to point out that the projection may not be accurate, and, in fact, the value may not increase at all.
   C. It is most important that the seller be aware of the expected market time if you are attempting to get the top dollar.
   D. Explain that the give-and-take in the discount sale requires a true discount. In essence, the buyer gives the buy-back because of the discount.
   E. Do not be the buyer of the discount sale. If you are the broker, it is wise not to buy the discount sale you have planned. No matter what happens in the future, you will not like the results. At best, you may be accused of structuring a deal to suit your own best interests. Remember, the buyer of a discount sale has very little to risk—and much to gain.

HOW TO SELL THE BUYER ON THE DISCOUNT SALE

In dealing with buyers, you must be firm in your understanding of what you are selling. If the discount is genuine and the terms of the buy-back or lease-back plausible, then stick to them. If the buyer wants to offer less, tell him that the discount is real and the proprety a "steal" at the price at which it is being offered. If he still wants to offer less, go on to another buyer. Some buyers think they can take advantage of every situation, and that all discount sales have to do with distressed properties or distressed sellers. This is not true, of course, and the discount sale is merely a problem-solver which works well in difficult times.

In your normal selling approach you will have comparable sheets on other similar properties in the market. These properties will give some indication as to the validity of the discount. If you are approaching knowledgeable buyers, these sheets and the buyer's expertise in the market should be enough.

The more difficult the property, the greater the discount needed to bring buyers into the transaction. Because of this and the fact that with too great a discount the seller may not be solving his problem, the other negotiating aspects of the discount sale may be brought into play. The buy-back option is almost a standard in the discount sale. In fact, there would be no real incentive to the seller to give the discount unless he has this option or another form of value.

The buyer may want to cut down on some of these future options on the transaction. This is not uncommon. But, you should again be firm if you have structured a transaction which is plausible. Naturally, if all your buyers balk at what you have presented, you may have to restructure the transaction and then go back to them. This is not a pleasant thing to do when you are trying to project an image of firmness. It is most important to set the right discount and terms initially.

"Other methods," such as the lease-back, first right of refusal, and lease with recapture, are all variables which may appeal to buyers in different forms. The right of refusal is the weakest value available to the seller. Here, he only has a right to meet an offer and may not see any profit.

Once you have set the groundwork, and convinced the buyer of the discount, the rest is easy. Remember, the buyer has very little to risk and a lot to gain.

Note: The buyer is, to some degree, gambling that the seller will not be able to exercise the option to buy back. This can occur for many reasons and is the true disadvantage to the seller. The land may not have appreciated to an amount above the option price, or not high enough to make the buy-back worthwhile to the seller. In the event the seller does not recapture, then the buyer has more to gain in later appreciation of the property.

SOME FINE POINTS IN THE DISCOUNT SALE

Because the seller is in a give-and-take situation by virtue of the discount on the price, he is able to negotiate terms not normally possible on the later buy-back, or lease-back and recapture. However, the buyer knows that the longer the time period of the option the less value the discount has, unless there is another counterbalance. It is possible to structure these counterbalances to provide some protection to the seller for a longer time, without unduly burdening the buyer.

The seller, for example, wants a ten-year option to buy back, a very long time for the discount sale. In this event, a number of factors can be brought into play to make it feasible:

1. The future price to be set at a predetermined base price, with an appraisal to be made at the tenth year, a future percent of which value shall be the buy-back price or the predetermined base price, whichever is greater. (The amount of the future percent will be another negotiating point, and should be no greater than 75% nor less than 50%. This limits the amount of profit the seller can take on the recapture.)

2. Give the buyer the right to ''buy out'' the option with a payment to the seller. This provision will allow the buyer, for a sum of money, to null and void the option. It is possible that the buyer may want to sell or even develop the property, and with the option over his head that may not be practical. The sum of the buy-out is normally at least the balance to the discount plus some profit. If the value was $100,000 and the discount sale was at $60,000, the buy-out may be at $45,000. However, this is a highly negotiable point.

3. First right of refusal. This may be all the seller can get, or may run with the property for a period of time after the option to buy back has expired.

4. Escalating option or lease price. The seller may agree to a series of higher prices in future options to buy back. The same may occur in the lease payments. This and other long-term options or provisions are used in vacant and other nonincome-producing properties more often than in income-producing property. The reason is the new owner may not properly maintain the structure if the option price prevents him from a recapture of his invested capital.

Most any other provisions which could be coupled to a normal sale, or option, can be used with some effect on the total overall discount sale. Keep in mind that the discount sale is more than just a lowered price.

Chapter 10

How to Use The Sale and Lease-Back In Real Estate

A sale and lease-back is the sale of an interest in realty and the subsequent leasing back of that same realty. The sale and lease-back is one of the best tools to use in generating more useful capital from one realty that can be used by the seller. This form of financing starts as a sale. The seller then agrees to lease-back the property being sold. Sometimes this lease-back can merely be a move to entice the buyer into the transaction. In its most effective form for the seller, however, the lease-back provides continued use of the property by him.

The property being sold can be all the realty, meaning land and buildings, or it may be just the buildings or just the land. Each aspect of the sale and lease-back can have different long-range results, depending on what portion of the realty is sold and then leased back.

HOW TO STRUCTURE THE LAND LEASE-BACK

The most basic of the sale and lease-backs is the land itself. It is very common in many parts of the world to have leased land under many types of buildings. These land leases generally began with a sale to one party, who then leases the land back to the seller. Over the years the owners of the leasehold change, but the lease remains.

In all lease-backs, and more particularly in the land lease, the ultimate title to the realty does not belong to the lessee. All the lessee owns is the leasehold interest. If the leasehold is later sold, the interest passed on is merely the remainder rights in the underlying lease or a portion of that lease. This factor creates many problems in land leases and leasehold interest, as it can cause difficulties in most conventional methods of financing buildings when the land is not owned in fee simple, but in leasehold.

THE SUBORDINATION FACTOR IN LAND LEASE

Because most lenders will not lend on buildings situated on leased land without that lease being subordinated to the mortgage, and because many owners of land are reluctant to lease land to someone who wants to put a huge mortgage over their legal position (due to the subordination), there is a natural reluctance to subordinate. Nonetheless, there are thousands of subordinated land leases in the United States and for the most part they are viable transactions, but not without risk.

Development on leased land requires the lessee to chose one or a combination of these three solutions: (1) use all cash with no lien; (2) obtain an insecured loan; (3) find a lender who will treat the leasehold as a fee simple. Taking the first solution, many builders do just that. They build with their own cash. It may be they have leased the land with options to purchase, and so they build without having to lay out the cash needed to buy the land. They pay the nominal rent during construction, and later, when the building is finished, obtain a mortgage, pay off the land by exercising an option to buy, and move on to another project. This is done in single-family housing where the builder can and does build the house quickly, and then sells it before many of the outstanding bills on it come due. In those cases, the overall cash outlay by the developer is not as great as if he had bought the land for cash.

An unsubordinated lease maintains the owner of the land in the first position. Any loans made subject to the lease are in a secondary position. To find a secondary loan to fund a major development on leased land without subordination is not impossible, but extremely difficult.

There are lenders, however, who approach the leasehold interest as being similar to fee simple. In some areas of the world a long-term lease of such a time period as to be beyond the normal life span of the building planned, may be accepted as being the same as completed ownership. Each lender will have a different opionion on this topic, and each situation must look to the substance of the lease itself. When the cost of the land lease is not excessive, a lender will often be willing to lend behind the lease.

LEASEHOLD VS. FEE SIMPLE VALUES

Unlike the creation of a normal lease, whether it be land or buildings, the sale and lease-back is unique. The previous owner, or fee owner, becomes the leasehold owner. It is this change of ownership which makes the sale and lease-back both dangerous and quite often rewarding.

A lease is accompanied by a rent, and the value of the lease is based on the ability of the lessee to pay the rent or the security he offers to support that ability to pay the rent. If the tenant, or lessee, fails to pay the rent, and the security is not sufficient to support the economic base of the property until another lesseee can be found, the lease may then become worthless. Of even more consequence, it may cost the lessor money to get the tenant out of the property.

If the building is a single-purpose structure and the tenant not very strong, then the ultimate ability to pay the lease and the long possible delay in finding another tenant could reflect on the value of the fee simple. An existing lease runs with the land, and a new buyer accepts the tenant on the remaining terms of the lease. The property may be worth $100,000, but if there is a 20-year lease at $3,000 per annum the value is not $100,000, due to the effect of the rent return. Also, if the rent were $10,000, but the tenant is always behind, the value may not be substantiated.

ESTABLISHING THE LEASEHOLD VALUE

The terms and conditions of the lease establish the value of the leasehold. It is clear, for example, that two identical parking lots, side by side on leased land, will have values depending on the terms of the underlying land leases. The parking lot which has an annual rent of $1,000 will be of far more value as a leasehold than the one which has an annual rent of $2,000. In reverse, the owner of the lots will find the lease which returns $1,000 per year is less valuable than the one which returns $2,000 per year. What is shown here is the variable between value of the lease and value of the leasehold. It is important, then, to distinguish these two values in each sale and lease-back situation. The sale and lease-back creates both events: the leasehold and the fee owner, or the lease.

HOW TO DETERMINE WHEN THE LEASE-BACK IS EFFECTIVE

The sale and lease-back is used in these situations:

1. When the use of the property has more value than owning the property.
2. To substantiate the value of the fee by creating a fixed return.
3. The need for capital makes the lease-back more economical than other forms of financing.

These three situations cover a lot of territory, and from a practical point of view, the latter two will be seen more often in real life. However, a quick look at the three gives some insight as to the use of the two aspects of this form: the value of the fee and the value of the leasehold.

WHEN THE VALUE OF THE USE EXCEEDS THE VALUE OF OWNING

A case history illustrates this point. Kayser had a small restaurant. He owned the land and building free and clear. He wanted to start another restaurant across town, but found he did not have sufficient capital to do this. Naturally, he looked to the normal forms of financing to raise this capital, so he visited the local banks and savings and loans. Even though his past record was good, he found that new restaurants are not easily financed because they are costly to start up. He did find that he could obtain new financing, up to a point, but the balance must be cash out of his pocket. Kayser counseled with his broker and discovered he could approach an investor to buy his present restaurant to create the new capital. His options on a lease-back showed he could set up a sale and lease-back on the land, or the buildings, or both. The final decision would depend on capital needed, on the value of the property, and the rent he was able to pay.

The value of the land was $135,000. This was based on other similar properties in the area. The buildings had been appraised at a value of $200,000. The new restaurant Kayser was planning was expected to cost about $400,000.

Kayser was sure he could support an overall debt service of $35,000 to $45,000 in annual payments with ease, once the second restaurant was built and operating. At present, he was making a good living from the first restaurant by taking home around $90,000 per year. He expected to make the same, or more, from the second one.

If Kayser were able to sell his first restaurant for $300,000 and lease it back on a net-net lease (he has to pay all maintenance, taxes, insurance, etc., as well as the lease), he should easily be able to borrow the remainder on the new property to finish the construction and provide working capital.

The broker knew that an investor would be inclined to buy the first restaurant since it had a good track record, and Kayser would be, after all, leasing the property back at a good return to the investor. That return, by the way, is subject to good, hard negotiation. There are many factors on which to bargain in sale and lease-backs, and the buyer and seller can find much to negotiate on before the final transaction is signed and sealed.

For Kayser, the value of owning has taken second place to the value of use of the property. As long as he has control of the restaurant, it may not make much difference if he owns or leases. His leasehold value becomes more apparent after he leases. In this case the lease-back was $30,000 per year, based on a sale at $300,000 as Kayser was netting $90,000 before the lease. The $60,000 he will net after the lease becomes the factor in establishing the economic value of the leasehold. As restaurants have a demand yield of about 15% to 20%, the leasehold value is from $300,000 to $400,000.

The investor has this leasehold value as additional collateral on the lease, as long as the business is good and Kayser can pay the rent.

HOW TO SUBSTANTIATE THE VALUE OF THE FEE BY CREATING A FIXED RETURN

In this event, Kayser might not want to build another restaurant at all. The fact of the matter could be that business is off, and for the past year the best he was able to take home was $40,000. In this situation, he may want to get cash out of the property for other reasons.

To substantiate the value of $300,000 on the sale, he agrees to lease the property back on a long-term lease. That pleases the investor, until the lease becomes worthless and Kayser goes off to another state to run a bar. Of course, the title to the bar is in his wife's name.

HOW TO USE THE SALE AND LEASE-BACK WHEN OTHER FORMS OF FINANCING ARE MORE COSTLY

In many situations you will encounter a client who needs to raise money, but has not thought of selling his property because it is his main source of income. He may, therefore, seek to borrow against that property to solve his cash needs.

If the money market will support his financial needs at reasonable rates through more conventional forms of mortgaging, there may be no need to look elsewhere. However, due to any number of circumstances, a reasonable or sufficient loan may not be available.

Specialty types of real estate fall into categories that many lenders will shy away from, or at best they'll quote high interest rates and low loan to value amounts. The combined effect of insufficient restructure of existing debt and high constant payments on the borrowed funds may put the borrower, your client, in deeper trouble than that in which he currently finds himself.

During this same time when the money market is tight, interest rates tough, and loans low or nonexistent, there may be a solution via the sale and lease-back. Your ability to determine the effectiveness of the sale and lease-back will require you to examine the effect the two forms available have on the client.

For example: Lloyd has a used car lot. He makes a good living from this business, but finds he needs cash to expand his inventory. He has approached a local lender and has found he can borrow only 75% of what he needs by placing a first mortgage on the property. Besides the insufficient sum of money available, there is a high point cost and interest is set at 5 points above prime.

On the other hand, a sale and lease-back may produce 100% or more of the cash needed at an overall interest rate that is lower than that charged by the lender. As Lloyd needs the property and has substantial records to show he can support the rent, he may, out of necessity, move in the direction of the sale and lease-back to solve his problems. He recognized that his ability to earn money on the input of new capital is greater than the cost of the land lease. As long as he has a prudent lease-back from his long-term growth, he will make this move.

Of course, he will be forced to look to some other form of financing, or capital seeking, if he cannot raise the money in the conventional money market. However, you should be the first to tell Lloyd that he should seek conventional sources as possible alternatives to his problem, if for no other reason than as a comparison to the sale and lease-back.

There Is A Risk In The Lease-Back

There are valid reasons for the lease-back. But the risk involved, due to the value adjustments, requires buyers to be rather cautious of overstated values of the fee or of the *leasehold*.

It is possible for the seller to substantiate the value of the fee by creating the fixed return with a minimum of risk to the buyer. This can be accomplished with lease insurance. The insurance will cover the rent in default should the seller/tenant get into trouble. What could be a bad deal can become a "Triple A" transaction.

THE VALUE OF ALL LEASES DEPENDS ON THESE SIX FACTORS

1. *The lessee:* Who or what is he? What is his past record, financial backing, and motivation? Will he sign personally? If not, why?
2. *The use:* Has it been successful? Is the operation well run, managed, and staffed? Is there a future for the present use? Does the use present unusual hazards to the property? Does the use limit the function and flexibility of the property?
3. *Lease conditions:* The term of years—too long or too short? Who pays taxes, utilities, assessments, repairs, maintenance, and other property costs? Is there a provision for increasing the rent due to cost of living increases? What other provisions can affect the future return to the owner (options, provisions for cancellations, etc.)?
4. *The performance:* What is the record of the lessee in making his rent payments? In new leases, this is a big unknown and only time will tell.
5. *The property:* Is the economic life of the property beyond that of the term of the lease? If so, the fact that a new tenant must someday be found or the same tenant enticed to stay can cause a problem in the future. Is the location suitable for the present tenant? Is the tenant suffering because of the property or the location?

6. *Fee vs. leasehold:* There must be a real value in both. The greater the value in the leasehold, the greater the security for the lessor. In the sale and lease-back, this apparent value in the leasehold should be carefully examined.

The value of the lease depends heavily on the use and the user. Artificial value can be generated in the leasehold by the lessee. This artificial value is, in essence, a burden to the property and results from pushing this form of financing.

THE NEED FOR CAPITAL

Need necessitates action, and a need for capital is generally the reason for the sale and lease-back. There are many more favorable forms of financing, if they can be obtained in the market. For example, there is no real reason why a seller who wants to use the property should take a sale and lease-back transaction, unless the economics of accepting another form are onerous or unavailable.

However, this does not make the sale and lease-back the last resort, and it should not be considered as a step down from something not available or economically unsound. It *can* be highly advantageous to the seller. If the seller cannot borrow the necessary funds and he needs the use of the property for economic reasons, then the sale and lease-back can solve these problems.

ADVANTAGES AND DISADVANTAGES OF THE SALE AND LEASE-BACK

Here are the advantages and disadvantages as they apply to both the seller and the buyer:

The Seller

Advantages:

1. Allows the seller to retain use of the property.
2. Allows the seller to negotiate the amount of the rent by offsetting the sale price.
3. Often, the terms of the lease are more flexible in the lease-back.
4. Can firm up the price and value.
5. Gives flexibility to difficult transactions since the land and improvements can be separated.
6. As the seller is the ultimate ten-

Disadvantages:

1. Seller gives up many benefits of ownership of improvements and land.
2. Future appreciation of land usually lost completely.
3. Leasehold value has a shorter life than the property.
4. A decline in leasehold value can be a total loss.

ant, he has great strength in dealing on the lease-back.

7. Can provide capital when all else fails.

The Buyer

Advantages:

1. Can provide an excellent tenant.
2. Offers some flexibility in price vs. rent negotiations.
3. In the case of unsubordinated land: (a) low risk investment, (b) future recoupment of improvements, and (d) appreciation.
4. If very carefully examined and secured, can offer an excellent investment potential.

Disadvantages:

1. Either the price or the rent will be to the seller's advantage; often both.
2. Too hard a push on the seller may give you an investment without a tenant.
3. A lease-back by a nonuser may be a good sign that the income won't support the value.
4. May have to step into a large mortgage to protect his interest.

To these advantages and disadvantages you can apply most pro and con aspects of any lease. One thing is definite, however. The sale and lease-back is more complicated than it appears on the surface. It requires good, sound advice and consideration. A broker should never walk his client, the seller, into the sale and lease-back unless there is absolute confidence on the part of the broker that the transaction is beneficial to both parties. It is far too easy to boost the value with this form of financing and take advantage of some buyer, not aware of the potential danger. Be sure all parties understand the pros and cons of the lease-back before you establish that transaction.

This form of financing has a place in real estate. It is used in commercial realty and other forms of development, land planning, and, of course, industrial realty. Lenders find it an ideal tool for securing their position in large development loans. Here the lender may take a land lease under a project he is financing. In this way he participates in the overall project to the degree that he will always own the land. In many cases, the developer may buy the land back in the future at an escalated price. Since the lender may not be extending more funds than he would have on just the loan, he has a strong advantage over the seller.

Yet the seller may not fare too badly either, as he can cash out ahead of the project and still own the improvements. The cost of carrying the land and paying off the mortgage may not have any higher constant than just the loan. Of course, the portion of debt service that applies to the land lease will never retire any principal, and the ratio of constant to remaining balance will increase faster than in a mortgage without a land lease.

HOW TO SET UP THE SALE AND LEASE-BACK

After counseling with your seller, and when you are sure the sale and lease-back is the proper way to go, carefully examine the two values involved:

1. The fee simple
2. The leasehold value

There will be some flexibility in the adjustment of these two values. This adjustment may have tax-saving results. For example, if the seller has a low base it may be possible to set a price which is near that base, and reduce the rent the seller will pay in the lease-back to offset the reduced price. Remember, the lower the rent paid by the seller the higher the value of the leasehold. Naturally, you cannot reduce the price to a point that is below the market value just to save on taxes. However, there is usually ample room in which to work in order to provide some flexibility in these negotiations.

It may be in the seller's best interest to attempt to establish the lowest value on the sale to reduce gains tax. The rent paid later on the lower base can, over a few years, make up the reduced sales price. On the other hand, if the capital gained from the sale is not sufficient, then the higher price, even with the tax, may be more prudent. Because the sale and lease-back can generally justify a higher price, the spread in the low to high value will be greater than in a normal sale. This high value is said to be somewhat artificial and warranted only on the basis of the lease-back.

Negotiating A Lower Price

This occurs because the buyer recognizes that he is buying at a good price and can adjust his income accordingly. The buyer should realize that the lower the rent, the higher the value of the leasehold. The higher the value of the leasehold, the more security to the buyer.

A buyer will find that the maximum security he can have on a lease-back is the lease insurance. This type of insurance is obtained by the tenant and insures the lessor in the event the lessee fails to pay his rent. It is not easily obtained, however, and is not used too often in sale and lease-back situations. But if the buyer wants the utmost in security, then this type of insurance will provide it.

If only the land is being leased and there is no subordination, the risk to the buyer is limited. If the price for the land is realistic and not inflated, then the buyer has a sound investment. There would be little reason to consider insurance with this type of transaction. In limited subordination, where the lessee has the right to put on a mortgage of limited proportions, the buyer will find his security waning. The amount of the mortgage, a percentage to the value of the property, will establish the value of the security. Should the lease-back carry full subordination, the risk to the buyer will be predicated on: (1) the success of the property, and (2) the ability of the lessee to pay the rent.

The buyer should realize that in the sale and lease-back the lessee may have made a profit, but may have no actual equity in the property or the leasehold. In this event, the loss to the lessee in a failure to perform on the lease may be small.

We have seen two values. The fee simple and the leasehold. In fact, there may be three values. The third being the value of the business itself. A retail shop, for example, may have a business value not dependent on the exact location or improvements. If the lessee can move his business with ease and retain its value, the security to the buyer is reduced unless he ties the lessee into the lease more stringently.

The ability of the seller-tenant to move the business does not in itself reduce the buyer's security, however; unless the improvements are single purpose and the new owner were to find it difficult to rerent the space should the lease-back tenant fail on his lease for some reason. The best security for the buyer in the sale and lease-back will always be *extreme caution.*

SALE AND LEASE-BACK HIGHLIGHTS

What it will do:	1. Generate cash.
	2. Provide terms on a lease to suit the lessee.
When to use it:	1. When value of use exceeds value of ownership.
	2. To substantiate value of fee.
	3. When borrowing to raise capital is not economically effective or available.
What to look for:	1. Seller who has successful use of property.
	2. A use that is potentially successful, but may need either time or capital or both.
Negotiating points:	1. Term of lease.
	2. Sale price.
	3. Other options, such as: (a) subordination, (b) recapture of ownership, (c) subdivision of property to separate lease (land or improvements).
Danger to seller:	1. Gives up advantages of ownership.
	2. Loses future appreciation of property.

Chapter 11

How to Design And Implement A Pyramid Investment Plan

There is no investment financing strategy that requires greater confidence in one's abilities than pyramiding. It is not a program for the investor who is unwilling to take a high risk.

Pyramiding is a form of financing best suited for a rising economy. It will not be effective in a declining economy, and the greater the pyramid the less the economy has to slip for the pyramid to collapse. In fact, with a broad-base pyramid, even a slowdown of a rising economy can bring financial disaster.

WHAT IS THE BASIS FOR PYRAMIDING?

Pyramiding is a form of leverage that is used in almost all forms of barter and sale. Its use in real estate has given it some very special attributes that are not found in other areas. In essence, pyramiding is using what you already own as collateral to obtain something more.

Ryan, for example, owns a small home he bought three years ago for $30,000. At that time he obtained a first mortgage of $25,000, which has since been reduced to $23,500. The value of the home is now $40,000. To pyramid, he has $16,500 of equity to use as collateral.

Ryan goes to McKay, the owner of a duplex that has an asking price of $30,000 and a first mortgage of $20,000. Ryan would pyramid if he could get McKay to take a second mortgage on the home for $10,000, the amount needed to swing the duplex.

Have Your Cake, And Eat It Too: The Real Benefit Of The Pyramid

The strategy of pyramiding is to move into new real estate transactions without capital outlay, or at least keep the actual dollars spent at a minimum. Because you are able to use apparent equity as a basis for the exchange, you retain ownership of the previous property and at the same time gain another.

Any owner with an equity can go into the marketplace and attempt to find someone who will take that equity as security for the property being sold. The difficulty, of course, is finding "that someone" who will, in fact, take the equity in the form of a second or third mortgage on a property other than that sold.

Generally speaking, there will always be properties available, because there are owners so highly motivated that they will do anything that offers an opportunity to relieve themselves of what they own. While many of these situations would fall into the category of distressed properties, sometimes it is the owner who is distressed and not the property.

Pyramiding Is A Risk That Can Be Worthwhile

You should not get the impression that pyramiding is to be avoided, as there are many situations that are acceptable for all parties. It is only necessary for you and the other participants in a pyramid to be aware of the risks involved. Without a doubt, pyramiding is one of the highest leverage forms of financing available to the broker or his client. There will be times when the risk is well worth the possible gain.

Because real estate has a special quality, appreciation, and is often very difficult to evaluate in exact terms, apparent equity can be generated in a very short time. This new equity, or surplus over what the owner has invested, becomes the power behind the pyramid. In a rising market, this value may have the promise of rising further, adding to the "security" of the junior mortgage to be used in the pyramid.

HOW TO BUILD A FORTUNE IN A HURRY BY PYRAMIDING EQUITY

The amount of risk the pyramider takes depends on the amount of equity he has to begin with. Because this is the total limit to his loss capability, except for time, pyramiding is obviously weighted in his favor. That is as it should be, of course, since pyramiding is primarily a buyer's tool. There is one exception to this rule, however, and later on we will see how a seller can use pyramiding to his advantage.

The best way to explain pyramiding is to go through an example. I have chosen an extreme example because it points out the many aspects and benefits of this exciting tool.

How One Investor Started His Pyramid With $30,000 And Ended Up With $510,000

Blackburn owned an apartment building worth $90,000. Against this value there was a first mortgage of $60,000 and he had a real equity of $30,000. His desire was to buy more properties, but he was limited by the capital he had to invest—only $30,000 in cash. While he could live without the income from his investments, he could not invest more cash than the $30,000. Blackburn's long-range plan was to build as much equity as possible, sell out, and retire to a ranch in Montana. Everything he had was dedicated to this goal.

In working with his real estate broker, several interesting apartment houses of varying sizes were located. Each needed some improvements to increase the income, but these repairs could and would substantially increase the value. The first property was a 10-unit building for sale at $100,000. The property had a recent first mortgage of $70,000.

Under the advice and counsel of his broker, Blackburn offered to buy the apartment house for the full price of $100,000. However, he did not invest cash, but assumed the first mortgage and gave the seller a second mortgage of $30,000 secured by his first apartment house. To this amount Blackburn added $8,000 in cash from his bank account to improve the property.

With the improvements made, the income was quickly improved and the fair market value of the 10 units increased to $130,000. It took Blackburn six months to accomplish this build-up of value, and at the end of this period the first apartment house had also increased in value by $5,000 due to an overall improvement of the market. Blackburn now had: (1) first apartment house ($95,000 value, against that total mortgages of $90,000 leaving an equity of $5,000); and (2) a 10-unit apartment house worth $140,000 with mortgages of $70,000 (equity in the 10 units was $60,000 plus a remaining cash amount of $22,000).

The next step: moving into another transaction. Next, the broker found a 20-unit apartment house also in need of repair. The estimated cost for repairs was $15,000. Although the seller was asking more, the broker knew he would sell for $180,000. There was a mortgage of $100,000 on the property.

Blackburn went to his banker and told him that he would like to borrow a net of $140,000 on the 20-unit complex. (An additional $4,000 was needed for closing costs to cover the lending expense, etc.; so the total loan required was therefore $144,000.) Blackburn explained to the banker that he would spend

$15,000 on the property after the closing, and with this improvement the property should be worth over $220,000. He showed the banker a *pro forma* the broker had worked out, indicating the rental potential after the minor improvements and repairs.

The banker agreed. Blackburn then offered the seller $25,000 cash, and a second mortgage on the 10 units of $55,000 to equal the seller's $80,000 equity. The total cash needed in this transaction was: $25,000 to the seller, $100,000 to pay off the existing mortgage, $4,000 for closing costs, and $15,000 for improvements ($25,000 + $100,000 + $4,000 + $15,000 = $144,000). Blackburn had made the transaction totally out of the new loan proceeds, and therefore did not have to touch his remaining cash in the bank.

What the pyramid looked like after 12 months. At the end of 12 months, the three properties were worth more and the picture looked like this. (The reduced mortgage amount is due to principal payments made).

Property	Present Value	Total Mortgages	Equity
1st apartment house	$100,000	$ 86,000	$14,000
10-unit complex	$130,000	$125,000	$ 5,000
20-unit complex	$220,000	$144,000	$76,000
Totals	$450,000	$355,000	$95,000

Plus $22,000 in cash.

In each of the above transactions, Blackburn had to be sure that the income from each property would cover the debt service being placed on it. Because the second mortgages are always from the previous purchase, Blackburn did not move on to other deals until there was income to support the new second to be used as part of his subsequent acquisitions.

Blackburn did not stop here, however, but continued to do the same thing on a larger scale.

Blackburn's broker shows him how to pyramid into a mini-warehouse. The broker found an old industrial building which would convert nicely into a mini-warehouse and storage facility. He knew Blackburn would have to put all his remaining cash into the renovations, but the deal looked promising. He outlined the plan to Blackburn and here is what happened.

Blackburn offered the owner a second mortgage of $75,000 secured by the 20-unit apartment house and assumed the existing mortgage on the industrial building of $325,000. He then went to the bank holding the mortgage on the building. He got them to extend the loan by the amount of interest for one year and at the same time put a one-year moratorium on principal payments. He told the bank he was going to put another $22,000 into the property and presented them with a detailed *pro forma* prepared by his broker showing how he expected to double the present revenue within 12 months. Since the bank was concerned about the future of the present loan, they liked Blackburn's idea and decided to work with him.

At the end of another year, Blackburn had increased the value of the warehouse to $550,000—with the promise that in a few years it would exceed $600,000.

If you succeed once, why not try again. Because of his luck in the last venture, Blackburn did the same thing across town. He bought an even larger industrial complex which had been vacant for over two years and put $100,000 into remodeling the buildings.

How did he get the $100,000? The complex was on the market at a rock-bottom price of $1,025,000. Blackburn knew his bankers would lend up to $750,000 since the existing loans on the property were only $255,000.

Blackburn and his broker went to the owners and explained what he wanted to do. He offered them a deal which, after much negotiation, ended up as follows:

$370,000	cash paid to the owners
$255,000	pay-off of existing mortgage
$150,000	second mortgage secured by the mini-warehouse
$775,000	total so far

Blackburn then offered the owners a land lease under the complex's property subordinated to a first mortgage not to exceed $750,000. The land could be purchased by Blackburn at any time within the next 20 years, or the lease would continue for a total of 40 years. Blackburn and the sellers agreed that any loan proceeds over the amount to be paid on the purchase price must go into improvements on the property. The amount of the lease was to be $24,000 per year. This amount was agreed to as being slightly over 8½% of the $275,000 remaining value of the land. The option to buy the land during the 20 years was at a flat $290,000. As an additional kicker for Blackburn, the rent did not start until 12 months after closing. The transaction went as follows:

$ 370,000	cash paid to the owners
$ 255,000	pay-off of existing mortgage
$ 100,000	improvements
$ 15,000	paid as loan cost
$ 10,000	legal and other closing costs
$ 750,000	amount borrowed from Blackburn's bank
$ 275,000	value of land Blackburn leased
$1,025,000	full asking price

At the end of 12 months, with the new complex fully rented and doing well,

Blackburn's overall financial picture, due to increases in value and principal reductions, looked like this:

Property	Market Value	Mortgages	Equity
1st apartment house	$ 105,000	$ 83,000	$ 22,000
10-unit complex	$ 135,000	$ 122,000	$ 13,000
20-unit complex	$ 230,000	$ 215,000	$ 15,000
Mini-warehouse	$ 575,000	$ 475,000	$100,000
Industrial complex	$1,110,000	$ 750,000	$360,000*
Totals	$2,155,000	$1,645,000	$510,000

*Buildings only

In only a few years, Blackburn had built his net worth from $60,000 to $510,000—with only equity and $30,000 in cash to work with. At this point he was generating a cash flow of about $55,000 per year. (All values used were based on the positive cash flow being just over 10% of the equity.) At this stage in Blackburn's plan, he could retire to Montana to live out his life punching cows—or stay in the pyramiding game a bit longer.

How the broker got $90,800 in fees. The total number of transactions that were accomplished in this pyramid were four. Hence, the broker collected four commissions. In two of the transactions he was able to collect his fee in cash at closing, while in the other two over a period of years.

1. The first transaction was the 10 units and had a fee of $6,000. As the seller did not receive cash, the broker collected the fee over a period of four years at a nominal interest.
2. In the second transaction, the 20 units, the fee of $10,800 was paid in cash at closing.
3. The third transaction was the mini-warehouse. Again, no cash transferred at closing, so the broker took his $24,000 fee over four years at nominal interest.
4. The last transaction in the pyramid was the industrial complex. Since the sellers received substantial cash, a flat fee of $50,000 was paid at the closing.

In all, $90,800 was paid to the broker—not counting the interest gained from the deferred fees.

How To Set Up The Most Profitable Pyramid For Your Client

There are two major factors to keep in mind when you approach pyramiding: (1) Pyramiding is highly risky; (2) The property taken in the pyramid should have the potential to substantiate the risk. Once these cautions are clear in your mind, you are ready to go to work to help your client make use of this high-leverage financing tool.

The six key steps in building a strong pyramid. In keeping with the step-by-step procedure, follow these six steps to pyramiding:

1. Find out the client's goal. Then work to that end.
2. Find out his ability to risk equity and/or cash.
3. Substantiate his equity by appraisals or *pro formas.*
4. Look for property within the ability of the client that has not reached peak income potential.
5. Make an offer.
6. Do not move on until the new property will support new pyramiding by carrying a secondary loan.

Suppose your client wants to build an estate. Together you determine that to build this estate quickly he can risk going into the pyramid program. The next step is to establish the value of the equity on which you plan to build. In Blackburn's case, he started with a $30,000 equity plus $30,000 cash. (Cash is not always a requirement, but some may be needed to improve the properties being acquired.)

An appraisal of one sort or another would be desirable to show the real equity in the property with which you plan to start. Appraisals generally work to the owner's advantage since it is rare for a property to sell for a price over the appraisal, and market value often lies somewhere below that appraised value. The appraisal, therefore, will give a value above the actual marketable sales price in the majority of cases. If you know that the market will support a higher price than that given by the appraiser, then be ready to support that price with hard facts.

Armed with this appraisal, the equity for the pyramid will be apparent. This equity will determine the strength of a second mortgage to be secured by it.

One of the best sources for properties that may be available for pyramid buying will be the local exchange group. In essence, the pyramid buyer is exchanging a mortgage in one property for equity in another. If you don't have an exchange group in your area you may find your job more difficult, but not impossible.

In either case, it would not be amiss to start with what the client would like to buy and what he is capable of managing or developing into a winner, or that you as a broker can help him develop. It may be possible to work out a transaction that blends the pyramid into a normal transaction. We saw how Blackburn was able to use the pyramid and give the seller cash by refinancing the existing mortgages. *Look to the combination of as many forms of financing as possible to meet the goals you have set.*

HOW TO PRESENT THE PYRAMID OFFER EFFECTIVELY

Once you have located one or more properties that seem to be worth considering, make an offer. Do not contact the owner and ask if he thinks he might be interested in taking a second mortgage on other property as a down payment on his sale.

What Not To Do

Salesman: "Mr. Owner, I notice you have an apartment house on 2nd Street that has a 'For Sale' sign in the yard."

Owner: "That's right."

Salesman: "I was wondering, you wouldn't be interested in taking a mortgage back on another property instead of cash down, would you?"

It is obvious that this type of approach is not professional or effective. However, because this *is* the approach that many salesmen *do* take, a brief analysis is needed. *Firstly*, very few sellers know what kind of transaction they will accept, until they actually accept one. *Secondly*, a negative approach (you wouldn't be interested, would you?) will invite a negative reply.

How To Present The Offer

Follow these key steps in presenting pyramid offers:

1. *Have a signed offer.* You should not even talk to the seller about the pyramid transaction until your contract is signed by your client. While this is very important in all real estate transactions, it is a must in pyramiding.
2. *Have all the data about the security on the property being used to leverage up in the pyramid.* Not only should you have the contract signed, but you should go to the value of the mortgage being offered. A survey, appraisal, income statements (if the property is an income producer), comparable sales values, and photographs are needed. Be ready to take the seller over to the property if he wants to see it for himself. Naturally, you will have the data on any superior mortgages that already encumber the property.
3. *Begin the presentation in a positive mood.* "Well, Mr. Seller, it looks as though we have been able to get your selling price." This positive mood will arouse his interest and help you through the tough part that comes next.
4. *Don't become defensive when the seller rejects the idea.* This is normal.

It is a natural reaction to what the seller wants, and most times you will get a first reaction that is negative.

5. *Agree with the seller that the offer does not satisfy his desire to receive cash instead of the mortgages.* But then restate his objection in a softer tone. "Mr. Seller, as you say, it would be better to get cash, but there are some aspects that deserve careful consideration." At this point, you should talk about the property being used as security for the mortgage. Go over some of the material you have brought for this purpose. From time to time, mention the buyer and what he plans to do with the new property. If cash has to be spent to upgrade it, say this. Call attention to the price. "While we were not able to get the cash you wanted, Mr. Seller, we held onto the price." This may mean more than you think.
6. *Go over the risks involved.* This will not cost you a deal, but will earn some respect for you in the long run. Point out that in a transaction where the seller does not get cash, but a mortgage, there is a risk that the mortgage will not be paid. Once you have said this, again go over the material you have on the property that will secure the pyramid. Try to show that risk is kept at a minimum.
7. *Call on your very best closing techniques; the rest is up to you.* When it gets down to this stage, there are no guidelines to follow. You must play it byear the rest of the way. Some sellers will have to sleep on the offer. Don't get pushy here, since pyramiding may be a very new concept to them. Other sellers may go to the dotted line right away.

HOW TO USE PYRAMIDING AS A SALES TOOL

There are times when a property is difficult to sell because of the low mortgages it carries. A free and clear property may be extremely difficult to sell unless there is some form of financing available, either from the seller or from other sources.

When a combination of the following factors is present, the pyramid can be used to benefit the seller.

The Seller's Checklist To See If Pyramiding Can Aid A Sale

1. The seller's equity presents a problem in the sale. This will occur in many situations where a high equity and minimal existing financing require a high capital investment on the part of the buyer.
2. The seller cannot or will not hold purchase money financing to facilitate the ultimate sale.
3. The conventional financing market does not offer effective refinancing of existing financing. This may be the major stumbling block in the sale

of the property in the first place. If the property is an income producer, a high interest rate and a high constant rate may not be absorbed in the net operating income to offer a respectable yield to the investor.

4. The seller wants to reinvest into more real estate. This factor makes the seller a buyer, and the pyramid program can be examined in detail to see how it can be used to satisfy all four of these criteria.

In a situation that involves a seller and where all four of these criteria can be met, you can then move into a pyramid.

The objectives of the pyramid for the seller are to help make the property more saleable, and at the same time reinvest the equity into more real estate. To follow this, I am presenting an example that shows a step-by-step application of these principles for the seller.

Bristow was the owner of a retail complex that consisted of seven shops. He is one of many investors that like to build and own with a high equity position. In this case, he had built the complex with his own cash and had no mortgage at all.

Over the years, he realized that his attitude toward real estate investing was not giving him the desired leverage on his capital. Thus, he wanted to sell the retail complex and build a larger one by using the capital from the first.

When I examined the property and his situation, I realized that his conservative approach would make the sale difficult. First of all, he needed to realize most of his equity to move ahead with his plan. Secondly, he therefore could not hold much paper, if any, at all. To test the third item on the check-list, calls to the local lenders were made. These indicated that while there was money available for mortgages on the present complex, they would be costly and could hurt the ultimate value since the constant rate was high.

The fourth item on the checklist was already met, as the seller was indeed ready to reinvest. There were numerous options to follow in a marketing plan. The property could be put on the market with new financing, but I felt that the loss of value, due to the cost of the money alone, would make this choice secondary if we could come up with another solution. To be specific, the value of the property was determined to be $250,000, based on the fact that the NOI was $25,000 and a 10% capitalization rate was felt to be warranted in this situation.

Commercial money was available at 9¾% interest per annum, over 17 years. This created an constant rate of 12.07%, or $22,631 per year (P&I) on the maximum loan of $187,500 (75% of the value). On top of this, the loan cost would be approximately $8,000.

With a NOI of $25,000 and a deduction of the annual debt of $22,631, a cash flow of only $2,369 would remain. If the investor wanted a 10% return, his total capital payment would have to be $23,690. But as $8,000 of that would go to the cost of the loan, the seller would receive the $187,500 plus $15,690, or $203,190. Thus, *with conventional financing the seller would get only $203,190* *for a $250,000 value.* A loss of over $46,000 was too much to take without further study.

How The Pyramid Got The Seller The Full $250,000 Value, And Made Another Sale For The Broker At The Same Time

I knew if financing could be put on the property that would provide a 10% constant, at no cost to the ultimate buyer or seller, the overall value of the complex could be sustained.

In counseling with the seller, I ascertained that he wanted to buy a vacant tract of land where he could build another, larger complex. He did, in fact, have several locations in mind, even though he had not negotiated on any of them. His conservative nature had kept him from buying until he sold. One site was a three-acre tract that was well suited for his needs. It was on the market for $210,000, a very fair price, and was, as much vacant property is, free and clear of any debt.

My first approach was to see if the owner would consider an exchange for the shops. An offer was presented in the normal exchange procedure. He would not exchange. Yet, I learned that he only wanted a secure return and would sell with a very low down payment and hold paper for the balance. However, this would not solve my investor's problem, as he needed the land free and clear to obtain a development loan and had to sell his property.

A pyramid was structured. We presented the seller of the three acres with a contract that would allow Bristow to meet his needs, if all went well. The owner of the three acres was to receive $10,000 cash and a first mortgage in the amount of $190,000 on the shops as the full price for the land. The mortgage was set up on these terms: 8% per year, interest only for the first three years, then an amortized pay-out over the remaining 25 years with a balloon on the fifteenth anniversary of the closing. The closing was to occur upon the sale of the retail complex, providing this sale could be accomplished within 60 days.

How The Pyramid Helped Sell The Retail Complex

In an instant, the retail property now had a $190,000 first mortgage that offered an investor excellent terms and potential for return. The interest only at 8% for the first three years meant that the annual debt service on the $190,000 would be $15,200. This would leave a cash flow of $9,800. If the property were to sell for $250,000, the down payment of $60,000 would show a 16.33% yield. This provided excellent leverage for those three years. At the end of the interest only period, the annual debt service would go to a 9.27% constant, or $17,613. If there were no improvement in the NOI (which was projected to go up), the cash flow would be $7,387 or a 12.3% yield on the original investment of

$60,000. The balloon did not hamper the sale of the property, as the time period allowed ample opportunity for future refinancing of the loan prior to its balloon. On this basis, the sale of the units was rather easy and was accomplished well within the 60-day period.

How The Broker And His Client Came Out

Each of us did nicely. Bristow sold the retail complex for its full value of $250,000. He took $10,000 of the $60,000 he received on the sale and paid that over to the seller of the three acres. Then, the $190,000 mortgage was established to the benefit of all the parties involved. Bristow now proceeded to develop a larger complex on the three acres which he owned free and clear.

The brokerage fee was $15,000 on the sale of the retail complex, which was paid at closing, and $20,000 on the sale of the three acres. Half of the latter was paid at closing and the remaining $10,000 over a three-year period. In all, $35,000 in fees was collected.

Had the pyramid not been used, there is no assurance the transaction would have been possible. To be sure, even if we had sold the retail complex, there is no telling whether we would have been in on the later purchase by Bristow. As it turned out, everyone was happy. The client took over the three acres and was able to use the equity in the land to mortgage out on the development of a 24,000 square foot retail center.

ADVANTAGES AND DISADVANTAGES IN PYRAMIDING

There are two factors which create a risk in pyramiding:

1. The ability to pay on the increased debt.
2. The danger of overleverage.

As you can see, both of these factors are related. If the client extends his value to equity ratio to the point where there is no real equity after the pyramid, his over-leverage may cause a toppling effect. But this risk may be slight to the buyer as he is extending equity that may not be real anyway. In Blackburn's case, he built a sizeable equity in several years by use of the pyramid. But, as you remember, all went well. If one of the later transactions had gone sour, part or all of the pyramid may have toppled. But since his gain would well offset the loss, his risk was justified.

What are the advantages and disadvantages? First of all, remember that two parties are involved. Each must look at the pyramid in a different light. Because of this double standard, the advantages and disadvantages are presented from the point of view of both the buyer and the seller.

The Buyer: The Client Who Instigates The Pyramid

ADVANTAGES	*DISADVANTAGES*
1. Expands holdings	1. Possibility of overleverage
2. A low-cost financing tool for reinvestment	2. One failure and the whole pyramid can fall
3. Establishes good "selling" terms	3. Buyer limited to fewer sellers
4. Fantastic estate builder	

In short, the buyer in the pyramid is a gambler full of confidence in his abilities. He is riding on an up market. But if he is not overly bright or has made a mistake about timing, he can lose the whole bundle even quicker than he put it together.

The Seller: The One Who Feeds The Pyramid

ADVANTAGES	*DISADVANTAGES*
1. Creates a sale	1. Sale generates paper, not cash
2. Tax advantages, due to spread of gain on the sale to the terms of the mortgage taken	2. Paper may not be secure
3. Provides long-term income	3. Another remote transaction could have a great effect on this security
4. Secured by other property with visible results	4. Paper is flexible in terms

The seller in the pyramid is generally a person highly motivated to sell. He considers and later accepts the offer for paper because it is the best deal offered. If you were to compare the pyramid offer to an all-cash offer of the same value, there could be no question as to the better, less risky transaction. However, this is not a proper comparison. The seller wants to sell and has a plausible offer. Hence, it may be worthy of acceptance and better than holding onto the property.

HOW TO MAKE THE TRANSACTION WORK FOR ALL PARTIES CONCERNED

The pyramid can be a very safe and profitable way to finance new acquisitions if used conservatively. This means the amount of real equity transferred via a mortgage should be kept at a low to moderate amount. In most cases, the total debt service on the property should not exceed 80% of the net operating income of that property. In very stable income properties this percentage may be extended to 90%. There should be a 10% or greater buffer between income and expenses. In taking over a new property, the buyer should consider out-of-pocket expenses to bring the income up, and this out-of-pocket must be taken into account *before* the transaction is completed. It should be figured into the total price or at least accounted for in later expenditures. If the buyer is able to generate this needed out-of-pocket cash from additional financing on the acquired property, then the total debt should be reasonable and not overlevereaged.

The market conditions themselves will provide some limitation to this overleverage, as it will be difficult for the buyer to obtain excessive financing on marginal properties. But the domino effect of the total pyramid can build up quickly if you are not careful.

The seller should exercise caution in any transaction that does not involve cash. However, that caution should not mean a pyramid transaction is not worth considering. To the contrary, the property being sold may not be saleable by any other method.

Chapter 12

How to Use Exchanges In Financing Real Estate

The movement of equity is in itself a form of financing, and for the real estate investor exchanging is a most viable way to accomplish what cannot be accomplished by other means. Naturally, exchanging will not fit all situations or even most. Yet, the advantages that are presented due to tax laws and market conditions make this form of financing worthy of more consideration.

The exchanging of real estate has grown into a major specialty. Exchanging clubs have been formed around the country. These clubs will be most useful to you once you understand their basic philosophy. Your ability to utilize exchanges as a way to solve problems will depend on your understanding of the ideal results you want from them and the general results you will obtain.

WHAT EXCHANGING IS ALL ABOUT

I have found that many professional exchangers find it difficult to properly answer questions about the reason for exchanging. Some exchanges happen without the broker fully understanding why, and most fail for the same reason. Some that look most difficult on the surface become workable once the broker or associate delves into the results desired and the willingness to make a "move." Other proposed exchanges just never make the contract stage because the basic concept of what exchanging should do—and what it is all about—is violated.

The purpose of this chapter, therefore, is to go into the basics of exchanging, and show you how to apply these techniques to financing. You will be able to recognize when exchanging is viable and when it is not. If an exchange appears to be of benefit to your client, then you will be able to make the proper moves to see that it is properly completed.

What Exchanges Do

Exchanges affect three parties. The owners of at least two properties involved and the broker. Therefore, the results of the exchange itself can be seen from two points of view. It is important that both points of view be analyzed briefly as this will help establish the proper attitude toward the exchanges you attempt, as well as your relationship with your clients.

What The Exchange Can Do For The Property Owner: Four Key Benefits

You should approach any exchange situation with a simple question: "Will the exchange solve or move the client closer to a solution of the problem at hand?"

To be able to answer this question, you must have a clear understanding of the problem. Previous chapters have dealt with fully understanding the problems of your clients. It is crucial to know where your client wants to go when it comes to exchanges. If the answer to the question stated above is "*No*, it does not solve the problem or move the client closer to a solution," then, obviously, the exchange should not be recommended.

Here are the four key ways in which exchanging can benefit property owners:

1. Tax free benefit. The present tax laws make exchanges of like property a possible way to avoid the payment of capital gains tax at the time the transfer takes place. This has been referred to as a "tax free benefit," but this is really a misnomer. The tax is merely *deferred* until ultimate sale of the received property. Should the device of exchange be utilized time after time, the tax on the gain continues to be put off until a final sale. The only way for the transaction to be free of gains tax would be for the owner to die. Upon death, of course, other taxes come into play. New tax laws for estates carry forward the old basis, which will have an affect on the later sale. Nonetheless, the tax law benefit has many applications and is one of the major reasons for exchanges. The law provides for the transfer of basis from the old property to the new property. Some tax may be due at the time of the transfer, but this will depend on a number of factors and will be covered later in this chapter in the discussion on the method of transferring the basis.

An exchange will be considered to be "tax free" when two or more properties are exchanged that are like property. The term "like property" has caused much consternation in real estate circles. Like property is the intent of use more than the physical characteristic. So, to be specific: *Like Property is any real interest which is held for use in a trade or business or held as an investment and was not acquired for resale.*

To simplify this definition, any property which is owned by a nondealer can be exchanged for any other kind of property to be used in the same category as the old property. For example, Roland owns several vacant lots which he uses for outdoor storage of his equipment. There is no question that an exchange of one of these lots for another lot (to be used for storage) in another town would meet the like for like portion of the law.

Another lot, however, also owned by Roland, has not been used for several years. He did not sell it because he decided it would be a good investment and would increase in value in the future. He exchanges this lot for an apartment building. As the apartment building can be construed as an investment, the exchange will meet the like property test.

There have been countless combinations of exchange in realty. In every instance, the like property test must be met for the exchange to have the deferment of tax at the time of the transfer. It is important for you to realize that this test need not be met by both parties, nor does it have to be met at all for an exchange to be beneficial. The advantage to the exchange, from a tax angle, will depend greatly on the situation and the individuals.

2. *Increase depreciation.* Because investment and busines property can be depreciated, there are times when exchanging is used with the primary reason being to increase the amount of depreciation the client is currently obtaining. This advantage is available because of the tax deferment ability, but has special significance to many transactions. The value of the depreciation itself may be taken into consideration if the client needs a tax loss.

For example: Keaster owns 100 acres of land and a old farm building which he has been leasing out along with the land. His base in the entire property is $45,000, having paid $60,000 nearly ten years earlier and depreciating the building to nearly zero. The value is $250,000 and he has a small $15,000 mortgage balance. Keaster exchanges his equity for a large apartment house worth $900,000 and having a first mortgage of $650,000. Keaster's new base is increased by cash paid plus the difference between the two mortgages. The subsequent depreciation will then be calculated on that base, less an allocation for the land.

What would have happened if Keaster had sold the farm and then bought the apartment house? Look at the two examples of this case study: (1) the exchange as it actually took place, and (2) the results from a sale and later purchase of the apartment house (Figure 12-1). The amounts shown are net sums, and brokers' fees are not shown at this time.

In comparing the two situations, you will see several important tax consequences. From the depreciation point of view, the new annual depreciation of $18,533 amounts to 123% of the cash paid ($15,000). The sale followed by the purchase of the apartment complex required $82,000 cash, and generates $24,000 of new annual depreciation or 29% ratio cash to depreciation.

The cash required to end up with the same property differs greatly, the reason being the tax which must be paid in the sale. Keaster had no tax to pay at

Figure 12-1.

THE EXCHANGE

Current Depreciation:	$ -0-
Current Equity:	$235,000
Existing Mortgages:	$ 15,000
Net Market Value:	$250,000

Exchange Equity of $235,000 for Apartment house (shown below):

Net Market Value:	$900,000
Existing Mortgages	$650,000
Equity (Apt.):	$250,000
Less Equity (Farm):	$235,000
Cash to Pay:	$ 15,000

ADJUSTMENT FOR NEW BASE

Old Base in Farm:	$ 45,000
Less Mortgage Amount on Farm:	$ 15,000
Plus New Mortgage on Apt. Bldg.:	+$650,000
Plus Cash Paid at Closing:	+$ 15,000
New Base:	$695,000

Ratio of value: Land vs. Bldg. (20% Land vs. 80% Bldg.)

New Base:	$695,000
Land:	$139,000
Building:	$556,000

AVERAGE RATE (ESTIMATED) DEPRECIATION

Straight line 30 years:	$ 18,533
Cash Paid in Transaction:	$ 15,000
Equity in Apt. Bldg.:	$250,000

A SALE AND THEN A PURCHASE

Current Depreciation:	$ -0-
Current Equity:	$235,000
Existing Mortgages:	$ 15,000
Net Market Value:	$250,000

Assume a sale at this price: Calculate Capital Gains Tax due at the close of the transaction.

Sales Price:	$250,000
Less Base:	$ 45,000
Gain:	$205,000

(Estimated capital gains tax based on 25% tax on first $50,000 of gain; balance at 35%)

Tax:	$ 67,000

Total Proceeds from Closing:

Cash Received by Seller:	$235,000
Less Capital Gains Tax:	$ 67,000
Net Cash to Seller:	$168,000

SELLERS NOW WANT TO BUY THE APT. HOUSE

Price of Apt. House:	$900,000
Less Total Mtg.:	$650,000
Cash Required:	$250,000
Cash from Sale of Farm:	$168,000
Additional Cash Needed:	$ 82,000
NEW BASE:	$900,000
Depreciation Base $900,000 × 80% =	$720,000

AVERAGE RATE OF DEPRECIATION

Straight line 30 years:	$ 24,000
Cash Paid in Transaction:	$ 82,000
Equity in Apt. Bldg.:	$250,000

the time of the exchange, so his adjustments in arriving at new basis did not reflect the addition of taxable gain.

3. Expand the market. If you have a property which is difficult to move for one reason or another, then exchanging may provide an increased market. The key to this is to determine what you plan to do with the proceeds of the sale. If you intend to reinvest the money or a major portion of it in more real estate, then the exchange will not only be the extension of the market, but a tax saver as well. There are many dealers in the exchange market who will take property in trade just to make a move. These people are generally brokers or associates that have taken property from previous exchanges as a part of their fee. This "Fee Property" becomes barter for these brokers, and exchanges within this area are more on the "I'd-rather-have-that-than-what-I've-got" basis.

The expansion of a market is most important. There are many investors locked into large capital gains who cannot sell their investments without having to pay the tax. These investors will look for exchanges to move their equity or to increase depreciation. It is not important at this point that you may not want what they have. Often, their property is highly marketable for cash—*they* just can't sell. But you can make the trade and then *you* can sell their property.

4. Cash-out. This occurs when the owner of a difficult-to-sell-or-finance property exchanges it for another property that is easy to sell or finance. The motivation and the benefit are cash, and not the property received in the exchange. Ramond owns a vacant lot, the value of which is $100,000. Ramond needs cash, but cannot sell or finance the vacant property. So, he exchanges it for a free and clear home. The home is easily financed, and once he has raised $70,000 on it he then puts it on the market at $85,000. The $15,000 down payment and reduced price is apt to produce a buyer, whereas the same reduction on the lot would not.

For a cash-out, the easiest property to exchange is a free and clear home up to $150,000. This home becomes prime cash-out potential for exchangers. Present one of these at any exchange club and it will produce a number of offers.

The benefit, the cash-out, is important. It is part of working with your client toward the desired goal. Investing in real estate is best done with some sort of plan. The desire to start here and end there may require more than one step or move. Exchanging should be considered as a part of the steps in a dance. Or would you prefer to sit this one out?

What Exchanging Can Do For The Broker

Exchanging can be the most exciting part of marketing property. As a financing tool, exchanging is valuable in many ways for adding that extra bit of creative thought to a well-rounded presentation or concept. The broker can expect to derive the following benefits from dealing in exchanging:

1. Increased commissions. Mentioned first because money is most certainly a motivating force. The advantage of having that extra knowledge will mean you will be able to make more deals than before. Exchanging is a way of life for some people and is not complicated. The basics covered in this chapter will get you started. The how to, where to, and when to exchange are not hard to understand. The only reason more brokers are not into exchanges is their own limitation in wanting to grasp something new.

2. Increased service to your clients. This is the most important reason for dealing in exchanges. It is crucial to know what the client's reason for selling is. If you find out the seller needs the cash because he wants to invest in larger properties, then you will be doing him a service if you suggest an exchange to save possible tax and to improve his reinvestment position. Brokers and associates often think the investor has the same knowledge that they have—or more. Often, this is the situation, since there are many very sophisticated investors in this field. However, there are many more investors who do not know the advantages of exchanging or how to go about structuring such a transaction.

3. Buyer-seller connection all at once. When you have a client ready to exchange, you have both a sale and a purchase staring you in the face. Two deals, two commissions, but most important in this context, you are developing a stable of sound investors who will deal with you again and again. Investors who exchange properties are movers. They are accustomed to making deals and like that part of the business.

4. Grow with your profession. This is part of the service line, but goes beyond that. When you get out and become part of a new area within your own field you will see that your fears of not having the expertise were unfounded. There are "super exchangers" to be sure, but most are dedicated, hard working people who are looking for new ways to make deals and to earn more commissions. Acquiring this knowledge is something that you can do over a period of time.

HOW TO GET STARTED IN EXCHANGING

The best way to get started in exchanging is to join a local exchange group in your area. There will be one somewhere nearby. These clubs are usually founded by brokers and associates of real estate firms in the community that deal in the exchange of properties. These clubs may be operating under the local Board of Realtors, but this is not always the case.

If you do not know if such a club exists, ask the nearest Board of Realtors to see if they have any information. If they cannot help, then look in the classified section of your local newspaper under "Exchange of Real Estate." If the newspaper does not have such a section, and you have not been able to find an exchange club in your area, and the local boards don't know of any, then you have just found the dream of all exchangers—a place in America where there is no competition for exchanging!

It is possible that there will not be a club, even though there will be fellow associates dealing in exchanges. If you are a novice and need to get some experience in exchanging, you can look to the state for this assistance. I don't know of one state that does not have at least one professional group dealing in exchanges of real property.

The importance of joining a group such as this is simply that the members will become your initial market. The cooperation that is common among salesmen and firms in the real estate business is even more evident in the exchanging field. The co-splitting of a fee in a transaction is an unwritten law that all exchangers learn to respect. Most exchangers do not try to hunt up both sides of the exchange themselves. If you go out and find another associate who can match your side of the deal, you will make more deals. It does not matter how many legs there are in making a transaction. All the fees are put into a pot and the total is divided by the number of firms participating. The size of the legs of the exchange doesn't make any difference. All firms participate equally.

For example, in a two-leg exchange there may be two firms, Firm A and Firm B. Each represents one of the parties to this two-way deal. The fee on each side is put together and then split 50/50. It doesn't matter that the fee on A was more than the fee on B.

Understanding The Philosophy Of Exchangers

Using exchanges to make deals work is just one way of putting transactions together. You should never use an exchange unless it accomplishes this major goal: "Does the exchange solve or move the client closer to a solution of his problems?"

Unfortunately, there are some brokers and associates who are only concerned with the benefits they can derive and do not fully understand the benefits to the property owners. With such a misunderstanding, this tool is apt to fail. For example, if you attempt to make exchanges and are not convinced that the tax savings or other benefits can be highly beneficial to your client, then you will approach the exchange as merely another, less attractive, method of reaching a desired goal and may have a tendency to set two values on the property. The property can be purchased for $200,000, some brokers say, but for exchange it has a value of $250,000. Setting a sales price below the exchange value may be wrong. The exchange may be more beneficial to the owner. If this is true, and it often is, then the exchange has value in itself. If you save your client money by using an exchange to reach the desired goal, you would have to get more in selling, not less.

This book will not change the many exchangers who use this double-form pricing. You will come up against this in exchange clubs and in dealing with the uninformed public. They will tell you that because this is the case, exchange properties are listed over their for-sale price and that the only way to counteract that distortion is to list over the value.

The overpricing of properties for exchange is something you will have to face. I do not recommend that you follow this seemingly common policy. There are many exchangers who will not quote two prices—ever. Your actions in this field should be governed by whether the exchange is good for your client or not. If it is good, then set a value that will stand up under the most stringent scrutiny. When you see this double standard being used, you will recognize an exchanger who would really rather sell or who doesn't fully understand the benefits of exchanging.

Some exchangers have the tendency to look only at the "most desperate" type of deal presented. The local club to which I belong has from time to time found itself running amok of the "desperate only" sort of deal, and I know of others having this problem. Most clubs have what they call a marketing session every month or even more often. It is during these sessions that the members "pitch" the listing to their fellow exchangers. This pitch allows the other members to examine the motivation of the owner and to ask questions to find out what type of property may be acceptable in exchange. When the questions asked begin with "How badly does he want to exchange?" then this is a sign that the club has fallen into the "desperate only" syndrome. What they are in effect saying is: "No one will exchange unless they are desperate." This is, of course, far from the truth.

Before we leave the realm of exchangers, don't get the impression I feel exchangers do a poor job. Exchangers and exchange clubs in particular are bringing the benefits of exchanges to more and more investors. The failings of a few exchangers will not deter this worthy movement from growing.

HOW TO PUT TOGETHER AN EXCHANGE

The pre-exchange procedure, the steps you must take to work up to the exchange, is most important. You will not be able to make an effective exchange presentation unless you have done the necessary homework; nor will you be able to get your client into the exchange in order to solve his problem or help him reach his goal.

Seven Key Steps In The Pre-exchange Procedure

1. Fully accept the concept and attitude that an effective exchange must help solve a problem or move your client closer to his desired goal. You must believe in what you are suggesting.

2. Know all the necessary facts about the person and the property. In the qualification process you will find out all the things about your client that will help you understand his goal or problem. If you don't have this clearly in mind, then your solutions will be off center and they could have harsh results. You should gather the following information:

A. Price of the property. Only one—for sale or exchange. If you do quote two, the for-sale price should be higher.
B. All facts pertinent to the existing financing.
C. The amount of the equity.
D. The amount of cash the client has to add to the deal. If he has none, then you will have to raise the cash to pay your fee out of the transaction or else wait.
E. What is the basis on the property? You should know this figure because it will affect your tax analysis. Don't take the amount the client gives you without being sure he knows what you are asking, and that he has checked to see how much he has depreciated his property over the past years.
F. Limitations which would cause certain properties to be unacceptable for exchange. Physical, psychological, and financial reasons might cause you to eliminate possible exchanges for your client, but only if you know his capabilities and abilities.

3. Condition your client to the workings of exchanges. Be sure he understands that the exchange may just be a method of expanding his market or moving him closer to his goal. It is most important that your client know that he will have to pay a fee, and that the fee will be the same as though he sold the property. You should tell the client that you will also obtain a fee from the other party, even though another broker is involved.

4. Ask the client if he already has a property picked out that he would like to own. Some of your clients will. This selection will give you an idea as to where to go and what kind of property the client would like. You might start out by attempting to make an exchange on that selected property. Do not get hung up, however, on this selection. Look for what the client believes this property will do for him, then look for other types of properties that will accomplish the same goals.

For example, I have a client who told me he had been looking at a small medical building. He told me he liked the idea of collecting rents from professional people who were apt to stay put rather than move every few years. Based on that input, I showed him a number of properties that had strong tenants who had been in the area for a long period of time and were not apt to move. He ended up with a restaurant leased to a national firm.

5. Review the benefits of exchanges in your own mind—*tax benefits, increase depreciation, expand the market, cash-out*. It is a good idea to have them written down.

6. Know how to do the math calculations. These will be shown later in this chapter. They include how to compute base, capital gain and balance of equity.

7. Examine the market for your needs. Once you have an idea of the type of property your client will accept in an exchange, the obvious next step is to find that property. As you can imagine, this is not as easy as it sounds. Three factors will make this task complicated: (1) the property you seek may not be available for exchange, (2) the other owner may not want your property, and (3) your client can't make up his mind about what he really wants.

Despite these complicating factors, you still have to go out and find what you can, and from that, try to narrow down to an acceptable deal. The exchange club will be a good start. But don't stop there. Look at all the listings you have access to. Even if the sellers of other properties have not told their agents they would consider an exchange, it is possible they will. Never be fearful of making an offer on a property that is listed for sale, even if the agent doesn't think the owner will exchange. You can be very successful by running ads in the local papers or following up on ads run by fellow exchangers. Of course, the type of property you have to deal with will differ, and so too the source for possible exchange. It should be assumed you would look to the obvious buyers for such properties. Where they may not be able to purchase or may not be motivated to buy . . . an exchange can bring out other motives or make the terms so easy they find the willingness to buy increased.

Partial exchanges are also ideal in this light. The owner may be willing to sell and at the same time accept part of the sale price in the way of a trade. When you visit the exchange club, you should be prepared to make a presentation of your property based on the outline which follows this discussion. Keep in mind that clubs differ in their form of presentation, and while all the data covered in this outline should be a part of their format, the order may vary. Once you have gone over the outline, you should make a separate card for each of the major topics to be covered so you can discuss them in the order preferred by the club. I would suggest you familiarize yourself with the club or group prior to making any presentation. Most clubs will require prior membership and some have rather strict rules, but others are very informal.

Marketing Session Presentation Checklist For Exchange Of Property

THE PROPERTY:

(1) Location.
(2) Very brief description.
(3) Price, mortgages, and equity.
(4) Have detailed listing sheet to pass out to members.

THE PERSON THAT OWNS PROPERTY:

(1) Type of entity that owns the property.
(2) How long have they owned the property?
(3) Motivation to sell or exchange.
(4) If there is special motivation to exchange, state what it is.
(5) What are the problems?
(6) Can the owner add cash, and, if so, how much?

THE WANT:

(1) What are the end results desired by your client?
(2) What types of property seem to fit that goal?
(3) Geographic limitations.
(4) Other limitations

Naturally, it will be helpful if you have this information organized in such a way that you can go over it quickly. The general course of action at most exchange clubs or groups is to have the presentation made by the lister, then go into a moderated session.

When you have finished with your presentation, the leader of the session will ask a few questions to see that everyone understands what you have and what you want. From there, members in the club may make suggestions, such as, contact this broker or that one as he may have what you want.

Your total time in front of the club will be about five to ten minutes. If there is any immediate interest from the members of the group, you may get what is called a mini-form. This mini-form is a short agreement signed by the lister. It indicates that one of the members (his name is shown on the form) has a client who may be interested in taking your property in exchange. This is a preliminary step to the exchange agreement. Mini-forms are used extensively, and when you receive one you should follow up with that broker to see if an exchange can be made.

Because exchanges are a two-way street, you must be attentive in exchange clubs. You never know when something that will appeal to one of your clients will come up in the presentations. If you hear of a property that will be attractive to your client, you may be tempted to offer a mini-form. But it's best to wait until after the session when you can sit down with the lister and find out more about the property. If it is local, visit it. You should refrain from offering your client a property that you have not seen, unless you know the client will accept anything or the property is distant and cannot be visited within a reasonable time.

Once you have a property that fits the general needs of your client, you are ready to proceed with the exchange. You should keep in mind that you can start the exchange from either side. If you represent the owner of an apartment house who wants to exchange for vacant property, it would be normal to have your client make the offer on any vacant property you locate. However, at times you may want the vacant property owner to initiate the offer. I will explain the reasons for this in an example after we look at the normal client-initiated offer.

Your Offer To Exchange: How To Get It In Writing And How To Present It

The motivation for exchanging is vastly different from that for selling. In selling you have to get a buyer to part with his money, but they are sometimes reluctant to do this. In exchanging you only have to get one party to give up what he already doesn't want for something else.

If you think about this, you will begin to grasp part of the difference. Logic, the sound argument of tax benefits, and 100% use of the value will help make many exchanges. However, the final decision made by the owners of the two properties in question will not depend on this sound advice alone. The other motivation, that of willingness or strong desire to get rid of the presently owned property, can be the most compelling factor in the exchange. This desire to get rid of a property is generally coupled to at least one other motivation. For example: If there is strong need for cash, the satisfaction of this desire is the exchange that will provide cash for your client. The owner that is fed-up with management will look to problem-free (people-free) property. Other reasons such as ill health, transfer, depreciation has run out, tax problems, geographic changes, and so on, are all coupled to the willingness to be rid of a property. Your ability to accept this and allow it to become a part of the exchange process is important—important for your client and for you if you expect to make many exchanges.

What this means is simply this: The logic behind exchanges is the basis to support the need to move equity from one property to another. As a broker, you may have to explain this logic to an unwilling exchanger. Once the decision has been made to exchange, then the important point is the strength of the motivation to make the move. If you want to convert a dog-hater into a dog-lover, you don't expound on the logical benefits of having a dog around the house. Dog-haters don't care about that sort of talk (they have heard it all before). What you do is give them a small puppy to hold. Once they have the puppy in their hands, then the logic can sink in.

Exchanging is very much the same. Get the property owner to grasp the idea of holding some other property.

How To Approach Your Client With A Property And Get The Offer

You have found a prime property for your client. The other listing agent has told you that he too feels there is a basis for exchange. So you want to get things started by having your client make an offer to exchange.

After sitting down with the client, you are ready to make the presentation to him. Here is what you do:

(1) Have a photo of the property you want to make the offer on.
(2) Have all the details and other data necessary to make a judgment as to the income, expenses, and so on.
(3) Set aside enough time to visit the property that day.
(4) Begin your conversation with your client in as positive a mood as you can. You will want to play on his strongest motivation. If he is motivated by the need for cash, you might start as follows: "Mr. Jones, I believe I have found a property that can generate the cash you need; and best of all, the owner may be willing to accept your property in trade." If your client is fed up with the management problems of small seasonal motels, your beginning may be something like this: "Mr. Jones, I believe I have found a property that has no management problems; and best of all, the owner may be willing to accept your property in trade." Or, how about the client that needs more depreciation: "Mr. Jones, I believe I have found a property that will increase your tax write-off by giving you increased basis for depreciation; and best of all, the owner may be willing to accept your property in trade."

Three things are obvious here. In each of the above conversations, the broker points out the desired solution and couples it with an explanation of the resulting action; indicates that the other party will accept the client's property; and encourages a positive reaction from the client even though he has not told him anything about the property other than that he believes it will do what he thinks the client wants the property to do.

In selling you have to deal with many emotions. The importance of getting the feel of a property is much more critical in selling than in exchanging. The exchange, after all is a two-sided coin where each party has to give up one property and accept another. The very fact that I am telling the client I have a property which may suit his needs and the owner of that property may accept his property in trade, gives the impression that we are half way or better to making a deal.

Naturally, it is important that you have some feeling about this mutual acceptance. It is in this way that the mini-forms have their real value. You can show your client a copy of this form, given to you by the listing agent for the other property indicating interest in the exchange, and can say: "See—this is from his agent."

Putting The Offer Down On Paper

By now, your client has asked you why the other party didn't make the offer first. This is natural, and you can say that all good things have to start somewhere. Of course, the best reason to give is that if he makes the offer then he will be in control of the first step. The important thing is to move forward, so don't dwell on the topic of who should go first. Just move on.

When you draw up an offer for exchange, you will want to use a standard form. These forms are available through the local exchange clubs or they can be obtained from the National Association of Realtors. Your lawyer may also have a form. I have not included a sample of any such form because you should use the particular form which is familiar to others in your community.

These forms are rather simple and are for the most part self-explanatory. The caution you exercise in filling them out will be no greater than you presently use in sales contracts. The most complicated part, and this is actually rather easy, is the balance of the equity. Each party should put in the same amount of equity, or equity-plus-boot.

Boot is any addition made to a transaction which is not real equity. If one party adds cash or gives a car or diamond ring as a part of the exchange, then this becomes boot for the receiver. It is rare for equities to balance without some boot added.

The balance of equity

Ernest Has:	A Medical Building:	Value	$300,000
		Mortgage	200,000
		Equity	$100,000
Fowley Has:	A Hotel:	Value	$1,050,000
		Mortgage	750,000
		Equity	$ 300,000

Ernest and Fowley are exchanging properties. There are many ways to balance these equities and two are shown below. The methods you use will depend on your imagination and the capabilities of your client. You can see that in between the two examples I have provided, you can have many variables of play in the cash and mortgages.

A cash balance

(ERNEST)			(FOWLEY)	
Equity:	$100,000		Equity:	$300,000
Cash to Balance:	200,000		Cash to Balance:	-0-
	$300,000	Equity now balances. Ernest pays Fowley the $200,000 in cash as a part of the trade.		$300,000

Mortgage balance

Equity:	$100,000		Equity:	$300,000
			Less additional financing held by Fowley:	$200,000
	$100,000	Equity now balances. Ernest owes Fowley $200,000, payable as per the terms of the extra financing held by Fowley.		$100,000

In the two preceding examples of equity balance, there are two examples of boot. The $200,000 cash or the mortgage becomes boot, because it is an extra amount received by Fowley.

Balancing the equity, as you can see, is not difficult. The problem of the boot is a tax problem, and even though the exchange may qualify under the tax law as a tax-free exchange, tax may still have to be paid on at least a part of the exchange. The only time it is possible to have an exchange where neither party has to pay tax is when two free and clear properties of equal value or exactly equal mortgage and equity are exchanged. Any difference in the amount of the two mortgages given or accepted will amount to "boot" received.

The calculation of gain realized and gain recognized is an important step in understanding this function of the tax law. The usual explanation of how this is calculated is most complicated. In an attempt to make this clear, I shall start with the most basic of exchanges and tax calculations and work forward. These computations are crucial to the whole exchange process, and unless you are fully competent in their manipulations, you will have a hard time with this form of financing.

How To Calculate The Tax Consequences Of An Exchange

Smyth and Greenbalm are our two owners. *Smyth owns 100 acres of land.* Its value is $200,000. He owns this land free and clear. He has a basis of $100,000. The rest is appreciation in the land over the past 12 years. *Greenbalm owns a 15-unit apartment house*. Its value is $200,000 and it too is free and clear. His basis is $140,000. This has occurred because he paid $180,000 for the property and has taken $20,000 in depreciation. Smyth and Greenbalm make a trade with no cash paid and no mortgages swapped. In other words, the exchange is *even*.

Smyth now owns the 15 units. His basis of $100,000 from the land has transferred over to the apartment house. As there were no mortgages, or cash transferred, or other boot, Smyth has no tax to pay. Greenbalm now owns the 100 acres of land. His basis from the apartment house of $140,000 has carried over to the land. He also has no tax to pay.

Now, let's examine another case study. Jones and Blackburn are our new owners. Jones owns 100 acres of land. Its value is $200,000. He has a first mortgage on the property in the amount of $50,000. His basis in the land is $100,000. Blackburn owns a 15-unit apartment house. The apartment house is valued at $300,000. Blackburn has a $200,000 mortgage on the property. His basis is $125,000. Jones and Blackburn want to exchange.

BALANCE OF EQUITY

Jones's Equity:		Blackburn's Equity:	
$150,000	Blackburn agrees to pay Jones the difference in cash in order to balance the two equities	$100,000	
		50,000	(cash added by Blackburn)
$150,000		$150,000	

The two case histories, illustrated in Figure 12-2, point out a common misconception about exchanging. First: It *is* possible to have an exchange where both parties have no tax to pay at the time of the transaction. Second: It is also possible to have an exchange where both parties *do* pay tax. The situation with Smyth and Greenbalm was clear-cut. Neither took any boot, nor were they relieved of mortgages. The equity was the same and the different basis had no tax consequenses in this transaction.

Jones and Blackburn were different. They both had a tax consequence and both saved on the tax as a result of the exchange. If Jones had sold his property, then paid the tax on the gain over his basis, he would not have had enough left to purchase Blackburn's property. This would hold true for the remaining three parties in these two transactions. To show this effect on a transaction to your client can be a major part of your "selling" the concept of the exchange. Emphasize that if you sell, then pay the tax due, you won't have the buying power you have with an exchange.

Figure 12-2: TAX CALCULATIONS IN TWO CASES

	Jones	*Blackburn*	*Smyth*	*Greenbalm*
Value of Property Received	$300,000	$200,000	$200,000	$200,000
ADD THE FOLLOWING:				
Cash Received	50,000	-0-	-0-	-0-
Other Boot Received	-0-	-0-	-0-	-0-
Mortgage Relief	50,000	200,000	-0-	-0-
SUBTOTAL	$400,000	$400,000	$200,000	$200,000
SUBTRACT FROM SUBTOTAL:				
Basis of the Time of Exchange	$100,000	$125,000	$100,000	$140,000
Amount of Mortgage Assumed	200,000	50,000	-0-	-0-
Amount of Cash Paid	-0-	50,000	-0-	-0-
Amount of Other Boot Given	-0-	-0-	-0-	-0-
GAIN REALIZED	$100,000	$175,000	$100,000	$ 60,000
TO COMPUTE AT THE TAXABLE GAIN:				
(1) Total Mortgages Relieved ..	$ 50,000	$200,000	$ -0-	$ -0-
(2) Less Total Mortgages Assumed	200,000	50,000	-0-	-0-
(If (2) is greater than (1) put 0 Amount)	$ -0-	$150,000	$ -0-	$ -0-
Less cash paid	-0-	50,000	-0-	-0-
Subtotal	$ -0-	$100,000	$ -0-	$ -0-
Plus Other Noncash Boot Received	-0-	-0-	-0-	-0-
Plus Cash Received	50,000	-0-	-0-	-0-
RECOGNIZED GAIN	$ 50,000	$100,000	$ -0-	$ -0-

Taxable Gain is the lower of Gain Realized or Recognized Gain. Note below calculation shows the Gain which is not taxed by virtue of the exchange.

GAIN REALIZED	$100,000	$175,000	$100,000	$ 60,000
Less Taxable Gain (Recognized) .	50,000	100,000	-0-	-0-
GAIN SAVED:	$ 50,000	$ 75,000	$100,000	$ 60,000

Following are the results of a sale. Note that no selling costs have been taken. We will later see a full calculation showing commissions.

	Jones	*Blackburn*	*Smyth*	*Greenbalm*
PRICE:	$200,000	$300,000	$200,000	$200,000
BASIS:	100,000	125,000	100,000	140,000
GAIN:	$100,000	$175,000	$100,000	$ 60,000
TAX CALCULATIONS:*				
First $50,000:	12,500	12,500	12,500	12,500
Over $50,000:	17,500	43,750	17,500	3,500
TOTAL TAX:	$ 30,000	$ 56,250	$ 30,000	$ 16,000
PRICE:	$200,000	$300,000	$200,000	$200,000
Less Tax:	30,000	56,250	30,000	15,000
GROSS PROCEEDS:	$170,000	$243,750	$170,000	$185,000
Less Mtg:	50,000	200,000	-0-	-0-
Spendable to reinvest:	$120,000	$ 43,750	$170,000	$185,000
Orig. Equity:	$150,000	$100,000	$200,000	$200,000
Amt. lost from Reinvestment Potential:	$ 30,000	$ 56,250	$ 30,000	$ 15,000
	(20% Drop)	(56¼% Drop)	(15% Drop)	(7½% Drop)

*Tax calculated on gain at 25% for first $50,000 and 35% on all gain over that amount. This is not to be considered the exact method, but should result in the maximum tax to be obtained in any situation. When compared to a sale, tax preference items could make the exchange even more desirable.

Loss in reinvestment potential from a sale can mean a 50% or better reduction in buying power. You do not have to show any further calculations to indicate the tax savings in exchanging. The advantages are there. As you can see, they do not have the same results for everyone. Greenbalm, for example, will only see a 7½% drop in his reinvestment capability in after-tax funds in a sale, while Blackburn takes a beating of a 56¼% drop. When you find a high gain and a low percent of equity in the same property, exchanges are highly beneficial. Low gain or no gain has little or no affect on the owner from a tax point of view.

It is not unusual to have an exchange where one of the properties is free and clear. When there is no mortgage relief—when the owner of a free and clear property exchanges for another property—the only gain that would be recognized would be the boot received. Most exchanges, however, do involve properties which are mortgaged. It will be necessary to use the charts shown in this chapter or other calculations to arrive at the realized gain and the taxable gain.

Thus far, I have mentioned only gain. However, it is possible to have a situation where there is a loss. When a property has a basis above the value in the exchange, the basis passes through to the new property as in the gain situations. The loss, however, is not recognized. The exchange benefits, due to the tax-free provisions of the law, allow gains to pass on in many situations without tax at the time of the transaction. However, the loss cannot be taken until disposition of the later property.

THE EFFECT THE EXCHANGE HAS ON DEPRECIATION

As previously mentioned, one of the benefits of exchanges is the enhancement of depreciation. This can be seen in the following actual history. Matthews owns a 100-unit apartment house. He built the complex 16 years ago and has a present basis of $900,000. His present annual depreciation is approximately $20,000 per year and declining. The present fair market value is $2,300,000. The total debt on the property is only $500,000. Matthews' desire is to exchange for more income-producing property. He wants to generate some cash and at the same time increase his tax shelter.

After examining a proposed sale, Matthews realizes that an outright cash sale would leave him with $1,233,750 for reinvestment.

SALES PRICE:	$2,300,000
Less Closing Cost and Commissions	125,000
Net Sales Price	$2,175,000
Less Adjusted Basis	900,000
GAIN*	$1,275,000
Tax on first $50,000 (25%)	$ 12,500
Tax on Balance (35%)	428,750
TOTAL TAX	$ 441,250
Restate Net Sales Price	$2,175,000
Less Total Tax	441,250
GROSS BALANCE FOR REINVESTMENT (Only if Free and Clear)	$1,733,750
If mortgaged, deduct mortgage balance	500,000
NET BALANCE FOR REINVESTMENT	$1,233,750

*No provision made for added tax due to tax preference item calculations.

Matthews knows the benefit of the exchange and the ability to use his full equity in making it. He can take a quick look at the amount of the tax ($441,250) and see that that power of reinvestment is lost in a sale. All this means a lot to Matthews, but his real motivation is to build up more tax shelter by increasing his basis.

The benefit of tax shelter, or the paper loss attributed to the effect of the accounting for depreciation, is very real. Because of this paper loss, income which would normally be taxed at earned income rates passes on to the owner untaxed. The ultimate pick-up on the previous depreciation is a capital gain rate. This occurs because when you depreciate a business item (building, furniture, etc., in this context), the amount of depreciation is taken as an expense. This expense is a deduction to income, thereby reducing the taxable income by that amount. The basis is the function of this depreciation against the capital investment. In essence, basis is what you pay for a property, what you add to it, less what amount you depreciate. If you sell a property you have owned for ten years for the same amount you paid for it ten years earlier, you will have a gain equal to the amount of the depreciation you may have taken. However the gain is taxed at capital gains rates instead of income rates, and this difference can be quite favorable to the owner.

When the owner of a property takes an accelerated form of depreciation, or is nearing the end of depreciation for major items in a property, this paper loss may drop to the point that the continued conversion of earned income to capital gains income is below desired levels. Couple this with the high gain on a sale, and you see that the exchange can increase depreciation and continue to transfer the earned income to capital gains.

How Matthews Made An Exchange To Increase His Depreciation

Matthews knew that he had a net equity (after closing cost and commissions) equal to the net sales price less his existing mortgages ($2,175,000–$500,000 = $1,675,000). He also knew that to increase his basis in an exchange he either had to: (1) pay addtional cash or other boot, or (2) assume mortgages greater than those that he had on his property. Now keep in mind that Matthews wanted to get some cash out of the deal—not only to pay his closing cost and commissions, but also to have a few dollars left over to cover possible taxes. This meant that he was not going to add cash.

Matthews' broker found him a moderate-size shopping center. Price: $3,750,000. Existing financing was $1,750,000, leaving the owner of that center with a $2,000,000 equity.

Remember, Matthews' net equity is only $1,675,000; gross equity is $1,800,000. Matthews felt he needed $125,000 for costs and fees plus $100,000 in cash. Therefore, he had to clear $225,000 in cash from the transaction.

EQUITY BALANCE FOR MATTHEWS

	(Mathews)	(Center Owner)
GROSS PRICE	$2,300,000	
Less Mortgages of Record	500,000	
PRESENT EQUITY	$1,800,000	
Less Cash Wanted (paid by other party)	225,000	
EQUITY AVAILABLE FOR EXCHANGE	$1,575,000	
GROSS PRICE		$3,750,000
Less Mortgages of Record		1,750,000
Present Equity		$2,000,000
BALANCE OF EQUITY		
Cash Received		
Mortgages Held by		425,000
EQUITY BALANCE	$1,575,000	$1,575,000
PARTIES GET		
Property Value	$3,750,000	$2,300,000
Cash	225,000	-0-
Other Boot	-0-	425,000
TOTAL	$3,975,000	$2,725,000
Less Existing Financing	1,750,000	500,000
Less new Financing	425,000	-0-
Less Cash Paid	-0-	225,000
Balance to Present Equity	$1,800,000	$2,000,000

Matthews has solved his part of the problem. The exchange was able to generate cash from the financing structure used. He merely gives the owner of the center a second mortgage in the amount of $425,000 so the equities balance. The calculations shown for Matthews will be helpful to you in balancing other equities where you must generate cash for your commission.

The exchange proposed by Matthews would no doubt cause problems for the other side. Where is the shopping center owner going to come up with the money to make the deal, even if he wants the exchange? This question did, in fact, become the selling factor in this case. Matthews did not want to refinance his center, but the fact was that he had obtained a commitment in the amount of $1,800,000. Once the center owner had the apartment units, he went to the same lender and obtained a loan for $1,800,000. He paid off the existing loan and the mortgage cost of $36,000. The amount he netted after the transaction looked like this:

New Loan Proceeds:	$1,800,000
Less:	
Cash paid to Matthews	225,000
Commission on his side	100,000
Mortgage cost	36,000
Pay off mortgage	500,000
NET CASH PROCEEDS	$ 939,000

What Did Matthews' Net Base Look Like, And How Much New Depreciation Did He Gain?

Reminder: Matthews' original basis was $900,000. His annual depreciation was down to $20,000 per year and declining. This is the result of a rapid write-off using an accelerated depreciation calculation.

What is his new base? To find a new basis you can follow this formula:

Begin with old basis of your old property	$ 900,000
Add Capitalized Closing Costs	125,000
TOTAL REPRESENTS ADJUSTED BASIS	$1,025,000
ADD: 1. Cash paid	$ -0-
2. Other non cash boot given	-0-
3. Existing financing assumed or taken over	1,750,000
4. New seller-held financing (or third party)	425,000
5. Amount of gain taxed	225,000
TOTAL	$3,425,000
THEN SUBTRACT:	
6. Mortgage or total financing existing on old property exchanged	500,000
7. Amount of cash received	225,000
8. Amount of noncash boot received	-0-
TOTAL REPRESENTS THE NEW BASIS IN THE PROPERTY RECEIVED	$2,700,000

Matthews' new basis was $2,700,000. It was allocated by further agreement with the owner of the center to reflect land at 20% and buildings and equipment at 80%. This gave Matthews $2,160,000 of depreciable property. He then set this up on a straight line scale and obtained $86,400 per year of depreciation expenses over the next 25 years.

New depreciation expense allowance	$86,400
Old depreciation expense	$20,000
Gain in Annual Depreciation	$66,400

Exchanges such as the one involving Matthews are not uncommon. You will have the ability to understand the various aspects that will come up in many other types of exchanges if you understand what happened with Matthews. The motivation and the goals desired were met without difficulty. The broker in the transaction collected two fees, since both parties in an exchange pay a fee. Each party obtained cash out of the transaction—Matthews from the primary exchange and the shopping center owner from the refinancing of the apartments.

SOME FINE POINTS OF EXCHANGING—AND HOW TO IMPROVE YOUR ABILITY IN MAKING MORE AND LARGER TRANSACTIONS

1. *Be on the lookout for exchanges wherever you go.* Any time you talk to an owner or prospective buyer of real estate, ask them if they have anything they would like to exchange. Sometimes the buyer will suggest a piece of property you have not been talking about and the seller is always a prime candidate for the tool.
2. *Learn to negotiate with other exchangers.* You will benefit from their experience, or at least will become comfortable in the language they use. It is a good idea to write up several hypothetical deals for self-practice before you sit down with your clients. If there aren't any advanced exchangers around to talk to, don't worry. See your attorney and have him go over one of the standard exchange forms with you so you will be able to use it properly. Tell him that you are going to make some big deals (you will if you try), and that as your business improves so will his.
3. *Don't get hung up on the math of the exchange.* First of all, it is not hard. You only have to follow the sequence, as shown in this chapter, to get at the right answers. Much of the time you will have help. When it comes to calculating the tax on the gain, you will have to pass that task on to the client's accountant anyway. The tax samples shown here are only estimates. You will never be able to arrive at the exact tax unless you have considerable knowledge of the client's other income. Whenever you do show a tax consequence, be sure to point out the assumptions you need. Once you have the client's accountant working with you, he will do the rest of the calculations. Keep in mind that in math, there are different ways of arriving at the same solution. Don't be quick to tell the accountant he has figured it out wrong, unless you see his calculations and know what assumptions he used.

4. *Use exchanges in other parts of financing.* This is a tool to be used for finding solutions to your clients' problems. You can and will find ways to mix this form with others. For example, it is possible to take a property and break it up into land and buildings. Once values are set, you can sell part and exchange the other. Sale and lease-backs can be intermixed into exchanging. A property can be sold, leased back, and the leasehold later exchanged for some other property. The possibilities are nearly endless.
5. *Don't become a professional exchanger.* There are a few people who have made that transition successfully. I am of the opinion, however, that this is just one way to skin the cat. If you rely on this format alone and are unwilling to consider the possibility that you or your client should not exchange, then you will not be objective in your service. Be flexible.
6. *Take the upper hand.* You can become experienced in exchanging in a very short time. Try to read more about the topic. Articles often appear in some of the major real estate publications. Look for these new ideas used by others. Watch for changes in the law that affect exchanges.

Chapter 13

Wrap-Around Mortgages: How to Use Them Effectively

No tool can be as effective in helping to solve your financing problems as the wrap-around mortgage. Wrap-around mortgages are, at the same time, one of the most misunderstood forms of financing. Yet, they are quite common and are found in all areas of financing.

WHAT IS A WRAP-AROUND MORTGAGE?

The wrap-around mortgage is any mortgage, no matter what its form is, that encompasses or wraps around other mortgages. For example, Norstead is selling his motel. He has first, second, and third existing mortgages on the property. He is going to hold paper in addition to the cash down. Instead of holding a separate document in the amount of the fourth mortgage, he holds a mortgage in the total amount of the existing financing, *plus* the amount of what would have been the fourth mortgage. This new mortgage is a wrap-around mortgage. The buyer will make one payment from which Norstead must then see that the existing mortgages are paid, and he keeps the difference. Norstead is in a fourth position of priority—the same rank as the fourth mortgage.

This capacity to wrap-around other financing will give added dimension to the application of some of the other forms of financing described previously. The wrap-around provision is adaptable to many situations and can have a varying effect on the parties involved. It is a form of financing that has positive benefits for both the mortgagor and the mortgagee (the buyer and the seller).

The purpose of this chapter is to detail the use of this truly creative form of financing. By going into its use and learning some of the fine points of the form, you will be able to generate sales and make deals that have eluded you in the past. The wrap-around can and does overcome many objections to seller-held financing, and can be the most important secondary financing tool you will use.

In continuing with a description of what a wrap-around is, it becomes necessary to tell you what it is not.

1. It is not a magic cure-all form of financing. No single form of financing can do as much as the wrap-around mortgage. Nonetheless, this fact does not make the wrap-around absolute. There will often be times when the situation will not lend itself to the application of this tool.

2. It is not a first mortgage. It is impossible for a wrap-around mortgage to hold a first position against all the property pledged as security. Because the mortgage by its description wraps around other mortgages, there must be at least one superior mortgage on at least part of the property pledged as security prior to the use of the wrap. All wrap-arounds are junior mortgages. The position for the mortgagee is one down from the lowest ranking existing mortgage. For example: If there is a $50,000 wrap-around that covers a $20,000 first, a $5,000 second, and a $4,000 third, you can see that the total existing financing is $29,000. There are three mortgages existing, so the position of the difference of $21,000 is a fourth position.

3. It is not required to wrap around all the financing. Nothing in the rule book says that you must wrap around all the financing. It is possible to allow the buyer to assume the first mortgage, and then wrap around the second and third. When there are numerous mortgages, it is possible to have the wrap cover only the bottom mortgages.

HOW A BROKER USED A WRAP-AROUND TO MAKE A SALE

Pallsen wanted to sell his large home for $155,000. He had a low interest rate existing mortgage in the amount of $75,000 with 20 years to go at only 7% per annum. At the time the property was listed the seller did not want to hold any paper, therefore the broker thought he had no choice but to anticipate a need to refinance conventionally to a new first mortgage. Beck, another broker, obtained an offer on the home that called for Pallsen to hold a second mortgage in the amount of $40,000, over 20 years at 9%. Beck had a buyer with $35,000 cash to put down. Pallsen balked at holding the balance of the deal in secondary paper. Beck asked him what he planned to do with the proceeds of the sale. Pallsen said he planned to reinvest, but at higher interest than that shown on the second mortgage. "How much higher?" Beck asked. "At least 11%," Pallsen replied. Beck, knowing about wrap-around mortgages, suggested a counteroffer to the buyer: Pallsen would accept $35,000 cash at closing as offered and would hold a wrap-around mortgage of $40,000 above the existing financing in the amount of $115,000. The terms of the wrap to be 8¾% per annum, based on a 25-year pay-out.

Before the seller could object, Beck went on to demonstrate how this would show a return to him of 11% with a big kicker. Beck explained: The buyer will make only one payment on the $115,000 wrap-around. That payment is based on the 8¾% interest and a 25-year amortization. Pallsen must make the payments due on the existing first and keep the balance. Beck reviewed with Pallsen the difference between the wrap and the existing mortgage. The wrap total is $115,000 less the existing total of $75,000. The difference is thus $40,000. This difference is the seller's principal position in the mortgage. "How much is 11% of $40,000?" Beck asked the seller. "$4,400," Pallsen replied. Beck then asked: "If I could show you 11% plus you would be interested, wouldn't you?" Beck made some notes and checked the payments in his amortization book. He then showed the following to the seller:

Annual payment made by the buyer on the wrap:	$11,350.50
Annual pay-out to be made on the existing first:	6,975.00
BALANCE TO SELLER:	$ 4,375.50
Or 10.9% of $40,000.	

The seller quickly pointed out that the $4,375.50 was not interest only, but the difference between the two mortgage payments. Beck agreed, and pointed out that the above calculations would hold true only for the term of 20 years. The remaining 5 years would not require the reduction by the amount of the first mortgage, as that mortgage was retired on the 20th year. The seller, therefore, would receive $11,350.50 for 5 more years, or $56,752.50. Deducting the $40,000 original, this left $16,752.50. This was a bonus. The total yield on this wrap-around is increased by the adjustment of this bonus. For the moment, however, the seller was getting the yield desired plus the future bonus.

Beck did not calculate this yield to the most accurate percent that he could have. He only wanted to move ahead with the contract at hand and present the wrap as an acceptable alternative to the seller, over his intended use of the funds he would obtain in the sale. Nonetheless, Beck was correct that the yield during the term of the 20 years would be almost 11% and that over the remainder of the 25 years the seller would obtain a bonus. The actual loan made to the buyer had a balloon on the 20th year which returned Pallsen his original capital difference and a bonus.

Transactions such as this reveal the key to the wrap-around in its seller-held usage. The ability to leverage over the interest rate charged against the existing financing is unique to this form of financing, and the net yield to sellers holding such mortgages can be incredible. The increase in interest from one to two points above the interest charged on the existing financing can mean total yields more than doubling the suspected yield.

THE 12 MOST COMMON USES OF A WRAP-AROUND MORTGAGE

1. Use this tool as a method of leveraging a seller's position upward with the idea of increasing the effective yield earned on the mortgage. The ability to increase the return on funds mortgaged is the primary benefit of the wrap-around.

2. To induce the seller to hold secondary paper. The benefits of the increased return may help a broker convince a reluctant seller to take treater paper, or any paper at all for that matter. Many transactions are saved simply because the sellers were made aware of the benefits of this tool.

3. When the existing financing is at a relatively low rate and the constant payment percentage is relatively low, the green flag is out that a wrap-around is potentially viable. The key factor here is the constant rate. More about that later.

4. If the existing financing has any provisions that make prepayment difficult or costly, then the wrap-around mortgage may provide an effective solution to the inability to economically obtain new primary financing. When there are several mortgages encumbering a property, there may be one or more with provisions that will create such problems. It is best to consider the wrap-around when such conditions are present. Sellers unwilling to approach the wrap-around should be made aware of the full impact of their present financing.

5. A nonassumption clause in the existing financing may be an indication that the wrap-around mortgage can be used. There are numerous lenders that have been using these provisions in their loans. When a property is sold, the buyer must make application to the lender to be permitted to assume the obligation. Some lending institutions have taken a harder stand than others, but most will attempt to implement such a provision if money is tight. The lenders often reserve the right to adjust the interest rate when such a new assumption takes place. Battles have been fought over this, both in court and out. The right of the lenders to require a new buyer to assume the obligation and their power to regulate the terms of the loan as a result of that are in question. Nonetheless, a wrap-around mortgage does not have the buyer assume the existing financing. This is a key factor in the whole structure of the wrap-around mortgage, and indirectly has created the difficulty for third parties to lend on the wrap. When a buyer purchases a property and gives the seller a wrap-around mortgage, the existing financing remains the obligation of the seller. The seller makes the payments directly or causes them to be made on the existing mortgages. Some secondary financing which may be encompassed within the wrap may have absolute provisions which would make the wrap-around difficult, but for the most part a nonassumption clause can be overcome by the use of the wrap if the mortgage is held by the seller. Some lenders have taken a new position in this battle against the wrap-around. At this time, clauses which require the mortgage

to be renegotiated in the event the property is sold are being tested. Time will tell, and I suggest you fight hard against such provisions being inserted in any primary financing you obtain.

6. The increase of cash flow is a definite benefit which can be accomplished by using the wrap. Therefore, when the sale of a property is hampered by a low cash flow, look to the wrap-around. In essence, there are only a few ways to increase cash flow. Assuming a status quo in all other factors, the increase of income will accomplish this. If this fails, a reduction of expenses will also increase the cash flow. Often, a combined effect of increased income (via more rents, etc.) and lowered expenses will solve the problem and make the wrap unnecessary. Normally, however, the seller is already maximizing income and minimizing expenses. The resulting Net Operating Income (NOI) can only show an increased cash flow based on lowered debt service. The yield resulting from the cash flow, based on the invested capital, must meet the demand rate. In the general marketing of an income property, the cash down is often based on the seller holding some paper, or with new financing necessary. The cash flow yield may be too low with this form of financing to warrant the investment. The wrap-around can, and often does, solve this problem nicely.

7. Tight mortgage markets bring out the best in the wrap-around. When you find yourself marketing a property which cannot be readily financed due to the current market conditions, you must look to all the possible alternatives. The toughness of the market need only be relative to the overall rate on the existing financing. This means that if you have a property that has very low rates, and the current market is a point or two above those rates, then you should examine the possibility of the wrap. Of course, the complete inability to refinance for any reason within the economics of the deal will bring the wrap into play more quickly and with more dramatic results.

8. Refinancing costs can sometimes be a major problem, and this factor can be a good reason to look to the wrap. The overall effect of placing a wrap-around mortgage is less costly to administer than new financing. The seller need only charge whatever legal cost is involved in the preparation of the loan document, and this should not be much more than the cost of preparing a standard form for a secondary loan.

9. Multimortgaged properties can often be very difficult to sell or market simply because of the number of mortgages present. If you have a property that has three or more existing mortgages, the wrap can convert these into one. The buyer, after all, makes only one payment on the wrap, even though the seller must direct payments out to the encompassed mortgages.

10. A short balloon in existing financing can create many difficulties in selling property. If the property is an income producer and the possibilities of refinancing it to cover the balloon payment are slim, then the wrap-around can

provide a solution. Naturally, the amount of the balloon must be considered. But if it is soon due to close and is not excessive, then the wrap may work out.

11. Marketing a property with sound financing can bring about a quicker sale and less negotiating of the price. When a property has only a moderate extension of financing, that is to say a low ratio of the loan to value, the seller's equity will come under attack by buyers anxious to buy at a lower price. It is obvious that a home offered at $100,000 with an $85,000 mortgage leaves only $15,000 to negotiate with. Buyers expect some equity, and will haggle on only the upper limits of such a transaction. The broker utilizes this technique and obtains a commitment from the seller (or a third party lender for that matter), and quotes the wrap-around mortgage in his presentations. This extending of the loan to value ratio will benefit the negotiations. As the buyer approaches the close of the sale, full ramifications of the underlying mortgages encompassed by the wrap will, of course, be disclosed. The first examination, however, need only show the higher wrap.

12. Buyers will look to the wrap as a tool to be used for their benefit as often as a seller. The buyers' benefits are in the overall comparison with the existing mortgage market, rather than in seller-held, conventional secondary financing. There are a few examples where the buyer will benefit from a wrap, such as when the seller will hold a usual second mortgage for the same terms and rates. The seller will, however, hold a wrap for longer, and often at lower rates than a usual second. Therefore, the buyer can benefit by approaching any situation that may call for refinancing and offer the seller terms only slightly less costly to the buyer in the general lending market. In this way he obtains better terms from the seller than he could at an institutional lender, saves the points, and at the same time passes on to the seller the full benefits of the wrap.

If the primary reason for using the wrap-around is to increase the cash flow on the income property for sale, there may be a sacrifice in some other area. The nature of the wrap-around and its effect on the dollar amounts paid and received by the seller or lender should be clearly understood. In the first place, it is normal for the balance of the "difference" owed to increase for a period of time. Remember, the word "difference" in wrap-around terms refers to the amount of the total wrap-around mortgage that is left whenever you deduct the then present amount owed to the existing financing. A wrap-around in the amount of $100,000 that encompasses a first and a second totaling $80,000 will have an original "difference" of $20,000. This term is not universal, and in some areas this amount the ($20,000) is called the "wrap difference," the "lender's position," or "new money." I shall continue to refer to it as the "difference." This difference will not remain constant throughout the mortgage and normally grows in the early years. To best illustrate what happens to this difference, examine the following case history.

THE FUNCTION OF THE AMORTIZATION AND ITS EFFECT ON THE DIFFERENCE IN WRAP-AROUND MORTGAGES

Hodges sold a shopping center for $2,500,000. He received $350,000 down and held a wrap-around for the balance. The wrap-around was for a face amount of $2,150,000, and was payable over a period of 20 years at 9% per annum in equal monthly installments which totaled $235,532.50. The existing financing was a first mortgage ($1,200,000) at 7½% with 19 years remaining. Annual payment was $120,492. There was a second mortgage in the amount of $700,000 payable over 15 years at 8%. The annual payment was $81,781.

	Mortgages	Face Amount	Annual Payments
	Wrap-Around	$2,150,000	$235,532.50
Less:	1st Mortgage	$1,200,000	$120,492.00
Less:	2nd Mortgage	$ 700,000	$ 81,781.00
Original Difference		$ 250,000	$ 33,259.50

The above calculation is correct only for the moment the wrap-around is made. Each year the balances due on the mortgage will alter. The payment allocation to the difference will also change when the existing mortgages retire.

Here's what occurs at the end of the first year:

	Mtg. Balance At Start Of 1st Year		Total Payment Principal	Total Payment Interest	Balance Owed At End of The 1st Year
	Wrap-Around	$2,150,000	$42,032	$193,500	$2,107,967
Less:	1st Mortgage	$1,200,000	$30,492	$ 90,000	$1,169,508
Less:	2nd Mortgage	$ 700,000	$25,781	$ 56,000	$ 674,219
	Difference	$ 250,000	($14,241)	$ 47,500	$ 264,240

What has happened is this: The balance owed on the wrap-around has declined by the principal paid of $42,032. However, the existing mortgages have declined $56,273. The total owed or remaining as a principal balance on the wrap is $2,107,967. If the mortgage were paid off by the buyer at that time and the existing mortgages satisfied, then $264,240 would remain to apply to the mortgagee or the seller. The original amount at the beginning of the year was only $250,000. The $264,240 is the difference at the end of the first year. This is ($14,241) greater than the original difference of $250,000. What happened shows up in the interest column. The interest on the wrap-around mortgage is $47,500 greater than the combined interest on the first and second mortgages. This $47,500 is net interest earned by the holder of the mortgage, but since he received only $33,259.50 (see previous chart) the total principal amortized on the existing financing exceeded that amortized on the wrap-around. The deficit ($14,241) had to be deducted from the total interest, then added to the balance owed. This constant adding of the deficit interest to the balance applicable to the difference will continue as the mortgage progresses. This is what happens in the second year.

	Mtg. Balance At Start of 2nd Year		Total Payment Principal	Interest	Balance Owed At End Of 2nd Year
	Wrap-Around	$2,107,967	$45,815	$189,717	$2,062,152
Less:	1st Mortgage	$1,169,508	$32,779	$ 87,713	$1,136,729
Less:	2nd Mortgage	$ 674,219	$27,843	$ 53,937	$ 646,375
	Difference	$ 264,240	($14,807)	$ 48,067	$ 279,048

The holder of the wrap still only gets the $33,259.50 cash left after the total payment is received less the existing payments on the first and second mortgages (see first chart). In this year, however, the balance applicable to the difference has grown to $279,048.

The reason for this build-up is not simply explained. It is a function of several factors that combine to create the major leverage to the difference. In the first place, leverage is present in the spread of mortgage rates. The interest charged on the wrap-around is greater than the combined effect of interest charges against the total existing financing. You should be cautioned at this point not to jump to conclusions that all the underlying mortgages must have interest rates below that of the wrap. It is the combined effect you must look at. In a multimortgaged property you may have one or more mortgages with greater interest rates than the wrap-around and still have a build-up of difference owed.

Therefore, the function of the amortization on the balance applicable to the difference will generally be that the amount owed will grow each year until there is a satisfaction of at least one existing mortgage. Keep in mind, however, that this is not always the case, and the actual calculation to determine this factor must be done. To recap the amortization of the wrap-around in this case study, I have provided a breakdown of the mortgages and the difference throughout the full term of the loan. This breakdown is necessary in the understanding of the effective yield gained on the wrap-around and will be used in the larger analysis of this yield later on. The amortization of the mortgages shown in Figure 13-1 gives the amounts owed at the end of the periods shown. Generally, you are dealing with amortizing loans which will have one constant monthly or annual payment that includes interest and principal. Because of this, neither the interest or the principal payments in each period are equal to other previous payments. Therefore, the corresponding balances of each mortgage and the difference must be calculated for each period. In analyzing a mortgage you can be fairly accurate with year-end totals. Only in this way will you know what the pay-off amount applicable to the difference is at any given point of time.

In Figure 13-1, each mortgage is shown with the principal balance outstanding at the end of each period. For example, at the end of 8 years the balance outstanding on the wrap-around mortgage is $1,686,446 (A), the 1st $881,469 (B) the 2nd $452,777 (C), and the difference has grown to $379,200 (E).

THE EFFECTIVE RATE EARNED ON THE WRAP-AROUND

This is the most difficult part of the wrap-around to fully comprehend. The big question is simply this: What is the real (or effective) return to the holder of the wrap?

In looking at the Hodges Shopping Center Analysis Sheet (Figure 13-1), we can see numerous yields. At first glance we see that the seller will receive, after all payments on the existing financing, a balance of $33,259.50 for the time that the existing mortgage debt service remains unchanged. This amount of return, in cash, represents 13.30% of the original balance of the difference ($33,259.50 ÷ $250,000 = 13.30%). However, the balance of the difference does not diminish during the period of full existing debt service. And should the mortgagor pay off the wrap before any of the existing debt is satisfied, the holder will obtain the full $250,000 plus a bonus of built-up interest which was earned but not received. This bonus is in addition to the interest of $33,259.50 received or retained. With this in mind then, until the outstanding difference drops below its original sum, we can treat the wrap as an interest-only return to the mortgagee with the effective yield being this original 13.30% plus the bonus rate.

Therefore, when analyzing the wrap-around there will be more than one rate which you must recognize. First, there is the rate on the retained cash. This represents that sum of money that is actually received net of payments on the existing financing less amortization of the difference. In Figure 13-1, the total cash received on the difference (Column F) is $33,259.50 for the term of the existing financing and will increase when the second is retired. As there is no amortization of the difference during this period, the Retained Total (H) equals Column F. Since the original investment by the mortgagee is $250,000, and that balance owed remains at or above that sum during the term of the existing financing, then the retained cash is 13.30% for that period of time only. This rate becomes the CAP rate of the difference.

In reference to Figure 13-1, you will notice that this annual payment of retained cash changes when the second mortgage is satisfied. All calculations on wrap-around effective rates must be broken down to the periods of the existing financing. When there is no amortization of the difference, which generally will occur only in the first period, the cash received will equal the retained cash. In addition to the effective rate of 13.30% for the retained cash, a bonus also occurs. This bonus is earned but not retained. It cannot be accurately computed until the mortgagee benefits from that sum at some time in the future.

FINDING THE OVERALL EFFECTIVE YIELD OF A WRAP-AROUND MORTGAGE

The first step in finding the effective yield of the bonus is to fill out the wrap-around analysis chart (Figure 13-1). In looking at the amortization chart for the wrap-around mortgage and the existing financing, you will be able to note the year in which the build-up of difference stops and amortization of that balance begins. This is significant since it establishes the year the bonus is benefiting the mortgagee. In the Hodges Shopping Center Case Study (Figure 13-1), this occurs on the 15th year. When there is a build-up or accrual of bonus, the change generally occurs when all or part of the existing financing retires. In some mortgages, the retirement of one mortgage is not sufficient to increase the payment to the difference.

Because the bonus amount is important, and because the data necessary to obtain an accurate effective rate of return is dependent on the Analysis Sheet (Figure 13-1), a brief discussion of how to fill out this sheet is in order. Examine the chart. Notice that there are columns A through J. These ten columns will accommodate a wrap-around and three existing mortgages. If you have a situation where you have more than three existing mortgages, you need to add D1, D2, etc., for each additional mortgage.

HOW TO USE THE WRAP-AROUND MORTGAGE ANALYSIS SHEET

COLUMN (A): The basic information needed which pertains to the wrap should be filled in at the top. The term of years, annual interest rate charged, and annual payment of P & I are important for reference. At the *End of Period O*, you should place the face amount or original balance owed on the wrap-around. In the following years, as the column extends down the page, you can put the principal balances owed at the end of each successive year. This is a purely mathematical calculation which can be done easily with a two-memory calculator or can be obtained from an amortization schedule. It should be noted that the years shown are the *end of that period,* and in order to find the balance owed at the *beginning of a year* you need to look to the balance owed at the end of the previous year.

COLUMNS (B), (C) & (D): These columns contain the same type of information as Column A, except that they are for the currently existing mortgages. Most sellers will have amortization schedules for this information.

Figure 13-1: HODGES SHOPPING CENTER—CASE STUDY ANALYSIS

End of Period	THE WRAP-AROUND PRINCIPAL BALANCE @ $2,150,000 Wrap-Around Mtg. Yrs. 20 Rate 9% Payment $235,532.50 (A)	EXISTING FINANCING PRINCIPAL BALANCE AT END OF PERIOD $1,200,000 1st Mtg. Yrs. 19 Rate 7½% Payment $120,492 (B)	$700,000 2nd Mtg. Yrs. 15 Rate 8% Payment $ 81,781 (C)	3rd Mtg. Yrs. ____ Rate ____ Payment ____ (D)
0	$2,150,000	$1,200,200	$700,000	
1	2,107,967	1,169,508	674,219	
2	2,062,152	1,136,792	646,375	
3	2,012,213	1,101,492	616,035	
4	1,957,780	1,063,612	583,828	
5	1,898,448	1,022,891	548,753	
6	1,833,775	979,115	510,872	
7	1,763,283	932,057	469,961	
8	1,686,446	881,469	452,777	
9	1,602,693	827,087	378,058	
10	1,511,403	768,627	326,522	
11	1,411,897	705,781	270,863	
12	1,303,435	638,223	210,750	
13	1,185,212	565,598	145,830	
14	1,056,348	487,525	75,715	
15	915,887	403,598	-0-	
16	762,785	313,376	-0-	
17	595,903	216,387	-0-	
18	414,002	112,124	-0-	
19	215,729	-0-	-0-	
20	-0-	-0-	-0-	
21				
22				
23				
24				
25				

	DIFFERENCE					
	Difference $250,000 20 Yrs. Varies	Total Cash Received on Difference $33,259.50	Difference Amortized	Retained Interest	Annual Interest Rate	Earned but Not Retained Bonus
	(E)	(F)	(G)	(H)	(I)	(J)
0	$250,000					
1	264,240	$33,259.50	-0-	$33,259.50	13.30%	$14,240
2	279,048	33,259.50	-0-	33,259.50	13.30%	29,048
3	294,416	33,259.50	-0-	33,259.50	13.30%	44,416
4	310,340	33,259.50	-0-	33,259.50	13.30%	60,340
5	326,804	33,259.50	-0-	33,259.50	13.30%	76,804
6	343,788	33,259.50	-0-	33,259.50	13.30%	93,788
7	361,265	33,259.50	-0-	33,259.50	13.30%	111,265
8	379,200	33,259.50	-0-	33,259.50	13.30%	129,200
9	397,548	33,259.50	-0-	33,259.50	13.30%	147,548
10	416,254	33,259.50	-0-	33,259.50	13.30%	166,254
11	435,253	33,259.50	-0-	33,259.50	13.30%	185,253
12	454,462	33,259.50	-0-	33,259.50	13.30%	204,462
13	473,784	33,259.50	-0-	33,259.50	13.30%	223,784
14	493,108	33,259.50	-0-	33,259.50	13.30%	243,108
15	512,289	33,259.50	-0-	33,259.50	13.30%	262,289
16	449,409	115,040.50	62,880	52,160.50	10.18%	199,409
17	379,516	115,040.50	69,893	45,147.50	10.05%	129,516
18	301,878	115,040.50	77,638	37,402.50	9.86%	51,878
19	215,729	115,040.50	86,149	28,891.50	9.57%	34,271
20	-0-	235,532.50	215,729	19,803.50	9.18%	
21						
22						
23						
24						
25						

COLUMN (E): This is the balance owed on the *Difference* and the most important part of this computation. If there is no amortization of the difference, as will usually be the case in early years, this amount will grow. The total in this column represents the net payoff to the mortgagee at the end of any given year. This column will indicate when the difference peaks out and begins to amortize. Subtracting the original balance of the *Difference* from the amount in this column at the end of any year will give you the amount of the *Bonus* thus far accrued (to be shown on Column J).

COLUMN (F): The *total cash received* on the difference is the amount of net cash left over after the existing mortgage payments are deducted from the payments received on the wrap-around. These payments will remain constant for the separate periods of the existing financing. If you have only one existing mortgage that is satisfied before the end of the wrap, you will have only two periods. This column is very easy to calculate and should present no difficulty.

COLUMN (G): Difference Amortized. This column will contain amounts only for the years when the difference is declining. These amounts are found by looking at Column E. In Column E you have the amount of the difference as it increases and then declines. You need not be concerned with the increase in the Column G calculation, only the decline. The amount amortized is the amount of decline each year as seen in the reduction of Column E. When the total in Column E does begin to drop, deduct the end of the year amount from the previous year.

COLUMNS (H) & (I): It is generally best to do these two columns as one calculation. The Retained Interest and Annual Interest Rate are found as follows: The Retained Interest—Column F (Total Cash Received on Difference) less Column G (Difference Amortized). The result will be the interest portion of the total cash actually received. In most all instances of a wrap-around, the amortization (G) occurs late in the term of the wrap.

The Annual Interest Rate is found by dividing the interest received by: (1) In the event of 0 amortization as seen in Column G, by the original balance of the Difference; (2) In the event of amortization, by the amount of the difference at the start of that year (end of the previous year). You may have a very low Annual Interest Rate when the total cash received in the early years is just above the existing mortgage payments. Therefore, a low Annual Interest Rate is not unusual.

COLUMN (J): Earned but Not Retained Bonus. This column need not be filled in completely. Its function is to show the amount of accrual of "extra lending." It represents the amount found in Column E (Difference) less the original balance of the Difference. You need only put in this calculation the year the difference peaks out. (The year before amortization begins on Column D, as shown in Column G.) This amount you will show in Column J is the total Bonus for that period. Generally, this is the only bonus you will have for a wrap-around.

In the example given in Figure 13-1, you will note that on the line which corresponds to the end of the 15th year under Column E the difference peaks out at $512,289. Further review of the remaining pay-out of the wrap-around and the existing financing indicates that the difference amortizes beginning the 16th year. The amount of the amortization (G) is simply found by subtracting the current year's balance from the previous year's balance. The retained interest total (H) is the total cash received (F) less the amount of amortization (G).

The Bonus Column (J) is the accrual of the earned but not retained portion of the difference. Of course, it peaks along with the difference. This bonus can be deemed to become a benefit at the time the difference begins to amortize. In essence, the return to the mortgagee can no longer be treated as interest only, as was done as the difference grew. Instead, the Annual Interest Rate must take into account the bonus. While the difference was growing, the Annual Interest Rate was found by dividing the retained interest by the original difference. Now, as the mortgagee is receiving benefit from a new difference, the Annual Interest Rates, for years when there is amortization, are found by dividing the retained interest by the balance of the difference owed at the end of the previous year. For example: At the end of the 15th year the difference was $512,289. During that year the difference had grown and there was no amortization. However, in the 16th year there was a reduction of $62,880 and the balance at the end of that year was $449,409. A total of $115,040.50 was kept by the mortgagee. Of that amount, the $62,880 is Principal Reduction of the New Difference (Benefit) and $52,160.50 Interest. The Annual Rate for this interest retained (I) is found by dividing $52,160.50 by $512.289. The result is 10.18%. In essence, for that year the mortgagee earned 10.18% on the mortgage of $512,289.00.

The following year shows a reduction of the New Difference by $69,893.00 and an Interest Retained of $45,147.50. The Annual Rate for the 17th Year is 10.05% (45,147.50 ÷ 449,409). This calculation is carried out each year until the balance of the wrap is satisfied. By doing these calculations, it is possible to complete the full analysis sheet and to proceed to the final calculation of the overall effective yield for the mortgage.

The first step is to arrive at the Primary Effective Rate which occurs during the early years when the difference is growing. To make this computation easier, I have provided a chart, Figure 13-2, to follow. (This chart shows Sections A and B of the necessary calculation.) The use of this chart is not as complicated as it may appear. Once Columns A through J have been filled, in simple math, the use of the sinking fund table provided in this book and a small calculator will make fast work of the Primary Effective Rate. It is important to note, however, that the Primary Effective Rate will not be the final answer unless the mortgage were to balloon during the period the difference is still growing.

Figure 13-2: PRIMARY EFFECTIVE RATE CALCULATIONS WHEN DIFFERENCE GROWS . . .

SECTION A

(A) Amount of Original Difference: $ ______

(B) Annual Cash Retained: $ ______

(C) Annual Interest Rate (Line B ÷ Line A) (state as decimal): ______

(D) Total New Difference: $ ______

(E) Amount of Bonus (D less A): $ ______

(F) % of Bonus (Line E ÷ A) (state as decimal): ______

(G) Total Years for Period: ______ # years.

(H) Total Benefit at Period (Line B × Years) + Line E: $ ______

(I) Average Annual Benefit (Line H ÷ Years): $ ______

(J) Average Rate (Line I ÷ Line A) (state as decimal): ______

Note: Primary Effective Rate will lie between Average Rate (Line J) and Annual Interest Rate (Line C).

SECTION B

The Formula to Find P.E.R. (Shown Below)

Primary Effective Rate — (% of Bonus* × 1 S_N) = Annual Interest Rate

*Shown as a Decimal

1. Target ______ Annual Int. Rate
2. Less ______ (A)
3.
4. ______ (B)

INTERPOLATION

$$PER = \_\_\_\_\_\_ + \frac{.01 \times (A)}{(B)}$$

PER = ______

Taking the known facts from the Hodges Shopping Center Case study, Figure 13-1, examine how the Primary Effective Rate for the first period was obtained. Note that the first period is the time the difference was still growing.

The Question Is Stated As Follows: If $250,000 is invested now and the investor receives $33,259.50 each year for 15 years, and at the end of the 15-year period has a return of his investment plus $262,289, what is the investor's effective rate of return? This data is found in the computations on the Analysis Chart (Figure 13-1). With this information, fill in and compute Section A of the Effective Rate Calculation.

Figure 13-3: PRIMARY EFFECTIVE RATE CALCULATIONS WHEN DIFFERENCE GROWS . . .

SECTION A

(A) Amount of Original Difference:	$250,000.00
(B) Annual Cash Retained:	$ 33,259.50 (Column F)
(C) Annual Interest Rate (Line B ÷ Line A) (state as decimal):	.1330 (13.3%)
(D) Total New Difference:	$512,289.00 (Column E at 15th yr.)
(E) Amount of Bonus (D less A):	$262,289.00 (Column J at 15th yr.)
(F) % of Bonus (Line E ÷ A) (state as decimal):	1.0492
(G) Total Years for Period:	15 yrs.
(H) Total Benefit at Period (Line B × Years) + Line E:	$761,181.50
(I) Average Annual Benefit (Line H ÷ Years)	$ 50,745.43
(J) Average Rate (Line I ÷ Line A) (state as decimal):	.202982 (20.2982%)

To complete the Primary Effective Rate calculation, it is necessary to complete Section B of the chart (Figure 13-4).

Since the following calculation requires an assumption to begin with, examine the relationship of the Annual Interest Rate and the Average Rate. The Annual Interest Rate shown is .1330 (or 13.3%) and the Average Rate is .202982 (or 20.298%). The Primary Effective Rate will lie somewhere between these two.

The formula is: P.E.R.—(% of Bonus × 1 S_N) = Annual Interest Rate. The calculation 1 S_N is found in the sinking fund table provided in this book. Because the P.E.R. is unknown, make a guess at a rate slightly less than halfway between the Annual Interest Rate and the Average Rate. In this case use .16 (16%) as a starting point. In completing the formula you will look in the sinking fund table under the rate you assume to be correct for the period of years which in this example would be .16 (16%). Look at the 16% table for the 15th year. The resulting number represents 1 S_N for 16% at 15 years. The number shown in the table is .019358. From the previous Section A of this chart on Line F, the percent of the Bonus has been found. That number, shown as a decimal, is 1.0492. The Annual Interest Rate, also found in Section A on Line C is .1330. Now complete the formula with the first assumed interest rate as shown on Figure 13-4, Line 1.

Figure 13-4: PRIMARY EFFECTIVE RATE CALCULATIONS WHEN DIFFERENCE GROWS . . .

SECTION B

The Formula to Find P.E.R. (Shown Below)

Primary Effective Rate—(% of Bonus* × 1 S_N) = Annual Interest Rate

*Shown as a Decimal

1.	.16 − (1.0492 × .019358) = .139689	Target:	.13300 Annual Interest Rate
2.	.15 − (1.0492 × .021017) = .127949	Less:	.12795
	.011740 (B)		.00505 (A)
3.			
4.			

INTERPOLATION

$$PER = \frac{.15}{} + \left(\frac{.01 \times .00505\ (A)}{.011740\ \ (B)}\right)$$

PER = .15 + .00430, thus PER = .1543 (PER = 15.43%)

The resulting Annual Interest Rate on the assumed P.E.R. of 16% exceeds the Target Rate. The Target Rate is the Actual Annual Interest Rate of .1330. Therefore, it is necessary to reduce the assumed rate. Try .15 (15%). In the table, locate 15% at the 15th year. The corresponding number is .02017. Therefore, the second part of the calculation would appear as .15 − (1.0492 × .02017) = .127949.

The Annual Interest Rate found with this assumed rate of 15% is less than the Target Rate. By subtracting the Annual Interest Rate on this lower interest from both the *Target Rate* (actual Annual Interest Rate) and Annual Interest Rate on the higher interest (16%), you can obtain the basis for Interpolation.

(1)	.16 − (1.0492 × .01968) = .139689	*Target:*	.13300
(2)	.15 − (1.0492 × .02017) = .127949		.127949
	.01 .011740 (B)		.00505 (A)

The Interpolation will approximate the Effective Rate once you have narrowed it down. In the lower tables, you can come very close to the actual rate and will not have to use a full point spread in your assumed rates. The formula for the Interpolation is:

$$\text{PRIMARY EFFECTIVE RATE} = \text{Lowest Rate Assumed} + \left(\frac{\text{Spread} \times \text{Difference A}}{\text{Difference B}}\right)$$

therefore . . .

$$\text{PRIMARY EFFECTIVE RATE} = .15 + \left(\frac{.01 \times .00505}{.011740}\right)$$

PRIMARY EFFECTIVE RATE = .1543 (stated as a % = 15.43%)

The Primary Effective Rate for the Case Study, as of the end of the 15th year, is 15.43%. If the mortgage were to balloon on that date, there would be no further calculations. If the mortgage were to be paid off earlier than the 15 years, the entire process would be computed on the balances and amounts applicable for the specific period of time.

Should the mortgage continue beyond the 15th year, the annual yield for each succeeding year would have to be added to the multiple of the Effective Rate thus far obtained and the years received. See these calculations on the consolidation section of the Effective Yield Calculation (Figure 13-5).

Figure 13-5: CONSOLIDATION OF YIELD

Period of Wrap-Around Analyzed	Effective Rate Per Period: Annual Interest Rate	Effective Rate Per Period: Primary Effective Rate	No. of Years Rate Earned	Rate × Yrs.
1st PERIOD		15.43	15	231.45
2nd PERIOD	10.18		1	10.18
3rd PERIOD	10.05		1	10.05
4th PERIOD	9.86		1	9.86
5th PERIOD	9.57		1	9.57
6th PERIOD	9.18		1	9.18
7th PERIOD				
8th PERIOD				
9th PERIOD				
10th PERIOD				
11th PERIOD				
12th PERIOD				
Combined Totals of Rate × Years: Total				280.29
Divide By Term of Years on Wrap: Effective Rate				14.015%

Figure 13-5 gives you the Effective Rate of Interest earned by the mortgagee over the term of the mortgage. This sum, 14.015% is the result of the leverage obtained over the existing financing. You can see that a balloon on the

15th year would have given an effective yield over those 15 years of 15.43%. The later years of this wrap-around gave a higher cash flow return than the early years. However, the benefit or bonus return accounted for the majority of that cash flow. It would have been best to have obtained the full benefit at the 15th year.

HOW TO USE THE EFFECTIVE RATE IN SELLING THE WRAP-AROUND CONCEPT TO A MORTGAGEE

Keep in mind that the majority of mortgagees you will deal with will be sellers. The wrap-around is a prime tool for increasing return to a seller, and this fact alone can convince many sellers who are reluctant to hold paper to do just that. To see this point clearly, examine the case study again (Figure 13-1). A wrap-around in the amount of $2,150,000 was created for 20 years at 9% per annum. The difference held by the seller was $250,000. Over the term of the loan the seller received a total annual yield of 14.015%. What this really means is that in order for the seller to have done as well he would have had to hold a fourth mortgage at that same interest rate or greater. A buyer offered that kind of financing may balk at such a high rate. The leverage shown in the case study was not exceptional for the wrap-around, and it is not uncommon for you to have much more dramatic results than that. Nonetheless, a 14.015% per annum return is not readily available and may be enough to motivate the seller. In third-party lending this same advantage will hold true. The third-party lender comes in and uses the same benefit to increase this overall yield on new money lent. The technique you use in convincing a seller of the advantages of holding the wrap-around, instead of normal secondary paper, will depend on your fully understanding this leverage. The seller may find it to his advantage to accept a little more or even a lot more paper in order to take this increased yield. Yet, there are also other advantages to the seller in holding a wrap. All of these are discussed in the next section.

ADVANTAGES TO THE SELLER OR OTHER MORTGAGEE AND HOW TO CAPITALIZE ON THEM

1. Effective yield increases. This is one of the most important advantages unique to the wrap-around. Great leverages in annual return are common-place in wraps. No form of secondary financing can be as productive in increasing yield for the lender.

2. Default notice. When a seller or other mortgagee holds a wrap-around mortgage, the owner of the property makes one payment to the mortgagee. From this payment the mortgagee then causes the existing mortgage payments to be made. Because the new owner has no control over this act, his default will come at the level of the wrap. In other words, if the new buyer falls behind in his payments the wrap mortgagee is the first to know. Action to collect, and even foreclosure if necessary, can be made at an early date—well before the existing mortgages themselves become overdue or go far in arrears. Of course, the mortgagee can easily step in and pay down the existing financing with no difficulty in the wrap. This advantage is considerable. If the mortgagor is going into arrears, it is not unusual for the mortgage having the lowest priority to be the last to be paid. It is possible and quite common, for example, for a new owner of multi-mortgaged property in financial difficulty to let the last mortgage (the third or fourth mortgage held by your seller) to go unpaid. In the meantime, this mortgagor may keep the first mortgage current for a while, then slip into problems. But if the seller-held mortgage is sizable, the mortgagor may keep that one current and let the first mortgages go into default. Even with provisions that lenders are to notify the other mortgagees of any default, this may not occur until a bad situation has advanced into a most impossible default.

The wrap-around solves this problem nicely. Point out the priority of a fourth mortgage to your seller and show him the possibility of not knowing about economic problems the new buyer is having until it is too late. With the wrap-around he still has the same position against the property, but he gets all the money and makes the payments himself.

3. The selling tool works for the seller. When you are marketing a property and have the ability to provide what appears to be an excellent mortgage, at terms under current rates and years longer than those available at local lenders, you have a good advantage in selling the property. This advantage goes to the seller. It is important to remember that you need not offer alternatives. A buyer may well understand the leverage of the interest on the existing mortgages and may not want to have that advantage pass on to the seller or some other party. In this event, he may ask the seller to hold secondary paper at a nominal interest rate and take over or assume the existing mortgages at their lower rate. The fact that the seller will hold a wrap, however, should become the new financing offered. Hence, the comparison that a buyer must make is not between the wrap and normal assumption of the existing mortgages and secondary paper, but between the terms offered on the wrap and the conventional terms available at local lenders. The wrap will compete favorably in almost any market, providing the existing financing can be wrapped around. In marketing a property with the wrap, you will find it easy to make this comparison: "Mr. Buyer, we have provided terms which are far better than those currently available at the local lenders. This fact, the ease in closing on the property due to this mortgage, and no points are to your advantage." So, while this is a seller's advantage it is a buyer's advantage as well.

4. Maintain installment sale. The wrap-around mortgage has a most important use that has nothing to do with leverage on rates or even its use as a marketing tool. When a property that has a very low basis is sold, there is a capital gain circumstance that can often be costly. If the owner of the property for sale has mortgages above the basis, simply to receive a sale, with no money down, can cause tax to be due. For example: Barkley owned a sizable office building for nearly 20 years. The current basis is only $50,000 even though the fair market value is over $500,000. He had placed new financing on the property a few years ago and currently owes $300,000 on it. He had a buyer willing to pay $500,000 with $100,000 down. Barkley determined that he would have a $425,000 adjusted gain in the sale and over $140,000 in capital gains tax. To make the sale would require him to come out-of-pocket over $40,000, plus fees, commissions, and other closing costs.

A wrap-around mortgage was established in the amount of $400,000, payable over 20 years at a nominal interest rate. As Barkley was still on the mortgage and the buyer did not assume the liability, he was not relieved of that amount of debt. The income that came in over the term of the wrap-around allowed Barkley to maintain an installment sale since he did not receive more than 30% in any year. The capital gains tax was still there, but now it was payable over the term as though a normal installment sale had taken place.

ADVANTAGES TO A BUYER OF PURCHASING WITH A WRAP

1. The best terms in town. The wrap-around is so flexible that a high effective yield can be passed on to the mortgagee even though the buyer has a better rate and years than available elsewhere. The buyer saves on points, and when given no alternative of closing with assumption of the existing financing and the seller holding normal secondary paper, he will choose the wrap. Of course, the wrap can also offer better terms than assumption and secondary paper. If the existing financing has a low interest rate, but also a short term to go, the annual payment may be just about as high as the buyer can pay or the property can stand. To place on top of that a second mortgage of even the most modest annual payment may be more than either the buyer or the property will pay. The wrap has the capability of having a very low retained interest on the difference. The build-up of the bonus and its later recoupment and greater yield are most unique to this form of financing. This factor can save many transactions that have a short balloon in one of the existing mortgages by having that mortgage amortized out of the total wrap and carrying forward the new difference to a later year.

Many buyers are cash flow conscious. They don't really look to the term of the mortgage. A 20-year mortgage is just 10 years less than a 30-year mortgage. When an investor is looking at how much cash he gets now on his down payment, then the wrap can keep the debt service at a more constant level, and often much lower than other forms of mortgages.

2. *Increase cash flow.* Because the wrap can provide a lower total annual payment (even though over a longer term) than a combination of existing financing and secondary financing, the advantage to a buyer in the case of income property can be considerable. A property with a NOI of $20,000 and existing debt service of $15,000 provides a cash flow of $5,000. If the investor demands a 10% cash flow yield he can pay $50,000 cash to the existing financing. However, the seller may want $60,000 to the existing financing. If the combined cash down and balance owed is within the fair market value range and the seller is firm on the price, the wrap can provide the answer. The question to answer here is: What total amount of wrap, at what interest rate, for how long, will cover the existing mortgage and its constant annual payment? Assume that the amount is $100,000 at 8% for approximately 10 years, and as the annual payment is $15,000 the constant annual payment is 15%. Also assume that the investor will pay up to $45,000 cash down.

A. Minimum Price	$160,000
B. Maximum Cash to Invest	$ 45,000
C. Amount to be Held as Wrap-Around	$115,000
D. NOI	$ 20,000
E. Cash Return Demanded (Line B × Rate Demanded)	$ 4,500
F. Amount Available for Debt Service	$ 15,500
G. Constant Annual Payment Percentage (Line F ÷ Line C)	13.479%
H. Minimum Years Possible (total yrs. of remaining pay-out on existing mortgage)	10 years
I. Nominal Rate on Highest Existing Mortgage	8%
J. Possible Terms	

	(1)	(2)	(3)	(4)
Nominal Rate	8% (same as I)	8¾%	9½%	10%
Years	12 years	12.5 years	13.5 years	14.5 years
Constant Shown	13.270%	13.471%	13.450%	13.353%
Annual Payment	$15,260.50	$15,491.65	$15,467.50	$15,355.96

To find J, refer to annual constant % tables. Begin at same rate shown in Line I. Find constant nearest to but no greater than constant rate shown in Line G. Check years and find actual annual payment by multiplying constant rate found in column by amount of wrap-around in Line C. Increase interest in increments of less than 1%, maintaining the same number of years or more as indicated on Line H, and a constant not more than that shown on Line G.

Any of the possible terms shown would offer a total debt service which would not exceed the maximum amount available for debt service (Line F). With a wrap-around on these terms, the minimum cash flow yield demanded by the investor would be met, and at the same time the seller would have obtained the total asking price desired.

The seller would no doubt look to the maximum interest rate which would still offer the annual payment as shown. The 10% over 14½ years would give the seller a greater overall effective yield than 8% over 12 years. The buyer would look to the smaller amount if he had his choice. When using this method, it is important to make sure that the annual payment on the existing debt service is met for the entire term of that mortgage. In a wrap-around with only one existing mortgage, it is only necessary to keep the rate at or above that charged on the existing mortgage to accomplish this. If, however, you have a wrap that encompasses several mortgages, using the highest rate on any existing one and the maximum terms on any other (even if they are not the same mortgage) will also accomplish this. It is possible to use an interest lower than the maximum rate on one of several existing mortgages, providing that the annual payment on the wrap does not fall below the combined annual payment on the existing mortgages and the unpaid balance of the wrap is equal to or larger than the declining balance of the existing financing. This will involve looking at the entire mortgage however, and if the first method (maximum rate and maximum years) is used this will automatically be accommodated.

3. Ease of payment. In multimortgaged property, nothing can be more annoying than to have to make several payments to different lenders each month. Keeping track of the amortization of each is a problem. With the wrap however, the buyer has only *one* payment to make and can look to *one* amoritzation schedule. The form of payment is very important, as this is the area where most objections arise. Because the buyer does not directly make the payments on the existing mortgages, he may be most concerned that those payments will in fact be made. There have been many cases of wrap-arounds where the buyer faithfully made his monthly payment, but only to find that the seller collecting that payment did not pay any of the existing mortgages. This is a nasty situation, and people that have experienced it have been needlessly hurt.

PAYMENTS SHOULD BE MADE TO AN ESCROW ACCOUNT—ALWAYS

When you set up a wrap-around mortgage it is imperative that the payments on it be made to an escrow agency, or collection agency. The agency would then make the existing mortgage payments, collect for taxes and insurance, and disperse the balance to the mortgagee. This makes the maintenance of the wrap relatively easy for all parties concerned, and assures the mortgagor that the existing payments which should go to the existing mortgages are made. This escrow agency, either a commercial bank, savings and loan association, or other third-party service, should be paid by the mortgagee, but it is not unusual that this cost is shared by the mortgagor as well.

HOW TO PROTECT THE MORTGAGOR AND THE MORTGAGEE IN THE ESCROW AGREEMENT

The escrow agent will only do what he is instructed, so it is important that he has complete and comprehensive instructions. The factors that need to be covered in this escrow agreement will be:

(A) How the fee is paid for the escrow service. The escrow agent will normally deduct his fee from the amounts collected. If the mortgagor is sharing this cost, his portion of the fee must be added to the total wrap payment.

(B) Collections for taxes and escrows covered in the wrap or existing mortgages. A first mortgage may have a constant monthly payment added each year to the amortization which accrues annual taxes, insurance, and other assessments. It is imperative that these provisions be made a part of the wrap document, and that the escrow agent be instructed to make those out payments as well. In the event of a future assessment, or changes in taxes or insurance that would alter this escrow collection, the wrap should provide for those changes and the agent instructed on how to notify the mortgagor of these additions or subtractions to his total payment.

(C) Prepayment provisions. Careful analysis of prepayment provisions in existing mortgages should be made and incorporated in the wrap-around. The holder of the wrap should provide an equal pro-rata reduction of both the existing financing as well as the wrap for all prepayments. For example: If the outstanding balance at the time of the prepayment is shown to be 80% to existing financing and 20% to the DIFFERENCE, then the prepayment of $20,000 would be divided by that ratio. 80% would then be prepaid to the holder of the existing financing. Of course, the entire 100% is reduced from the wrap balance, and new calculations would occur. The prepayment in full is the same as a balloon with regard to the effective yield rate.

(D) Grace Period. There should be a shorter grace period on the wrap than on the existing financing. This will assist in notification of default ahead of due dates on the existing financing. When there is a very short grace period on any of the existing financing, it may be desirable to allow a build-up on one period to accrue in the escrow account in order to advance the lead time on default on the existing financing. For example: If a second mortgage has a 10-day grace period, the mortgagee may find it to his advantage to allow collections, less dispersements, to build up to an amount equal to one period payment on that second. If it is a monthly payment, then the grace period allowed to the mortgagee is now one month plus 10 days.

(E) Automatic foreclosure by underlying mortgages. In an multimortgaged property, the first mortgage may have a provision which provides that it will automatically be in default and foreclosable in the event that any secondary lender file foreclosure proceedings. There is no real justification in this, but some lenders have this provision in their loans. It is far more important that the inferior loans have this provision, in the event the existing mortgagee or superior mortgagees file foreclosure. As the mortgagee in the wrap pays the existing mortgages, he knows when a default will occur. However, since he has the ability to make the existing payments on the existing mortgages, he can keep them current even though the wrap goes into default. Should he file foreclosure proceedings against the mortgagor, and should the existing mortgage have this automatic foreclosure provision in their loan, they too may file foreclosure, even though they are current. In this event, the escrow agent must be instructed not to file such proceedings without obtaining an agreement from the existing mortgage lenders that they will not file as long as they keep current. Most lenders, even if they have this provision of automatic foreclosure, will go along with such a request.

(F) Maintain integrated accounts. The escrow agent should keep one account for the funds. The account should be in the name of the mortgagee. If the agent is a bank or other lending institution with savings accounts or checking accounts, then all the funds collected should be paid into that account. Then, the agent will pay out the funds required for the existing financing. Have your lawyer draw up this escrow agreement. It is a very important part of the wrap process and is highly recommended. Naturally, this is not a necessity, yet to have a wrap without collections made by a third party can be less than prudent for the mortgagor.

THE WRAP-AROUND CAN PRESENT UNIQUE PROBLEMS FOR THE THIRD-PARTY LENDER

When a wrap-around mortgage is given to a third-party lender, such as a commercial bank or mortgage company, some unique problems occur. Take this situation as an example: Midwest Central Bank examines a potential lending situation that will involve a wrap-around mortgage. They have concluded that by lending new money to a buyer of property and wrapping around the existing mortgage they will leverage their yield to above 12%. Assume that the new money they lend is $100,000. At the end of the first year of the loan they will receive their total investment of $100,000 plus $12,000. The mortgage they are wrapping around has a one-time payment (shown as follows).

	Face Amount	Rate	Term	Due at End of Term
(1) Existing Mortgage	$400,000	7%	1 Year	$428,000
(2) New Money	100,000	?	1 Year	?
(3) Wrap Total	$500,000	8%	1 Year	$540,000

TOTAL Principal and Interest Return on Wrap-Around, End of 1st Yr.	$540,000
LESS Total Pay-out, 1st Mortgage	428,000
TOTAL Principal and Return on New Money	112,000
LESS Original Principal on New Money	100,000
TOTAL Return on New Money	$12,000
EFFECTIVE RATE OF RETURN on New Money at End of 1st Year	12%

The third-party lender has lent only $100,000 in this transaction. He has not had any obligation to pay the original first mortgage of $400,000. If he makes the wrap-around loan with the existing owner and original mortgagor on the existing mortgage, or a new owner that has assumed the first mortgage, he is advancing only new money with no liability on the existing financing. Courts have contended that in these situations the return to the lender *is* 12% and if the sum is usurious the loan is not valid.

In the wrap-around mortgages we have concluded it is possible to leverage a yield much higher than the 12% shown in this example. Nonetheless, in many states a 12% return may be usurious. Therefore, this examination of return must be considered as a major problem for the third-party lender. The real advantages for a third-party lender are the leverage and the increased yield. If in making these loans the courts determine that usury is present, the loan can be null and void and the lender face loss of the sum lent and have a penalty placed on him as well.

The face rate of the wrap-around is only 8%, well below usury in most states. But since the lender has no obligation to pay the existing financing, *no risk* as it were, the actual yield can be considered the effective rate of return.

HOW TO AVOID USURY ON WRAP-AROUND LOANS BY THIRD PARTIES

The actual answer to this is not clearly defined by the courts. However, it does seem that if the third-party lender can place himself in the same shoes so to speak as a seller holding a wrap, then this problem can be averted. To do this will require the lender to assume the full obligation of the existing financing being wrapped around. When the lender has liability against the existing loans, then he may well be in the same position the seller would be in by holding the wrap-around.

It is hoped that in the near future this matter of possible usury on third-party loans will be more clearly defined by the courts. In the meantime, third-party lenders must accept the advice of their legal advisors on this matter. There are numerous cases which have occurred in various states that indicate the above solution is perhaps the answer. But states may vary in this regard, so it is best to take a close look at what has happened in your state.

HOW TO CALCULATE INTEREST EARNED FOR ANNUAL INCOME ACCOUNTING

It is necessary to know how to account for interest earned in the wrap-around for income tax purposes. In essence, the interest earned on the wrap-around mortgages will be the interest to be reported as income. Deductions of interest to be reported as income and deductions of interest paid against the underlying existing mortgages will offset that total interest as long as the tax laws permit deduction of interest.

For example:

Total Interest collected at end of 1st year on a $500,000 existing wrap at 8% per year	$40,000
less	
Total Interest paid out on existing mortgage, assuming a $400,000 existing mortgage at 7% per year	28,000
Net difference:	$12,000

Income to be reported	$40,000
Interest Deduction	28,000
Taxable	$12,000

Note: Watch tax laws that may limit or remove interest deductions on real estate mortgages.

HOW TO TELL IF A SITUATION IS IDEAL FOR A WRAP-AROUND MORTGAGE

There will be definite signs which should indicate to you if a situation is right for the use of the wrap-around mortgage. Your ability to recognize these signs will aid you in reaching the conclusion that the wrap will help achieve the goals of your client. Listed below are some of the primary signs that you will encounter. At times they will present themselves alone, while at other times in combination with each other.

The Signs That Indicate The Need For A Wrap-Around

(1) Existing loan constant annual payment percentage relationship to maximum loan potential: Take a look at the total annual payment of the existing mortgages. Then find the constant payment percentage this represents of the total loan potential. If this constant is *below* a normal loan constant, you have a prime candidate for a wrap. For example: The total loan payment on three existing mortgages is $15,000 per year starting the first year. The property is priced at $225,000, therefore a normal loan may be 80% of that amount or $180,000. The $15,000, existing loan payment represents 8.33% of the total loan potential. A look at constants available in the market for new money may show as 11% annual constant to be reasonable. The spread of 2.67% in constants for the first year is tremendous. In fact, a spread of 2.67% in constants for the first year is tremendous. In fact, a spread of only .5% would be sufficient to warrant a further look to see if the wrap would be desirable. If you find that the constant annual payment on the existing financing is higher than the present market constant, a wrap-around may not be effective.

*(2) A forced wrap-around:*If you have existing financing that cannot be assumed and a refinancing of the property is not possible due to market conditions or economic cost, then the wrap-around sign is very strong.

(3) Reinvestment goal of the seller: The leverage gained on the yield may be most attractive to the seller, and could be a primary sign that the wrap should be considered. Keep in mind that the constant spread indicated in the first item (above) should be favorable for the leverage to occur.

HOW TO USE THE WRAP-AROUND TO MAKE MORE SALES

You should have a good understanding for what the wrap will do, should do, and can do. The ability to take this tool and apply it to the selling of property will depend on whether you can sell the concept to the parties involved. The proficiency with which you accomplish this will therefore depend on how comfortable you feel in dealing with this tool. I suggest that the first step is to take several properties you presently have listed and restructure the existing financing via wrap-around to see what happens to their marketability. If you see that you can offer a property with better financing and increase the cash flow, you are on the way to having a better inventory and making more sales.

You will have only relative difficulty in selling this concept to the buyer. After all, this depends on the alternatives offered to him. If he can buy with the wrap, instead of conventional financing, and the wrap offers better terms than the present market, then he will go with it.

The seller must also see the advantages it has to offer him. This chapter has given you all the ammunition to make that part of the sale easier than it might have been otherwise.

The wrap-around is a fine tool in the hands of the real estate broker or associate. It is most effective as a selling tool, and while third-party loans may become more frequent in the future, the major lenders will continue to shy away from this format. Do not let that aspect dismay you however, since the third party lender has problems that are unique to the wrap that the seller does not have. Unfortunately, however, the power third parties exert in the lending area has been to hold down wider use of the wrap by sellers and brokers.

Remember: The wrap-around is merely a tool. It has limitations and drawbacks. The return to the mortgagee is often postponed until the future, and though the yield is leveraged upward, the funds may not be available for use when they are needed. This factor should be considered as the major disadvantage to the wrap from a seller's point of view.

Figure 13-6 which follows is a blank Wrap Analysis Chart (see Figure 13-1 for one filled out). Have this reproduced along with the other charts shown in this chapter for analyzing the Effective Rate on the wrap-around.

Figure 13-6: THE PRIMARY ANALYSIS CHART

(The calculation of mortgage amortizations using complicated formulas is no longer the drudgery it once was. The chart used to set down the pertinent data on the wrap-arounds, enabling you to find the pay off amounts and calculate yields, is shown below.)

THE WRAP-AROUND PRINCIPAL BALANCE @ | DIFFERENCE

End of Period	Wrap-Around Mtg. Yrs. ____ Rate ____ Payment ____	1st Mtg. Yrs. __ Rate __ Payment ____	2nd Mtg. Yrs. __ Rate __ Payment ____	3rd Mtg. Yrs. __ Rate __ Payment ____	Difference Column A Less B, C, and D	Total Cash Received on Difference Payment A Less Paymts. B, C, and D	Difference Amortized Amount of Column "E" Paid Off	Retained Interest	Annual Interest Rate	Earned but Not Retained Bonus
	(A)	(B)	(C)	(D)	(E)	(F)	(G)	(H)	(I)	(J)
0										
1										
2										
3										
4										
5 etc.										

Chapter 14

When, Why, and How To Discount a Mortgage

The ability to increase the yield on a mortgage by selling it below face value can be utilized in many ways. The concept of mortgage discounting is widely used in the government loan programs and has applicability to the private sector as well. The *discounting of a mortgage* is when the holder of the mortgage sells the note to either the maker or a third party at an amount less than the principal plus interest owed. The result is that the buyer would, upon satisfaction of the note at its contract rate and terms, receive a greater yield than the original holder.

WHEN A MORTGAGE SHOULD BE DISCOUNTED FOR CASH

A mortgage should be discounted whenever the need for cash, or the yield which can be obtained with the cash, exceeds the return on the mortgage. Naturally, there are other alternatives, such as obtaining a loan against the mortgage or seeking the funds elsewhere. These alternatives, which may be highly desirable solutions in normal circumstances, may not work quickly enough or produce the desired results as effectively as a discounting of the mortgage.

The cash discount is a sale of the paper at a reduced price to enable the buyer to have an overall yield greater than the contract rate on the mortgage. This cash sale of the paper can occur at any time after the mortgage is written and up until the date it is satisfied. A mortgage which has some maturity is considered to have a performance record, and hence may be discounted less than if it had no record of payment. Mortgages discounted in the early years will generally have an additional penalty for this lack of seasoning. This will depend on the type of mortgage and the position in rank. It is obvious that a second mortgage will not be as saleable as a first mortgage on the same property. Therefore, it may require a greater discount. Yet, a third mortgage on one property may be more marketable than a first mortgage on another property. The loan to value ratio is important throughout this ranking process. If a property is valued at $100,000 and there is a first mortgage of $40,000, the loan ratio is 40% and the equity ratio is 60%. That same property with an additional loan (second) of $20,000 would have a loan ratio of 60% to value and the equity ratio of 40%. Therefore, the loan to value ratio is crucial and the remaining equity ratio essential to determine the "risk" factor to the mortgage.

For example: Castelle had taken back a third mortgage when he sold his home nearly two years earlier. The mortgage now had ten years to go and the unpaid balance was $10,500. The contract rate was 8% and the monthly payment to amortize the balance was $152.88. Castelle felt that he would be able to sell the mortgage if he could discount it to show an investor 10% on the invested capital. This meant that the investor could not pay more than $9,639 for it to have that yield. The first investor looked at the discounted price and was interested. He asked Castelle what were the loan percentages and equity percentage ratios. Castelle wasn't sure what the investor meant, so they figured them out together. The estimated value on the property was $60,000.

The mortgage represented 17.5% of the total value and the superior financing totalled $42,500 or 70.8% of the value. This meant there was a total of 88.3% financing and 11.7% equity. The investor decided that with only 11.7% equity between the mortgage and foreclosure, he needed a 12% return. The mortgage would have to sell for $6,993 to show a 12% yield. Castelle decided to keep the mortgage, since his need for cash would not generate a 12% return.

However, later in the same year Castelle found a small apartment building he could buy if he had cash to the mortgages. The apartment building should throw off nearly 13% cash. He tried to get the owner of the building to take the mortgage as part of the transaction. Failing in that, he went back to the investor and discounted the mortgage to come up with the cash to buy the apartments. Castelle now had a greater use for the cash than the present return generated from the yield on paper.

WHEN SHOULD A MORTGAGE BE DISCOUNTED IN EXCHANGE

In the previous example, Castelle attempted to get the owner of a property he wanted to buy to take paper he held. This was a step to exchange the paper at its face amount. Later in the negotiations Castelle tried to make the paper more attractive by discounting the face amount, but the apartment owner had a need for cash that overshadowed the yield any reasonable discount could generate.

While Castelle failed in the exchange of the paper, he was at least on the right track in trying to better the buying power of the paper by using it as a part of a transaction rather than discounting it.

When an investor attempts to buy a property it is wise to offer as a part of the total transaction any paper being held, especially if the paper has a yield less than the expected return on the property being purchased. Yet, even though the yield on the paper is greater than the overall yield, the leverage gained in the purchase terms may make the use of the paper desirable.

Redding, an investor, offered to buy a strip store. He had $75,000 in cash and $50,000 in paper he was holding on a vacant piece of land he had sold the year before. The strip store had a first mortgage of $300,000 and an annual debt service of $33,000. The NOI of the store was $45,500, or a cash flow of $12,500 on a total offering of $125,000 cash to the mortgages. The $50,000 in mortgages Redding was offering would yield nearly 12%. Nonetheless, Redding was most interested in the strip store because of yields other than just the cash flow. In the first place, the tax shelter boosted the yield as did the principal build-up. Appreciation was that added bonus that he was not getting in the mortgage.

There are two ways to discount a mortgage in an exchange. The first is in adjusting the total price offered, still showing the mortgage at its face amount. The second is adjusting the price and showing the mortgage at a discounted value.

Here's an actual example. Rosenbloom wanted to acquire a vacant parcel of land to build on. The asking price was $100,000. Rosenbloom had cash and, in addition, a $15,000 mortgage he was holding from the sale of another property. He decided he would not pay more than $80,000 cash plus his mortgage.

FIRST OFFER: ADJUSTED PRICE WITH FIRM FACE VALUE ON PAPER

The offer would read as follows:

Price	$95,000
Cash	$80,000
Mortgage in Exchange	15,000
Total	$95,000

SECOND OFFER: ADJUSTED PRICE AND DISCOUNTED VALUE OF PAPER

Price	$90,000
Cash	80,000
Mortgage in Exchange	10,000
Total	$90,000

It would appear that the proper method would be the first offer. After all, it is argued, the higher price is the best way to go. This may be true in many circumstances. However, if this is the maximum which can be offered, that is $80,000 in cash and the balance in the paper, and the face amount of the paper is $15,000, then there is little room for negotiation.

Therefore, I suggest that in the offering of paper in exchange for a part of the transaction that the paper be generously discounted right at the start. If the above $15,000 paper yields 8% at its face amount, and assume that if discounted to $10,000 it will yield 16%, you have removed the primary argument of the value of the paper before the seller can settle in on that portion of the negotiations. If he were to counter at a higher price, you could merely remind him that in fact there was another $5,000 in face value in the paper anyway.

In Rosenbloom's situation, he knew the maximum he wanted to pay for the property and that he wanted to use the paper as a part of the transaction. Generally, sellers will absorb part of a bigger deal in old paper, thereby removing the paper from the buyer's portfolio.

HOW TO DETERMINE THE AMOUNT OF A DISCOUNT

This is a two-part problem. The first is the market condition. What amount of discount is necessary to make the paper saleable? The second part of the problem is the actual computations to arrive at the discount.

HOW TO ANALYZE THE MARKET FOR A DISCOUNTED MORTGAGE

To some degree it is the old story of how long must your legs be. The answer of course is long enough to reach the floor. In the discounting of mortgages the amount of the discount must be sufficient to market the paper. Investors dealing with the purchase of paper look to a demand rate that is generally greater than the yields on the property securing the paper. If the mortgage is a first mortgage and there is a low loan to value ratio, the discount will be reduced as the risk is lessened. On the other hand, if the mortgage is a second or third mortgage and the total loan to value ratio is high, equity is therefore low and the discount must be increased.

The motivation of the seller of the paper must be considered as the most important factor. If the seller must have cash, then he has little choice but to increase the discount until the paper sells. But if his need for cash is limited to a portion of the mortgage, he may be able to borrow the needed funds by placing the mortgage up as security for the loan. The interest paid on such a loan can be greater than the yield offered in the discount, and yet the total cost is less than if the mortgage were discounted.

When you deal in the discount mortgage market it is a good idea to establish a few buyers for such paper. You need to have a list of such investors on hand in case you need one. It seems that the need arises when time is short, and an attempt to find a buyer then can be difficult. The investors will dictate the amount of discount needed from their point of view. Unless you are able to dispose of the paper through other means, the general market will be your only hope—and they set the terms.

HOW TO FIND THE DISCOUNT

Constant annual percent tables are provided in this book. These tables have many uses, one of which is an easy way to arrive at the discount amounts for mortgages. The method of finding the discount is explained in the example below.

Williams needed cash and had a mortgage to sell. The principal amount was $50,000 over fifteen years at 8% annum. The monthly payment was $478. Once the pertinent data is given, the next step is to find the current constant annual percentage of the mortgage. The monthly payment is $478, therefore twelve times that would give the annual sum of $5,736. The annual sum is then divided by the face amount of the mortgage (that amount still unpaid) and this gives the current constant annual percentage ($5,736 ÷ $50,000 = .1147). This should be stated as a percentage (in this case 11.47%). This represents the percent of the total annual payment in relation to the outstanding balance for the years remaining. With the constant annual percent known, the remaining calculation is quite simple. In this example, assume the yield the investor demands is 12%. We know the mortgage has 15 years to go. Find the constant annual percentage which corresponds to 12% for 15 years.

In the table of constant annual percentages you would look in the 12% interest column for the 15 years. The answer would be 14.40% (some tables may vary based on the full calculations made). Now complete this formula:

$$\frac{\text{Constant Annual Percent on Mortgage at Contract Rate}}{\text{Demand Rate Constant}} = \text{Discounted Percentage}$$

$$\frac{11.47}{14.40} = 79.65\%$$

To apply these results multiply the face amount of the mortgage by the discounted percentage ($50,000 × 79.65% = $39,326). The $39,326 is the value of the mortgage to an investor demanding a 12% yield. To find the percentage of the discount, subtract the discounted percentage from 100% (100% − 79.65% = 20.35% discount).

Fig. 14-1: MORTGAGE DISCOUNT SHEET WHEN DEMAND RATE IS KNOWN

1. Face Amount of Mortgage (Present Balance Owed) . . . . $________
2. Contract Rate . . . . ________%
3. Payment (Monthly ___, Quarterly ___, Semi-Annual ___, Annual ___; check one) . . . . $________
4. Constant Annual Percent Annual Adjustment of Line 3 Divided by Line 1 . . . . ________%
5. Demand Rate . . . . ________%
6. Term of Years of Mortgage . . . . ________years
7. Constant at Demand Rate. Find by Looking in Demand Rate Column for Number of Years . . . . ________%
8. A. $\frac{\text{Line 4}}{\text{Line 7}}$ = Discounted Value % . . . . ________%
9. Discount Percent (Subtract Line 8 from 100) . . . . ________%
10. Amount of Discount (Line 9 × Line 1) . . . . $________
11. Amount to be Paid at Discount . . . . $________

    A. Line 1 less Line 10
    or as check

    B. Line 1 × Line 9
    or as check

Figure 14-1 offers a computation chart to facilitate these calculations.

When you are computing a mortgage that has payments which are other than monthly or does not have equal payments over the term, this method of arriving at the discount will cause errors. However, when the payments are equal but not monthly you can still compute the constant percent for that mortgage by using the table for payment at a given rate.

For example: Assume a mortgage is paid semi-annually at 8% over 15 years. To find the constant annual percentage, look in a table for semi-annual mortgages at 8% for 15 years. The semi-annual payment is $57.83 for each $1000 of the mortgage, or $2,891.50 twice a year for a $50,000 mortgage. This totals $5,783 per year or a constant semi-annual percent (per annum) of 11.57%, whereas the monthly constant was 11.47%. To find the constant rate, take the payment ($57.83), multiply it by 2, and move the decimal to the left one place. Since this mortgage is payable semi-annually, you need to take the demand rate from the same table. As the demand rate is 12%, look under 12% for 15 years. This indicates a $72.65 semi-annual payment per $1,000. Multiply the payment by 2 (72.65 × 2 = 145.3) then move the decimal to the left one place (14.5). The end result is the constant annual percent of the demand rate based on a semi-annual payment. The formula can now be completed as in the first instance. However, remember that different payment schedules at the same contract rate and term of years will have different constants.

Mortgages with unequal payments require rather complicated calculations. However, it will be possible to obtain an estimate for such mortgages by totaling the payments received on a mortgage with equal principal plus interest. This will provide an average constant. The following calculations are for a $10,000 mortgage.

Estimate Constant Annual Percent for Mortgages with Constant Principal plus Interest on the Unpaid Balance

EXAMPLE: Assume $10,000 mortgage, $1,000 per year and interest at 8% per annum. 10-year payment.

STEP 1: Compute total interest for term of loan.
FORMULA: Principal Amount × (Term + 1) × Rate ÷ 2.
$10,000 × (10 + 1) × .08 ÷ 2 = $4,400
TOTAL INTEREST PAID: $4,400

STEP 2: Add Principal Amount.

Interest:	$ 4,400
Principal:	$10,000
TOTAL:	$14,400

STEP 3: Divide by years (term of loan). This gives the average annual payment.

$14,400 ÷ 10 = $1,440

STEP 4: Divide average annual payment by original principal amount of loan and convert to a percentage.

$1,440 ÷ 10,000 = .1440

Converted to % = 14.40%

This results in the Constant Annual Percent for the Mortgage: 14.40%.

In this example, assume the demand rate is 12% as in the other examples. Because we have adjusted the payment of the mortgage to show an annual average payment of $1,440, you can use the annual payment table for 12% to find the demand constant. Using the table you will find $176.98 is the annual payment for $1,000 for 10 years at 12%. It is not necessary to multiply this by 2 as with the semi-annual payment—merely move the decimal one place to the left: 17.7% (rounded off). Complete the formula:

$$\frac{14.4}{17.7} = 81.35$$

The 81.35% is the discounted price of the mortgage in this estimate (81.35% × $10,000 = $8,135). Remember that this is just an *estimate*. It is not accurate because the constant annual percent is based on averages only.

HOW TO FIND THE INTEREST YIELD ON A MORTGAGE WHICH IS DISCOUNTED

It will be necessary from time to time to know how to calculate the yield on a mortgage that is offered at a discount. For example: Sterling has a $50,000 mortgage with 15 years remaining at 8%. The payment is $478 per month (same as Williams' mortgage mentioned earlier). Sterling is offering this mortgage for sale at a 20% discount. The purchase price of the mortgage is therefore 80% of the face amount ($50,000 × 80%= $40,000). What is the yield to an investor?

The following chart will assist in this calculation. Note that it is very similar to the previous discount chart but with one important difference—we do not know the demand rate. The formula in this computation is:

$$\frac{\text{CONSTANT ANNUAL PERCENT}}{\text{DISCOUNTED VALUE PERCENT}} = \text{CONSTANT AT YIELD RATE}$$

The chart has been worked out below. Review it and make your own by using it as a guide.

Yield On A Discounted Mortgage

1. Face Amount of Mortgage (Present Balance Owed)	$50,000	
2. Contract Rate	8	%
3. Payment (Monthly √ , Quarterly ___, Semi-Annual ___, Annual ___; check one)	$478	
4. Constant Annual Percent Annual Adjustment of Line 3 Divided by Line 1	11.47	%
5. Discount Rate (known factor)	20	%

6. Discounted Amount Ratio
   100 Less Line 5 — 80 %

7. A. Constant Annual Percent

$$\frac{\text{Constant Annual Percent (Line 4)}}{\text{Discounted Amount Ratio (Line 6)}} = \text{At Constant Yield R}$$

   B.

$$\frac{11.47}{80} = 14.33\%$$

8. Find Yield from Tables:
   Locate Closest Constant Rate at 15 Years.

	Constant Rate Found:	Corresponding Yield:
A.	13.64	11%
B.	14.40	12%
C.		

9. Estimate Yield at nearly 12%

HOW SELLERS CAN USE DISCOUNTED MORTGAGES TO HELP THEM SELL THEIR PROPERTY

Given a standard set of circumstances, any buyer will pay more for a property on terms than he will pay if he must invest 100% of the price in cash. This conclusion is based on two major assumptions: (1) the buyer can earn a greater yield on his capital from the income of the property or from other sources than the cost of the financing; and (2) the buyer has the alternative of paying cash, such as obtaining financing from the seller.

The seller now has the opportunity to use this factor to his best advantage. If the buyer wants to pay cash, there is no problem and the discounted mortgage aspect does not enter into the picture. However, to broaden the market, or to create a market for a property that is difficult to sell, the seller may offer reasonable financing.

Robinson owns a 50-acre tract of land. It has been on the market for $20,000 per acre ($1,000,000) for nearly six months. His broker suggests that the terms he wants (50% down and short pay-out) are the major drawback. Robinson, however, needs cash for another venture and agrees to reduce the price to $18,000 per acre to move the property ($900,000), but he still needs 50% down. His broker examines the situation and proposes that Robinson keep the price at $20,000 per acre since it is reasonable for the market, but that he be willing to accept only 10% down. The balance of 90% will be broken into two mortgages: a first mortgage in the amount of $500,000 and a second in the amount of $400,000.

The terms are to run concurrently for fifteen years at 6% on the first at normal amortization with monthly payments and 8% interest only due on the second for the fifteen years. The broker then suggests that Robinson look to a discount of the first mortgage to generate the cash required.

The first mortgage will pay out at the rate of $4220 per month over the fifteen years. The mortgage is saleable if it will yield 10% in the general market, as it is only 50% of the total value and represents low risk. The broker calculates the sale price to be $392,600, so Robinson would clear this amount on the sale of the mortgage. He would also receive $100,000 down on the property and then have a total of $492,600 (before he pays his broker his fee). Also, he still is owed $400,000 which is earning interest at 8% per annum.

Had Robinson offered the property at $900,000, it is unlikely that it would have moved. Instead, the broker used creative financing to convert a difficult property into a more easily marketable one. The buyer needed only $100,000 down, and had a low interest first mortgage and an interest-only second mortgage—both highly acceptable forms of financing for a buyer. Also, since the seller was offering the property with 90% financing, little room was left for negotiations by the buyer to reduce the price.

The buyer of the mortgage obtained a good yield at a fairly safe risk. In Robinson's case, the land was at a fair value so the risk was slight. Robinson came out better than he had thought in that the package produced a sale. Had he received 50% down at a price of $900,000 he would have had $450,000 in cash, whereas with the $100,000 price and the discount he had $492,000.

The trade-off of a discounted mortgage, instead of lowering the price, will work in many areas of real estate. A free and clear property where the seller can use a first mortgage for the discount, as did Robinson, is best for such a transaction, but the secondary mortgages can be discounted as well.

HOW TO FIND INVESTORS WHO WILL BUY DISCOUNTED MORTGAGES

There are several markets for mortgages. The most organized is that consisting of mortgage brokers. These professional people make their living by placing and making mortgages. They deal with private investors as well as institutional funds and will act on their own behalf or as broker-agents. Because they have daily contact with this field, they are a prime source for discounted mortgages.

Locating these sources is relatively easy. Most will be listed in your phone book. You can also obtain the names of others who are outside your area from your banking sources. The contact you make with them is important.

It should be noted that not all the mortgage brokers you may contact will be viable. Some don't have the contacts that others may have, or may find dealing with you uncomfortable. I presume that you will not be dealing as a mortgage broker and as a real estate broker at the same time. You should make your situation clear to the mortgage broker right away. Your interest in dealing with discounted mortgages is merely to help your client reach a desired goal. Unless you are licensed as a mortgage broker, you may not be entitled to receive a fee. The mortgage broker knows this and will be relieved that you also understand the situation. Those of you who may have both types of licenses already know how to get the cooperation of your fellow mortgage brokers. Therefore, I shall leave that topic alone.

Mortgage brokers are but one source. Trust departments and pension funds that may be located in your area are also candidates for good mortgages, and they like the idea of leveraging up on a discounted mortgage. These sources are found in your local commercial banks and insurance companies. The commercial bank is the best place to start and you might as well go right to the top—the secretary of the president. This astute lady will direct you to all the right people. Often, a recommendation from her to the person you want to deal with is more important than if the president himself called the trust officer and said you were on your way. How so? Follow this suggestion: meet and establish good rapport with the bank's president. This is essential to other dealings you will have in the community anyway. Go over some of the services that the bank offers. Do they have a trust department? If so, what type of trust services do they give? Once you have had two or three meetings with this bank president, you will have made contact with his secretary. Be sure she knows who you are and that you are on friendly terms with her boss.

The day you want to sit down with the trust officer, give the president's secretary a call and ask her the name of the trust officer in charge: "Is it a Mr. Rankin?" you might ask. Then ask her if she would mind giving Mr. Rankin a call as an introduction for your appointment that day. She usually will and will also have something nice to say about you.

Once you are with the trust officer ask him about his services. He will become a salesman, giving you data about his department. Do not rush in to a trust officer you have never seen and confront him with a discounted mortgage you must sell by that afternoon or else blow a big deal.

Question him about the mortgage brokers he must deal with in buying private mortgages for the trust account or pension fund they represent. If he gives you some names remember them, but the important thing you have learned is that the bank does buy such mortgages. Ask the trust officer who approves such private mortgage purchases how you would go about presenting a package to them.

Private investors are numerous, although very difficult to cultivate. Earlier chapters have dealt with this private investor in mortgages. But to be somewhat repetitive, remember the private investor in mortages is not greatly unlike the investor in real estate. They both recognize the advantage of realty as a security. However, the mortgage investor is willing to take a lower yield at a reduced risk than the real estate investor.

Some of your realty buyers may like to sink some of their portfolio into mortgages, so don't overlook your own buyers of real estate as possible investors. To some degree, this source comes out of your back pocket because you will not receive a fee for placing such an investment. But the sale of the mortgage may close another deal. Besides, passing a good mortgage at a high yield on to a past investor will be appreciated and the favor will be returned.

Look in the mirror. The person looking back at your may be a prime discounted mortgage buyer. It is not impossible that you may look to the mortgage as the total commisison or at least a part of your fee. Sellers will often ask you to take part or all of a mortgage as your fee. Your ability to plan for this possibility and to have the mortgage discounted will depend on your willingness to take the paper.

If you approach the possibility of discounting a mortgage as part of a cash-out program for the seller, you should speak to him early and tell him that at times your firm will buy mortgages as an investment or take the paper as all or part of the fee. Do this only if you are prepared or if your firm is willing to do it. The opposite is also necessary. Tell the seller that your firm is not in a position to take paper on such a discount, but you will do all you can to help him dispose of the mortgage.

To avoid mention of one of these two possibilities will leave the suggestion up to the seller. Refusing to take the paper at that moment in time may cast doubts in the seller's mind about your earlier suggestions that he make such a transaction and hold such paper in the first place.

Don't forget the mortgagor. He may be a prime buyer for a discounted mortgage. Naturally, in these situations the seller of the mortgage is the mortgagee. He may be holding paper from a previous sale or may be investor who bought a mortgage from you or someone else. Before you run off and seek out other investors, offer the discount to the guy who makes the monthly payment. By giving him a break in the pay-off, he may become a good client later on. In any event, the buyer of the mortgage makes little difference to the mortgagee selling the paper—it is the cash that is important.

A Review Of The Sources That Will Buy Discounted Mortgages

1. *Mortgage Brokers:* For the broker who will not deal frequently with discounted mortgages, this source can be consistent and easy to approach.
2. *Trust Funds and Pension Funds:* A little harder to approach, but one of the prime sources used by the mortgage broker. These sources are found at your commercial banks and insurance companies.

3. *Private Investors:* Look first at your own realty investors. Some of these clients may like a good discounted mortgage. Other private investors will advertise in local papers or can be found through your bank or savings and loan.
4. *You:* Take a discounted mortgage as part of your fee. However, be careful you don't have to give a discount yourself to buy the mortgage. Early disclosure of your firm's attitude to mortgages as part of your fee will help in dealing with the seller.
5. *The Mortgagor:* Never overlook the person who writes out the monthly check that pays off the loan.

A Partial Discount To The Mortgagor

It may be possible to raise some quick cash by going to the mortgagor and suggesting a discount on the future payments if he will prepay some of the outstanding principal. I was involved in such a case some time ago. Emory was holding a $45,000 second mortgage on a business he had sold several years earlier. The mortgage had fifteen years remaining at 8½% interest per annum. The annual payment was based on monthly payments of $443.25. The constant annual percent on this mortgage is 11.82 (found in constant table sunder 8½% at fifteen years). Emory needed a quick $15,000 and found that if he were to discount the mortgage the yield necessary would be 12%. This meant the sale price would be $36,936 (11.82 ÷ 14.40 × 45,000). Emory felt this was too great a discount to take in order to obtain the $15,000 needed.

He approached one of the local mortgage brokers to see whether he could borrow against the mortgage, but that did not produce any positive results. By the time Emory called me, he was at his wits end. "I need the cash by the end of the week," he said, "and it seems that the more I need it, the tougher it becomes to get it." Sounds very familiar, I know.

After counseling with Emory, I suggested we make the following proposal to the mortgagor. The mortgagor would prepay $15,000 on the outstanding mortgage. This would bring the unpaid principal balance down to $30,000. Based on this balance, the monthly amortization would be reduced to $295.50. As an inducement or bonus to the mortgagor, Emory agreed to reduce the interest rate on the mortgage to 6½% rather than the 8½% for its remaining term. This gave a new constant of 10.45 and a monthly payment of $261.25 instead of the $295.50. What this meant was that the mortgagor was obtaining a discount for the remaining balance by the prepayment of the $15,000. Over the balance of the term the mortgagor would save $6,165. The cost to Emory was not really the $6,165 however, as the reduction of the interest lowered his pretax income and converted future pay-back (the mortgage) into ready cash. A discounting of the mortgage would have caused a greater reduction of total earnings, and hence all parties benefited.

There were many other ways to approach the benefit Emory had given the mortgagor, but this solution seemed to be the best for Emory. The mortgage, as it turned out, was paid off four years later when the property was sold by the mortgagor. No doubt the low interest on the second was somewhat instrumental in attracting a buyer, even though the property was refinanced anyway. The gamble Emory took in reducing the interest rate was well calculated. Had he reduced the principal amount in the discount, that sum would have been a lost item regardless of when the mortgage was paid back. The reduced interest was an expense to Emory only as long as the mortgage was in force. Emory knew that most mortgages have a maximum life span of 7 to 10 years in the type of busines he had. The life span of mortgages is important in discounting. The early retirement of a mortgage will boost the yield to the holder when the face amount is discounted.

The bonus yield that comes when a discounted mortgage is paid off cannot be calculated except by experience in the loan market for the area. Some savings and loans and commercial banks will give you the statistics on their type of loan history, but many feel this is confidential information. Here's why:

Assume that Emory had sold his $45,000 mortgage at a discount which would have yielded 12%. As we saw in the example the price would have been $36,936. Remember, the face amount on the mortgage is $45,000. If the loan were paid off at the end of the first year the new mortgagee (the investor who bought the mortgage from Emory) would have been paid approximately $48,800. As the investor paid only $36,936 for the paper, his return on his investment for one year would be $11,864, or a yield of 32.12%. Each year this bonus will decline, and by the fifteenth year the yield is down to the 12% discounted yield. The incredible bonus interest that comes with this early prepayment is one of the real advantages of the discounted mortgage and should never be taken lightly.

Examination of the total financing on the property may disclose a potential necessity for refinancing in which a mandatory prepayment of a mortgage may be imminent. For example: A first mortgage is offered for discount. It is a 20-year mortgage at a moderate interest rate. Because of the term of years, the discount will be rather high. The mortgage broker examines the underlying mortgages and finds a large second mortgage which is interest only for three years with a balloon payment. The combined financing is less than 60% of the value and the second mortgage is nearly half that total. The mortgage broker concludes that the owner of the property will refinance all of the mortgages into one new first mortgage before the end of the three years when the second mortgage balloons. Not only is such a mortgage a good risk, but the discount and probable bonus will give an exceedingly high yield.

Another situation would be when the discounted mortgage is a second mortgage behind a low interest rate first mortgage that is nearly paid off. Such mortgages have a high constant rate and become prime candidates for refinancing even though the new interest rate would be higher. The constant rate for income property is often more important than the interest rate. Once the mortgage is refinanced, the second mortgage would automatically be paid off.

The combinations are endless. The motivation of the mortgagor is also important. Some mortgagors have a history of early prepayment. If you have this information, it's worth its weight in discounted mortgages.

Chapter 15

Five Additional Key Methods Of Financing Real Estate

In the writing of this book, there were several forms of financing that did not seem to constitute a complete chapter. Nonetheless, they are all very important and have some special use either as a complete form of financing in themselves or when used in combination with other forms. They can often mean the difference between making or not making a deal. Therefore, I have put these five forms into this chapter. They are not placed in order of importance. Each is equally important.

These five methods of financing are:

1. Mortgage and Lease Insurance
2. Leasehold Financing
3. Percent of Income
4. Land Lease
5. Co-ventures & Syndicates

The purpose of this chapter is to cover these five methods of financing—to enable you to see how they are used, what they do to help you make more transactions, and when to bring them into play.

MORTGAGE AND LEASE INSURANCE

There are two basic forms of mortgage insurance. The largest is the government VA and FHA programs. This insurance allows lenders to make loans which would not be available without the upper portion of the loan being insured by the government. A previous chapter which dealt with VA and FHA covered this form of insurance. The second form of this mortgage insurance (plus the added bonus of lease insurance) comes from private companies which offer these services to the public. Naturally, I use the term "private" meaning non-governmental. Most of these insuring firms are public corporations with considerable background in the insurance industry.

This section of this chapter will deal solely with this non-governmental insurance—what it does, how much it costs, where you can get it, and how it will help you make deals.

What Mortgage And Lease Insurance Is, And What It Does

Insurance on a mortgage or a lease will cause that mortgage or lease to become less risky. The fact that the mortgage or lease no longer has the stigma of excessive risk will generally lead to more favorable terms.

The insurance companies differ in the exact types of insurance they will provide. The cost likewise varies on programs offered by the same firm as well as from company to company. Most of the firms, however, do provide similar coverage at a reasonable cost. They insure mortgages on single-family homes and apartment houses (up to four units). The single-family units can be homes or apartments. Many firms offer insurance for mobile home mortgages as well. Other firms have programs which include mortgages on commercial properties and other nonresidential investments. The lease insurance can cover almost any form of lease on almost any type of property. However, not all insuring firms provide all these services.

A buyer in need of a high loan to value ratio has the alternative of obtaining a VA or FHA insured loan or a private form of insurance. If he does not qualify for VA, or the seller will not pay the points, or the time to qualify for FHA is not available, the buyer can look to private insurance to assist in conventional financing. Once the buyer has been qualified by the insuring company and he has chosen the program offered, the insurance will then cover the upper limits of the amount to be lent. Usually, the insuring firm issues a binding agreement to insure the buyer's loan and sets forth the limits and amounts which will be covered. The lender uses this insurance to make his loan less risky, knowing that in the event of a foreclosure he will be covered for 20 or 25% of the loss. This additional coverage is usually sufficient to make the foreclosure possible without loss to the lender.

The advantage of dealing with this type of insurance is its speed and low initial cost. Unlike FHA, the private firms pride themselves in their ability to respond to the submission within a few days. Some offer one-day service, and if you live in an area where they have an office and don't have to rely on the mails, that may be possible. Keep in mind that they don't approve everyone and are usually more selective than the FHA program. You can get a "no" quickly too.

The cost is not high either. For example, one company has a wide variety of payment plans for its 95% loan insurance that covers the top 25% of the loan.

The borrower can pay: 1% plus $20 appraisal review fee for the first year with ¼% for each renewal year thereafter; or ½% for each of the first three years and then ¼% each year thereafter; or for one payment premium, 1-¾% plus $20 appraisal review fee to cover six years, while 2-½% plus $20 appraisal review fee would cover ten years.

Because the buyer is using this form of insuring a loan, rather than the FHA program, sellers will often pay for this initial premium which is less than the FHA discount. In any event, the front dollars necessry to close with the private insurance can be less than that required by FHA. Of course, this will vary from company to company and will also depend on whether the seller is picking up the initial premium. You can see, however, that if the loan is $30,000 and the FHA has 5 points on the discount, the seller would receive $1,500 less than he was asking. For the private insurance, an initial premium of 1% plus $20 for appraisal would total $320. It is far easier to get the seller to pay the $320 than the $1,500. The buyer must pay the higher, more conventional loan rates on the normal loan obtained with the private insurance instead of the FHA maximum rate. But with the insurance, the lender will generally keep the loan interest rate as low as possible, and a fraction of a percent may be the only difference between the two forms.

Where To Get This Type Of Insurance

Most lenders have connections of their own. Mortgage brokers provide this service and it is also possible to deal directly with the companies on lease insurance and some of the nonresidential types of insurance. If none of the lenders in your area know of any private firms, you can contact one of those mentioned at the end of this section to see if they can be of any assistance.

The lenders generally run the credit reports on the applicants and fill out the necessary documents. These are then sent to the insurer for approval. Often, the slowest part of this process is the lender. As a broker you can speed things up considerably by making sure your client has all the necessary documentation ready for the lender. Following is a list of the exhibits required by one such insurer:

1. A Completed Application for Insurance:
   A. General data on applicant
   B. Type of commitment requested
   C. Appraised value of property (appraisal made by the lender)
   D. Sales price or proposed cost
   E. Amount of loan and terms
   F. Borrower's equity
   G. Age and description of the property
2. Current Appraisal with Photo
3. Current Borrower's Credit Report

4. Sales Contract
5. Income Verification (if borrower is self-employed, provide income statement and balance sheet—include spouse)
6. Copies of Other Data Required by Lender

How Mortgage Or Lease Insurance Can Help You Make More Deals

In mortgaging, it will help put that finishing touch to the sale. When VA or FHA just don't provide the answer, private insurance steps in. In many situations it will alleviate the difficulties of closing in a hurry with only 5 or 10% down.

Lease insurance is one of the best aids to the real estate profession. With this insurance, an owner of an office building may take good local tenants and by requiring each of them to provide lease insurance end up with triple-A tenants. This ability of the lease insurance to increase the value of the tenant will in turn increase the loanability of the lease—and in the future lead to a more profitable sale. A builder interested in building a factory may require the future occupant to provide fifteen-year lease insurance. The builder is now able to borrow the funds to build the building. Without the insurance, the lease may not have fulfilled the lenders' ideals of a "good" tenant and the loan may not have been made.

Keep in mind that these programs have not been around for a very long time. Some of the largest firms in the business have existed for less than fifteen years. Because of the newness, not all lenders are fully comfortable in dealing with this form of financing. However, most of the savings and loans provide such private insurance and many private banks offer some form of it through an affiliated firm.

You should learn more about the programs offered in your area. Find out which firms your savings and loans deal with and contact them to get full details. They will be more than happy to send you the information you need.

Firms That Offer Insurance For Mortgages Or Leases

The following are some of the firms that may provide this insurance. I have given only the addresses of their headquarters even though they may have offices in your state:

American Mortgage Insurance Company
3948 Browning Place
P. O. Box 27387
Raleigh, North Carolina 27611

United Guaranty Corporation
826 N. Elm
P. O. Box 21567
Greensboro, North Carolina 27420

Commercial Credit Mortgage Insurance
201 N. Charles Street
Baltimore, Maryland 21201

PMI
Mortgage Insurance Company
555 California Street
San Francisco, California 94104

Continental Mortgage Insurance
150 East Gilman Street
Madison, Wisconsin 53701

Foremost Guaranty Corporation
131 West Wilson Street
Madison, Wisconsin 53703

Liberty Mortgage Insurance Corporation
Ashwood Building
11353 Reed Hartman Highway
Blue Ash, Ohio 45241

Mortgage Guaranty Insurance Corporation
MGIC Plaza
Milwaukee, Wisconsin 53201

Ticor Mortgage Insurance
5900 Wilshire Boulevard
Los Angeles, California 90036

LEASEHOLD FINANCING

A leasehold is the ownership of a right to use a specific property for a term of years for which the lessee pays rent. The tenant has a leasehold interest in the property or space, and as long as the terms of the lease are met that interest is real and can be pledged as security on loans. Some types of leasehold interests are more valuable than others, and this value depends on the following factors:

1. The type of property leased: It should be obvious that different properties will have different values. If all other aspects are equal, lease on an office building should be more valuable than a lease on vacant land. A lender looking at the possibility of making a loan on a leasehold will look very strongly to the value of the space or property. If the leasehold loan is for improvements in a boutique in a shopping center, the usefulness of that space for other types of businesses will be important. The economics of the property will be most important in the evaluation of real equity.

2. The annual rent of the lease: The lease is the document which will create the actual value. The leasehold equity will become the security for the unsubordinated loan, and leasehold equity is found by appraising the space or property and deducting a capitalized value of the rent from that amount. For example: FPA Corp. has a 60-unit hotel on the beach. It is located on leased land. FPA Corp. owns the right to use the property—for which they pay an annual rent of $26,500. Assume they had no financing and built the hotel with cash. The finished value of the building was $1,050,000 and the land is worth $875,000. Therefore, the total combined value is $1,925,000. As FPA Corp. pays $26,500 in rent, this amount can be said to represent a cost of a capital investment. Setting a cap rate of 10% on this cost would make the investment $265,000. An 8% cap rate would increase the investment to $331,250. See the computations below to determine the leasehold equity at 10% and 8% cap rates with a leasehold mortgage of $800,000.

	10%	*8%*
1. Annual Rent on Lease of Land	$ 26,500	26,500
2. Capital Investment of Cap Rate to Provide Rent	265,000	331,250
3. Combined Value of Land and Buildings	1,925,000	1,925,000
4. Less Existing Financing	800,000	800,000
5. Gross Equity Before Adjustment for Land Lease	$1,125,000	1,125,000
6. Less Amount from Line 2	265,000	331,250
7. Total Leasehold Equity	$ 860,000	793,750
8. Less Capital Investment	100,000	100,000
9. Leasehold Equity Appreciation	$ 760,000	693,750

It should be clear that the cost of the lease, in terms of annual rent, must be capitalized to give an adjustment in the equity. The rate which is used may vary from property to property and from lender to lender. It is a good idea to show the leasehold equity at two different rates and then take the lower rate in your loan package. In any event, the fact that FPA Corp. is leasing the land at $26,500 per year, and the land has a current value of $875,000, is some indication that you will have excellent leasehold appreciation and equity. Yet, the leasehold equity must consider the improvements and their existing financing.

3. The period of time remaining on the lease: If the lease expires in one year, the leasehold equity will be that equity which can be substantiated economically over the remaining term of the lease. The hotel owned by FPA Corp. on leased land will continue to have value, as will the land. FPA's leasehold value, however, will begin to decline at a point in time when the remaining term of the lease does not allow return of capital at a reasonable rate of return for that remaining period. For example: The hotel has a value based on the economic return. In most income properties this economic value is the more important of all value approaches, and should be close to or below the replacement cost evaluation. If the replacement value were lower than the economic value, it might be more prudent to build a new hotel. Nonetheless, this economic return may continue for twenty years in a reasonable projection. However, FPA Corp. may have only ten years in which to enjoy the benefit of their leasehold if their lease expires at the end of that time. An investor interested in purchasing the leasehold from FPA Corp. would analyze the yield only for the remaining term, giving little credit to the actual value of the property. A lender would look at the leasehold equity in the same way.

4. The conditions and provisions of the lease: Each lease is a new ball game. There are many provisions or conditions which can make it desirable or undesirable. Rights to sublet, diversity of use, high maintenance costs and the like will be examined carefully by any lender prior to a loan. Because these terms are so important in possible financing, a lessee should make every effort to create a lease that will offer a good basis for leasehold financing.

5. The use of the property: Is the building a single-purpose structure or is it easily adaptable to other uses? Is the use economically sound or not? These are important factors to the lender, not only because he may end up with the building, but for the tenant to survive and the leasehold equity to be maintained the economics of the operation must be in the tenant's favor.

6. The tenant: Of course, the lender will always take a good long look at the tenant. After all, it is the tenant that wants to borrow the money. All lenders are very interested in the person they lend money to.

These six factors will be the main criteria which will create leasehold financing. Each factor is important on its own, but it is the combined effect of all six that will provide a package that is financeable.

Leasehold financing comes in two forms: *subordinated fee* and *unsubordinated fee*. There is a considerable amount of money lent in both types, but the majority of the larger loans are on leasehold interests with subordinated fee. The situation of FPA Corp. with their hotel on leased land is a good example. The land lease had a provision which enabled FPA to obtain a first mortgage that would be secured by the improvements as well as the land. The owners of the land subordinated their interest to the lender on the first mortgage and took a second position. The lender could foreclose on both the improvements and the land if FPA Corp. defaulted on the mortgage and the land owners did not step in to take it over.

This adds to the land owner's risk of course, and increases the value of the lease as less equity is needed to build the hotel. Any increase in appreciation in the combined package will be leveraged upward due to this financing. The lender generally looks to the subordinated land lease as secondary financing behind his loan.

Many owners do not want to subordinate their land or other interests so that the leasehold owner can use their equity to obtain a loan. After all, when the land is subordinated, the lender will look to the real value of land and buildings without deducting the capitalized rent cost to arrive at a leasehold equity. If the owner does not subordinate the fee to the lender, then the financing must be made with unsubordinated fee.

The terms of the lease become most important here. If the lease is for a very long term (usually the term of the loan plus a sufficient remaining term to allow the investor to benefit from a build-up of equity, say 150% of the mortgage life) and the payments on it are not onerous, then the lender will look to these leasehold interests as a pseudo-fee. This fee or ownership of the land is seen as a clear use of the land, and if all other factors work out a loan can be made without the subordination.

There are some areas in the world where almost all the land is leased and most all real estate financing is leasehold. Hong Kong and Hawaii are good examples of places where leasehold financing is rather prominent.

How Leasehold Financing Can Be A Deal Maker

The ability to pull apart a property to a fee equity and a lease-hold equity can be used in many different forms. A sale and lease-back, for example, is generally the sale of a property and then the leasing back of it by the seller. It may be feasible to sell the land to one party and lease that back and sell the building to another investor and lease it back. These two separate types of leases each have different values. First, the land lease could have excellent terms for the new owner of the land, thereby giving him a secure return for which he will accept the lower rate you want. The investor looking for tax shelter, and not much cash flow, may like the idea of owning a building. The fact that it is on leased land may add rather than subtract from his desire to buy. He cannot depreciate the land, but can deduct the rent on it.

The ability to obtain new financing on leased land or on leasehold space in other buildings will depend on your contacts in the money market. It will also depend on the total combined effect of the six factors shown in the earlier part of this section.

The rise and decline of the leasehold equity is, of course, the most important aspect of leasehold financing. The security offered by this equity, along with other risk reducers such as personal signature and guarantee on the note and pledge of other collateral or security, makes the leasehold mortgage a most interesting form of financing.

The sources for such finance monies are commercial banks and mortgage bankers and brokers. These sources do most of the lending in this form of financing, yet the savings and loans associations and insurance companies are effective in leasehold financing on a larger scale. All loan sources have dealt with one form of leasehold money at one time or another and continue to do so.

If you are financing on subordinated fee to a leasehold, then the lender will approach the loan as though the property is owned in fee simple rather than a leasehold. In that event, seek the normal lender for the type of property you have.

PERCENT OF INCOME

This form of percent taking is far more frequent than the sharing of actual ownership. In this form of financing the lender will receive his normal payment of interest and principal. But in addition to those payments, he will also receive a bonus of all or part of the income above a set standard. For example: Insurance Company A loans all the money needed to build a major shopping center. Their loan provisions indicate that they will receive a bonus of 20% of all income above a gross revenue of $2,500,000. Another lender, REIT B., has just financed a ten-story office building. Their loan states they get a bonus of 3% of the gross income above $200,000.

Both of these situations required the borrower to pay a percent of the income on the project to the lender. These types of loans are very similar to rents under leases that require the tenant to pay a bonus or percent of the gross income. Sometimes the lender will look to these leases as a source of the bonus on the mortgage. If the tenants in a center average 3% overages on their leases (that is to say, the leases are set at 3% of gross income against a minimum rent), then once the base rent is reached by the calculation of the 3% of gross income, all income above that will earn the bonus of 3% to the landlord. If the lender is participating in the income with the developer, then one method may be to split or in some way divide the over-ride of gross income on the leases.

Lenders usually have a cutoff on this revenue to assure that they do not exceed the usury for the area. For example, if the maximum interest which could be charged was 12%, then the total interest earned by the lender for that year could not exceed 12%. In most areas there is a difference in usury between private parties and corporations, with the corporation having the highest chargeable interest. Because of this, most lenders wishing to participate in ownership or percent of income will require the borrower to be a corporation. This will give them a higher amount of interest that they can receive and an additional buffer between earning and potential earning.

Offering a percent of the income on a property as an incentive to the lender to give good terms has its merit. If the base income passes through without any bonus to the lender, then only that income that may come because of improvement or appreciation in the property will go to him. And since the investment and cash flow are improved for the buyer, he also benefits from the transaction.

Using this same principle, it is possible to entice a seller to hold a good second mortgage on the sale of an income property. For example: Wilton wants to buy a small shopping center that Miles owns. Miles is asking $650,000 with $225,000 cash to his existing $425,000 mortgage. The existing cash flow based on the current debt service is $24,000. However, Miles is sure that the income will increase, as there are several vacant stores and rents will undoubtedly go up with new tenants. Wilton, however, demands at least a 12% return on his invested cash and can't quite see how to get it out of this center.

I took a look at the situation nearly four weeks after Wilton had given up on the Miles center. Wilton had come to me to see if I had anything else he might like to buy. During the several visits we made to other centers, he kept talking about Miles's center. I asked him why he was unable to put it together. "Miles won't take paper" was the reply. I spoke with the broker that had shown Wilton the Miles center and we agreed that if I could get Wilton back there and show Miles how a deal could be made, we would split the fee.

The first step was to go visit Miles with the other broker. I wanted to see how strongly Miles felt about the future of the center, and what was his motivation to sell. It turned out that Miles was motivated to sell because of an inability to cope with the problems of the center. He was not management oriented, and the tenants had quickly found that they could get what they wanted by bugging Miles to death. Yet, he did feel strongly about the future of the center and knew that if someone had the knowledge to manage it properly it would show a greater return than it presently did.

Based on this information, Wilton and I went over the income statement of the center. Wilton agreed that the income could be increased, but he had to be sure of a 12% return.

Here is what Wilton did: He offered the full price of $650,000 since it was a fair price. He was to pay $150,000 cash at closing and give Miles a $75,000 second mortgage to make up the balance. The pay-out of the second mortgage was as follows: ten-year interest only at 7% per annum. At the end of the ten years the total outstanding balance would be paid (Wilton would refinance the first mortgage at that time). As an inducement, Wilton added the provision that Miles would receive an additional bonus of 25% of all cash flow above $24,000.

Aside from some minor changes added by Miles to clarify the term "cash flow," we were able to sell him on the contract. Wilton could not prepay the second mortgage without a stiff penalty so Miles is still collecting on it. The income is over the original estimate and the property is throwing off better than a $33,500 cash flow. Miles is receiving an annual bonus of $2,375 along with his interest only payment of $5,250, giving him a total yield of 10.17%. In addition, the income is apt to increase before the mortgage is paid off.

The use of percent of ownership or percent of income as negotiating points will depend on their introduction at the right time. At times, the adversary in the negotiations brings these factors into the picture when you don't want them. A lender, for example, may want a piece of the action, but your client has not anticipated this possibility and has not allowed for such an eventuality. Many brokers do not know how to handle this type of situation and become confused by the lender's suggestion. Many lenders will look you right in the eye and tell you that they all want this kind of action. That may be true, of course. They may want it, but not all lenders demand it. Stick to your guns when you are unwilling to give up a piece of the action, but don't close the door. See what the lender is willing to do to get it.

LAND LEASES

The creation of a land lease is often one of the best methods of generating cash. This tool, when used properly, can be better than a mortgage and have a longer lasting effect. For example, Victor owned a large hotel with over 100 rooms. He had a good first mortgage and a satisfactory second mortgage. The total loan to value ratio was only 60% financing, as the property had appreciated greatly since Victor had financed it originally. He needed to generate some ready cash for improvements to the hotel.

In counseling with Victor, I asked him how much cash he needed to generate and what return he felt it would create for him in the improvement of the hotel. He said he needed $240,000 and that most of that would go into a complete refurnishing of the building. He expected the increased income from these improvements to be in the neighborhood of $50,000 to $60,000 per year.

We ruled out the possibility of refinancing the hotel, as the existing financing was at very low rates and the cost of new money was excessive. Points would have to be paid on the funds just to pay off the first and second, plus the extra money. Victor ruled out financing or leasing the furniture as too costly. And anyway, that would not cover the other work that needed to be done.

I suggested that Victor consider selling the land under the hotel and then leasing it back. After several conversations with him and his lawyer, it appeared that this was the best way to go.

A document was drawn up and the land was offered at $310,000 with an annual lease of $31,000 net, net, net. Victor had an option to recapture the land any time after the sixth year and before the fourteenth year for $31,000 plus $500 for each year after the sixth.

An investor bought the land and entered into the lease. The lease was subordinated to both the first and the second mortgages, but then these mortgages did represent a low percentage of the total value since the land value alone was in excess of $500,000. Victor could have obtained more for the land lease, but his payment would have been greater. The lease suited his needs and in fact generated more cash than required for the improvements.

Owning Land Or Leasing—How To Determine Which Is Best

The question of leasing instead of owning (or the other way around) has caused many brokers to pull their hair out by its roots. There is no clear-cut answer unless you have a multitude of facts about the situation. In an attempt to shed some light on this matter, I have provided the following guidelines as a method of giving economic justification to either the ownership or leasing of land. If we asusme that a buyer of an income property can either buy the land under the improvements or lease that land, we can see the need for the buyer to make this determination.

First, let's look at the economic factors that affect the land:

1. Land has no depreciation. In some types of land, mainly mineral or organic producing land, there is a depletion allowance which has a similar affect as depreciation. However, in land under income property, the land itself will produce no tax shelter.

2. The capital investment in land does not produce income. It is the use of the land that produces the income. If there is a medical complex on top of the land, or a parking lot or a hotel, it is the improvements and the use that produce income. The use of the land is not dependent on ownership. All value will ultimately depend on the use. Even when land is rented or leased, it is not the land that produces the income. It is the use that gives it value and warrants a lease, which in turn throws off income to the owner even though he may not be the user.

3. A capital investment in land must be offset by the economic rent which can be allocated to that investment. This economic rent is the income which that capital investment would earn if invested at the maximum or nominal rate which the investor could obtain elsewhere. If an investor buys land under an office building at the same time he buys the office building, he has both the use of the land and the ownership of the land. The cost of the land, or his capital investment which can be allocated to the land, must carry this economic rent expense for the ownership to be feasible. If the investor is able to earn 9% on his investments outside the investment in the land, this rate of 9% would be his economic rent expense.

4. Ownership and leasing must be considered on the life of the economic use and the value at the end of that use to be comparable. It should be obvious that ownership is infinite whereas a lease terminates. However, if the lease is for a sufficient time period to encompass the economic use of the improvements and has a value at the end of that time, there will be economic justification in the lease.

5. Use extends beyond the physical manipulation of the site. The right to mortgage, develop, sell, transfer, and so on, are all values which must be

considered in the analysis of a lease. Ownership generally has these provisions, whereas a lease is usually limited in some degree. This limitation will deduct from the value of the lease.

6. The continued cost of the lease over its term will no doubt fluctuate in most cases. The economic rent of land in ownership also fluctuates and must be considered. For example: Ownership costs the economic rent based on the reinvestment rate. As this increases, the capital tied up in the land also increases in cost. The appreciation of the land by normal processes increases the amount of capital tied up and therefore pushes the economic rent even higher. If Liggett paid $100,000 for land ten years ago, and the economic rent was 11% then, his cost was $11,000 per year. If the land has a present value of $150,000 and the reinvestment rate is now 12%, the cost of the land is $18,000 per year.

7. Because ownership of land requires a major capital investment, whereas the lease is generally limited to a fraction of that capital cost, the initial economics will often depend on the initial capability of the investor. If the investor is capable of buying the land, he may still choose to lease it for economic reasons. On the other hand, if the land cannot be purchased and is available for lease only, then the investor must weigh the value of the lease in connection with the cost of the improvements. For each situation there will be a point at which the lease becomes economically feasible. This may, of course, require adjustments in the one factor which is flexible—the price of the improvements.

For example: Heathcote was negotiating on a hotel and found that the improvements were on leased land. The lease did not provide for a recapture of the land so he could not buy it. He could only buy the improvements on the leasehold. The NOI of the hotel before land lease was $100,000 and the land was $20,000 per year. The price asked on the hotel (subject to the lease) was $700,000. The cash flow on this free and clear property was 11.42% per year. There was no question about buying the land, but had it been available it would have been worth nearly $300,000. In adjusting the investment then, if Heathcote had been able to buy both the land and the improvements at the price of $1,000,000, he would have had a NOI of $100,000 or a yield of 10% per year. This would place the economic rent at 10% of the reinvestment capital of $300,000. The economic rent would therefore be $30,000, whereas the actual rent on lease was only $20,000. This produces one of the economic criteria in determining the value of leasing over owning. If the economic rent is higher than the actual cost, the lease may be more desirable than if the leasehold will sustain its value through the economic life of the hotel and retain value beyond that time.

This of course raises the question: How do you determine the economic life of a property and the value thereafter? This will call for a projection based on known facts. You must find out how quickly the investor wants to have the return of his capital investment, what yield he wants in the meanwhile, and what appreciation he feels he should obtain on his investment. If Heathcote invests $700,000 in obtaining the hotel on the leased land, and then demands an 11.42% cash flow, wants to see a complete return of his capital within 15 years, and also wants an annual appreciation simple of 3%—these would be the factors to analyze.

Heathcote has set a 15-year economic life on his investment. Therefore, he knows that a buyer must be able to pay a price at that time which would give him his capital investment plus, and that the property would have to have remaining life to warrant an investor paying the required purchase price. Heathcote's price in 15 years is easily calculated since he has purchased the property free and clear. Three percent per year appreciation times 15 years would give a simple interest appreciation of 45%. The price at the end of 15 years would therefore have to be $1,015,000. This would mean that the cash flow would have to increase by the same 3% for a buyer to reap the same yield on his investment as Heathcote has. The feasibility of this will depend on the property and the economic condition of the location 15 years from now. This is a most difficult factor to project—but possible based on past trends.

However, 15 years from now, a new buyer will look at the property at $1,015,000 and make a similar analysis. The economic value of the property must project a higher return in future years to enable this new investor to recoup his investment plus some appreciaiton. If the original lease was for 30 years at the time Heathcote purchased the property, the new investor must obtain all his return and recoup capital plus appreciation out of the income from the property, as there would be no possibility of selling the leasehold once it has terminated. If the remaining life cannot support this estimated value, even with optimistic projections, then the original lease-hold purchased by Heathcote was excessive, or his projections on yield demanded and appreciation anticipated were too high.

Therefore, it is important that all situations which provide the opportunity to lease instead of purchase land, or when the land is leased and ownership is not available, be analyzed with the total return capability over the economic life with sufficient time to provide return of capital and appreciation. To make this analysis as easy as possible, I have provided two checklists which can be filled out to determine if the economic situation favors leasing or ownership. Keep in mind that the economics alone will not be sufficient to determine the acceptability of the lease; the other factors mentioned must be considered as well. Nonetheless, if the economic value does not favor the lease, there must be adjustments in the price of the improvements to bring about a change to make the lease acceptable. If these changes are not possible, then either the buyer must accept the lease as it is, often due to the inability to raise sufficient capital to buy the land, or the investor must pass on the transaction.

Checklist One. This list of calculations would be used when the land is offered either as a part of the purchase price or with an option to lease instead. To understand the use of this list, look at the facts of this case study and then see the checklist in Figure 15-1:

> Ambrose is looking at an office building which can be purchased for \$700,000 with a \$20,000 per year land lease, or for \$1,000,000 including the land. The property has a NOI of \$77,000 and an existing mortgage of \$400,000 payable at \$40,000 per year. Ambrose must find the cash flow yield for both situations and establish the economic rent expense of the land.

Figure 15-1: CHECKLIST FOR WHEN THE LAND CAN BE LEASED OR PURCHASED

NOI: \$77,000 DEBT SERVICE: \$40,000	PURCHASE ON TERMS	PURCHASE WITH 100% EQUITY
1. The total purchase price of land and improvements	\$700,000	\$700,000
2. Less total financing available	400,000	0
3. Total cash down	300,000	700,000
4. Less reduction of cash down if land is leased	200,000	200,000
5. Cash down if land is leased	100,000	500,000
6. Annual lease payments on land	(A) 20,000	20,000
7. Cash flow before land lease (NOI less debt service)	37,000	77,000
8. Cash flow after land lease (line 7 less line 6)	17,000	57,000
9. Cash flow yield (no land lease) (line 7 ÷ line 3)	(B) 12.33%	11%
10. Cash flow yield with land lease (line 8 ÷ line 5)	(C) 17%	11.4%
11. Economic rent expense of land if owned (line 4 × line 9)	(D) 24,660	22,000

In reviewing the checklist, notice blocks A, B, C, and D. Block A is the annual lease payment or the rent cost of the lease. Block D represents the economic rent expense of the land if the land is owned. Whenever A is lower than D the primary indication would be that the lease is economically more feasible than ownership, all other things being equal. Blocks B and C show the cash flow yields on the investment without the lease and with the lease respectively. The greater the percent in C, the more desirable the lease.

You will note that the analysis was done in two stages—first with the terms offered and then as though the price were 100% down. It is necessary to show both these calculations, since the debt service on the existing financing may be excessive during the early years of the purchase and the premise shown above would reverse itself. For example: If the annual debt service were $56,000, lines 6 through 11 would show the following:

6. 20,000 (A)
7. 21,000
8. 1,000
9. 7% (B)
10. 1% (C)
11. 14,000 (D)

This would cause A to be greater than D, and B to be greater than C. If the 100% calculation also showed the same status, this would mean that even though the amounts would be different, the lease was not more favorable than ownership from an economic point of view. If the 100% investment varies from the purchase with terms, this indicates there is a negative leverage present, and it is the terms of the financing that have caused the lease vs. ownership calculations to be misread. Naturally, if the terms on the financing cause the cash flow on line 7 to be less than the land lease payments, then the economic structure of the lease is not possible without greater capital investment or a restructuring of the financing terms.

Once a determination has been made as to the favorability of the lease over ownership, the full criteria of the lease can be analyzed. Does the lease provide transferability or mortgagability and will the economic life allow for a recoupment of capital? If not, the original economic favorability must give way to the overall analysis of the lease and its effect on the future return of capital plus appreciation. Sometimes, the buyer has no option except to buy with the land lease. It is not uncommon to have property with existing land leases. In these situations there is no option to buy land or not. The calculations are centered around the need to know if the total price for the improvements needs adjustment to make the land lease economically feasible.

This case study involves these facts: A motel is listed at $600,000 and is on leased land. There is an existing land lease of $24,000 per year and an existing mortgage of $450,000 (75% of the price of the improvements) payable at $45,000 per year. The NOI is $87,000 per year and shows a cash flow after debt service and land lease of $18,000. (Figure 15-2.)

Checklist Two. This list (Figure 15-2) is also computed with the purchase on the terms stated, and again with 100% equity. This will provide a check against a misread check if the debt service is the culprit in the land lease showing up as unfavorable to ownership of the land.

In the first analysis (Figure 15-1), we can see that under the terms offered with the land lease the economic rent expense (block D) is far less than the actual cost of the land lease. Also, the cash flow for the project without the land lease is greater than with it, based on the hypothetical purchase of the land and the

Figure 15-2: CHECKLIST TWO FOR WHEN THE LAND CAN ONLY BE LEASED

NOI: $87,000* DEBT SERVICE: $45,000 NEW MTG. DEBT SERVICE		PURCHASE ON TERMS (B) $ 62,000	PURCHASE WITH 100% EQUITY
1. Total purchase price of improvements		600,000	$600,000
2. Less total financing available		450,000	0
3. Cash down		150,000	600,000
4. Annual payment of land lease	(A)	24,000	24,000
5. Current cash flow (or projected)		18,000	63,000
6. Cash flow yield with land lease (line 5 ÷ line 3)	(B)	12%	10.50%
7. Estimated value of *land* alone		225,000	225,000
8. *Total* purchase price of land and improvements (est.)		825,000	825,000
9. Less estimated total financing available if land could be purchased (75% of new value)		618,750	0
10. Cash down (which would include land) (line 9 less line 10)		206,250	825,000
11. Cash down allocated to land (line 10 less line 3)		56,250	225,000
12. Cash flow adjustment to estimated financing (NOI less new debt service (B))		25,000	87,000
13. Cash flow yield (no land lease) (line 12 ÷ line 10)		12.12%	10.54%
14. Economic rent expense of the land (line 11 × line 13)	(C)	681.75	23,715

*Before land lease cost has been deducted.

estimated financing which would be available. Of course, it is important that this estimated financing be real to the market conditions. To determine if the financing is creating this disfavor of the land lease, the computations are done again with 100% equity. The same result is seen; however, not as dramatically as before. The result clearly indicates that the land lease is not desirable under the price and terms of the purchase.

Of course, in this circumstance the land lease is already set and cannot be altered. Therefore, the price must be the basis for negotiations. There are two places in which adjustments can be made which would cause the calculations to favor the land lease. The first and most obvious would be the purchase price and adjustments of financing; and second, the amount down and adjustments of financing. Because both of these methods can be attacked in many different ways since the cash flow is dependent on the debt service, it will be necessary to have some adjustment in that area.

How To Use Land Lease As A Financing Tool To Help Sell Property

Because the use of land leases reduces the initial capital requirement on the purchase price, the land lease could be considered as an alternative to second mortgages held by the seller. Or, it could be sold to another party, thereby generating cash for the seller. As long as the economics of the land lease are favorable, as seen in Figure 15-1, then the buyer can rationalize the use of this tool as beneficial to increasing the yield on his investment.

The land lease has many advantages for the seller holding it after a sale over the junior mortgages, and because of this a lower annual payment will usually result for the buyer. For example: a $200,000 value can be seen as both a second mortgage and as a land lease. If the buyer gives a second mortgage in the amount of $200,000 payable over 20 years at 8½% per annum, the annual payment would be slightly over $21,000. A land lease based at 9% of the value would be $18,000. The obvious difference is that the land lease continues beyond the mortgage pay-out whereas the mortgage terminates at the end of the 20-year term. Many investors assume that this factor alone will cause the land lease to be more onerous than a mortgage. This, however, may not be true. Examine the illustration which follows:

WALTERS HAS THE OPTION OF PAYING A LAND LEASE OF $18,000 PER YEAR OR A SECOND MORTGAGE OF $21,000 PER YEAR. HOW DOES HE COME OUT?

The Second Mortgage:	
1. Total payments over 20 years	$420,000
2. Amount which can be deducted	220,000
3. Tax rate (assume 50% in this study)	50%
4. Amount of deduction	110,000
5. Total after tax payment (1 less 4)	310,000
The Land Lease:	
1. Total payments over 20 years	360,000
2. Amount which can be deducted	360,000
3. Tax rate (assume 50% in this study)	50%
4. Amount of deduction	180,000

5.	Total after tax payment (1 less 4)	180,000
6.	Overage available for reinvestment (amount of mortgage payment less lease payment)	3,000 per yr.
7.	Rate of investment	8% (assumption)
8.	Future value of line 7 at the end of 20 years	137,285
9.	Less capital reinvestment for period	60,000
10.	Amount of interest on reinvestment	77,285
11.	Amount of tax paid or payable	38,643
12.	Total gain on reinvestment after tax	98,642
13.	Actual cost of land lease at same annual investment as second mortgage (line 5 less line 12)	81,358
14.	Original cost of land (as a mortgage)	200,000
15.	If bought at end of 20 years total paid	281,358

This analysis assumes a tax rate of 50% and a reinvestment rate of 8%. It should be obvious that if the investor is paying $21,000 each year in both situations, he will have $3,000 left to reinvest after the land lease is made. Of course, the major argument in this analysis in favor of the second mortgage would be that the investor may not be able to purchase the land at $200,000 in 20 years. This is true, but then the purchase could be as high as $238,642 for the calculations to equal the amount paid on the second mortgage.

If the investor had purchased the land in the form of a second mortgage, when he went to sell the property he would have to obtain a higher price to receive this capital. But if the lease continued for the new buyer, the sale might be easier as the total price would be less and, assuming no increase in income, the yield would be greater. If the investor did sell on the twentieth year and the buyer assumes the land lease, the total paid out would be only $81,358 on the land lease, assuming the reinvestment of $3,000 per year at 8% instead of $320,000 on the second mortgage (all figures are after taxes).

The holder of the second mortgage has not done badly, of course. He took in $420,000 over the 20 years and paid tax on a portion of that amount which represented interest. If he were a seller, a portion of the balance may have been taxable under capital gains rates. However, the lessor, the same seller perhaps, took in $360,000 in rent payments and will take in another $360,000 the following 20 years. One day, he or his estate may get the entire property back when the lease terminates.

It is not unusual for the lessee to obtain an option to buy the land at some time in the future. This option may be tied to some form of price escalation, such as the cost of living or a set scale.

CO-VENTURES AND SYNDICATES CAN BE NOVEL WAYS TO FINANCE PROPERTY

These two forms of financing will be discussed together since they both involve some similar techniques. To some degree they can be the same thing, depending on your point of view.

A *co-venture* is a joint effort by two or more people who combine abilities or capabilities. In real estate, the co-venture can take many forms. It may be a land owner who joins up with a developer. The land owner puts up the land and the builder his knowledge of building, and together they develop the land. Or, it could be two doctors who join forces to buy a lot to build a medical complex.

A *syndicate*, on the other hand, is generally thought of as a group of people who combine their monetary ability to buy land or other property for a mutually profitable end result. As you can see, the syndicate is a form of joint venture, even though not all co-ventures take the syndication route.

There are numerous legal forms of ownership for both types of investing and financing. Limited partnerships have been used for both co-ventures and syndicates and have special tax privileges which, to some degree, still hold up under the new tax laws. Investment trusts, corporations, professional associations, and partnerships all are legal forms of ownership which can be used in both of these creative forms of financing.

The purpose of this section of this chapter is not to make you an expert in co-venture enterprises or syndications. This takes considerable study and knowledge. Instead, the brief passages on these topics are meant to spark your interest in these exciting fields.

What Co-Ventures And Syndicates Can Do For You And Your Clients

There will be times when the price or size of a property you represent is beyond the capability of the average investor. When this situation presents itself, the solution may be to divide the ownership interest among several buyers. This division of ownership could take the form of a syndication and you would become the syndicator. The end result of the transaction would be a sale of the property and a fee earned. On the other hand, you may find one buyer that would like to develop the property, and his capability is such that he can handle the project if the seller will co-venture it with him. In this situation you have a co-venture transaction and you would act much like a syndicator, except that once the deal is put together you are no longer involved in it. Or, you may become part of the venture yourself. It is not unusual for the real estate broker to go into a deal as a co-venture partner.

Remember, no matter which form of financing you use, the goals of your clients are the first factor to consider. If all parties are suited for a co-venture, then this tool can be used satisfactorily. However, the co-venture transaction will keep the seller in (if the seller is a co-venture partner, of course) and this fact may not provide the desired results.

From the broker's point of view, any form of financing which will give reasonable results should be attempted. The broker knows that the exact goal may never be attained, so he should try to come as close as possible to it as he can.

Where Do You Find Partners For Co-Ventures?

They are almost everywhere. The first step is to determine the probable use of the property. Once you know, or at least have some idea of, the use which would be economically feasible, you will know where to go to find a partner for the transaction. For example, if you represent the owner of a tract of land that is suitable for construction of a shopping center, you would look to developers of shopping centers as possible partners.

Your build-up of contracts in other areas will help. Mortgage bankers, mortgage brokers, architects, and general contractors all have leads that can direct you to someone actively looking for such a transaction.

What You Can Do To Make The Transaction More Appealing To The Possible Co-Venture Partner

This is the most important part of the process. Once you have a property and feel that the co-venture is best suited for your seller, the move you make to entice the developer into the transaction may mean the difference between a deal that will work and one that will not.

The complete understanding and approval of the seller is crucial. Many brokers go off with the feeling that their client will do anything to make a deal and start looking for a co-venture partner. At the final moment, they find that the seller will do almost anything except go into a partnership. Get this understanding early and keep your seller informed of your progress. Be sure he understands the type of deal you hope to make and see if he finds it feasible from his point of view.

There are many ways to structure a co-venture deal, and the actual transaction itself can vary from the original plan with just minor changes. Most sellers are not aware of the special clauses which are often inserted in such transactions. Many make the deal workable, others just complicate it. All are important, however. Some of the more important fine points are the following:

Five Important Features in Co-Ventures

1. The preferred return. Often, one of the partners will demand a preferred return on his investment. Either the seller or the other partners can request this, but it is generally the money partner who will prevail. The seller may offer this as an inducement to get big money investors. The preferred return, in essence, is a condition that allows the first percent of the income to go to this investor. The percent can be a set percentage, such as 12%, or some other percentage based on income gross. For example: Reynolds invests $100,000 into a co-venture deal and is preferred 12% on his investment. This means he will get the first $12,000 of income. The other partners then get the next $12,000 and the overage is split based on other provisions of the agreement.

2. *The guaranteed return.* This is much stronger than the preferred return and is not used too often. The same occurs as in the above situation, except that Reynolds will be *guaranteed* the return of 12%. What would happen if the income did not total enough to pay his return would depend on the balance of the terms of the agreement. However, a guaranteed return may constitute a security and should be used only in situations where the sellers can sell securities under the laws of the state in which they act and meet Federal Security Laws as well. It is best to seek the advice of a lawyer on this matter. This type of agreement is widely used outside the United States, and is seen in international real estate transactions frequently.

3. *Accural of unpaid but earned return.* This can be used with both the preferred return and the guaranteed return. Here, the investor will not be paid the amount of the preference or guarantee, either because of a lack of income from the project or his desire not to receive the funds. The amount of his investment is then increased by the amount not paid, thus increasing his later return. For example: Reynolds was not paid $12,000 this year because the income and expenses broke even. His total investment is now calculated at $112,000 and his preference or guaranteed income will be based on that amount, instead of the original investment of $100,000.

4. *Subordinate interest.* While either party can subordinate its interest, it is generally the seller who is called on to do this. The seller puts up all or a part of his equity in the transaction behind financing to be obtained. This will allow the co-venture to benefit from the full equity and obtain the maximum mortgage available. This requires the party giving the subordination to accept higher risk, but may be warranted if the transaction is economically feasible.

5. *Land bank.* At times, the owner of a tract of land may be willing to carry the cost of the land while the co-venture partner gets the development ready. In essence, the cost of carrying the land will become an additional expense for the owner, but land banking is sometimes essential for obtaining the other partner. It is usually used when the time needed to bring the property to development cannot be determined, or is already known to be such that immediate development will not be possible, and when the co-venture partner does not want to hold land.

Your ability to use these features to make the co-venture attractive for developers or investors will depend on your understanding of the area's and the investors' needs. For example, it would not be productive to look for a developer for a hotel if hotels cannot be financed or are in disfavor in your area for some reason. Also, the use of the property must be almost immediate. However, remember that the time it takes to develop a shopping center is much longer than the time it takes to build a strip store. Because of this, the time needed to begin construction will vary. A major center will take at least two years from the word "go" to the word "open."

What You Can Do To Become Involved With Syndications And Co-Venture Deals

The first step may be this book. It contains most of the tools used by both the syndicator and the broker to put together co-ventures. Study these tools and see how they can be used in these forms of financing. The application of all the aspects of financing will be no more difficult when dealing with a group of buyers for a syndication or a builder for a co-venture than when dealing one-to-one with a buyer. The only difference may be the size of the commission, which might be greater in the syndication or co-venture.

Ask your lawyer to help you with the syndication or to give you some information about the co-venture deals he has put together. If you can read over some actual co-venture and syndication prospectuses you will learn a great deal.

Be careful of the legal requirements in syndication. There are many laws which control the sale of securities and most syndications will fall within one or more of these laws. Real estate professional bodies are presently seeking more clarification of some of these laws which are not precise as to their interpretation, so don't be surprised if you get several different answers to some of your questions.

Do not become a professional syndicator. This is the guy who does nothing but syndications. He is generally not highly regarded in the industry since he will syndicate anything to make a deal. However, this certainly does not hold true for all professional syndicators. The best syndicators are those knowledgeable brokers and associates who use syndications as a tool to build their own wealth. Remember, you should want to invest in real estate yourself if this is your profession. And what better way to do this than to bring in other investors to help you.

Look around your market area and see who is involved in syndicating. If you can locate several brokers, talk to them and see what they feel you could do to get started. Some will be candid and offer you help in this direction while others won't encourage competition.

At this time, I feel it is important to mention one of my basic philosophies of this business. Real estate is my profession, and I am in the business of helping my clients reach their goals. Therefore, I believe it is necessary to offer all properties that are good buys to my clients first—before I consider buying any of them for my own portfolio. You will find that when you follow this practice, you can pass on to your clients the best of what you might later buy if they do not. This reasoning also takes care of the client who will say: "OK, if this is such a hot buy who don't you buy it yourself?" Or the other client who says: "I know this is hot, but not hot enough for you to buy it." Or the last one who says: "You always gobble up the good ones yourself."

For example: I once saw a tract of land that I knew was priced to sell. I sweated out three weeks of showing it to nearly 40 of my prospective buyers, none of which could or would see the value. I bought the property myself (after having told all of them I had this in mind) and sold it two years later at a 400% profit. They all later became good clients and now act quickly when I show them a property with high recommendations.

Chapter 16

Refinancing Real Estate

Why should you or your client sell or dispose of property if a refinancing of the existing mortgages will solve the problem? The answer to this question may seem obvious, yet it is too often overlooked as a way of solving the client's problems. The fact is there are many prospective sellers who should be "keepers."

Many brokers close their eyes and ears to the possibility of telling a seller he should not sell. After all, a broker usually makes his money by selling property and he may find little or no monetary reward in convincing sellers to keep their property. Right? Wrong! Brokers will find that a satisfied client is money in the bank. If you can help your client reach his goals, in the best way, then you will benefit later if not at present.

With this in mind, this section is devoted to the concept that some sellers should not or need not sell or dispose of their property in order to reach their goals. Some of the techniques which will be used in the solving of problems in this manner have been discussed in previous chapters. This section will give you guidelines to follow which will indicate when a seller should keep his property. You will then learn how to best use the tools of real estate financing to solve sellers' problems.

THE FIRST STEP: DETERMINING THE PROBLEM AND THE GOAL

Of course, this is the first step in all problem solving. You must fully understand the problem and the desired goal. The first three chapters of this book are devoted to finding the problem and setting up the groundwork for reaching the desired goal. Most of this book is directed toward methods that produce commissions. However, you must keep an open mind to the fact that the seller need not sell at all. This is often very hard to do for several reasons.

1. The seller is often convinced that he must sell.
2. The salesman will usually reinforce that conviction.
3. If a salesman tells his client he should not sell and cannot offer a plausible alternative, the client, convinced that he must sell, will go somewhere else.
4. Salesmen are reluctant to tell a client he should not sell because they will have to forfeit their commission.

FOUR QUESTIONS TO ASK TO DETERMINE IF THE SELLER SHOULD KEEP HIS PROPERTY OR NOT

1. Why does the seller believe a sale (or other disposition) of the property is the proper method of solving the problem? Some sellers know exactly why they feel this way, others don't know or can't pinpoint the reason. This answer will be a clue to the preconditioning of the client by other sources. If the client has a good reason for feeling the disposition of the property is proper, or the situation is clear without asking the question, then you may be able to stop here. On the other hand, if the answer is vague and the client isn't sure why he feels the sale or disposition is best for him, proceed to the next question.

2. Restate the problem as you feel you understand it and ask: "If I can show you how we can reach a solution to your problem without selling or disposing of the property, would this interest you?" At this time, the client may bring up other reasons for wanting to dispose of the property and the whole problem may become clearer to both of you. A prospective seller of a small motel may have a plausible problem and reason for selling. When presented with a possible solution that requires him to keep the property, he may then disclose another reason for wanting to sell. The actual reason is important, of course, but more important here is the fact that he may just want to get rid of the property. In any event, you will proceed to the next question to close the gap.

3. In the second question results in a "yes," answer, restate the problem again, but make your restatement positive and inclusive of the client retaining the property. For example: If the problem is a desire to have more motel units, a client may have first thought he had to sell the existing property to buy a larger complex. You have determined by virtue of a "yes" to Question 2 that the client would keep his property. If you can solve that desire, your follow-up statement would be: "As one possible solution to your desire to have more units (the problem), you would keep your present units if we could refinance them to provide for additional ones?" Using this process, you look for acceptance of this

statement. If you get a rejection, ask for a clarification and continue to restate the problem in a positive way until there is an acceptance of your understanding of the situation. Once you have done this, you have discovered if the client can meet his needs as he sees them and in doing so keep the existing property. This does not solve the problem, of course, but gives you room to move in that direction.

4. If the answer to Question 2 was a "no," you have a client that has reasons for wanting to sell different from those originally given. A "no" to Question 2 will allow you to go back to the first question. With this new reason and a possible change in the original problem, you may get a better idea of why the client feels a sale or other disposition is required or necessary. Unless there is some obvious reason to doubt the sincerity of the client or the circumstances of the transaction, you can conclude that the need or want to dispose of the property will out-weigh any other possible solution.

Once you have come to the conclusion that the client has no real basis for selling, other than possible preconditioning, and he has agreed that a solution that includes his keeping the property would be acceptable, you can proceed to the task of finding that solution and then determining if it is plausible.

EXAMINING THE PROPERTY FOR REFINANCING

The next step in this process is to examine the property. There will be six factors to look at and analyze.

1. The economic benefit of the property. You must ascertain the economic benefit of the existing property from the client's point of view. As you are looking at refinancing as well as a sale as possible solutions in this situation, the economics of the property will play a great role in both. If the income is not sufficient to support new or adjusted financing, then refinancing may not work. At the same time, if the economics are such that the property is a drain on the client, no matter how good the future income or profit may be, the lapse of income could augment the problems of the client and cause the refinancing plan to fail in obtaining its objectives.

2. The economic ability of the client. What can the client do or afford to do within the scope of possible refinancing? If he is in need of considerable cash, but cannot support lending outside the ability of the property to repay, then the full advantage of maximum leverage may be lost. Of course, the maximum leverage with extended debt may not be prudent in any event, even if the economics of the property warrant that move but the client does not.

3. The economic need of the client. What does he need monetarily to solve his problem? Keep in mind that the problem will change somewhat when the client decides to keep the property rather than sell or dispose of it. If he wants more units and at first felt he had to sell the existing ones in order to buy a larger project, his need for cash would be greater than if he kept the units he had and added to them. On the other hand, if he is moving out of town and the home he has is a burden and he wants to replace the drain with a cash flow, the need may exceed the ability of the property if rented.

4. The reinvestment capability to replace or better the yield obtained from the existing investment. If the client cannot find a reinvestment as good as the one he has, then there may be no reason to sell. Once the client is aware of his net funds for reinvestment (after cost and tax), his original thoughts of what he can buy may be altered.

5. The market conditions for disposition of the property. If the market is down, a disposition at this time may not produce the highest and best price. At the same time, the desired reinvestment may be up and the cost difference in the replacement of the funds may be to the client's disadvantage.

6. The current financing on the property. This gets right down to the equity position and a determination as to the possibility of refinancing above that equity. If the present equity position is weak, new financing may be difficult to find and harder to place. Adjustments in existing financing may be possible, but that alone may not solve the problem.

The combined effect of these six factors will aid you in deciding on the possibility of refinancing. This end result will be determined by the type of refinancing available and its overall impact on the client when compared with possible disposition. After all, your solution should be the best possible one for reaching the client's goals. You may find that refinancing does not move the client as close to his desired goals as a sale would.

HOW REFINANCING CAN ALLOW THE CLIENT TO KEEP HIS PROPERTY AND SOLVE HIS OTHER PROBLEMS AT THE SAME TIME

The answer for solving the problem may be in several alternate methods of using the financing tools given you in this book. I have provided a list of possible solutions which can be used in refinancing.

Twenty Ways The Owner Can Keep His Property By Refinancing

1. *Sell the land and lease it back.*
2. *Obtain secondary financing to generate cash.*
3. *Pyramid with a second mortgage to gain buying power.*
4. *Refinance the existing financing into a new first mortgage.*
5. *Sell the entire property, lease back with an option to buy.*
6. *Renegotiate the existing financing to lower the constant rate.*

7. *Seek a moratorium on the existing mortgage for either interest or principle or both.*
8. *Refinance with use of real estate bonds.*
9. *Bring in a partner through a syndication or joint venture.*
10. *Plan addition and refinance total package.*
11. *Buy adjoining property and refinance total package.*
12. *Discount existing financing for cash.*
13. *Sell chattels and lease them back.*
14. *Seek unsecured financing.*
15. *Refinance with blanket mortgage adding other security.*
16. *Rent to cover expenses and debt service.*
17. *Prepay rent or mortgage to obtain better terms.*
18. *Sell only a portion of the property or interest.*
19. *Sublease a portion of the property or interest.*
20. *Look to a wrap-around mortgage to generate required capital.*

How One Broker Turned One Client That Shouldn't Sell And Another That Wouldn't Sell Into Buyers

Silvers was the owner of a 57-unit oceanfront motel in the Ft. Lauderdale area. His business had been great for the three years that he had owned the property—so much so that he wanted to buy a larger building. His first thought was to buy something not only larger, but newer than his 17-year-old facility. He went to Richman, a broker in town, to see what the market looked like for his 57 units. He hoped that with the cash from the sale, and about $150,000 he had, he could buy something larger. As it turned out, Silvers had bought his property in the right way and had considerable equity in it due to the appreciation of land on the ocean.

Richman was glad to see a motivated ''seller'' walk into his office and went through the motions of taking the listing. They arrived at a price after the second meeting and Richman proceeded to market the motel, while at the same time looking for something containing around 80 units or more for Silvers. There were several near deals on the motel, but Silvers kept firm on his price and was cool to negotiation since he had not yet found anything else. He did not want to sell and not have another property sewed up.

One day it dawned on Richman that if he could get the adjoining property next to Silvers's motel, the two properties combined would total nearly 85 units. That could solve the problem. At first he hesitated to even mention the idea to Silvers because it seemed so obvious. So, instead he contacted the owner of the adjoining property who lived out of town. The motel was managed by a long-time friend of the owner who Richman knew to be highly protective of his job.

The owner said he didn't want to sell the motel under any condition and that he was happy with the type of operation he had. This was a blow to Richman and seemed to be the end of that idea. Nonetheless, he followed up his call with a letter thanking the owner for his time and offering his services should he need any help in real estate in the area.

A month passed by, and not much happened. Silvers was becoming disappointed about not finding anything to replace the 57 units and was wondering if he should sell after all. Richman then took another stab at the owner of the adjoining property. This time he asked the owner if he would be interested in buying Silvers's motel. He leveled with the owner and told him what Silvers wanted to do. He also told him that at first he thought if Silvers could add to his existing property by buying the adjoining property it would solve the problem. In any event, as the owner didn't want to sell perhaps he would want to do the same thing that Silvers wanted to do. The owner said it was a good idea, but if anything he would want a smaller operation and not a larger one. Lights began to flash, and Richman asked the owner why he didn't sell and buy something smaller. The owner said his tax situation would not permit a sale as his basis was so low he would have too much to pay in tax. Richman then suggested an exchange.

The owner came to town and looked at several smaller properties that were on the market. It seemed his real interest was to find something that had a large apartment for his own use when he was in town. He picked out one that was just right for his needs.

Richman then went to Silvers and told him he had the solution to his problem—the adjoining property was available. Also, the combination of the two properties would give him the right size operation. He could capitalize on the business he had built up in the location over the past three years.

To make the deal work, Silvers would buy the property the other owner had picked out and then exchange it for the motel adjoining his. This would satisfy the exchange requirements for the owner and at the same time solve the problem Silvers had.

The cash needed to make the deal, and the funds required to put both properties into first class condition, was obtained by refinancing the new combined package of the two motels Silvers now had. The transaction was a buy, exchange, and refinancing. All aspects of the transaction were tied to the ultimate mortgage that Silvers would get on the last leg of the deal.

Richman ended up with two deals. He had converted one seller into a keeper and one keeper into an exchanger. In essence, both of these clients bought other properties and each solved a problem.

Another Seller Becomes A Keeper

Harris had a nice home on one of the islands in town. It was a smaller, older home. The lot under it had most of the value. I had known Harris only socially and had not done any business with him until this occasion. After several meetings with him and his wife, I came to the conclusion that since their desire was to have a more modern home, they should keep what they had and remodel. They could not sell in the present market and reinvest the return from a sale in a location as valuable and buy a home as nice. We decided that to completely remodel the home would be a good investment because if they wanted to sell later on they could get all the cost back and some profit to boot.

They decided to do exactly that and spent the next six months remodeling. I had introduced them to a builder in town that specialized in that type of work and they were most satisfied with the results. The basic house was so designed that with some simple changes a dramatic result was obtained.

Harris worked for an international company. One day he called and said he was being transferred to London and could we sell his home for him. Of course we could, I told him, but what about the future? What did he plan to do after London? Was London to be permanent or just temporary? He wasn't sure, but he felt that he wanted to eventually retire to Florida.

With this in mind, I suggested he consider renting the home as his first choice. If he could get enough rent to carry his mortgage and throw off a little extra, he would be ahead of the game. He said that was reasonable, but just in case a tenant didn't come along we set a price for sale anyway.

The home was rented and Harris went off to London. We had included a provision in the lease that it could be terminated with a three-month notice should the job in London become more temporary than was anticipated.

Six months later, Harris called me and said he was being transferred back to Miami! Fortunately, he had a home to return to. The tenant, though surprised about the lease being terminated, understood and moved out.

In looking back over the whole series of events, if Harris had sold the home in the first instance, long before his move to London, he would have bought another home and most likely would have had a large mortgage and more invested in it than he did in his older, now remodeled home. That would have made the later move to London very difficult. Then, of course, had he sold the home when he did move to London, his reinvestment might have been in London, hence complicating the later move to Florida again.

It would have been very easy for our firm to have sold his home at any stage, but that was not in his best interest. Harris realizes that, and the goodwill gained has far exceeded the fee our firm would have earned on a sale.

How Refinancing Can Improve The Owner's Situation

Often, a prospective seller wants to sell what he has in order to buy a more productive property. This might mean moving either up or down, depending on the type of investment and the capabilities the client feels he can handle. Notice I say "feels he can handle," since many clients don't know the true capability of their investment capital. They will usually underestimate the ability to buy and overestimate the ability to make more than they are presently making with their existing property. By examining the various tools of financing, we have seen that it is possible to increase the cash flow on income property by adjusting the debt service on that property. Often, through a creative application of financing, the income can be so improved that the reinvestment capability of the capital in the event of a sale would not produce as good a cash flow yield as the existing property would.

The needs of any property owner must be considered in making the decision to keep or to sell. In fact, any investment must be examined in terms of these following four points:

1. The risk to the owner. Risk is relative. Some people can risk greater capital than others. The amount of staying power may cause one investment to have very little risk, since the investor can wait out a bad market or provide sufficient capital to build up the operation quickly. But another investor, with less venture capital, may find his ability to feed the investment to be limited and the risk of losing it greater. All real estate, as with all types of investing, has some risk. The risk quotients are not to be underestimated nor limited to a loss of money. The loss of time must also be considered. If it takes two years for a business or investment to fail, and the time put in by the investor was merely that when signing the check, then the amount of time lost is negligible. However, if two years of hard work, worry, and effort went into the operation and the same result were to occur, then the risk involved more than just money.

A decision to sell or to refinance a property to obtain needed cash must be analyzed by comparing the effect on both the property and the person of each of the proposed transactions. If refinancing serves the need of the owner by generating cash, and the result of the new mortgage is not burdensome to the property, then risk may be reduced. However, if new financing causes the property to be overloaded with debt service, and the future of holding onto the property is placed in jeopardy, then the risk is substantially increased.

A sale, however, may not generate an appreciable amount of cash after tax and commissions are paid. And reinvestment of this cash may not acquire comparable value with the property sold. The amount of real equity left in a property refinanced, even though overburdened with a high mortgage and heavy debt service, may be a reasonable risk under these circumstances simply because the cash obtained solved the problem. As refinanced cash is not taxed at the time the loan is made (if ever), these funds are often worth much more than proceeds from a sale.

Each possible transaction should be looked at closely, comparing it with the present situation, the situation after sale and the situation after refinance. Only by comparing these three situations can you see the relative risk factors.

2. The second point is the time involved. Time is money, but more important is the fact that money can be replaced, whereas time cannot. If the property is a home, the return of capital in any investment will depend on the time necessary for appreciation, establishment of value, and marketability. Some properties have a slow appreciation schedule for the first years after purchase, but others may rise suddenly. This factor should be considered prior to any disposition. It could well be that the greater rise in value is about to occur, and rather than sell now, a short holding period can often mean the difference between a good profit and a great profit (or the difference between a loss and a profit).

The same can be said for the income picture. The longer an income property can maintain a steady increase in NOI, the easier its marketability will be. Obviously, given a standard demand rate, a greater NOI will indicate a higher value.

The discount sale recapture option is one method of allowing the owner to sell the property to generate cash now, and later capitalize on a sudden rise in value. This form will work within the scope of refinancing, since the client gives up title only as a way to meet his ends. Of course, if the rise in value does not come as anticipated, then the seller need not exercise his option to recapture the property.

We have all seen the situation where the seller sold too soon. The buyer often makes a quick killing at the expense of the seller who needs a fast deal to solve other problems. An analysis of the situation after it has happened does not do the seller any good. Usually, thinking about the matter early in the game and analyzing all the alternatives will give a clue as to the time factor and its effect on the value of the property in the near future.

3. The third aspect is the actual need. The importance of the client's need has been discussed in other chapters, and methods of finding the need, goals, and motivation have been presented. Here, the need must be known by both the client and the salesman in order to determine whether to sell or keep the property. No alternative can be wisely selected or rejected unless this need is clear.

Usually, the need can be related to a dollar amount. When this is possible, the solution and therefore the alternatives will be more obvious.

4. The last factor to consider is the composite of alternatives available to the client. These alternatives take three forms: (1) the alternatives of refinancing, (2) the alternative methods of selling or disposing of the property, and (3) the alternative reinvestment capability for the investor. Each of these three forms will affect the overall outlook on the situation. Remember, it is very important to compare other possibilities in each of these three alternatives prior to selecting the one that obviously seems to be the best choice.

Summary On Refinancing Your Client Out Of A Sale And Into Keeping The Property

Whenever you tell a client he is better off keeping his property rather than selling it, you will be entering a world not often visited by real estate brokers and salesmen. Naturally, you will not do this unless you have a good reason for feeling this way—and then with the idea that you can help the client solve his problems.

There is no question that at times the problem will be beyond the capability of the property, either by refinancing or by disposition. In these situations, the best advice will only come close to solving the problem. For example, a need for more cash than can be generated by a sale or refinancing can obviously not be met by the property. Nonetheless, you can help the client move in the right direction, since it is more important than ever that in a partial solution the proper use of the existing equity be made. If a sale doesn't solve the problem, and it appears that if the client will hold on for a little longer a combination of refinancing, improved income, and appreciation will move the property into a position where it can be sold for a sufficient amount to solve the problem, then the decision is clear.

In consulting for large firms or lending institutions, such as REITS and insurance companies, the decision to hold or sell can in itself be the purpose for your fee. Often many firms have numerous properties across the country and are unable to decide for themselves which should be sold and which should be kept. If you are able to ascertain which of the two is the best for your client, then you may find the opportunity to offer that service at a reasonable fee.

Your full understanding of the market's capacity to absorb the property in question will no doubt be important. The marketing program needed to move a property, the time involved, and the reinvestment capability of the net proceeds from the disposition will add the final touches to a full and comprehensive program in consulting.

The ability to carry out the actual marketing program will depend on your intent. Often, all you need to do is make the determination, or at least give the client the proper input so he can make a selection from the available alternatives. The advice should also include who can best carry out the alternatives presented. If the solution is to be a refinancing program, the logical tie-in should be where, how, and with whom the refinancing package should be made. Your connections with mortgage bankers, mortgage brokers, and other lending sources will play an important role in this aspect.

You should also be in a position to know of and admit to your own ability or inability to market. If your client has property which you cannot sell, suggest the proper course for marketing it. I have, for example, been a consultant for international companies in this context. If at the end of the consultation I advised them the best solution would be to sell, I would recommend the firms which I felt would be best equipped to handle the marketing of the specific type of property. You usually know ahead of time if you will be able to market the property, and should determine your fee prior to entering into an advisory capacity with the client.

In the end, if you play your cards correctly and have the interest of your client foremost in mind, you will turn what might be a free consultation into a fee.

Chapter 17

How to Deal with Foreclosure

Like "bankruptcy," the word "foreclosure" has a ring of failure about it. In financing, foreclosure is the one thing that investors and borrowers alike seem to fear. The fact of that matter is, however, that foreclosure is not the evil monster that most borrowers believe it to be. Lenders, on the other hand, have good reason to be fearful of its consequences.

WHAT IS FORECLOSURE?

In essence, the act of foreclosure is the legal process which is begun by a mortgage or lien creditor to gain title to property owned by the mortgagor. The foreclosure of the interest of the mortgagor is to defeat that interest or redemption of equity so that the mortgagee may have title to the property without any obligations to or interference from the mortgagor. The reasoning behind the law is usually to protect both the mortgagee and the mortgagor.

We all remember the stories of the banker calling on the window who was two days behind in the monthly mortgage payment. The sinister banker would twirl his waxed mustache and then boot the old gal out onto the dusty front steps. To many, this is foreclosure at its finest hour. Yet, this is not foreclosure at all. How about this old gal? She pledged the equity in her ranch on a moderate percentage loan to value, and now just because she is behind in the payment is she to lose everything? I think not, and the courts would agree. Today, even with all the inequities and problems in the foreclosure laws, they are still much more protective of the mortgagor's rights than is generally believed.

In essence, no mortgagor, by right of most foreclosure laws, can be deprived of interest or equity redemption which may exceed the amount of the debt (plus cost and interest outstanding of course) without due process of law. The laws, while different for many states, generally agree that the right of this possible redeemable equity should be retained by the mortgagor. The purpose of this chapter is to take a close look at foreclosure—to see if it is such a terrible animal, and if so, whom does it bite the hardest. An in-depth look at how to avoid foreclosure will be examined, and some sure-fire steps for moving from possible foreclosure to positive cash flow for income properties will be provided.

BEFORE FORECLOSURE THERE MUST BE A DEFAULT IN THE MORTGAGE

The language used in mortgages to describe default and to pinpoint when default occurs will vary. Some mortgages will provide a grace period for payments. This allows the mortgage to enter a period during which the payment is due but actual default has not occurred. These grace periods can be long or short, or there may be none at all for that matter. Even without a grace period, a mortgagee will generally allow a reasonable time for default since notice and legal action to precede foreclosure would take time, and if the mortgage were brought current prior to a foreclosure being filed, the matter could be mute.

Everyone who seeks to borrow money should understand that the lender expects the funds to be repaid. The absence of personal liability on the note or mortgage does not lessen the lender's desire to be repaid, even though it may reduce the obligation for repayment from a legal point of view. In a loan where security is pledged and the borrower gives a mortgage to the lender to evidence the security, the lender will look to the mortgagee's loss of the security as the primary basis for the loan to be repaid. If the loan is not repaid, the security may or may not compensate the lender for the problems he must go through to collect his due. The lenders rights, or ability to collect beyond the security, are seriously hampered, even when there are personal signatures guaranteeing the note.

Lenders often find it difficult to collect beyond the security, as there are numerous ways a borrower can isolate himself from this further action. Courts sometimes do not look favorably on deficiency judgments against borrowers on primary loans, and almost never on purchase money financing held by sellers. There are both pro and con arguments to the controversy, but I prefer to simply state the status quo rather than enter into the battle for or against deficiency judgments.

Therefore, when there has been a breach in the contract between the lender and the mortgagor, the mortgagee has the right to seek foreclosure as a means of collecting his funds. Or, he can sue in a court of law on the debt (the note), attempt to attain a judgment against the mortgagor, and then execute the judgment on property owned by the mortgagor.

Foreclosure then is a process that must first be preceded by a default. It is not the only process of remedy the mortgagee can seek to collect on the unpaid mortgage. Because default must come first, the simplest way to avoid a foreclosure is to never go into default. This may sound obvious, but isn't. It is possible to obtain many concessions from the mortgagee for allowing the mortgage to slip into actual default under the terms of the contract (note and mortgage) without default being claimed. These concessions will be discussed in detail later on in this chapter, but you should know that most mortgagees will do almost anything to stop a property from going into foreclosure. Highly institutionalized lenders will generally work with the average borrower. Private lenders, on the other hand, have a tendency of acting quicker to foreclose, as they either want to take over the property or to protect the possible advance of loss should the payments continue to go unpaid.

Once a default occurs, and the lender does not agree to an extension of the grace period, the mortgagee is in a position to call on his rights to foreclose. Prior to the actual foreclosure, however, there is generally a period of foreclosure assertions. That is, the mortgagee threatens to foreclose unless the mortgage payment is made. This pre-foreclosure period is a maze of typical first, second, and final notices, then letters from the lawyer, and so on—all steps lenders take to avoid having to file foreclosure. Finally, there's the nice phone call from the executive vice-president in charge of collections at the bank to ask if you are having problems.

It is during this time that deals can often be made that would curl your hair. But never count on that last ditch transaction to save the whole ball of wax. Foreclosure proceedings have a tendency of being drawn-out affairs that can be most unpleasant. Dealing with the respective parties during this period of actual foreclosure is often far more difficult than when the property was only on the verge of going into foreclosure. The pre-foreclosure period is when the mortgagee hopes or believes that the mortgagor will still make the payments. But when the mortgagor does not make the payments, the mortgagee realizes he must now make good the threats to foreclose.

FORECLOSURE AS SEEN BY THE LENDER

The attitudes taken by lenders, of course, will vary. The majority of all foreclosures are made by institutional lenders, so let's look at foreclosure from their point of view. Once the mortgagor knows how the lender looks at this final stage is of the lending cycle, he will have some understanding of what to expect. Most institutional lenders (as well as many noninstitutional lenders) divide the foreclosure action into four periods.

The Four Foreclosure Periods

1. The collection period
2. The pre-foreclosure period

3. The foreclosure
4. The post-foreclosure period

Depending on the size of the lender and the staff available, a standard operating procedure is designed to take care of these four periods. (An outline of this procedure follows.) Note that the institutionalized approach to this very critical event is impersonal. The people involved have very little actual knowledge of the person who borrowed the money or the property pledged as security.

The collection period:

A. Check calendar to see if payment arrived on time; if not, make note to follow-up within three days.
B. If follow-up indicates payment still overdue, then send out courtesy reminder that payment is due (*first notice*).
C. Continued late payments will be followed five to seven days after the first notice with another notice, indicating the date which terminated the grace period (*second notice).*
D. Follow-up calls to insure the borrower is aware the grace period has terminated. (*third notice*).
E. If the payment is 30 days past due, an inspection is generally ordered to determine if the property has been vacated or if there are other problems.
F. If the property appears not to have been vacated, a registered letter is sent from the legal department advising the borrower that his loan is in jeopardy of being foreclosed (*fourth notice*).
G. No response to the registered letter within seven days will cause the matter to be placed in the pre-foreclosure period.

The pre-foreclosure period:

A. A notice is sent to the collection department to the effect that no payments on this loan will be processed without approval, since the loan has gone into default.
B. A second letter may be sent to the borrower asking for a conference to discuss the status of the loan and to see if anything can be done to avoid foreclosure (*fifth notice*).
C. The lender now prepares for the possible foreclosure:
   1. Note and mortgage are reviewed and sent to legal department.
   2. Records are examined; insurance and other matters pertaining to the maintenance of the file and the property are checked.
   3. A field report is made showing the status of the property (occupied, maintenance of property, etc.).
D. A review of the situation is made by the proper authority and a decision is reached on the basis of the alternatives given or proposed by the borrower. If none are offered or they are not plausible, then *foreclosure is filed.*

The foreclosure period:

A. An appraisal of the property is made.
B. Accounting and collection departments prepare the status of the loan—total unpaid balance and other costs, indicating the bottom line needed by the association for their bid at auction, and the top line to cover their total cost bid by others.
C. The file and report are reviewed by the foreclosure panel and the top bid the association plans to make is decided; authorization is given to the officer or trustee of the association to make the bid as stated.
D. The sale takes place; the property is purchased either by the association or by another party who makes a higher bid.

The post-foreclosure period:

A. If the property were purchased by someone other than the lender, then the funds received are processed and the loan closed.
B. If the lender purchased the property, then the appropriate departments process the property and files to account for the change in ownership.
C. The property is then turned over to the proper department for marketing.

The four periods described vary from lender to lender. A foreclosure of a second or junior loan would require a slightly different procedure. If the first or superior mortgages are not joined in the foreclosure and the foreclosure was made subject to those loans, then the junior lender would make sure the superior loans were kept current during the entire process. Once the junior lender has made a successful bid on the property, he would take the necessary steps to assume the existing superior loans or give notice that he is the new owner.

It has been stated earlier that the lender will generally do all he can to prevent the property from going into foreclosure. Of course, there is a limit to how far he will or can go. Nonetheless, if the borrower has shown good intentions in the past and has not been late in making payments, the lender will go a long way to keep the loan from foreclosure.

Why Lenders Will Avoid Foreclosure If At All Possible

In almost all states, the foreclosure process is often long and burdensome. The time element is the most costly of all, since much can happen to the value of the property while the foreclosure grinds to the eventual sale or redemption of equity. At best, it is not a simple event. At worst, years can pass before the final document is filed and title is granted to the winning bidder at the foreclosure sale. Many arguments have been made for changes in the law and a speeding up of the process. Also, the law often seems to protect the less scrupulous mortgagor more than the one who attempts to do his best to pay back the monies owed.

If the property is an income producer, the mortgagor can slip behind in his payments, wait out the pre-foreclosure period, and prolong that by attempting to work out a settlement or payment plan. Then, in the end he will let the lender foreclose, knowing that without any debt service during this period of time he can milk the property until the lender can either foreclose or have a receiver or trustee appointed to operate it until the foreclosure is complete and settled.

Seasonal properties are most vulnerable to this type of "milking," and lenders are most cautious about lending in these areas when the equity is either vague or slight. Even then, the loan can be in jeopardy in a hurry since a milked hotel can drop 20% in value over the season. Good-will can be destroyed and the property itself left in disrepair. Hotels and other volatile properties that depend on limited times of operation (e.g., amusement parks and recreational facilities) will generally have mortgages that have strong default provisions. These provisions, however, do not always provide sufficient security to prevent "milking."

The speed with which the mortgagee can remove the mortgagor's control of the property will vary. In some states this removal can be accomplished in a relatively short time, while in others the time required will be longer. It may be possible for a mortgagor to claim that the mortgage interest is usurious or other aspects of the loan are onerous, and hence request the loan to be set aside. Such actions may cause the entire matter to go to court. But in the meanwhile, the mortgagor may be left in control of the property. Because the matter of foreclosure is a legal one, lawyers can often find many ways to delay the process. Lenders know this, of course, and while they may ultimately win the case, it may be only a paper victory.

It is often thought that the only type of property immune to the effect of mortgagor control is vacant land. Today, however, vacant land can become a victim of the timekeeper as well. In many communities there are movements to change zoning. Usually, zoning changes have considerable effect on the value of property. Since most zoning changes affect vacant land, they can make the land gain as well as lose value. Most rezoning provisions allow for a time period of adjustment. They usually permit an owner to file for building permits under the old zoning by a cutoff date. However, it is obvious that if the land is in the midst of a foreclosure this would not be possible. And once the foreclosure sale occurs the value of the land may be less than the amount of the mortgage.

In most office buildings and other income properties, where the gross income is gained from rents collected from tenants in the building, the mortgagee will have assignments of the leases. These assignments will permit him to step in and collect the rents in the event of a default. The owner and mortgagor may still have physical control of the building, but he no longer has control over the income from the property. The mortgagee will generally deduct from those rents the payments due and turn over the balance to the mortgagor while the foreclosure is proceeding. Keep in mind that once the mortgage has gone into default and a foreclosure has been filed, the only redemption may be for the mortgagee to pay off the entire loan and not just to bring the payments up-to-date.

OPTIONS OPEN TO THE LENDER AND THE BORROWER IN THE EVENT OF A DEFAULT ON A MORTGAGE

1. The lender agrees to wait for the payment or payments.
2. The borrower brings the mortgage current for interest but holds up on the principal portion of the payment.
3. A partial payment of interest is made.
4. A lump sum of interest and principal is made and the mortgage is adjusted to change the overall terms to provide relief for later payments.
5. The mortgagor turns over all income, less operational expenses gained on the property, for application against the debt service.
6. The lender agrees to refinance the loan to provide needed capital to bring the project back to its feet.
7. The lender advances funds on a secondary loan to cover the debt service.
8. The mortgagor adds additional security, the loan is extended into a blanket mortgage, and additional cash is added by the lender to cover the debt service.
9. The mortgagor can give up partial ownership in favor of the lender for a reduction of the debt.
10. A portion of the property can be deeded over to the lender as a partial or full satisfaction of the debt.
11. The mortgagee allows you time to try to sell your interest in the property to someone else.
12. Seek secondary financing from another lender.
13. A deed in lieu of foreclosure (often called voluntary deed) is granted by the mortgagor to the lender and the debt is satisfied.
14. Foreclosure.

The first twelve of these options can occur alone or in combinations. The willingness of the lender or the mortgagor to enter into any of these options will depend on the nature of the property and the history of the mortgagor. If the property is not worth the mortgagor's efforts to pull it out of default or he has a history of going into default in the past, then the matter may be mute and the lender may look to only the last two options.

The deed in lieu of foreclosure is a most attractive way out for the lender in many situations. The borrower may also look to this as a way of saving face in the community or meeting his moral obligations if all else fails, especially if the impending foreclosure suit does not appear to offer the opportunity for the mortgagor to gain in overage at the sale. After all, by the time the property is about to go into foreclosure, most mortgagors have tried almost everything to sell it so the market has been tested to some degree. Of course, if the mortgagor is behind in the payments by a wide margin, the cost to bring the property current, just in past due interest alone, may make the sale preforeclosure difficult. More on this aspect later.

A deed in lieu of foreclosure is a way the mortgagor can get out from under the mess of foreclosure and allow the mortgagee to enter the property without a long battle. If the property has several mortgages, all in default, and the first mortgage holder takes the property back by deed in lieu, then that mortgagee is assuming the obligations of the junior mortgagees. In foreclosure and a forced sale, the junior mortgagees would have to either protect their interest by bidding in above the first mortgagee or hope other buyers bid in sufficiently to cover their position. Often, this will not happen. Hence, the first mortgagee must decide if the junior mortgagee will in fact protect his interest by bidding in or attempting to obtain a deed in lieu himself, thereby assuming the existing mortgage or foreclosing subject to the superior mortgage and keeping that mortgage current. Frequently, the circumstances do not favor the first mortgagee allowing the property to foreclose if he can obtain a deed in lieu, even if that means he is assuming the junior mortgages.

If the property is seasonal in nature and the season is just around the corner, the mortgagee may pay the mortgagor to sell the deed in lieu of foreclosure. The fact that the mortgagor is behind in payments and owes the mortgagee money, does not mean that the mortgagor has any equity in the property. To avoid the cost and time of foreclosure and the loss of seasonal income, the payment to the defaulting mortgagor can expedite the end result and perhaps allow him to receive some cash out of the mess.

WHAT A MORTGAGOR SHOULD DO IF HE FEELS HE MAY GO INTO DEFAULT

When all good planning and hope fails, and the cash just isn't there for the next mortgage payment, there are several things the mortgagor can do to hold off foreclosure.

Steps To Hold Off Foreclosure

The Preventive Measures:

1. Develop a good pay-back record. This means more than just paying on time. Whenever possible, get in the habit of paying early. Mortgages, credit card payments, and the like all fall into this category. If you have never borrowed large sums of money before, you have no real credit rating with the banks on

your pay-back ability. One client of mine has never had to borrow money, but he has made it a practice to borrow up to $50,000 at once from one of the commercial banks in the area. He does this on his own signature and asks for the money for six months, but he pays it back in less than a month. The total cost to him is not that much since he manages to get interest on the amount borrowed from another bank. He says he doubts the bank would ever turn him down now if he really needed money. I don't recommend that you follow this lead, but a loan every once in a while will establish a good credit rating if you pay the money back promptly or early.
2. Don't attempt to overextend the loan to value ratio. Remember, the best way to keep from going into default is to be able to afford the debt service in the first place. Naturally, few investors would be able to carry all or at least a major portion of the debt service, so look to a prudent demand rate and safe mix of extension and leverage. When you buy, try to take into account the possibility of a reduced income, look at the break-even point, and be ready to risk some capital.
3. Know your abilities. This means staying away from investments you know nothing about unless you are sure you can rely on your advisors and/or partners. Most bad real estate investments are really good investments, but are made by underexperienced investors. Don't look across the fence and think the grass is greener on the other side. Those investors who are experts in their field make their jobs look easy. In fact, however, some areas of real estate are very difficult and take years of training and experience to understand and master. In Florida, as I am sure elsewhere, bars, lounges, motels, and restaurants are the big thing. Investors often feel that anyone can run a bar, lounge, and so on. Wrong!
4. Get to know the lenders you are dealing with. It is a good idea to be on speaking terms with them. Keep an account at all banks or savings and loans where you borrow. Drop in every now and then and talk to the officers about anything except foreclosure. If you are on friendly terms with them when you are making your payments, that rapport will carry over to a pre-foreclosure period if it shold ever come along.

What to do when default is on the way but has not yet occurred:

1. If you know you won't be able to make the next payment on time, there are two things you can do. First, if the payments are over short periods, such as monthly or quarterly, it is a good idea to call the bank or savings and loan president and let him know you have a problem. This is just to inform him that you are concerned about your inability to pay on time. Second, if the payments are over long periods, such as semi-annually or annually, you may not want to give prior notice that you may be late: Lenders who wait for long time periods between mortgage payments have a tendency to become very

nervous when informed that a payment for which they have waited a whole year may not be in on time. These lenders will think the worst right away and may start planning what they will do the very moment the payment is not in.

The rapport between the mortgagor and the mortgagee is very important. The record of past performance is likewise crucial, since a poor record will cause the lender to be most unsympathetic to tales of economic problems. Keep in mind that lenders have heard every story that exists, so keep the sob stories to a minimum, even if they are true. Remember, honesty usually works best when all else fails.

2. If you think you will be delayed in making your next payment, send the lender a letter outlining very briefly your inability to make the payment on time. If there is a good reason for the delay, state it. If not, then merely say that you will be unable to make the payment on time but that you hope to have the money before the grace period is up.
3. Review your situation and look at all the possible alternatives you may be able to use to solve your problem. The fourteen options listed previously are open to you. Look at each one and play with the figures to see if any are plausible.

What to do when default comes and you have no real prospect of pulling out without help:

1. By now, you may have tried to sell your interest but to no avail. This is the time for you to make the decision to hold onto the property or to attempt to make a settlement with the lender which will allow you to back out. Many mortgagors hang on too long, even when the property is not worth the effort or aggravation. The time to settle on a deed in lieu will depend on the property of course, but you should make that decision early in the default rather than wait until foreclosure is already filled, since it may be too late by then. On a very large property, however, your lawyer may advise you that if you do hang on you may be able to pull the loose ends together.
2. Assuming you decide to try to keep the property, this is a good time to sit down with the lender and work out a deal which will give you time or release you from the burden of the debt service, perhaps by some alteration of the mortgage. Sitting back and ignoring the lender's letters will not help your situation at all, and could show a lack of good faith on your part. If you are willing to cooperate, this probably will work to your advantage.
3. Have a plausible program which you feel will work. You may need help in putting this program together, so seek it. If you are representing a client in such a predicament, then you will do all you personally can to find a solution and will speak to those contacts you feel can help as well.
4. If there is a valuable equity in the property, and you have a reasonable solution which will solve the problem but the lender refuses to go along, you

may want to look to bankruptcy as another alternative. A Chapter 11, for example, if acceptable in your situation, would hold off foreclosure and permit a settlement of the economic problems. This possibility should be considered at any rate, at least so you will know what the option is and how it will affect you. Don't feel that bankruptcy is something you should avoid, especially if it is your only chance to protect all the creditors. Remember, if the first mortgage forecloses and the market sale does not produce an overage above it, then those creditors may be wiped out. The bankruptcy, however, may allow a partial settlement as a minimum for those creditors.

WHERE AND HOW THE BROKER FITS IN TO FORECLOSURES

A broker will enter the picture in at least two instances. The first is generally when the client is approaching default and wants to sell the property quickly. The second instance is when the property has been foreclosed and the lender has it back on the market.

Let's look at the first instance.

How To Approach A Sale Of A Property Nearing Foreclosure

The unfortunate part of this situation is that the broker is usually unaware of the real predicament as far as the impending foreclosure is concerned. The seller has not told him the truth about the economics of the situation and the default is sprung on him at the last moment.

I have seen many clients, both mine and those of other brokers, swear that they are solvent and the mortgages are in good standing right up to a default. Naturally, some of these clients have a false hope they will be able to make the payments when they are due and hence will not go into default at the last moment. Others just don't want to admit that they have economic difficulties. When the payments are monthly, the default comes quickly. Of course, the seller may quietly work out some delay with the lender and then not inform the broker of this. But if the payments are already in arrears, then the wheels of foreclosure may already be turning and the task of selling in these circumstances is immense. Some of the surprises of economic collapse can be anticipated by brokers if they follow these steps at the time the listing is taken.

Three steps to take at the time a listing is taken:

1. Get full data on the outstanding mortgages.
2. Obtain a letter from the seller permitting you to request information from lenders as to outstanding balances and mortgage status.
3. Ask the seller if there is any reason to believe that the future mortgage payments may not be covered.

Having the permission to obtain mortgage data will do you no good unless you use that permission and contact the lender. If the lender is a private person, as would be the case for a purchase money mortgage and other types of loans, the status of the loan is more crucial since these lenders may be less cooperative in the event of a default.

No matter when you find out about an impending foreclosure, once you know, the problem will be how to deal with it. To be sure, the marketing program will be apt to change. Follow these steps once you know the seller will not be able to meet the next payment or is already in default.

Five steps to follow once you know your seller is approaching a foreclosure:

1. Find out the amount of money needed to carry the property until:
   A. The property can be sold, given a reasonable marketing program and an adequate amount of time.
   B. An economic turnaround can occur which will remove the burden of the present economic crisis.
   C. Bring the mortgage current and provide for a limited amount of time to sell under economic duress.
   D. A buyer can close if a sale is obtained within a very short time.
2. Ask the seller what he can do to help you renegotiate the existing financing by ascertaining:
   A. The seller's net worth.
   B. The other security which can be pledged.
   C. The present economics of the property (if an income property).
   D. Will the seller risk additional capital, and if so how much?
   E. What else is past due besides the mortgage payments?
   F. What plan can the two of you come up with to present to the lenders?
3. Ask the seller if he is willing to walk away from the property.
4. Ask the seller if he is willing to sell under economic duress, and hence at a great reduction in order to salvage something out of the mess.
5. Plan your actions based on your assessment of the first four steps.

If the seller is willing to salvage whatever he can, then you have a tough job cut out for you. A sale under such circumstances tends to bring out the sharks looking for a wounded seller. Sales pre-foreclosures are most difficult, but can be accomplished if some relief can be obtained from the lenders or enough time is available to effect the sale. These two prerequisites are often not obtainable however.

How To Approach The Sale Once The Property Is In Foreclosure

In most states, the mortgagee can redeem the property out of foreclosure at any time up until the sale. This law will vary of course, but some time for that equity redemption is permitted in almost all states. Therefore, it is possible to sell the property even though it has gone into foreclosure. The prospective buyers, however, realize that they may be able to make a better deal with the mortgagee than with the mortgagor at this time. Hence, they will look to the lender as the primary seller even though title has not transferred to the mortgagee.

If the possible equity is high enough and the seller can hold off the final effect of the foreclosure, a sale may be prudent and possible. However, this task is almost impossible in the vast majority of cases and must be examined very carefully. It may be to the seller's best interest to try to work out a deed in lieu at this stage of the game, or at least to obtain permission from the lender to try to sell prior to the actual filing of the foreclosure. Failing in this, the broker must decide if he can effectively sell at this time. If the property is multimortgaged, the foreclosure may be needed to clear it of the cumbersome debt service. It is difficult to approach a prospective buyer when you have such a situation and advise him to enter into a transaction that you know will be a far better deal once the foreclosure is over. The time element will play a major role though. If the foreclosure will be long and drawn out, then an immediate deal could be best for all parties concerned. An attempt to discount some of the debt may be prudent and possible.

If all fails and the lender picks up the property by way of deed in lieu of foreclosure or at the forced sale, then the broker should make his move to represent the sale at that stage.

Representing Lenders In The Sale Of Their Foreclosed Properties

This is a big market for many brokers across the country. Banks, savings and loans, REITS, as well as other lenders have a normal portfolio of foreclosed properties. They are motivated sellers and can provide a good source of prime listings. These sellers have the unique ability of holding financing that is often quite flexible.

The price of foreclosed properties will often come down as well. Through the foreclosure, the underlying liens and junior mortgages may have been eliminated, thus making the economics of the sale more reasonable. Of course, some of these properties may be in an unfinished state. In the case of the REIT foreclosures, projects that have just been started may be available. The ability to sell these properties will call for considerable expertise, usually lacking in the organization that is holding the property.

Most banks and savings and loans have their own departments that handle the sale of these properties. However, this is not the best way for these organizations to approach this problem. Hence, an enterprising broker is needed who can convince such institutions that they should seek outside help in turning these properties into cash. Even if you are unable to obtain exclusive lisings on these properties, you will obtain the data necessary to give you additional inventory to add to your list of available properties. The simple fact that these sellers are highly motivated to sell will warrant your efforts in such cases.

Table A: CONSTANT ANNUAL PERCENT
EXPRESSING THE SUM OF 12 EQUAL MONTHLY PAYMENTS
NEEDED TO AMORTIZE A PRINCIPAL AMOUNT

INTEREST YEARS	5½%	5¾%	6%	6¼%	6½%	6¾%	7%	7¼%	7½%
0.5	203.26	203.38	203.55	203.67	203.84	203.96	204.13	204.26	204.42
1.0	103.02	103.15	103.30	103.42	103.57	103.70	103.84	103.97	104.12
1.5	69.62	69.75	69.89	70.02	70.16	70.29	70.43	70.56	70.70
2.0	52.92	53.05	53.19	53.32	53.46	53.59	53.73	53.86	54.00
2.5	42.91	43.04	43.18	43.31	43.45	43.58	43.72	43.86	44.00
3.0	36.24	36.37	36.51	36.64	36.78	36.92	37.06	37.19	37.33
3.5	31.48	31.61	31.75	31.89	32.03	32.16	32.30	32.44	32.58
4.0	27.91	28.05	28.19	28.32	28.46	28.60	28.74	28.88	29.02
4.5	25.14	25.28	25.42	25.55	25.69	25.83	25.97	26.11	26.25
5.0	22.93	23.06	23.20	23.34	23.48	23.62	23.76	23.90	24.05
5.5	21.12	21.25	21.39	21.53	21.68	21.82	21.96	22.10	22.25
6.0	19.61	19.75	19.89	20.03	20.17	20.32	20.46	20.60	20.75
6.5	18.34	18.48	18.62	18.76	18.91	19.05	19.19	19.34	19.49
7.0	17.25	17.39	17.53	17.68	17.82	17.97	18.11	18.26	18.41
7.5	16.30	16.45	16.59	16.74	16.88	17.03	17.18	17.32	17.47
8.0	15.48	15.63	15.77	15.92	16.07	16.21	16.36	16.51	16.66
8.5	14.76	14.90	15.05	15.20	15.35	15.49	15.64	15.79	15.95
9.0	14.11	14.26	14.41	14.56	14.71	14.86	15.01	15.16	15.31
9.5	13.54	13.69	13.84	13.99	14.14	14.29	14.44	14.59	14.75
10.0	13.03	13.17	13.32	13.47	13.63	13.78	13.93	14.09	14.25
10.5	12.56	12.71	12.86	13.01	13.17	13.32	13.48	13.63	13.79
11.0	12.14	12.29	12.44	12.59	12.75	12.90	13.06	13.22	13.38
11.5	11.75	11.91	12.06	12.21	12.37	12.53	12.69	12.84	13.00
12.0	11.40	11.56	11.71	11.87	12.02	12.18	12.34	12.50	12.66
12.5	11.08	11.24	11.39	11.55	11.71	11.87	12.03	12.19	12.35
13.0	10.79	10.96	11.10	11.26	11.42	11.58	11.74	11.90	12.07
13.5	10.51	10.67	10.83	10.90	11.15	11.31	11.47	11.64	11.80
14.0	10.26	10.42	10.58	10.74	10.90	11.06	11.23	11.39	11.56
14.5	10.02	10.18	10.34	10.50	10.67	10.83	11.00	11.16	11.33
15.0	9.81	9.97	10.13	10.29	10.45	10.62	10.79	10.95	11.12
15.5	9.60	9.76	9.93	10.09	10.26	10.42	10.59	10.76	10.93
16.0	9.41	9.57	9.74	9.90	10.07	10.24	10.41	10.58	10.75
16.5	9.24	9.40	9.56	9.73	9.90	10.07	10.24	10.41	10.58
17.0	9.07	9.23	9.40	9.56	9.73	9.90	10.08	10.25	10.42
17.5	8.91	9.08	9.24	9.41	9.58	9.75	9.93	10.10	10.28
18.0	8.76	8.93	9.10	9.27	9.44	9.61	9.79	9.96	10.14
18.5	8.63	8.79	8.96	9.13	9.31	9.48	9.65	9.83	10.01
19.0	8.50	8.66	8.83	9.01	9.18	9.35	9.53	9.71	9.89
19.5	8.37	8.54	8.71	8.88	9.06	9.24	9.41	9.59	9.78
20.0	8.26	8.43	8.60	8.77	8.95	9.12	9.30	9.48	9.67
20.5	8.15	8.32	8.49	8.66	8.84	9.02	9.20	9.38	9.57
21.0	8.04	8.21	8.39	8.56	8.74	8.92	9.10	9.29	9.47
21.5	7.94	8.11	8.29	8.47	8.65	8.83	9.01	9.19	9.38
22.0	7.85	8.02	8.20	8.38	8.56	8.74	8.92	9.11	9.29
22.5	7.76	7.93	8.11	8.29	8.47	8.65	8.84	9.02	9.21
23.0	7.67	7.85	8.03	8.21	8.39	8.57	8.76	8.95	9.14
23.5	7.59	7.77	7.95	8.13	8.31	8.50	8.68	8.87	9.06
24.0	7.51	7.69	7.87	9.05	8.24	8.42	8.61	8.80	9.00
24.5	7.44	7.62	7.80	7.98	8.17	8.36	8.55	8.74	8.93
25.0	7.37	7.55	7.73	7.92	8.10	8.29	8.48	8.67	8.87
25.5	7.30	7.48	7.67	7.85	8.04	8.23	8.42	8.61	8.81
26.0	7.24	7.42	7.60	7.79	7.98	8.17	8.36	8.56	8.75
26.5	7.18	7.36	7.55	7.73	7.92	8.11	8.31	8.50	8.70
27.0	7.12	7.30	7.49	7.68	7.87	8.06	8.25	8.45	8.65
27.5	7.06	7.25	7.43	7.62	7.81	8.01	8.20	8.40	8.60
28.0	7.01	7.19	7.38	7.57	7.76	7.96	8.16	8.35	8.55
28.5	6.96	7.14	7.33	7.52	7.72	7.91	8.11	8.31	9.51
29.0	6.91	7.09	7.28	7.48	7.67	7.87	8.07	8.27	8.47
29.5	6.86	7.05	7.24	7.43	7.63	7.82	8.02	8.23	8.43
30.0	6.81	7.00	7.20	7.39	7.59	7.78	7.98	8.19	8.39
35.0	6.44	6.64	6.84	7.05	7.25	7.46	7.67	7.88	8.09
40.0	6.19	6.39	6.60	6.81	7.03	7.24	7.46	7.68	7.90

From *Realty Blue Book;* Professional Real Estate Publishing Co., P.O. Box 4187, San Rafael, Cal. 94903.

Table A (cont.)

INTEREST / YEARS	7¼%	8%	8¼%	8½%	8¾%	9%	9¼%	9½%	9¾%
0.5	204.55	204.71	204.87	205.00	205.16	205.29	205.45	205.58	205.74
1.0	104.25	104.39	104.54	104.67	104.81	104.95	105.09	105.22	105.37
1.5	70.83	70.97	71.11	71.25	71.39	71.52	71.66	71.79	71.94
2.0	54.14	54.28	54.42	54.55	54.69	54.82	54.96	55.10	55.24
2.5	44.13	44.27	44.41	44.54	44.68	44.82	44.96	45.10	25.24
3.0	37.47	37.61	37.75	37.88	38.02	38.16	38.30	38.44	38.58
3.5	32.71	32.85	33.00	33.13	33.28	33.41	33.56	33.70	33.84
4.0	29.16	29.30	29.44	29.58	29.72	29.86	30.01	30.15	30.29
4.5	26.39	26.54	26.68	26.82	26.97	27.11	27.25	27.40	27.54
5.0	24.19	24.33	24.48	24.62	24.77	24.91	25.06	25.20	25.35
5.5	22.39	22.54	22.68	22.83	22.97	23.12	23.27	23.41	23.56
6.0	20.89	21.04	21.19	21.33	21.48	21.63	21.78	21.93	22.06
6.5	19.63	19.78	19.93	20.08	20.23	20.38	20.53	20.68	20.83
7.0	18.55	18.70	18.86	19.00	19.16	19.31	19.46	19.61	19.77
7.5	17.62	17.77	17.93	18.08	18.23	18.38	18.54	18.69	18.85
8.0	16.81	16.96	17.12	17.27	17.43	17.58	17.74	17.89	18.05
8.5	16.10	16.25	16.41	16.56	16.72	16.88	17.03	17.19	17.35
9.0	15.47	15.62	15.78	15.94	16.09	16.25	16.41	16.57	16.73
9.5	14.91	15.06	15.22	15.38	15.54	15.70	15.86	16.02	16.18
10.0	14.40	14.56	14.72	14.88	15.04	15.20	15.36	15.53	15.69
10.5	13.95	14.11	14.27	14.43	14.59	14.76	14.92	15.09	15.25
11.0	13.54	13.70	13.86	14.02	14.19	14.35	14.52	14.69	14.86
11.5	13.17	13.33	13.49	13.66	13.82	13.99	14.16	14.33	14.50
12.0	12.83	12.99	13.16	13.32	13.49	13.66	13.83	14.00	14.17
12.5	12.52	12.68	12.85	13.02	13.18	13.35	13.53	13.70	13.87
13.0	12.23	12.40	12.57	12.73	12.91	13.08	13.25	13.42	13.60
13.5	11.97	12.14	12.31	12.48	12.65	12.82	13.00	13.17	13.35
14.0	11.73	11.90	12.07	12.24	12.41	12.59	12.76	12.94	13.12
14.5	11.50	11.67	11.85	12.02	12.20	12.37	12.55	12.73	12.91
15.0	11.30	11.47	11.64	11.82	11.99	12.17	12.35	12.53	12.71
15.5	11.10	11.28	11.45	11.63	11.81	11.99	12.17	12.35	12.53
16.0	10.92	11.10	11.28	11.45	11.63	11.81	12.00	12.18	12.37
16.5	10.76	10.93	11.11	11.29	11.47	11.65	11.84	12.02	12.21
17.0	10.60	10.78	10.96	11.14	11.32	11.51	11.69	11.88	12.07
17.5	10.46	10.64	10.82	11.00	11.18	11.37	11.55	11.74	11.93
18.0	10.32	10.50	10.68	10.87	11.05	11.24	11.43	11.62	11.61
18.5	10.19	10.37	10.56	10.74	10.93	11.12	11.31	11.50	11.69
19.0	10.07	10.25	10.44	10.63	10.81	11.00	11.19	11.39	11.58
19.5	9.96	10.14	10.33	10.52	10.71	10.90	11.09	11.28	11.48
20.0	9.85	10.04	10.23	10.41	10.60	10.80	10.99	11.19	11.38
20.5	9.75	9.94	10.13	10.32	10.51	10.70	10.90	11.09	11.29
21.0	9.66	9.85	10.04	10.23	10.42	10.62	10.81	11.01	11.21
21.5	9.57	9.76	9.95	10.14	10.34	10.53	10.73	10.93	11.13
22.0	9.48	9.67	9.87	10.06	10.26	10.45	10.65	10.85	11.06
22.5	9.40	9.60	9.79	9.99	10.18	10.38	10.58	10.78	10.99
23.0	9.33	9.52	9.72	9.91	10.11	10.31	10.51	10.72	10.92
23.5	9.26	9.45	9.65	9.85	10.05	10.25	10.45	10.65	10.86
24.0	9.19	9.38	9.58	9.78	9.98	10.18	10.39	10.59	10.80
24.5	9.12	9.32	9.52	9.72	9.92	10.13	10.33	10.54	10.75
25.0	9.06	9.26	9.46	9.66	9.87	10.07	10.28	10.48	10.69
25.5	9.01	9.21	9.41	9.61	9.81	10.02	10.23	10.43	10.65
26.0	8.95	9.15	9.35	9.56	9.76	9.97	10.18	10.39	10.60
26.5	8.90	9.10	9.30	9.51	9.71	9.92	10.13	10.34	10.56
27.0	8.85	9.05	9.26	9.46	9.67	9.88	10.09	10.30	10.51
27.5	8.80	9.01	9.21	9.42	9.63	9.84	10.05	10.26	10.48
28.0	8.76	8.96	9.17	9.38	9.58	9.80	10.01	10.22	10.44
28.5	8.71	8.92	9.13	9.34	9.55	9.76	9.97	10.19	10.40
29.0	8.67	8.88	9.09	9.30	9.51	9.72	9.94	10.15	10.37
29.5	8.63	8.84	9.05	9.26	9.47	9.69	9.90	10.12	10.34
30.0	8.60	8.81	9.02	9.23	9.44	9.66	9.87	10.09	10.31
35.0	8.31	8.52	8.74	8.96	9.18	9.41	9.63	9.86	10.09
40.0	8.12	8.34	8.57	8.80	9.03	9.26	9.49	9.72	9.95

TABLE A (cont.)

INTEREST / YEARS	10%	11%	12%	13%	14%	15%	16%	17%	18%
0.5	205.88	206.49	207.07	207.66	208.25	208.84	209.44	210.04	210.64
1.0	105.50	106.07	106.63	107.19	107.75	108.31	108.88	109.45	110.02
1.5	72.07	72.63	73.18	73.74	74.30	74.86	75.43	76.00	76.57
2.0	55.37	55.93	56.49	57.05	57.62	58.18	58.76	59.33	59.91
2.5	45.37	45.94	46.50	47.07	47.64	48.21	48.79	49.38	49.97
3.0	38.72	39.29	39.86	40.43	41.01	41.60	42.19	42.79	43.36
3.5	33.98	34.56	35.13	35.72	36.30	36.90	37.50	38.11	38.72
4.0	30.44	31.02	31.60	32.19	32.79	33.40	34.01	34.63	35.25
4.5	27.69	28.28	28.87	29.47	30.08	30.69	31.32	31.95	32.58
5.0	25.50	26.09	26.69	27.30	27.92	28.55	29.18	29.82	30.47
5.5	23.71	24.32	24.93	25.54	26.17	26.81	27.45	28.11	28.77
6.0	22.23	22.84	23.46	24.09	24.73	25.37	26.03	26.70	27.37
6.5	20.98	21.60	22.23	22.87	23.52	24.17	24.84	25.52	26.20
7.0	19.92	20.55	21.18	21.83	22.49	23.16	23.83	24.52	25.22
7.5	19.01	19.64	20.28	20.94	21.61	22.29	22.98	23.68	24.39
8.0	18.21	18.85	19.50	20.17	20.85	21.53	22.23	22.95	23.67
8.5	17.51	18.16	18.82	19.50	20.18	20.88	21.59	22.31	23.05
9.0	16.89	17.55	18.22	18.90	19.60	20.31	21.03	21.76	22.51
9.5	16.35	17.01	17.69	18.38	19.09	19.81	20.54	21.28	22.04
10.0	15.86	16.53	17.22	17.92	18.63	19.36	20.10	20.86	21.62
10.5	15.42	16.10	16.79	17.50	18.23	18.96	19.72	20.48	21.26
11.0	15.02	15.71	16.41	17.13	17.86	18.61	19.37	20.15	20.93
11.5	14.67	15.36	16.07	16.80	17.54	18.29	19.06	19.85	20.65
12.0	14.34	15.04	15.76	16.50	17.25	18.01	18.79	19.58	20.39
12.5	14.04	14.75	15.48	16.22	16.98	17.75	18.54	19.35	20.16
13.0	13.77	14.49	15.22	15.97	16.74	17.52	18.32	19.13	19.96
13.5	13.53	14.25	14.99	15.75	16.52	17.31	18.12	18.94	19.77
14.0	13.30	14.03	14.78	15.54	16.33	17.12	17.94	18.77	19.61
14.5	13.09	13.83	14.58	15.36	16.15	16.95	17.77	18.61	19.46
15.0	12.90	13.64	14.40	15.18	15.98	16.80	17.62	18.47	19.33
15.5	12.72	13.47	14.24	15.03	15.83	16.65	17.49	18.34	19.20
16.0	12.55	13.31	14.09	14.88	15.69	16.52	17.37	18.22	19.10
16.5	12.40	13.16	13.94	14.75	15.57	16.40	17.25	18.12	19.00
17.0	12.25	13.03	13.81	14.62	15.45	16.29	17.15	18.02	18.91
17.5	12.12	12.90	13.69	14.51	15.34	16.19	17.06	17.93	18.83
18.0	12.00	12.78	13.58	14.41	15.24	16.10	16.97	17.86	18.75
18.5	11.88	12.67	13.48	14.31	15.15	16.02	16.89	17.78	18.69
19.0	11.78	12.57	13.38	14.22	15.07	15.94	16.82	17.72	18.63
19.5	11.67	12.48	13.30	14.14	14.99	15.87	16.76	17.66	18.57
20.0	11.58	12.39	13.21	14.06	14.92	15.80	16.70	17.60	18.52
20.5	11.49	12.30	13.14	13.99	14.86	15.74	16.64	17.55	18.47
21.0	11.41	12.23	13.06	13.92	14.80	15.69	16.59	17.51	18.43
21.5	11.33	12.15	13.00	13.86	14.74	15.63	16.54	17.46	18.39
22.0	11.26	12.09	12.94	13.80	14.69	15.59	16.50	17.43	18.36
22.5	11.19	12.02	12.88	13.75	14.64	15.54	16.46	17.39	18.33
23.0	11.13	11.96	12.82	13.70	14.59	15.50	16.42	17.36	18.30
23.5	11.07	11.91	12.77	13.65	14.55	15.47	16.39	17.33	18.27
24.0	11.01	11.86	12.72	13.61	14.51	15.43	16.36	17.30	18.25
24.5	10.96	11.81	12.68	13.57	14.48	15.40	16.33	17.28	18.23
25.0	10.90	11.76	12.64	13.53	14.45	15.37	16.31	17.25	18.21
25.5	10.86	11.72	12.60	13.50	14.41	15.34	16.28	17.23	18.19
26.0	10.81	11.68	12.56	13.47	14.39	15.32	16.26	17.21	18.17
26.5	10.77	11.64	12.53	13.44	14.36	15.29	16.24	17.20	18.16
27.0	10.73	11.60	12.50	13.41	14.33	15.27	16.22	17.18	18.15
27.5	10.69	11.57	12.47	13.38	14.31	15.25	16.20	17.17	18.13
28.0	10.66	11.54	12.44	13.36	14.29	15.23	16.19	17.15	18.12
28.5	10.62	11.51	12.41	13.33	14.27	15.22	16.17	17.14	18.11
29.0	10.59	11.48	12.39	13.31	14.25	15.20	16.16	17.13	18.10
29.5	10.56	11.45	12.37	13.29	14.23	15.19	16.15	17.12	18.09
30.0	10.53	11.43	12.34	13.27	14.22	15.17	16.14	17.11	18.09
35.0	10.32	11.24	12.19	13.14	14.11	15.08	16.06	17.05	18.03
40.0	10.19	11.14	12.10	13.07	14.05	15.04	16.03	17.02	18.01

TABLE A (cont.)

INTEREST YEARS	19%	20%	22%	24%	26%	28%	30%	35%	40%
0.5	211.23	211.83	213.04	214.24	215.44	216.65	217.86	220.91	223.97
1.0	110.59	111.16	112.32	113.47	114.64	115.81	116.99	119.96	122.97
1.5	77.14	77.72	78.88	80.04	81.22	82.41	83.61	86.64	89.73
2.0	60.49	61.08	62.26	63.45	64.65	65.87	67.10	70.22	73.43
2.5	50.56	51.16	52.36	53.58	54.82	56.07	57.33	60.57	63.89
3.0	43.99	44.60	45.83	47.08	48.35	49.64	50.94	54.28	57.73
3.5	39.33	39.96	41.22	42.50	43.80	45.13	46.47	49.93	53.50
4.0	35.88	36.52	37.81	39.12	40.46	41.82	43.21	46.77	50.46
4.5	33.23	33.88	35.20	36.54	37.92	39.31	40.74	44.40	48.21
5.0	31.13	31.79	33.14	34.52	35.93	37.36	38.82	42.59	46.50
5.5	29.44	30.12	31.50	32.91	34.35	35.82	37.31	41.17	45.19
6.0	28.05	28.74	30.15	31.59	33.06	34.57	36.10	40.05	44.17
6.5	26.90	27.60	29.04	30.51	32.02	33.55	35.12	39.16	43.36
7.0	25.93	26.65	28.11	29.61	31.15	32.71	34.31	38.44	42.72
7.5	25.11	25.84	27.33	28.86	30.42	32.02	33.65	37.85	42.21
8.0	24.40	25.14	26.66	28.22	29.81	31.43	33.09	37.37	41.79
8.5	23.79	24.55	26.09	27.67	29.29	30.94	32.63	36.97	41.46
9.0	23.26	24.03	25.60	27.21	28.85	30.53	32.24	36.64	41.19
9.5	22.80	23.58	25.17	26.80	28.47	30.18	31.91	36.37	40.98
10.0	22.40	23.19	24.80	26.46	28.15	29.88	31.63	36.15	40.80
10.5	22.05	22.85	24.48	26.16	27.87	29.62	31.40	35.96	40.65
11.0	21.73	22.54	24.20	25.90	27.63	29.40	31.20	35.81	40.53
11.5	21.46	22.28	23.95	25.67	27.42	29.21	31.03	35.68	40.44
12.0	21.21	22.04	23.73	25.47	27.24	29.05	30.88	35.57	40.36
12.5	20.99	21.83	23.54	25.30	27.09	28.91	30.76	35.48	40.29
13.0	20.79	21.64	23.37	25.15	26.95	28.79	30.65	35.40	40.24
13.5	20.62	21.48	23.22	25.01	26.83	28.68	30.56	35.34	40.20
14.0	20.46	21.33	23.09	24.89	26.73	28.59	30.48	35.28	40.16
14.5	20.32	21.19	22.97	24.79	26.64	28.52	30.41	35.24	40.13
15.0	20.19	21.08	22.87	24.70	26.56	28.45	30.36	35.20	40.11
15.5	20.08	20.97	22.78	24.62	26.49	28.39	30.31	35.17	40.09
16.0	19.98	20.87	22.69	24.55	26.43	28.34	30.26	35.14	40.07
16.5	19.89	20.79	22.62	24.49	26.38	28.29	30.23	35.12	40.06
17.0	19.80	20.71	22.55	24.43	26.33	28.26	30.20	35.10	40.05
17.5	19.73	20.64	22.50	24.38	26.29	28.22	30.17	35.08	40.04
18.0	19.66	20.58	22.44	24.34	26.26	28.19	30.15	35.07	40.03
18.5	19.60	20.52	22.40	24.30	26.22	28.17	30.13	35.06	40.03
19.0	19.54	20.47	22.36	24.27	26.20	28.15	30.11	35.05	40.02
19.5	19.49	20.43	22.32	24.24	26.17	28.13	30.09	35.04	40.02
20.0	19.45	20.39	22.28	24.21	26.15	28.11	30.08	35.04	40.07
20.5	19.41	20.35	22.26	24.19	26.13	28.10	30.07	35.03	40.01
21.0	19.37	20.32	22.23	24.16	26.12	28.08	30.06	35.02	40.01
21.5	19.34	20.29	22.20	24.15	26.10	28.07	30.05	35.02	40.01
22.0	19.31	20.26	22.18	24.13	26.09	28.06	30.04	35.02	40.01
22.5	19.28	20.23	22.16	24.11	26.08	28.06	30.04	35.01	40.01
23.0	19.25	20.21	22.15	24.10	26.07	28.05	30.03	35.01	40.00
23.5	19.23	20.19	22.13	24.09	26.06	28.04	30.03	35.01	40.00
24.0	19.21	20.17	22.12	24.08	26.05	28.04	30.02	35.01	40.00
24.5	19.19	20.16	22.11	24.07	26 05	28.03	30.02	35.01	40.00
25.0	19.17	20.14	22.09	24.06	26.04	28.03	30.02	35.01	40.00
25.5	19.16	20.13	22.09	24.06	26.04	28.02	30.02	35.01	40.00
26.0	19.14	20.12	22.08	24.05	26.03	28.02	30.01	35.00	40.00
26.5	19.13	20.10	22.07	24.04	26.03	28.02	30.01	35.00	40.00
27.0	19.12	20.09	22.06	24.04	26.03	28.02	30.01	35.00	40.00
27.5	19.11	20.09	22.05	24.03	26.02	28.01	30.01	35.00	40.00
28.0	19.10	20.08	22.05	24.03	26.02	28.01	30.01	35.00	40.00
28.5	19.09	20.07	22.04	24.03	26.02	28.01	30.01	35.00	40.00
29.0	19.08	20.06	22.04	24.02	26.01	28.01	30.01	35.00	40.00
29.5	19.07	20.06	22.04	24.02	26.01	28.01	30.00	35.00	40.00
30.0	19.07	20.05	22.03	24.02	26.01	28.01	30.00	35.00	40.00
35.0	19.03	20.02	22.01	24.01	26.00	28.00	30.00	35.00	40.00
40.0	19.01	20.01	22.00	24.00	26.00	28.00	30.00	35.00	40.00

Table B: CONSTANT ANNUAL PERCENTS FOR LOANS WITH ANNUAL PAYMENTS

INTEREST / YEARS	6%	6¼%	6½%	6¾%	7%	7¼%	7½%	7¾%	8%
1.0	106.001	106.250	106.501	106.751	107.001	107.251	107.500	107.751	108.000
1.5	71.692	71.901	72.112	72.323	72.533	72.744	72.954	73.166	73.376
2.0	54.544	54.735	54.926	55.118	55.309	55.501	55.693	55.885	56.077
2.5	44.261	44.441	44.622	44.803	44.983	45.164	45.345	45.526	45.708
3.0	37.411	37.584	37.758	37.932	38.105	38.280	38.454	38.629	38.803
3.5	32.522	32.691	32.860	33.029	33.198	33.368	33.538	33.709	33.879
4.0	28.859	29.025	29.190	29.357	29.523	29.690	29.857	30.024	30.192
4.5	26.014	26.177	26.340	26.504	26.669	26.834	26.999	27.164	27.330
5.0	23.740	23.901	24.064	24.226	24.389	24.553	24.717	24.881	25.046
5.5	21.882	22.043	22.204	23.366	22.528	22.690	22.853	23.017	23.181
6.0	20.336	20.496	20.657	20.818	20.980	21.142	21.305	21.468	21.632
6.5	19.031	19.190	19.351	19.511	19.673	19.835	19.997	20.161	20.324
7.0	17.914	18.073	18.233	18.394	18.555	18.718	18.880	19.043	19.207
7.5	16.947	17.107	17.267	17.428	17.590	17.752	17.915	18.078	18.243
8.0	16.104	16.263	16.424	16.585	16.747	16.910	17.073	17.237	17.401
8.5	15.361	15.521	15.682	15.843	16.006	16.169	16.332	16.497	16.662
9.0	14.702	14.863	15.024	15.186	15.349	15.512	15.677	15.842	16.008
9.5	14.115	14.275	14.437	14.600	14.763	14.927	15.092	15.258	15.425
10.0	13.587	13.748	13.911	14.074	14.238	14.403	14.569	14.735	14.903
10.5	13.111	13.273	13.436	13.600	13.764	13.930	14.097	14.264	14.433
11.0	12.679	12.842	13.006	13.170	13.336	13.502	13.670	13.838	14.008
11.5	12.287	12.450	12.614	12.780	12.946	13.113	13.282	13.451	13.621
12.0	11.928	12.092	12.257	12.423	12.590	12.759	12.928	13.098	13.270
12.5	11.599	11.763	11.929	12.096	12.264	12.434	12.604	12.775	12.948
13.0	11.296	11.462	11.628	11.796	11.965	12.135	12.306	12.479	12.652
13.5	11.017	11.183	11.351	11.519	11.689	11.860	12.033	12.206	12.380
14.0	10.759	10.926	11.094	11.264	11.435	11.607	11.780	11.954	12.130
14.5	10.519	10.687	10.856	11.027	11.199	11.372	11.546	11.721	11.898
15.0	10.296	10.465	10.635	10.807	10.979	11.154	11.329	11.505	11.683
15.5	10.089	10.259	10.430	10.602	10.776	10.951	11.127	11.305	11.483
16.0	9.895	10.066	10.238	10.411	10.586	10.762	10.939	11.118	11.298
16.5	9.714	9.886	10.059	10.233	10.408	10.586	10.764	10.944	11.125
17.0	9.545	9.717	9.891	10.066	10.243	10.421	10.600	10.781	10.963
17 5	9.385	9.559	9.733	9.910	10.087	10.266	10.447	10.629	10.812
18.0	9.236	9.410	9.585	9.763	9.941	10.121	10.303	10.486	10.670
18.5	9.095	9.270	9.446	9.625	9.804	9.985	10.168	10.352	10.537
19.0	8.962	9.138	9.316	9.495	9.675	9.857	10.041	10.226	10.413
19.5	8.837	9.014	9.192	9.372	9.554	9.737	9.922	10.108	10.296
20.0	8.718	8.896	9.076	9.257	9.439	9.624	9.809	9.997	10.185
20.5	8.607	8.785	8.966	9.148	9.331	9.516	9.703	9.891	10.081
21.0	8.500	8.680	8.861	9.044	9.229	9.415	9.603	9.792	9.983
21.5	8.400	8.580	8.763	8.947	9.132	9.319	9.508	9.699	9.891
22.0	8.305	8.486	8.669	8.854	9.041	9.229	9.419	9.610	9.803
22.5	8.214	8.396	8.580	8.766	8.954	9.143	9.334	9.526	9.721
23.0	8.128	8.311	8.496	8.683	8.871	9.062	9.254	9.447	9.642
23.5	8.046	8.230	8.416	8.604	8.793	8.984	9.177	9.372	9.568
24.0	7.968	8.153	8.340	8.528	8.719	8.911	9.105	9.301	9.498
24.5	7.894	8.079	8.267	8.457	8.648	8.841	9.036	9.233	9.431
25.0	7.823	8.009	8.198	8.389	8.581	8.775	8.971	9.169	9.368
25.5	7.755	7.943	8.132	8.324	8.517	8.712	8.909	9.108	9.308
26.0	7.690	7.879	8.069	8.262	8.456	8.652	8.850	9.050	9.251
26.5	7.629	7.818	8.010	8.203	8.398	8.595	8.794	8.994	9.196
27.0	7.570	7.760	7.952	8.147	8.343	8.541	8.740	8.942	9.145
27.5	7.513	7.704	7.898	8.093	8.290	8.489	8.689	8.892	9.096
28.0	7.459	7.651	7.845	8.041	8.239	8.439	8.641	8.844	9.049
28.5	7.408	7.600	7.795	7.992	8.191	8.392	8.594	8.798	9.004
29.0	7.358	7.552	7.747	7.945	8.145	8.346	8.550	8.755	8.962
29.5	7.310	7.505	7.702	7.900	8.101	8.303	8.508	8.714	8.921
30.0	7.265	7.460	7.658	7.857	8.059	8.262	8.467	9.674	8.883
35.0	6.897	7.101	7.306	7.514	7.723	7.935	8.148	8.363	8.580
40.0	6.646	6.857	7.069	7.284	7.501	7.720	7.940	8.162	8.386

Table B (cont.)

INTEREST	8½%	8½%	8¾%	9%	9¼%	9½%	9¾%	10%	10¼%
YEARS									
1.0	108.251	108.501	108.750	109.001	109.250	109.501	109.750	110.001	110.250
1.5	73.588	73.799	74.010	74.221	74.432	74.644	74.855	75.067	75.278
2.0	56.270	56.462	56.654	56.847	57.040	57.233	57.426	57.619	57.812
2.5	45.890	46.072	46.254	46.436	46.618	46.801	46.984	47.167	47.350
3.0	38.979	39.154	39.330	39.506	39.682	39.858	40.035	40.212	40.389
3.5	34.050	34.221	34.393	34.565	34.737	34.909	35.082	35.255	35.428
4.0	30.360	30.529	30.698	30.867	31.036	31.206	31.377	31.547	31.718
4.5	27.497	27.664	27.831	27.998	28.166	28.334	28.503	28.672	28.841
5.0	25.211	25.377	25.543	25.709	25.876	26.044	26.211	26.380	26.548
5.5	23.346	23.511	23.676	23.843	24.009	24.176	24.343	24.511	24.680
6.0	21.796	21.961	22.126	22.292	22.458	22.625	22.793	22.961	23.129
6.5	20.489	20.654	20.819	20.985	21.152	21.319	21.486	21.655	21.823
7.0	19.372	19.537	19.703	19.869	20.036	20.204	20.372	20.541	20.710
7.5	18.408	18.573	18.739	18.906	19.074	19.242	19.411	19.580	19.750
8.0	17.567	17.733	17.900	18.068	18.236	18.405	18.574	18.744	18.915
8.5	16.828	16.995	17.163	17.331	17.500	17.670	17.840	18.012	18.183
9.0	16.175	16.342	16.511	16.680	16.850	17.021	17.192	17.364	17.537
9.5	15.593	15.761	15.930	16.101	16.271	16.443	16.615	16.789	16.963
10.0	15.071	15.241	15.411	15.582	15.754	15.927	16.100	16.275	16.450
10.5	14.602	14.773	14.944	15.116	15.285	15.463	15.637	15.813	15.989
11.0	14.178	14.349	14.522	14.695	14.869	15.044	15.220	15.396	15.574
11.5	13.793	13.965	14.139	14.313	14.488	14.664	14.841	15.019	15.198
12.0	13.442	13.615	13.790	13.965	14.141	14.319	14.497	14.676	14.857
12.5	13.121	13.296	13.471	13.648	13.825	14.004	14.183	14.364	14.545
13.0	12.827	13.002	13.179	13.357	13.535	13.715	13.896	14.078	14.261
13.5	12.556	12.733	12.911	13.089	13.269	13.450	13.633	13.816	14.000
14.0	12.306	12.484	12.663	12.843	13.025	13.207	13.390	13.575	13.760
14.5	12.076	12.255	12.435	12.616	12.799	12.982	13.167	13.353	13.539
15.0	11.862	12.042	12.223	12.406	12.590	12.774	12.960	13.147	13.336
15.5	11.663	11.845	12.027	12.211	12.396	12.582	12.769	12.958	13.147
16.0	11.479	11.661	11.845	12.030	12.216	12.404	12.592	12.782	12.972
16.5	11.307	11.491	11.675	11.862	12.049	12.238	12.427	12.618	12.810
17.0	11.146	11.331	11.517	11.705	11.893	12.083	12.274	12.466	12.660
17.5	10.996	11.182	11.370	11.558	11.748	11.939	12.131	12.325	12.520
18.0	10.856	11.043	11.231	11.421	11.612	11.805	11.998	12.193	12.389
18.5	10.724	10.913	11.102	11.293	11.485	11.679	11.874	12.070	12.267
19.0	10.601	10.790	10.981	11.173	11.367	11.561	11.757	11.955	12.153
19.5	10.485	10.675	10.867	11.060	11.255	11.451	11.648	11.847	12.047
20.0	10.375	10.567	10.760	10.955	11.150	11.348	11.546	11.746	11.947
20.5	10.273	10.465	10.660	10.855	11.052	11.251	11.450	11.651	11.854
21.0	10.176	10.370	10.565	10.762	10.960	11.159	11.360	11.562	11.766
21.5	10.084	10.279	10.476	10.674	10.873	11.074	11.276	11.479	11.684
22.0	9.998	10.194	10.391	10.591	10.791	10.993	11.196	11.401	11.606
22.5	9.916	10.113	10.312	10.512	10.714	10.917	11.121	11.327	11.534
23.0	9.839	10.037	10.237	10.438	10.641	10.845	11.050	11.257	11.465
23.5	9.766	9.965	10.166	10.368	10.572	10.777	10.984	11.192	11.401
24.0	9.697	9.897	10.099	10.302	10.507	10.713	10.921	11.130	11.340
24.5	9.631	9.832	10.035	10.240	10.446	10.653	10.862	11.072	11.283
25.0	9.569	9.771	9.975	10.181	10.388	10.596	10.806	11.017	11.229
25.5	9.510	9.713	9.918	10.125	10.333	10.542	10.753	10.965	11.178
26.0	9.454	9.658	9.864	10.072	10.281	10.491	10.703	10.916	11.130
26.5	9.400	9.606	9.813	10.021	10.231	10.443	10.655	10.870	11.085
27.0	9.350	9.556	9.764	9.974	10.184	10.397	10.611	10.826	11.042
27.5	9.301	9.509	9.718	9.928	10.140	10.354	10.568	10.784	11.002
28.0	9.256	9.464	9.674	9.885	10.098	10.312	10.528	10.745	10.963
28.5	9.212	9.421	9.632	9.844	10.058	10.273	10.490	10.708	10.927
29.0	9.170	9.381	9.592	9.806	10.020	10.236	10.454	10.673	10.893
29.5	9.131	9.342	9.555	9.769	9.984	10.201	10.420	10.640	10.860
30.0	9.093	9.305	9.519	9.734	9.950	10.168	10.387	10.608	10.830
35.0	8.799	9.019	9.241	9.464	9.688	9.914	10.141	10.369	10.598
40.0	8.611	8.838	9.066	9.296	9.527	9.759	9.992	10.226	10.461

Table C: ANNUAL SINKING FUND TABLES
WRAP-AROUND YIELD CALCULATION FOR 6-30YEARS

YEARS	6%	6¼%	6½%	6¾%	7%	7¼%	7½%	7¾%	8%	8¼%	8½%
1	1.000000	1.000000	1.000000	1.000000	1.000000	1.000000	1.000000	1.000000	1.000000	1.000000	1.000000
	.485437	.484848	.484262	.483676	.483092	.482509	.481928	.481348	.480769	.480192	.479616
	.314110	.313341	.312576	.311812	.311052	.310293	.309538	.308784	.308034	.307285	.306539
	.228591	.227745	.226903	.226064	.225228	.224396	.223568	.222742	.221921	.221103	.220288
	.177396	.176513	.175635	.174760	.173891	.173025	.172165	.171308	.170456	.169609	.168766
6	.143363	.142463	.141568	.140679	.139796	.138918	.138045	.137177	.136315	.135459	.134607
	.119135	.118230	.117331	.116439	.115553	.114674	.113800	.112933	.112072	.111218	.110369
	.101036	.100133	.099237	.098349	.097468	.096594	.095727	.094867	.094015	.093169	.092331
	.087022	.086126	.085238	.084358	.083486	.082623	.081767	.080919	.080080	.079248	.078424
	.075868	.074982	.074105	.073237	.072378	.071527	.070686	.069853	.069029	.068214	.067408
11	.066793	.065919	.065055	.064201	.063557	.062522	.061697	.060882	.060076	.059280	.058493
	.059277	.058417	.057568	.056730	.055902	.055085	.054278	.053481	.052695	.051919	.051153
	.052960	.052116	.051283	.050461	.049651	.048852	.048064	.047288	.046522	.045767	.045023
	.047585	.046757	.045940	.045137	.044345	.043565	.042797	.042041	.041297	.040564	.039842
	.042963	.042151	.041353	.040567	.039795	.039035	.038287	.037552	.036830	.036119	.035420
16	.038952	.038158	.037378	.036611	.035858	.035118	.034391	.033678	.032977	.032289	.031614
	.035445	.034668	.033906	.033159	.032425	.031706	.031000	.030308	.029629	.028964	.028312
	.032357	.031598	.030855	.030126	.029413	.028714	.028029	.027359	.026702	.026059	.025430
	.029621	.028880	.028156	.027447	.026753	.026074	.025411	.024762	.024128	.023507	.022901
	.027185	.026462	.025756	.025067	.024393	.023735	.023092	.022465	.021852	.021254	.020671
21	.025005	.024300	.023613	.022943	.022289	.021651	.021029	.020423	.019832	.019256	.018695
	.023046	.022360	.021691	.021040	.020406	.019788	.019187	.018602	.018032	.017478	.016939
	.021278	.020611	.019961	.019329	.018714	.018116	.017535	.016971	.016422	.015889	.015372
	.019679	.019029	.018398	.017784	.017189	.016611	.016050	.015506	.014978	.014466	.013970
	.018227	.017595	.016981	.016387	.015811	.015252	.014711	.014186	.013679	.013187	.012712
26	.016904	.016290	.015695	.015119	.014561	.014021	.013500	.012995	.012507	.012036	.011580
	.015697	.015100	.014523	.013965	.013426	.012905	.012402	.011917	.011448	.010996	.010560
	.014593	.014013	.013453	.012913	.012392	.011890	.011405	.010938	.010489	.010056	.009639
	.013580	.013017	.012474	.011952	.011449	.010964	.010498	.010050	.009619	.009204	.008806
	.012649	.012103	.011577	.011072	.010586	.010120	.009671	.009241	.008827	.008431	.008051

YEARS	8¾%	9%	9¼%	9½%	9¾%	10%	10¼%	10½%	10¾%	11%	11¼%
1	1.000000	1.000000	1.000000	1.000000	1.000000	1.000000	1.000000	1.000000	1.000000	1.000000	1.000000
	.479042	.478469	.477897	.477327	.476758	.476190	.475624	.475059	.474496	.473934	.473373
	.305796	.305055	.304136	.303580	.302846	.302115	.301386	.300659	.299935	.299213	.298494
	.219477	.218669	.217864	.217063	.216265	.215471	.214680	.213892	.213108	.212326	.211548
	.167927	.167092	.166262	.165436	.164615	.163797	.162984	.162175	.161371	.160570	.159774
6	.133761	.132920	.132084	.131253	.130428	.129607	.128792	.127982	.127177	.126377	.125581
	.109527	.108691	.107860	.107036	.106218	.105405	.104599	.103799	.103004	.102215	.101432
	.091499	.090674	.089857	.089046	.088241	.087444	.086653	.085869	.085092	.084321	.083557
	.077607	.076799	.075998	.075205	.074419	.073641	.072870	.072106	.071350	.070602	.079860
	.066610	.065820	.065039	.064266	.063502	.062745	.061997	.061257	.060525	.059801	.059085
11	.055715	.056947	.056187	.055437	.054696	.053963	.053240	.052525	.051819	.051121	.050432
	.050397	.049651	.048914	.048188	.047471	.046763	.046565	.045377	.044697	.044027	.043366
	.044289	.043567	.042854	.042152	.041460	.040779	.040107	.039445	.038793	.038151	.037518
	.039132	.038433	.037745	.037068	.036402	.035746	.035101	.034467	.033842	.033228	.032624
	.034734	.034059	.033396	.032744	.032103	.031474	.030855	.030248	.029651	.029065	.028490
16	.030951	.030300	.029661	.029035	.028420	.027817	.027225	.026644	.026075	.025517	.024969
	.027673	.027046	.026432	.025831	.025241	.024664	.024099	.023545	.023003	.022471	.021952
	.024815	.024212	.023623	.023046	.022482	.021930	.021391	.020863	.020347	.019843	.019350
	.022309	.021730	.021165	.020613	.020074	.019547	.019033	.018531	.018041	.017563	.017096
	.020102	.019546	.019005	.018477	.017962	.017460	.016970	.016493	.016028	.015576	.015134
21	.018149	.017617	.017098	.016594	.016102	.015624	.015159	.014707	.014266	.013838	.013421
	.016415	.015905	.015409	.014928	.014460	.014005	.013563	.013134	.012718	.012313	.011920
	.014870	.014382	.013909	.013449	.013004	.012572	.012153	.011747	.011353	.010971	.010601
	.013489	.013023	.012571	.012134	.011710	.011300	.010903	.010519	.010147	.009787	.009439
	.012251	.011806	.011376	.010959	.010557	.010168	.009792	.009429	.009079	.008740	.008413
26	.011140	.010715	.010305	.009909	.009527	.009159	.008804	.008461	.008131	.007813	.007506
	.010140	.009735	.009345	.008969	.008606	.008258	.007922	.007599	.007288	.006989	.006702
	.009238	.008852	.008481	.008124	.007781	.007451	.007134	.006830	.006538	.006257	.005988
	.008423	.008056	.007703	.007364	.007040	.006728	.006429	.006143	.005868	.005605	.005354
	.007686	.007336	.007001	.006681	.006373	.006079	.005798	.005528	.005271	.005025	.004789

Table C (cont.)

YEARS	11½%	11¾%	12%	13%	14%	15%	16%	17%	18%	19%	20%
1	1.000000	1.000000	1.000000	1.000000	1.000000	1.000000	1.000000	1.000000	1.000000	1.000000	1.000000
	.472813	.472255	.471698	.469483	.467290	.465116	.462963	.460829	.458715	.456621	.454545
	.297776	.297062	.296349	.293522	.290731	.287976	.285257	.282573	.279923	.277308	.274725
	.210774	.210003	.209234	.206194	.203205	.200265	.197375	.194533	.191738	.188991	.186289
	.158982	.158194	.157410	.154314	.151284	.148315	.145409	.142564	.139778	.137050	.134380
6	.124791	.124006	.123226	.120153	.117158	.114236	.111390	.108615	.105910	.103274	.100706
	.100655	.099884	.099118	.096111	.093192	.090360	.087613	.084947	.082362	.079855	.077424
	.082799	.082048	.081303	.078387	.075570	.072850	.070224	.067690	.065243	.062885	.060609
	.069126	.068399	.067679	.064869	.062168	.059574	.057083	.054690	.052395	.050192	.048079
	.058377	.057677	.056984	.054290	.051714	.049252	.046901	.044657	.042515	.040471	.038523
11	.049751	.049079	.048415	.045841	.043394	.041068	.038861	.036765	.034776	.032891	.031104
	.042714	.042071	.041437	.038986	.036669	.034480	.032415	.030466	.028628	.026896	.025265
	.036895	.036282	.035677	.033350	.031164	.029110	.027184	.025378	.023686	.022102	.020620
	.032030	.031446	.030871	.028668	.026609	.024688	.022898	.021230	.019678	.018235	.016893
	.027924	.027369	.026824	.024742	.022809	.021017	.019358	.017822	.016403	.015092	.013882
16	.024432	.023906	.023390	.021426	.019615	.017947	.016414	.015004	.013710	.012523	.011436
	.021443	.020944	.020457	.018608	.016915	.015366	.013952	.012662	.011485	.010414	.009440
	.018868	.018397	.017937	.016201	.014621	.013186	.011885	.010706	.009639	.008676	.007805
	.016641	.016196	.015763	.014134	.012663	.011336	.010142	.009067	.008103	.007237	.006462
	.014705	.014286	.013879	.012354	.010986	.009761	.008667	.007690	.006820	.006045	.005357
21	.013016	.012623	.012240	.010814	.009545	.008416	.007416	.006530	.005746	.005054	.004444
	.011539	.011169	.010811	.009480	.008303	.007265	.006353	.005550	.004846	.004229	.003690
	.010243	.009896	.009560	.008319	.007231	.006278	.005447	.004721	.004090	.003542	.003065
	.009103	.008778	.008463	.007308	.006303	.005429	.004673	.004019	.003454	.002967	.002548
	.008098	.007794	.007500	.006426	.005498	.004699	.004013	.003423	.002919	.002487	.002119
26	.007210	.006926	.006652	.005655	.004800	.004069	.003447	.002918	.002467	.002086	.001762
	.006425	.006159	.005904	.004979	.004193	.003526	.002963	.002487	.002087	.001750	.001467
	.005730	.005482	.005244	.004387	.003665	.003010	.002548	.002121	.001765	.001468	.001221
	.005112	.004881	.004660	.003867	.003204	.002651	.002192	.001810	.001494	.001232	.001016
	.004564	.004349	.004144	.003411	.002803	.002300	.001886	.001545	.001264	.001034	.000846

YEARS	21%	22%	23%	24%	25%	26%	27%	28%	29%	30%
1	1.000000	1.000000	1.000000	1.000000	1.000000	1.000000	1.000000	1.000000	1.000000	1.000000
	.452489	.450450	.448430	.446429	.444444	.442478	.440529	.438596	.436681	.434783
	.272175	.269658	.267173	.264718	.262295	.259902	.257539	.255206	.252902	.250627
	.183632	.181020	.178451	.175926	.173442	.170999	.168598	.166236	.163913	.161629
	.131765	.129206	.126700	.124248	.121847	.119496	.117196	.114944	.112739	.110582
6	.098203	.095764	.093389	.091074	.088819	.086623	.084484	.082400	.080371	.078394
	.075067	.072782	.070568	.068422	.066342	.064326	.062374	.060482	.058649	.056874
	.058415	.056299	.054259	.052293	.050399	.048573	.046814	.045119	.043487	.041915
	.046053	.044111	.042249	.040465	.038756	.037119	.035551	.034049	.032612	.031235
	.036665	.034895	.033208	.031602	.030073	.028616	.027231	.025912	.024657	.023463
11	.029411	.027807	.026289	.024852	.023493	.022207	.020991	.019842	.018755	.017729
	.023730	.022285	.020926	.019648	.018448	.017319	.016260	.015265	.014331	.013454
	.019234	.017939	.016728	.015598	.014544	.013559	.012641	.011785	.010987	.010244
	.015647	.014491	.013418	.012423	.011501	.010647	.009856	.009123	.008445	.007818
	.012766	.011738	.010791	.009919	.009117	.008379	.007701	.007077	.006405	.005978
16	.010441	.009530	.008697	.007936	.007241	.006606	.006027	.005499	.005017	.004577
	.008555	.007751	.007021	.006359	.005759	.005216	.004723	.004277	.003874	.003509
	.007020	.006313	.005676	.005102	.004586	.004122	.003705	.003331	.002994	.002692
	.005769	.005148	.004593	.004098	.003656	.003261	.002909	.002595	.002316	.002066
	.004745	.004202	.003720	.003294	.002916	.002581	.002285	.002023	.001792	.001587
21	.003906	.003432	.003016	.002649	.002327	.002045	.001796	.001578	.001387	.001219
	.003218	.002805	.002446	.002132	.001858	.001620	.001412	.001232	.001074	.000937
	.002652	.002294	.001984	.001716	.001485	.001284	.001111	.000961	.000832	.000720
	.002187	.001877	.001611	.001382	.001186	.001018	.000874	.000750	.000644	.000554
	.001804	.001536	.001308	.001113	.000948	.000807	.000688	.000586	.000499	.000426

Note 1
Calculations will result in slight error if mortgages calculated are less than annual payments. However, the error will not be sufficient to warrant that the table not be used.

Note 2
A constant annual payment percentage is that percentage which when multiplied by the loan balance will give an amount representing the annual payment of principal including interest. The table given will allow the user to take the interest rate to be paid, locate the term of years, and determine the constant annual percentage. This percentage multiplied by the principal owed will give the total annual payment which, in the case of Table A, is made up of 12 monthly installments. It is important to remember that the constant interest rate changes each year whereas the amount paid does not. This is due to the fact that the principal owed and years remaining diminish each successive year of the loan.

Index

D

G